Information Theory, Coding and Cryptography

Arijit Saha
Associate Professor,
Department of Electronics and Communication Engineering,
B. P. Poddar Institute of Management and Technology, Kolkata

Nilotpal Manna
Head,
Department of Electronics and Instrumentation Engineering,
JIS College of Engineering, Nadia, West Bengal

Surajit Mandal
Professor,
Department of Electronics and Communication Engineering,
B. P. Poddar Institute of Management and Technology, Kolkata

Pearson

ISBN 978-81-317-9749-5

First Impression

Published by Pearson India Education Services Pvt. Ltd, CIN: U72200TN2005PTC057128.

Head Office: 15th Floor, Tower-B, World Trade Tower, Plot No. 1, Block-C, Sector 16, Noida 201 301, Uttar Pradesh, India.
Registered Office: 7th Floor, SDB2, ODC 7, 8 & 9, Survey No. 01 ELCOT IT/ ITES-SEZ, Sholinganallur,
Chennai – 600 119, Tamilnadu, India.
Phone: 044-66540100
Website: in.pearson.com, Email: companysecretary.india@pearson.com

Printed in India at Repro India Limited

CONTENTS

FOREWORD

The knowledge of information theory and coding has become a necessity not only for the electrical communication engineers, computer scientists, and information technologists but also for all others dealing with information, data, and signal flow. To know the principles of operations, to work for research and developments, to know more about applications, and to work with new futuristic topics such as nanotechnology, bioinformatics, etc., a thorough knowledge of information theory and coding is essential. Shannon's theorem has given a beginning to this subject area which later on led to the development of several breakthrough concepts. Coding of information, data (audio, video, multimedia), and signals has become a necessity not only for error-free transmission/reception but also for reduction in storage space and for security of data/information. Cryptography, steganography, and watermarking are some of the examples of information security.

Prof. Arijit Saha, Prof. Nilotpal Manna, and Prof. Surajit Mandal are involved in teaching this subject for many years to the senior undergraduate students of B. P. Poddar Institute of Management and Technology and JIS College of Engineering both affiliated to West Bengal University of Technology, Kolkata. This book is the result of their sincere teaching using several books and journal papers. This book will address the needs of students studying this subject so that they get the study material in one source. The authors tried to cover the syllabi of all major universities and institutes of India, in general, and West Bengal University of Technology, in particular. In addition, they have included several advanced topics so that the book is suitable as a reference book for post-graduate students and practicing professionals. Some prominent aspects of the book are as follows:

- A brief but enough discussion on the mathematical and other prerequisites of the subject.
- Detail discussion on the theory and applications of all the topics, namely information theory, source codes, error control codes, linear block codes, cyclic codes, BCH codes, convolution codes.
- Discussions on advanced topics such as adaptive Huffman code, predictive code, LWZ code, MPEG, Dolby, interleaving techniques, CIRC coding, etc.
- A large number of solved examples to illustrate the concepts and at the end of each chapter, a large number of multiple choice questions with answers in each chapter, and a large number of problems in each chapter for practice.
- A good balance between theoretical and practical aspects of the subject. It provides a solid foundation of the subject for practicing professionals.
- Coverage of almost all the information of this subject area.

I am sure this book will serve the needs of the student community and will find an important place in Libraries.

Dr B. N. CHATTERJI
Former Professor and Head of the Department of Electronics and Electrical Communication Engineering and Former Dean, Academic Affairs of IIT Kharagpur
&
Presently Professor of Electronics and Communication Engineering and Dean, Academic Affairs of B. P. Poddar Institute of Management and Technology, Kolkata

PREFACE

Information lost means no information. A reliable transmission of information is the basic requirement of communication system. In spite of all the efforts given to the error-free transmission, noise is attributed to communication channel, causing erroneous data at the receiver. It is important that the information at the receiving end is error-free, or if any error occurs, the receiver must detect, locate, and correct the error. Search for the techniques to achieve reliable transmission over noisy communication channel is based on Shannon's theorem at late 1950 that reliable transmission can be achieved with the selection of proper encoding and decoding system, if the signalling rate is less than the channel capacity. This leads to the study of information theory and search for good efficient coding and decoding methods. Both the fields require the extensive background in applied mathematics, modern algebra, and probability theory. Since their inception, these have broadened to find applications in many areas, including data compression, error correction, statistical inference, natural language processing, cryptography, neurobiology, the evolution and function of molecular codes, model selection in ecology, thermal physics, quantum computing, plagiarism detection, and other forms of data analysis.

This book is intended to provide a comprehensive knowledge on information theory, study of different codes and decoding techniques with methods of error correction, and cryptography. The fundamentals of the subject are explained in this book with mathematical illustration wherever necessary. The book is designed in three parts with nine chapters. Part A presents the concepts of information theory and source coding consisting of three chapters; Part B consists of five chapters illustrating different types error control coding and decoding techniques; and Part C provides the basic concepts of cryptography.

In Part A, Chapter 1 provides the fundamentals of probability and random variables. Random processes and noise behaviour are also included in this chapter. Chapter 2 presents the concepts of information theory and channel characteristics with basic theorems and mathematical illustration. Chapter 3 illustrates various types of source codes, their classifications, and algorithms for formatting the codes with necessary mathematical background.

Part B is divided into five chapters, Chapter 4 through Chapter 8. Chapter 4 provides the theory behind error control codes, types of codes, types of errors, and strategies. These are elaborated with mathematical fundamentals and arithmetic of binary field. Galois field and vector spaces related to coding theory are also explained. Linear block codes, cyclic codes, BCH codes, and convolution codes have been illustrated in Chapter 5 through Chapter 8, respectively. Each chapter provides the mathematical background, generation of codes, types of encoders, decoding techniques, error correction, and application for the respective codes.

Part C consists of Chapter 9 that only devotes to cryptography and cryptosystems. This chapter provides the basic principles and fundamentals of cryptography and cryptosystems. Different types of encryption and decryption techniques and algorithms behind them are discussed in this chapter.

Simple lucid language is used throughout the book. Clear diagrams and numerous examples are provided for all the topics to facilitate easy understanding of the concepts. This book can be used as a text for an introductory course on information theory, error-correcting codes, and their applications at graduate or post-graduate level. The book is also designed as self-study guide for engineers in industry who wants to learn the error control codes, their correction techniques, and cryptography.

The authors are greatly thankful to all those who provided help and encouragement during the writing of this book. The authors are thankful to the publisher Pearson Education for providing the wonderful opportunity for publishing the book. The authors express their thanks to their wives and children for their continuous support and enormous patience during the preparation of this book.

Suggestions and corrections are welcome for the improvement of the book.

Arijit Saha
Nilotpal Manna
Surajit Mandal

part

A

INFORMATION THEORY AND SOURCE CODING

Chapter 1 Probability, Random Processes, and Noise

Chapter 2 Information Theory

Chapter 3 Source Codes

chapter 1

PROBABILITY, RANDOM PROCESSES, AND NOISE

1.1 INTRODUCTION

Any signal that can be uniquely described by an explicit mathematical expression, a well-defined rule or a table look-up, is called a *deterministic signal*. The value of such signals is known or determined precisely at every instant of time. In many practical applications, however, some signals are generated in a random fashion and cannot be explicitly described prior to their occurrence. Such signals are referred to as *nondeterministic* or *random signals*. An example of random signal is *noise*, an ever-present undesirable signal that contaminates the *message signal* during its passage through a communication link and makes the *information* erroneous. The composite signal, the desired signal plus interfering noise components at the input of the receiver, is again random in nature. Although there is an uncertainty about the exact nature of the random signals, probabilistic methods can be adopted to present their general behaviour. This chapter aims at presenting a short course on theory of probability, random processes and noise, essential for extracting information-bearing signals from noisy background.

1.2 FUNDAMENTALS OF PROBABILITY

Probability is a measure of certainty. The theory of probability originated from the analysis of certain games of chance, such as roulette and cards. Soon it became a powerful mathematical tool almost in all branches of science and engineering. The following terms are useful in developing the concept of probability:

Experiment—Any process of observation is known as an experiment.

Outcome—It is the result of an experiment.

Random Experiment—An experiment is called a *random experiment* if its outcome is not unique and therefore cannot be predicted with certainty. Typical examples of a random experiment are tossing a coin, rolling a die or selecting a message from several messages for transmission.

Sample Space, Sample Point and Event—The set S of all possible outcomes of a given random experiment is called the *sample space, universal set,* or *certain event*. An element (outcome) in S is known as a *sample point* or *elementary event*. An event A is a subset of a sample space ($A \subset S$).

In any random experiment, we are not certain as to whether a particular event will occur or not. As a measure of the probability, we usually assign a number between 0 and 1. If we are sure that the event will occur, the probability of that event is taken as 1 (100%). When the event will never occur, the probability of that event is 0 (0%). If the probability is 9/10, there is a 90% chance that it will occur. In other words, there is a 10% (1/10) probability that the event will not occur.

The probability of an event can be defined by the following two approaches:

1. *Mathematical or Classical Probability*—If an event can happen in m different ways out of a total number of n possible ways, all of which are *equally likely*, then the probability of that event is m/n.

2. *Statistical or Empirical or Estimated Probability*—If an experiment is repeated n times (n being very large) under homogeneous and identical conditions and an event is observed to occur m number of times, then the probability of the event is $\lim_{n\to\infty} (m/n)$.

However, both the approaches have serious drawbacks, as the terms 'equally likely' and 'large number' are vague. Due to these drawbacks, an *axiomatic approach* was developed, which is described in Sec. 1.2.2.

1.2.1 Algebra of Probability

We can combine events to form new events using various set operations as follows:

1. The *complement* of event $A(\overline{A})$ is the event containing all sample points in S but not in A.
2. The *union* of events A and B ($A \cup B$) is the event containing all sample points in either A or B or both.
3. The *intersection* of events A and B ($A \cap B$) is the event containing all sample points in both A and B.
4. *Null* or *impossible event* ($\varnothing$) is the event containing no sample point.
5. Two events A and B are called *mutually exclusive* or *disjoint* ($A \cap B = \varnothing$) when they contain no common sample point, i.e., A and B cannot occur simultaneously.

Example 1.1: Throw a die and observe the number of dots appearing on the top face. (a) Construct its sample space. (b) If A be the event that an odd number occurs, B that an even number occurs, and C that a prime number occurs, write down their respective subsets. (c) Find the event that an even or a prime number occurs. (d) List the outcomes for the event that an even prime number occurs. (e) Find the event that a prime number does not occur. (f) Find the event that seven dots appear on the top face. (g) Find the event that even and odd numbers occur simultaneously.

Solution:

(a) Here, the sample space is $S = \{1,2,3,4,5,6\}$.
It has six sample points.

(b) $A = \{\text{oddd number}\} = \{1,3,5\}$
$B = \{\text{even number}\} = \{2,4,6\}$
$C = \{\text{prime number}\} = \{2,3,5\}$.

(c) $B \cup C = \{2,3,4,5,6\}$.

(d) $B \cap C = \{2\}$.

(e) $\overline{C} = \{1,4,6\}$.

(f) This is a null or impossible event ($\varnothing$).

(g) Since an even and an odd number cannot occur simultaneously, A and B are mutually exclusive ($A \cap B = \varnothing$).

1.2.2 Axioms of Probability

Let $P(A)$ denote the probability of event A of some sample space S. It must satisfy the following axioms:

$$0 \le P(A) \le 1 \tag{1.1}$$

$$P(S) = 1 \text{ (sure event)} \tag{1.2}$$

$$P(A \cup B) = P(A) + P(B), \text{ if } A \cap B = \varnothing \tag{1.3a}$$

$$P(A \cup B \cup C \cup \ldots) = P(A) + P(B) + P(C) + \ldots, \text{ if } A, B, C, \ldots \text{ of } S \text{ are mutually exclusive events} \tag{1.3b}$$

1.2.3 Elementary Theorems on Probability

Some important theorems on probability are as follows:

$$P(\varnothing) = 0 \tag{1.4}$$
$$P(\overline{A}) = 1 - P(A) \le 1 \tag{1.5}$$
$$P(A) \le P(B), \text{ if } A \subset B \tag{1.6}$$
$$P(A \cup B) = P(A) + P(B) - P(A \cap B) \tag{1.7a}$$
$$P(A \cup B) \le P(A) + P(B), \text{ since } P(A \cap B) \ge 0 \tag{1.7b}$$
$$P(A \cup B \cup C) = P(A) + P(B) + P(C) - P(A \cap B) - P(B \cap C) - P(C \cap A) + P(A \cap B \cap C) \tag{1.8}$$

Example 1.2: Determine the probability for the event that the sum 8 appears in a single throw of a pair of fair dice.

Solution: The sum 8 appears in the following cases:

(2,6), (3,5), (4,4), (5,3), (6,2), i.e., 5 cases

Total number of outcomes is $6 \times 6 = 36$

Thus, $P(\text{sum } 8) = \dfrac{\text{Favourable cases}}{\text{Total outcomes}} = \dfrac{5}{36}$

Example 1.3: A ball is drawn at random from a box containing 5 red balls, 4 green balls, and 3 blue balls. Determine the probability that it is (a) green, (b) not green, and (c) red or blue.

Solution:

(a) **Method 1**

Let R, G, and B denote the events of drawing a red ball, green ball, and blue ball, respectively.

Then $P(G) = \dfrac{\text{Ways of choosing a green ball}}{\text{Total ways of choosing a ball}} = \dfrac{4}{5+4+3} = \dfrac{1}{3}.$

Method 2

The sample space consists of 12 sample points. If we assign equal probabilities 1/12 to each sample point, we again see that $P(G) = 4/12 = 1/3$, since there are 4 sample points corresponding to green ball.

(b) $P(\text{not green}) = P(\overline{G}) = 1 - P(G) = 1 - \frac{1}{3} = \frac{2}{3}.$

(c) **Method 1**

$$P(\text{red or blue}) = P(R \cup B) = \frac{\text{Ways of choosing a red or blue ball}}{\text{Total ways of choosing a ball}} = \frac{5+3}{5+4+3} = \frac{2}{3}.$$

Method 2

$$P(R \cup B) = 1 - P(G) = P(\overline{G}) = 1 - \frac{1}{3} = \frac{2}{3}.$$

Method 3

Since events R and G are mutually exclusive, we have

$$P(R \cup B) = P(R) + P(B) = \frac{5}{12} + \frac{3}{12} = \frac{2}{3}.$$

Example 1.4: Two cards are drawn at random from a pack of 52 cards. Find the probability that (a) both are hearts and (b) one is heart and one is spade.

Solution: There are $\binom{52}{2} = 1326$ ways that 2 cards can be drawn from 52 cards.

(a) There are $\binom{13}{2} = 78$ ways to draw 2 hearts from 13 hearts.

Thus, the probability that both cards are hearts $= \dfrac{\text{Number of ways 2 hearts can be drawn}}{\text{Number of ways 2 cards can be drawn}} = \dfrac{78}{1326}$

$= \dfrac{1}{17}$

(b) As there are 13 hearts and 13 spades, there are $13 \times 13 = 169$ ways to draw a heart and a spade.

Thus, the probability that one is heart and one is spade $= \dfrac{169}{1326} = \dfrac{13}{102}$

Example 1.5: A telegraph source emits two symbols, dash and dot. It was observed that the dash were thrice as likely to occur as dots. Find the probabilities of the dashes and dots occurring.

Solution: We have, $P(\text{dash}) = 3P(\text{dot})$.

Now the sum of the probabilities must be 1.

Thus,

$$P(\text{dash}) + P(\text{dot}) = 4P(\text{dot}) = 1$$

or

$$P(\text{dot}) = \frac{1}{4} \text{ and } P(\text{dash}) = \frac{3}{4}$$

Example 1.6: A digital message is 1000 symbols long. An average of 0.1% symbols received is erroneous. (a) What is the probability of correct reception? (b) How many symbols are correctly received?

Solution:

(a) The probability of erroneous reception $= P(A) = 0.1\% = \dfrac{1}{10 \times 100} = 0.001$

Thus, the probability of correct reception $= P(\overline{A}) = 1 - P(A) = 1 - 0.001 = 0.999$

(b) The number of symbols received correctly $= 1000 \times 0.999 = 999$.

1.2.4 Conditional Probability

The *conditional probability* of an event A given that B has happened $(P(A/B))$ is defined as follows:

$$P(A/B) = \frac{P(A \cap B)}{P(B)}, \text{ if } P(B) > 0 \tag{1.9}$$

where $P(A \cap B)$ is the *joint probability* of A and B.

Similarly,

$$P(B/A) = \frac{P(A \cap B)}{P(A)}, \text{ if } P(A) > 0 \tag{1.10}$$

Using Eqs. (1.9) and (1.10) we can write

$$P(A \cap B) = P(A/B)P(B) = P(B/A)P(A) \tag{1.11}$$

or

$$P(A/B) = \frac{P(B/A)P(A)}{P(B)} \tag{1.12}$$

This is known as *Bayes rule*.

Example 1.7: Consider the following table:

Sex	Employed (*E*)	Unemployed (*U*)	Total
Male (*M*)	250	50	300
Female (*F*)	150	100	250
Total	400	150	550

(a) If a person is male, what is the probability that he is unemployed? (b) If a person is female, what is the probability that she is employed? (c) If a person is employed, what is the probability that he is male?

Solution:

(a) $P(U/M) = \dfrac{\text{Unemployed and male}}{\text{Male}} = \dfrac{P(U \cap M)}{P(M)} = \dfrac{50}{300} = \dfrac{1}{6}$

(b) $P(E/F) = \dfrac{P(E \cap F)}{P(F)} = \dfrac{150}{250} = \dfrac{3}{5}$

(c) $P(M/E) = \dfrac{P(M \cap E)}{P(E)} = \dfrac{250}{400} = \dfrac{5}{8}$.

1.2.5 Independent Events

Two events A and B are said to be (*statistically*) *independent* if

$$P(B/A) = P(B) \tag{1.13}$$

or

$$P(A/B) = P(A) \tag{1.14}$$

i.e., the occurrence (or non-occurrence) of event A has no influence on the occurrence (or non-occurrence) of B. Otherwise they are said to be *dependent*.

Combining Eqs. (1.11) and (1.13), we have

$$P(A \cap B) = P(A)P(B) \tag{1.15}$$

Example 1.8: Determine the probability for the event that at least one head appears in three tosses of a fair coin.

Solution: Using Eq. (1.15) we have $P(\text{all tails}) = P(TTT) = P(T)P(T)P(T) = \dfrac{1}{2} \times \dfrac{1}{2} \times \dfrac{1}{2} = \dfrac{1}{8}$.

$$P(\text{at least one head}) = 1 - P(TTT) = 1 - \frac{1}{8} = \frac{7}{8}.$$

Example 1.9: An experiment consists of observation of five successive pulse positions on a communication link. The pulses can be positive, negative or zero. Also consider that the individual experiments that determine the kind of pulse at each possible position are independent. If the probabilities of occurring a positive pulse and a negative pulse at the ith position (x_i) are $p = 0.5$ and $q = 0.2$, respectively, then find (a) the probability that all pulses are negative and (b) the probability that the first two pulses are positive, the next two are zero and the last is negative.

Solution:

(a) Using Eq. (1.15), the probability that all pulses are negative is given by

$$P[(x_1 = -\text{ve}) \cap (x_2 = -\text{ve}) \cap \ldots \cap (x_5 = -\text{ve})]$$
$$= P(x_1 = -\text{ve})\, P(x_2 = -\text{ve}) \ldots P(x_5 = -\text{ve}) = q^5 = (0.2)^5 = 0.00032$$

(b) $P(x_i = 0)$
$= 1 - p - q$
$= 1 - 0.5 - 0.2$
$= 0.3$

Hence, the probability that the first two pulses are positive, the next two are zero and the last is negative is given by

$$P[(x_1 = +\text{ve}) \cap (x_2 = +\text{ve}) \cap (x_3 = 0) \cap (x_4 = 0) \cap (x_5 = -\text{ve})] = p^2(1 - p - q)^2 q$$
$$= (0.5)^2(0.3)^2(0.2) = 0.0045$$

1.2.6 Total Probability

Let $A_1, A_2, \ldots, A_n$ be mutually exclusive ($A_i \cap A_j = \varnothing$, for $i \neq j$) and *exhaustive* ($\cup_{i=1}^{n} A_i = S$). Now B is any event in S.

Then
$$P(B) = \Sigma_{i=1}^{n} P(B \cap A_i) = \Sigma_{i=1}^{n} P(B/A_i)P(A_i) \tag{1.16}$$

This is known as the *total probability* of event B.

If $A = A_i$ in Eq. (1.12), then using (1.16) we have the following important theorem (*Bayes theorem*):

$$P(A_i/B) = \frac{P(B/A_i)P(A_i)}{\Sigma_{i=1}^{n} P(B/A_i)P(A_i)} \tag{1.17}$$

Example 1.10: In a binary communication system (Figure 1.1), either 0 or 1 is transmitted. Due to channel noise, a 1 can be received as 0 and vice versa. Let m_0 and m_1 denote the events of transmitting 0 and 1, respectively. Let r_0 and r_1 denote the events of receiving 0 and 1, respectively. Given $P(m_0) = 0.5$, $P(r_1/m_0) = 0.2$ and $P(r_0/m_1) = 0.1$, (a) find $P(r_0)$ and $P(r_1)$. (b) If a 1 was received, what is the probability that a 1 was sent? (c) If a 0 was received, what is the probability that a 0 was sent? (d) Calculate the probability of error, P_e. (e) Calculate the probability (P_c) that the transmitted signal correctly reaches the receiver.

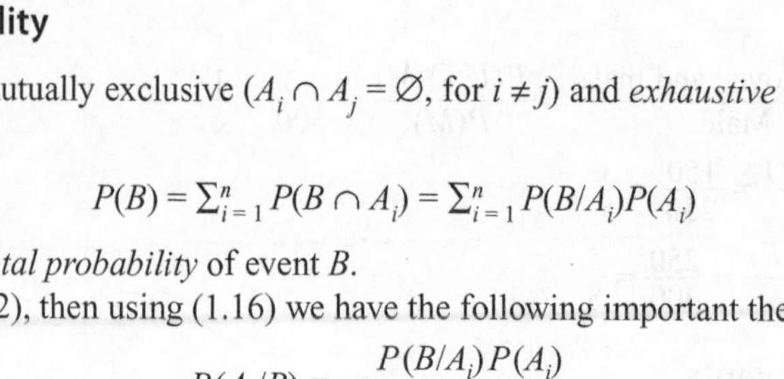

Figure 1.1 *A Binary Communication System*

Solution:

(a) We have, $P(m_1) = 1 - P(m_0) = 1 - 0.5 = 0.5$

$$P\left(\frac{r_0}{m_0}\right) = 1 - P\left(\frac{r_1}{m_0}\right) = 1 - 0.2$$
$$= 0.8$$
$$P\left(\frac{r_1}{m_1}\right) = 1 - P\left(\frac{r_0}{m_1}\right) = 1 - 0.1$$
$$= 0.9$$

Using Eq. (1.16), we have

$$P(r_0) = P\left(\frac{r_0}{m_0}\right)P(m_0) + P\left(\frac{r_0}{m_1}\right)P(m_1) = 0.8 \times 0.5 + 0.1 \times 0.5$$
$$= 0.45$$
$$P(r_1) = P\left(\frac{r_1}{m_0}\right)P(m_0) + P\left(\frac{r_1}{m_1}\right)P(m_1) = 0.2 \times 0.5 + 0.9 \times 0.5$$
$$= 0.55$$

(b) Using Bayes rule (1.12), $P(m_1/r_1) = \dfrac{P(m_1)P(r_1/m_1)}{P(r_1)} = \dfrac{0.5 \times 0.9}{0.55} = 0.818$

(c) Proceeding similarly, $P(m_0/r_0) = \dfrac{P(m_0)P(r_0/m_0)}{P(r_0)} = \dfrac{0.5 \times 0.8}{0.45} = 0.889$

(d) $P_e = P\left(\frac{r_1}{m_0}\right)P(m_0) + P\left(\frac{r_0}{m_1}\right)P(m_1) = 0.2 \times 0.5 + 0.1 \times 0.5$

$$= 0.15$$

(e) $P_c = 1 - P_e = 1 - 0.15 = 0.85$

This can also be found as follows:

$$P_c = P\left(\frac{r_0}{m_0}\right)P(m_0) + P\left(\frac{r_1}{m_1}\right)P(m_1) = 0.8 \times 0.5 + 0.9 \times 0.5$$
$$= 0.85$$

1.3 RANDOM VARIABLES AND ITS CHARACTERISTICS

The outcome of an experiment may either be a real number or be a symbol. An example of the former case is the roll of a die and that of the latter is the toss of a coin. However, for meaningful mathematical analysis, it is always convenient to deal with a real number for each possible outcome. Let $S\,[= \{s_1, s_2, s_3, \ldots\}]$ be the sample space of some random experiment. A *random* or *stochastic variable* $X(s_i)$ (or simply X) is a single-valued real function that assigns a real number to each sample point s_i of S, and the real number is called the value of $X(s_i)$. Schematic diagram representing a random variable (RV) is shown in Figure 1.2.

The sample space S is known as the *domain* of the RV X, and the collection of all values (numbers) assumed by X is called the *range* or *spectrum* of the RV X. RV can be either discrete or continuous.

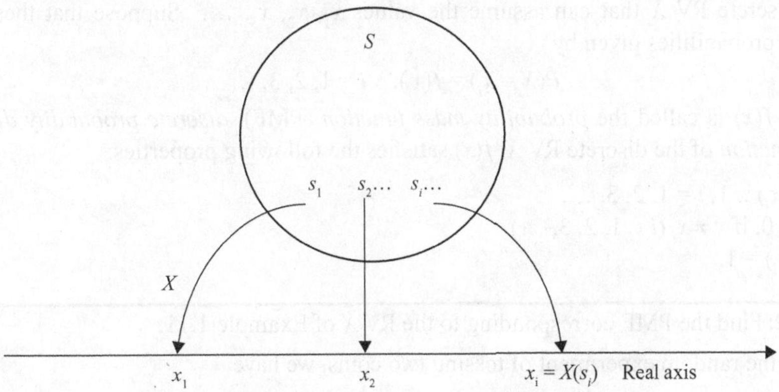

Figure 1.2 *The Random Variable X(s)*

1. *Discrete Random Variable*—A random variable is said to be discrete if it takes on a finite or countably infinite number of distinct values. An example of a discrete RV is the number of cars passing through a street in a finite time.
2. *Continuous Random Variable*—If a random variable assumes any value in some interval or intervals on the real line, then it is called a *continuous RV*. The spectrum of X in this case is uncountable. An example of this type of variable is the measurement of noise voltage across the terminals of some electronic device.

Example 1.11: Two unbiased coins are tossed. Suppose that RV X represents the number of heads that can come up. Find the values taken by X. Also show schematically the mapping of sample points into real numbers on the real axis.

Solution: The sample space S contains four sample points.

Thus, $$S = \{HH, HT, TH, TT\}.$$

Table 1.1 illustrates the sample points and the number of heads that can appear (i.e., the values of X). The schematic representation is shown in Figure 1.3.

Table 1.1 *Random Variable and Its Values*

Outcome	Value of X (Number of Heads)
HH	2
HT	1
TH	1
TT	0

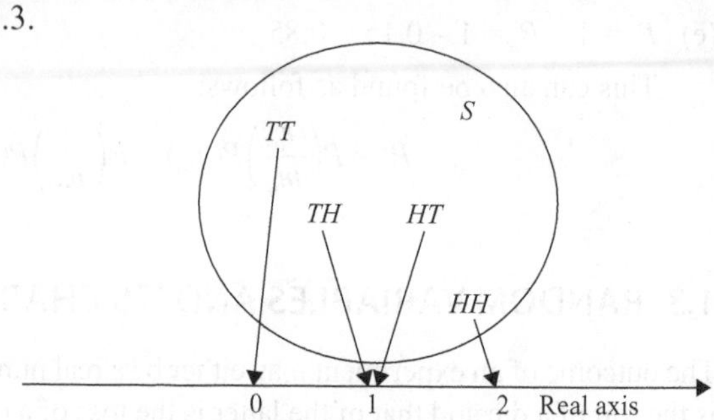

Figure 1.3 *Mapping of Sample Points*

Note that two or more different sample points may assume the same value of X, but two different numbers cannot be assigned to the same sample point.

1.3.1 Discrete Random Variable and Probability Mass Function

Consider a discrete RV X that can assume the values $x_1, x_2, x_3, \ldots$ Suppose that these values are assumed with probabilities given by

$$P(X = x_i) = f(x_i), \quad i = 1, 2, 3, \ldots \tag{1.18}$$

This function $f(x)$ is called the *probability mass function* (PMF), *discrete probability distribution* or *probability function* of the discrete RV X. $f(x)$ satisfies the following properties:

1. $0 \le f(x_i) \le 1, i = 1, 2, 3, \ldots$.
2. $f(x) = 0$, if $x \ne x_i$ $(i = 1, 2, 3, \ldots)$.
3. $\sum_i f(x_i) = 1$.

Example 1.12: Find the PMF corresponding to the RV X of Example 1.11.

Solution: For the random experiment of tossing two coins, we have

$$P(HH) = \frac{1}{4}, P(HT) = \frac{1}{4}, P(TH) = \frac{1}{4}, P(TT) = \frac{1}{4}$$

Table 1.2 *Tabular Representation of PMF*

x_i	0	1	2
$f(x_i)$	$\frac{1}{4}$	$\frac{1}{2}$	$\frac{1}{4}$

Thus,
$$P(X=0) = P(TT) = \frac{1}{4}$$
$$P(X=1) = P(HT \cup TH) = P(HT) + P(TH) = \frac{1}{4} + \frac{1}{4} = \frac{1}{2}$$
$$P(X=2) = P(HH) = \frac{1}{4}$$

Table 1.2 illustrates the PMF.

1.3.2 Cumulative Distribution Function

The *cumulative distribution function* (CDF) or briefly the *distribution function* of a continuous or discrete RV X is given by

$$F(x) = P(X \le x), -\infty < x < \infty \tag{1.19}$$

The CDF $F(x)$ has the following properties:

1. $0 \le F(x) \le 1$.
2. $F(x)$ is a monotonic non-decreasing function, i.e., $F(x_1) \le F(x_2)$ if $x_1 \le x_2$.
3. $F(-\infty) = 0$.
4. $F(\infty) = 1$.
5. $F(x)$ is continuous from the right, i.e., $\lim_{h \to 0^+} F(x+h) = F(x)$ for all x.

1.3.3 Distribution Function for Discrete Random Variable

The CDF of a discrete RV X is given by

$$F(x) = P(X \le x) = \Sigma_{u \le x} f(u), -\infty < x < \infty \tag{1.20}$$

If X assumes only a finite number of values $x_1, x_2, x_3, \ldots$, then the distribution function can be expressed as follows:

$$F(x) = \begin{cases} 0, & -\infty < x < x_1 \\ f(x_1), & x_1 \le x < x_2 \\ f(x_1) + f(x_2), & x_2 \le x < x_3 \\ \vdots & \\ f(x_1) + \cdots + f(x_n), & x_3 \le x < \infty \end{cases}$$

Example 1.13: (a) Find the CDF for the RV X of Example 1.12. (b) Obtain its graph.

Solution:

(a) The distribution function is

$$F(x) = \begin{cases} 0 & -\infty < x < 0 \\ \frac{1}{4}, & 0 \le x < 1 \\ \frac{3}{4}, & 1 \le x < 2 \\ 1, & 2 \le x < \infty \end{cases}$$

(b)

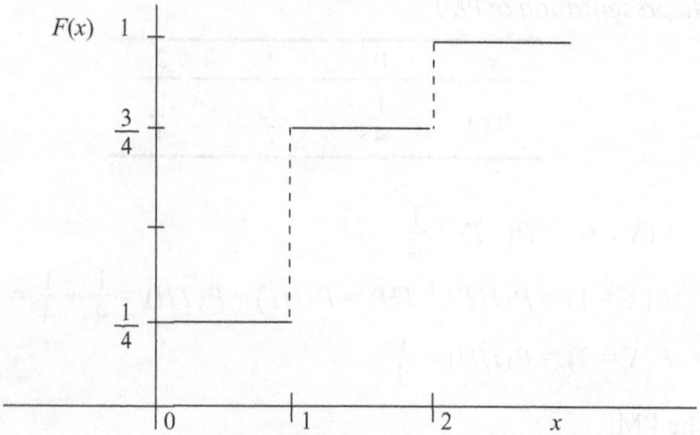

Figure 1.4 *The CDF*

1.3.4 Continuous Random Variable and Probability Density Function

The distribution function of a continuous RV is represented as follows:

$$F(x) = P(X \leq x) = \int_{-\infty}^{x} f(u)\,du, \quad -\infty < x < \infty \tag{1.21}$$

where $f(x)$ satisfies the following conditions:

1. $f(x) \geq 0$.
2. $\int_{-\infty}^{\infty} f(x)\,dx = 1$.
3. $P(a < X < b) = \int_{a}^{b} f(x)\,dx$.

   $f(x)$ is known as the *probability density function* (PDF) or simply *density function.*

1.4 STATISTICAL AVERAGES

The following terms are important in the analysis of various probability distributions:

Expectation—The expectation or *mean* of an RV X is defined as follows:

$$\mu = E(X) = \begin{cases} \Sigma_i x_i\, f(x_i), & X\text{: discrete} \\ \int_{-\infty}^{\infty} x f(x)\,dx, & X\text{: continuous} \end{cases} \tag{1.22}$$

Variance and Standard Deviation—The variance of an RV X is expressed as follows:

$$\operatorname{Var}(X) = \sigma^2 = E[(X-\mu)^2] = \begin{cases} \Sigma_i (x_i - \mu)^2 f(x_i), & X\text{: discrete} \\ \int_{-\infty}^{\infty} (x-\mu)^2 f(x)\,dx, & X\text{: continuous} \end{cases} \tag{1.23}$$

Eq. (1.23) is simplified as follows:

$$\sigma^2 = E[X-\mu)^2] = E[X^2] - \mu^2 = E[X^2] - (E[X])^2 \tag{1.24}$$

The positive square root of the variance (σ) is called the *standard deviation* of X.

1.5 FREQUENTLY USED PROBABILITY DISTRIBUTIONS

Several probability distributions are frequently used in communication theory. Among them, *binomial distribution, Poisson distribution* and *Gaussian* or *normal distribution* need special mention.

1.5.1 Binomial Distribution

In an experiment of tossing a coin or drawing a card from a pack of 52 cards repeatedly, each toss or selection is called a *trial*. In some cases, the probability associated with a particular event (such as head on the coin, drawing a heart etc.) is constant in each trial. Such trials are then said to be independent and referred to as *Bernoulli trials*. Let p be the probability that an event will occur in any single Bernoulli trial (probability of success). Therefore, $q = 1 - p$ is the probability that the event will fail to occur (probability of failure). The probability that the event will occur exactly k times in n trials (i.e. k successes and $(n - k)$ failures) is given by the probability function

$$P(X = k) = \binom{n}{k} p^k q^{n-k}, \quad k = 0, 1, \ldots, n \tag{1.25}$$

where $0 \le p \le 1$ and $\binom{n}{k} = \dfrac{n!}{k!\,(n-k)!}$ is known as the binomial coefficient. The corresponding RV X is called a *binomial RV* and the CDF of X is

$$F(x) = \Sigma_{k=0}^{m} \binom{n}{k} p^k q^{n-k}, \quad m \le x \le m + 1 \tag{1.26}$$

The mean and variance of the binomial RV X are, respectively,

$$\mu = np \text{ and } \sigma^2 = npq$$

The binomial distribution finds application in digital transmission, where X stands for the number of errors in a message of n digits.

Example 1.14: A binary source generates digits 1 and 0 randomly with probabilities 0.7 and 0.3, respectively. What is the probability that three digits of a five-digit sequence will be 1?

Solution: $$P(X = 3) = \binom{5}{3} (0.7)^3 (0.3)^2 = 0.3087$$

1.5.2 Poisson Distribution

Let X be a discrete RV. It is called a *Poisson RV* if its PMF is expressed as

$$P(X = k) = e^{-\alpha} \frac{\alpha^k}{k!}, \quad k = 0, 1, 2, \ldots \tag{1.27}$$

where α is a positive constant. The above distribution is called the *Poisson distribution*. The corresponding CDF is given by

$$F(x) = e^{-\alpha} \Sigma_{k=0}^{n} \frac{\alpha^k}{k!}, \quad n \le x \le n + 1 \tag{1.28}$$

The mean and variance in this case are, respectively,

$$\mu = \alpha \text{ and } \sigma^2 = \alpha$$

Poisson distribution finds application in monitoring the number of telephone calls coming at a switching centre during different intervals of time. Binomial distribution fails to solve the problem of the transmission of many data bits, where the error rate is low. In such a situation Poisson distribution proves to be effective.

1.5.3 Gaussian Distribution

The PDF of a Gaussian or *normal* RV X is given by

$$f(x) = \frac{1}{\sqrt{2\pi\sigma^2}} e^{-(x-\mu)^2/(2\sigma^2)}, \quad -\infty < x < \infty \tag{1.29}$$

where μ and σ are the mean and standard deviation, respectively. The corresponding CDF of X is as follows:

$$F(x) = \frac{1}{\sqrt{2\pi\sigma^2}} \int_{-\infty}^{x} e^{-(u-\mu)^2/(2\sigma^2)} du = \frac{1}{\sqrt{2\pi}} \int_{-\infty}^{(x-\mu)/\sigma} e^{-\mu^2/2} du \tag{1.30}$$

Eq. (1.30) cannot be evaluated analytically and is solved numerically. We define a function $Q(z)$ such that

$$Q(z) = \frac{1}{\sqrt{2\pi}} \int_{z}^{\infty} e^{-u^2/2} du \tag{1.31}$$

Thus, Eq. (1.30) is rewritten as follows:

$$F(x) = 1 - Q\left(\frac{x-\mu}{\sigma}\right) \tag{1.32}$$

$Q(z)$ is known as the complementary error function. Figure 1.5 illustrates a Gaussian distribution.

The normal distribution is useful in describing the random phenomena in nature. The sum of a large number of independent random variables, under certain conditions, can also be approximated by a normal distribution (*central-limit theorem*).

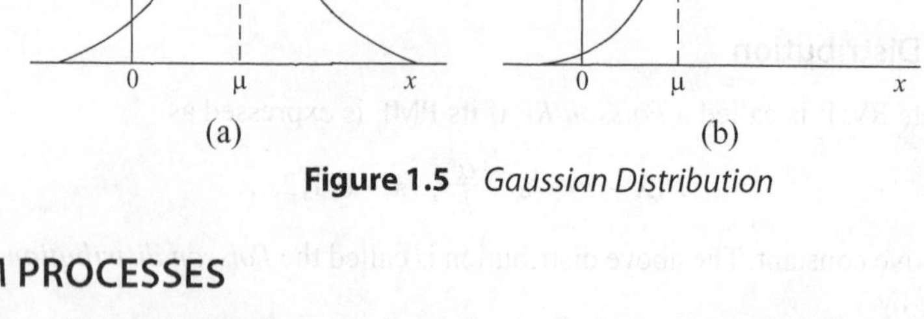

Figure 1.5 *Gaussian Distribution*

1.6 RANDOM PROCESSES

In the context of communication theory, an RV that is a function of time is called a *random process* or a *stochastic process*. Thus, a random process is collection of an infinite number of RVs. Any random signal such as noise is characterized by random process. In order to determine the statistical behaviour of a random process, we might proceed in either of the two ways: We might perform repeated measurement of the same random process or we might take simultaneous measurements of a very large number of identical random processes.

Let us consider a random process such as a noise waveform. To obtain the statistical properties of the noise, we might repeatedly measure the output noise voltage of a single noise source or we might make simultaneous measurements of the output of a very large collection of statistically identical noise sources. The collection of all possible waveforms is known as the *ensemble* ($X(t, s)$ or simply $X(t)$), and a waveform in this collection is a *sample function* or *ensemble member* or *realization of the process*.

Stationary Random Process—A random process is called *stationary random process* if the statistical properties of the process remain unaltered with time.

Strict-Sense Stationary—A random process is said to be strict-sense stationary if its probability density does not change with shift of origin, i.e.,

$$f(x_1, x_2, \ldots, t_1, t_2, \ldots) = f(x_1, x_2, \ldots, t_1 + \tau, t_2 + \tau, \ldots)$$

Wide-Sense Stationary—A random process is called *wide-sense stationary* if its mean is a constant and autocorrelation depends only on time difference.

Thus,

$$E[X(t)] = \text{constant}$$

and

$$E[X(t), X(t+\tau)] = R_X(t_1, t_2) = R_X(t_1 - t_2) = R_X(\tau)$$

Ergodic Process—A stationary process is known as ergodic process if the ensemble average is equal to the time average. The time-averaged mean of a sample function $x(t)$ of a random process $X(t)$ is given by

$$\langle x(t) \rangle = \lim_{T \to \infty} \frac{1}{T} \int_0^T x(t)\, dt$$

Thus, in this case,

$$E[X(t)] = \langle x(t) \rangle$$

The process which is not stationary is termed as *non-stationary*.

1.7 NOISE

The term *noise* encompasses all forms of unwanted electrical signal that corrupt the message signal during its transmission or processing in a communication system. Along with other basic factors, it sets limits on the rate of communication. However, it is often possible to suppress or even eliminate the effects of noise by intelligent circuits design. Thus, the study of fundamental sources of noise and their characteristics are very much essential in the context of communication.

1.7.1 Sources of Noise

Noise arises in a variety of ways. Potential sources of random noise can be broadly classified as external noise and internal noise.

1. *External Noise*—This noise is generated outside the circuit. It can be further classified as
   (i) *Erratic natural disturbances or atmospheric noise or static noise*—Natural phenomena that give rise to noise include electric storms, solar flares, lighting discharge during thunderstorm, lightning, intergalactic or other atmospheric disturbances and certain belts of radiation that exist in space. This type of noise occurs irregularly and is unpredictable in nature.

Noise arising from these sources is difficult to suppress and often the only solution is to reposition the receiving antenna to minimize the received noise, while ensuring that reception of the desired signal is not seriously impaired.

(ii) *Man-made noise*—This noise occurs due to the undesired interfering disturbances from electrical appliances, such as motors, switch gears, automobile, fluorescent lighting, leakage from high-voltage transmission line, faulty connection, aircraft ignition, etc. It is difficult to analyze this noise on analytical footing. However, this type of noise is under human control and, in principle, can be eliminated. The frequency range of this noise lies between 1 and 500 MHz.

2. *Internal Noise*—We are mainly concerned with the noise in the receiver. The noise in the receiving section actually sets lower limit on the size of usefully received signal. Even when ample precautions are taken to eliminate noise caused by external sources, still certain potential sources of noise exist within electronic systems that limit the receiver sensitivity. Use of amplifier to amplify the signal to any desired level may not be of great help because adding amplifiers to receiving system also adds noise and the signal to noise may further be degraded.

   The internal noise is produced by the active and passive electronic components within the communication circuit. It arises due to

   (i) thermal or Brownian motion of free electrons inside a resistor
   (ii) random emission of electrons from cathode in a vacuum tube, and
   (iii) random diffusion of charge carriers (electrons and holes) in a semiconductor.

   Some of the main constituents of internal noise are *thermal noise, shot noise, partition noise* and *flicker noise*.

1.7.2 Thermal Noise

In a conductor, the free electrons are thermally agitated because heat exchange takes place between the conductor and its surroundings. These free electrons exhibit random motion as a result of their collisions with lattice structure. Consequently, there exists a random variation in the electron density throughout the conductor, resulting in a randomly fluctuating voltage across the ends of the conductor. This is the most important class of noise in electronic circuits and known as thermal noise or *Johnson noise* or *resistor noise*.

Thermal noise can be best be described by a zero mean Gaussian process and has a flat type of *power spectral density* over a wide range of frequencies.

1.7.3 Shot Noise

Shot noise appears in all amplifying and active devices as a random fluctuation superimposed on the steady current crossing a potential barrier. The effect occurs because electrical current is not a continuous but discrete flow of charge carriers. In vacuum tubes, shot noise is caused by random emission of electrons from cathode. In semiconductor devices, it is generated due to the random variation in the diffusion of minority carriers (holes and electrons) and random generation and recombination of electron–hole pairs. As lead shots from a gun strike a target, in a similar way, electrons from the cathode strike the anode plate in a vacuum tube; hence, the name shot noise. Although shot noise is always present, its effect is significant in the amplifying devices.

The fluctuating component of current ($i_n(t)$) which wiggles around the mean value I_{dc} is the shot noise. Thus, the total current $i(t)$ is expressed as follows:

$$i(t) = I_{dc} + i_n(t)$$

Like thermal noise, shot noise also has flat type of *power spectrum* (power spectral density) except in the high microwave frequency range. For diodes, the rms shot noise current is given by

$$I_n^2 = 2I_{dc}qB,$$

where I_{dc} is the direct diode current, q is the electronic charge (= 1.6×10^{19} C) and B is the bandwidth of the system.

1.7.4 Partition Noise

Partition noise is generated in multi-grid tubes (tetrode, pentode, etc.) where current divides between two or more electrodes due to random fluctuations of electrons emitted from cathode among various electrodes. In this respect, a diode would be less noisy than a transistor. Hence, the input stage of microwave receivers is often a diode circuit. Very recently, GaAs field effect transistors have been developed for low-noise microwave amplification. The spectrum for partition noise is also flat.

1.7.5 Flicker Noise or 1/*f* Noise

At low audio frequencies (less than few kilohertz), another type of noise arises in vacuum tubes and semiconductor devices, the power spectral density of which is inversely proportional to frequency. This noise is known as flicker noise or $1/f$ noise. In vacuum tubes, it stems due to gradual changes in the oxide structure of oxide-coated cathodes and due to the migration of impurity ions through the oxide. In case of semiconductor devices, it is produced due to contaminants and defects in the crystal structure.

1.8 SOLVED PROBLEMS

Problem 1.1: What is the probability that either a 1 or 6 will appear in the experiment involving the rolling of a die?

Solution: Since each of the six outcomes is equally likely in a large number of trials, each outcome has a probability of 1/6.

Thus, the probability of occurrence of either 1 or 6 is given by

$$P(A \cup B) = P(A) + P(B) = \frac{1}{6} + \frac{1}{6} = \frac{1}{3}.$$

Problem 1.2: Consider an experiment of drawing two cards from a deck of cards without replacing the first card drawn. Determine the probability of obtaining two red aces in two draws.

Solution: Let A and B be two events 'red ace in the first draw' and 'red ace in the second draw', respectively.

We know that $P(A \cap B) = P(A)P(B/A)$

The relative frequency of $A = P(A) = \frac{2}{52} = \frac{1}{26}$.

$P(B/A)$ is the probability of drawing a red ace in the second draw provided that the outcome of the first draw was a red ace.

Thus, $$P(B/A) = \frac{1}{51}.$$

Hence, $$P(A \cap B) = P(A)P(B/A) = \frac{1}{26} \times \frac{1}{51} = \frac{1}{1326}.$$

Problem 1.3: The random variable X assumes the values 0 and 1 with probabilities p and $q = 1 - p$, respectively. Find the mean and the variance of X.

Solution:

$$\mu = E(X) = 0(p) + 1(q) = q$$

$$E[X^2] = 0^2(p) + 1^2(q) = q$$

Hence,

$$\sigma^2 = E[X^2] - \mu^2 = q - q^2 = q(1 - q) = pq$$

Problem 1.4: A fair die is rolled 5 times. If 1 or 6 appears, it is called *success*. Determine (a) the probability of two successes and (b) the mean and standard deviation for the number of successes.

Solution: We apply binomial distribution.

(a) Here, $n = 5$, $p = \frac{2}{6} = \frac{1}{3}$ and $q = 1 - p = \frac{2}{3}$

Thus, $P(X = 2) = \binom{5}{2}\left[\frac{1}{3}\right]^2\left[\frac{2}{3}\right]^{5-2} = \frac{80}{243}$

(b) $\mu = np = 5 \times \frac{1}{3} = 1.667$

and $\sigma = (npq)^{\frac{1}{2}} = \left(5 \times \frac{1}{3} \times \frac{2}{3}\right)^{\frac{1}{2}} = 1.054.$

Problem 1.5: When n is very large ($n >> k$) and p very small ($p << 1$), prove that the binomial distribution can be approximated by the following Poisson distribution:

$$P(X = k) \approx e^{-np}\frac{(np)^k}{k!}, \quad k = 0, 1, 2, \ldots$$

Solution: From binomial distribution, we write

$$P(X = k) = \binom{n}{k}p^k q^{n-k}, \quad k = 0, 1, \ldots, n$$

$$= \frac{n!}{k!\,(n-k)!}p^k q^{n-k}$$

$$= \frac{n(n-1)\ldots(n-k+1)}{k!}p^k q^{n-k} \tag{1.33}$$

Since $n >> k$ and $p << 1$, then

$$n(n-1)\ldots(n-k+1) \approx n \cdot n \cdot \ldots \cdot n = n^k$$

and

$$q = 1 - p \approx e^{-p}$$

Thus,

$$q^{n-k} \approx e^{-(n-k)p} \approx e^{-np}$$

Substituting these values into Eq. (1.33) we get

$$P(X = k) \approx e^{-np}\frac{(np)^k}{k!}.$$

MULTIPLE CHOICE QUESTIONS

1. Two cards are drawn at random from a pack of 52 cards. The probability that both are spades is
   (a) 1/15 (b) 2/17 (c) 1/17 (d) 2/15
   Ans. (c)
2. A ball is drawn at random from a box containing 6 red balls, 4 white balls, and 5 blue balls. The probability that it is red is
   (a) 2/5 (b) 4/15 (c) 1/3 (d) 2/3
   Ans. (a)
3. In the above problem, the probability that the ball is red or white is
   (a) 2/5 (b) 2/3 (c) 7/15 (d) 1/5
   Ans. (b)
4. Three light bulbs are chosen at random from 15 bulbs out of which 5 are defective. The probability that exactly one is defective is
   (a) 24/91 (b) 45/91 (c) 67/91 (d) none of these
   Ans. (b)
5. In the above problem, the probability that none of the three bulbs is defective is
   (a) 13/91 (b) 67/91 (c) 55/97 (d) 24/91
   Ans. (d)
6. Let A and B be two events with $P(A) = \frac{3}{8}$, $P(B) = \frac{1}{2}$, and $P(A \cap B) = \frac{1}{4}$. The value of $P(A \cup B)$ is
   (a) 5/8 (b) 1/3 (c) 1/2 (d) 3/8
   Ans. (a)
7. The probability of a 4 turning up at least once in two tosses of a fair die is
   (a) 11/36 (b) 17/36 (c) 13/36 (d) 19/36
   Ans. (a)
8. A class has 12 boys and 4 girls. If three students are selected at random from the class, the probability that they are all boys is
   (a) 19/28 (b) 3/28 (c) 17/28 (d) 11/28
   Ans. (d)
9. A box contains 7 red marbles and 3 white marbles. Three marbles are drawn from the box one after the other. The probability that the first two are red and the third is white is
   (a) 1/12 (b) 2/9 (c) 7/40 (d) 13/40
   Ans. (c)
10. The expectation of the sum of points in tossing a pair of fair dice is
    (a) 9 (b) 5 (c) 6 (d) 7
    Ans. (d)
11. In the above problem, the variance is
    (a) 37/6 (b) 35/12 (c) 35/6 (d) none of these
    Ans. (c)
12. A random variable X has the following density function:

$$f(x) = \begin{cases} \frac{1}{4} & -2 \le x \le 2 \\ 0 & \text{otherwise} \end{cases}$$

    Var (X) is
    (a) 1 (b) 2 (c) 3 (d) 4
    Ans. (a)

13. A random variable X has $E(X) = 2$, $E(X^2) = 8$. The standard deviation is
    (a) 1 (b) 2 (c) 4 (d) 10

    Ans. **(b)**
14. A random variable X is such that $E[(X - 1)^2] = 10$, $E[(X - 2)^2] = 6$. $E(X)$ is
    (a) 7/2 (b) 5/2 (c) 3/2 (d) 8/3

    Ans. **(a)**
15. In the above problem, Var (X) is
    (a) 17/4 (b) 15/4 (c) 13/4 (d) none of these

    Ans. **(b)**

REVIEW QUESTIONS

1. (a) Define following terms:
   (i) conditional probability
   (ii) independent events
   (iii) probability mass function
   (iv) cumulative distribution function
   (v) probability density function
   (vi) expectation.
   (b) State Bayes theorem.
2. What is the chance that a leap year selected at random will contain 53 Wednesdays?
3. If A and B are mutually independent events, then show that the following pairs are independent:
   (a) $\overline{A}$ and $\overline{B}$,
   (b) A and $\overline{B}$,
   (c) $\overline{A}$ and B.
4. If A, B and C be mutually independent events, then prove that
   (a) A and $B + C$ are independent
   (b) $\overline{A}$, $\overline{B}$, and $\overline{C}$ are mutually independent.
5. In a bolt factory, machines A, B, and C manufacture 25%, 35%, and 40% of the total of their output, respectively. Out of them, 5%, 4%, and 2% are defective bolts. A bolt is drawn at random from the product and is found to be defective. What are the probabilities that it was manufactured by machines A, B, and C?
6. A box contains 5 defective and 10 non-defective lamps. Eight lamps are drawn at random in succession without replacement. What is the probability that the eighth lamp is the fifth defective?
7. Three groups of children contain three girls and one boy, two girls and two boys, and one girl and three boys. One child is selected at random from each group. Show that the chance that the three selected children consisting of one girl and two boys is 13/32.
8. Two persons A and B throw alternatively with a pair of dice. A wins if he throws 6 before B throws 7 and B wins if he throws 7 before A throws 6. If A begins, find his probability of winning.

9. A variable X has the density function

$$f(x) = \begin{cases} \frac{x}{2}, & 0 \le x \le 1 \\ \frac{1}{2}, & 1 < x \le 2 \\ \frac{1}{2}(3 - x), & 2 < x \le 3 \end{cases}$$

Find the mean and variance of X.

10. For a random variable X, Var $(X) = 1$, find Var $(2X + 3)$.
11. If X has binomial distribution with parameter n and p, then show that
    (a) its mean is np
    (b) its variance is npq, where $q = 1 - p$.
12. A car-hire firm has two cars, which it hires out day by day. The number of demands for a car on each day is distributed as a Poisson distribution with average number of demand per day being 1.5. Calculate the proportion of days on which neither car is used and the proportion of days on which some demand is refused ($e^{-1.5} = 0.2231$).
13. If X is normally distributed with zero mean and unit variance, find the expectation of X^2.
14. If X is a Poisson variate such that $P(X = 1) = 0.2$ and $P(X = 2) = 0.2$, find $P(X = 0)$.
15. Show that for a Poisson variate standard deviation = $\sqrt{\text{mean}}$.

chapter 2

INFORMATION THEORY

2.1 INTRODUCTION

It is well-known that the performance of any communication system is determined by the available signal power, the presence of undesirable background noise, and limited bandwidth. Naturally, the questions that come to our mind are whether there is any ideal system that can reliably send messages over a communication channel with all its inherent physical limitations and how the message should be represented for reliable transmission over the channel. Recognizing the fact, Claude Shannon developed a completely new theory of communication in 1948 which he called *A Mathematical Theory of Communication* in which he established the basic theoretical bounds on the performances of communication systems. In his pioneering work, he emphasized that the message should be represented by its *information* rather than by the signal. His groundbreaking research was soon renamed as *Information Theory*—a hybrid area of mathematics and engineering. It combines noise protection and efficient use of the channel into a single theory.

Information theory deals with three basic concepts: (a) the measure of source information (the rate at which the source generates the information), (b) the information capacity of a channel (the maximum rate at which reliable transmission of information is possible over a given channel with an arbitrarily small error), and (c) *coding* (a scheme for efficient utilization of the channel capacity for information transfer). These three concepts are tied together through a series of theorems that form the basis of information theory summarized as follows:

If the rate of information from a message-producing source does not exceed the capacity of the communication channel under consideration, then there exists a coding technique such that the information can be sent over the channel with an arbitrarily small frequency of errors, despite the presence of undesirable noise.

The surprising fact of this statement is that it promises error-free transmission over a noisy communication channel with the aid of coding. Optimum coding matches the source and channel for maximum reliable information transfer, similar to impedance matching for maximum power transfer in electrical circuits. A typical communication system with both source and channel encoding/decoding is shown in Figure 2.1.

The channel encoder/decoder performs the task of error-control coding. An optimum channel coding yields an equivalent noiseless channel with a well-defined capacity of information transmission. The source encoder/decoder is then used to match the source to the equivalent noiseless channel, provided that the source information rate falls within the channel capacity.

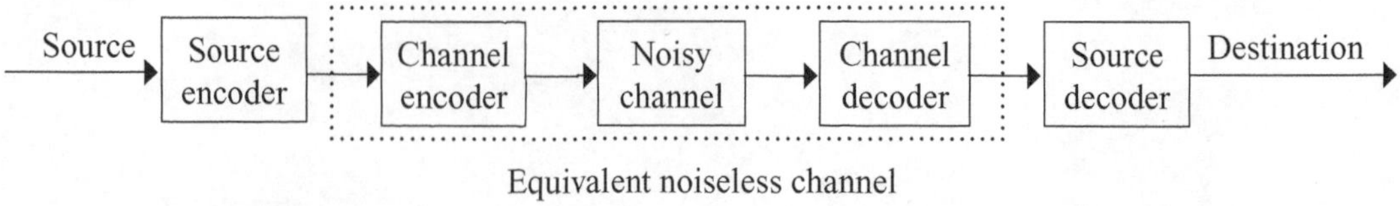

Figure 2.1 *A Communication System with Source and Channel Decoding*

In this chapter, fundamentals of information theory are discussed in detail. Source coding techniques have been discussed in chapter 3. Various channel coding techniques have been described in chapters 5, 6, 7 and 8.

2.2 MEASURE OF INFORMATION

In a communication system, information is something that is transmitted from the source to the destination, which was previously unavailable to the end user; else nothing would be transferred. Any information source, be it analog or digital, produces message (or event), the outcome of which is selected at random according to a probability distribution. Let us start with the measure of information. Information measures the *freedom of choice* exercised by the source in selecting a message from many different messages and the user is highly uncertain as to which message will be selected. A message containing knowledge of low probability of occurrence conveys more information than one with a high probability of occurrence. This can be best appreciated with the help of the following example.

One of the basic principles of the media world is: 'if a dog bites a man, it's no news, but if a man bites a dog, it's a news'. The first part, 'a dog bites a man', is quite common and seldom constitutes a headline in the newspaper, i.e., it is not a news at all! Technically, the probability of a dog biting a man is rather high; hence, it provides virtually no information. On the contrary, what really catch the reader's fancy are the last few words, 'a man bites a dog'. Had a man bitten a dog, it would have occupied the front page of the newspaper. Since the probability of a man biting a dog is almost zero (a rare and unexpected event), a large amount of information is carried by this message. Thus, information is inversely related to the probability of occurrence or directly related to the uncertainty. The less likely the message, the more information it conveys and vice versa.

Let a digital source generate a message *m* having a probability of occurrence *p*. The measure of information was quantitatively defined by Shanon as follows:

$$I = \log_b\left(\frac{1}{p}\right) = -\log_b p \tag{2.1}$$

where I is the *self-information* of the message *m*, and *b* is the logarithmic base. Since $0 \le p \le 1$, $I \ge 0$, i.e., the information is non-negative. The amount of information in a message depends only on its probability of occurrence rather than its actual content or physical interpretations. Although the probability is a dimensionless quantity, a unit is assigned to I. For the logarithmic base $b = 2$, the unit of I is *bit* (*binary unit*, different from *binary digit*). When the base is '*e*', the unit is *nat* (natural unit), and for $b = 10$, the unit is *decit* or *Hartley*. When no base is mentioned, the unit of the information is taken to as bit, i.e., $b = 2$. The information given in one unit can be expressed in other unit by the following relationships:

$$\log_2 a = \frac{\ln a}{\ln 2} = \frac{\log a}{\log 2} \tag{2.2}$$

For a *discrete memoryless source* (DMS), each message emitted is independent of the previous message(s). When such a source sends a number of independent messages $m_1, m_2, \ldots, m_M$ with their probabilities of occurrence $p_1, p_2, \ldots, p_M$, respectively, and the messages are correctly received, the information measure in the composite message is given by

$$I = \log_2\left(\frac{1}{p_1}\right) + \log_2\left(\frac{1}{p_2}\right) + \ldots + \log_2\left(\frac{1}{p_M}\right) = \sum_{j=1}^{M} \log_2\left(\frac{1}{p_j}\right) = I_1 + I_2 + \ldots + I_M \tag{2.3}$$

where $p_1 + p_2 + \ldots + p_M = 1$.

2.3 ENTROPY

The *average information* per individual message emitted by a source is known as the *entropy* of the source. However, the term 'average information' is used to indicate 'statistical average' and not 'arithmetic average'. To understand the fact, we consider the following example:

Let us calculate the average mass of M number of students in a class. If the mass of the jth student be m_j ($j = 1, 2, \ldots, M$), then the average mass of all students is given by

$$\overline{m_j} = \frac{\sum_{j=1}^{M} m_j}{M}$$

It can be noted that arithmetic average is applicable for the quantities which are deterministic in nature and hence are to be considered just once. Let us now consider the problem of information associated with every transmitted message (symbol) which is a non-deterministic (probabilistic, statistical) quantity. If there are M messages and the information associated with jth message is I_j, then using the previous definition of arithmetic average the average information per transmitted message is given by

$$\overline{I_j} = \frac{\sum_{j=1}^{M} I_j}{M}$$

However, the above calculation is wrong as the messages are not transmitted just once; they are transmitted many times and the number of times a message emitted is determined by its probability of occurrence. Hence, the above method is not valid and we adopt the following method to obtain the statistical average.

Let us consider M number of different messages $m_1, m_2, \ldots, m_M$ having their probabilities of occurrences $p_1, p_2, \ldots, p_M$, respectively. The source generates a sequence of L-independent messages over a long period of time such that $L >> M$. The number of messages m_1 within L messages is p_1L and the amount of information in each m_1 is $\log\frac{1}{p_1}$. The total amount of information in all m_1 messages is $p_1L\log\frac{1}{p_1}$. Thus, the total amount of information in all L messages comes out as follows:

$$I_t = p_1L\log\left(\frac{1}{p_1}\right) + p_2L\log\left(\frac{1}{p_2}\right) + \ldots + p_ML\log\left(\frac{1}{p_M}\right) \tag{2.4}$$

and the average information per message or entropy is

$$\begin{aligned} H = \frac{I_t}{L} &= p_1\log\left(\frac{1}{p_1}\right) + p_2\log\left(\frac{1}{p_2}\right) + \ldots + p_M\log\left(\frac{1}{p_M}\right) \\ &= \sum_{j=1}^{M} p_j\log\left(\frac{1}{p_j}\right) \\ &= -\sum_{j=1}^{M} p_j\log p_j \text{ bits/message} \end{aligned} \tag{2.5}$$

If $M = 1$, i.e., there is only a single possible message and $p_j = p = 1$, then

$$H = p_1\log\left(\frac{1}{p_1}\right) = 1\log\left(\frac{1}{1}\right) = 0$$

Under such situation, the message carries no information.

Example 2.1: Verify the equation $I(x_ix_j) = I(x_i) + I(x_j)$, if x_i and x_j are independent.

Solution: As x_i and x_j are independent, $P(x_ix_j) = P(x_i)P(x_j)$

From Eq. (2.1),

$$
\begin{aligned}
I(x_ix_j) &= \log \frac{1}{P(x_ix_j)} \\
&= \log \frac{1}{P(x_i)P(x_j)} \\
&= \log \frac{1}{P(x_i)} + \log \frac{1}{P(x_j)} \\
&= I(x_i) + I(x_j)
\end{aligned}
$$

Example 2.2: DMS X produces four symbols x_1, x_2, x_3, and x_4 with probabilities $P(x_1) = 0.5$, $P(x_2) = 0.2$, $P(x_3) = 0.2$, and $P(x_4) = 0.1$, respectively. Determine $H(X)$. Also obtain the information contained in the message $x_4x_3x_1x_1$.

Solution:

$$
\begin{aligned}
H(X) &= -\textstyle\sum_{j=1}^{4} P(x_j)\log_2[P(x_j)] \\
&= -0.5\log_2(0.5) - 0.2\log_2(0.2) - 0.2\log_2(0.2) - 0.1\log_2(0.1) \\
&= 1.76 \text{ bits/symbol}
\end{aligned}
$$

$$P(x_4x_3x_1x_1) = (0.1)(0.2)(0.5)^2 = 5 \times 10^{-3}$$

Thus, $I(x_4x_3x_1x_1) = -\log_2(5 \times 10^{-3}) = 7.64$ bits/symbol

Example 2.3: A binary memoryless system produces two messages with probabilities p and $1 - p$. Show that the entropy is maximum when both messages are equiprobable.

Solution:

$$H = p\log\left(\frac{1}{p}\right) + (1-p)\log\left(\frac{1}{1-p}\right)$$

In order to obtain the maximum source entropy, we differentiate H with respect to p and set it equal to zero.

Now,

$$
\begin{aligned}
\frac{dH}{dp} &= \frac{1}{\ln 2}\left[p \times p\left(-\frac{1}{p^2}\right) + \ln\left(\frac{1}{p}\right) + (1-p)(1-p) \times \frac{1}{(1-p)^2} - \ln\left(\frac{1}{1-p}\right)\right] \\
&= \frac{1}{\ln 2}\left[\ln\left(\frac{1}{p}\right) - \ln\left(\frac{1}{1-p}\right)\right] = 0
\end{aligned}
$$

Thus, $p = 1 - p$

or, $p = \dfrac{1}{2}$

Thus, the entropy is maximum when two messages are equiprobable. It can be shown that the second derivate of H is negative.

The maximum value of the entropy is given by

$$H_{\max} = \left(\frac{1}{2}\right)\log 2 + \frac{1}{2}\log 2 = 1 \text{ bit/message}$$

A plot of H as a function of p is shown in Figure 2.2. Note that H is zero for both $p = 0$ and $p = 1$.

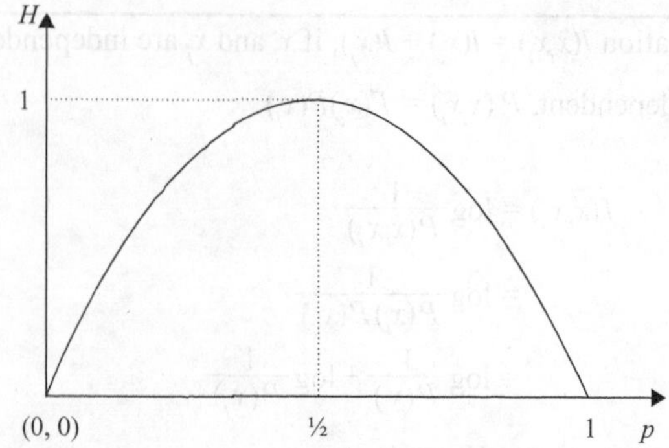

Figure 2.2 *Average Information H for Two Messages as a Function of Probability p*

Example 2.4: Consider that a digital source sends M independent messages. Show that the source entropy attains a maximum value if all the messages are equally likely.

Solution: Let the respective probabilities of occurrence of the messages be denoted as $p_1, p_2, \ldots, p_M$. Then the source entropy

$$H = p_1 \log_2\left(\frac{1}{p_1}\right) + p_2 \log_2\left(\frac{1}{p_2}\right) + \cdots + p_M \log_2\left(\frac{1}{p_M}\right)$$

with $\sum_{j=1}^{M} p_j = 1$. The partial derivatives $\partial H/\partial p_1, \partial H/\partial p_2, \ldots, \partial H/\partial p_M$ are equated to zero to get a set of $(M-1)$ equations. Setting the first partial derivative equal to zero, we obtain

$$\begin{aligned}\frac{\partial H}{\partial p_1} = & \left[p_1 \times p_1 \times \left(-\frac{1}{p_1^2}\right)\log_2 e + \log_2\left(\frac{1}{p_1}\right)\right] \\ & + \left[(1-p_1-p_2-\cdots-p_{M-1})^2 \times \frac{1}{(1-p_1-p_2-\cdots-p_{M-1})^2} \times \log_2 e \right. \\ & \left. -\log_2 \frac{1}{(1-p_1-p_2-\cdots-p_{M-1})}\right] = 0\end{aligned}$$

or

$$\log_2\left(\frac{1}{p_1}\right) = \log_2 \frac{1}{(1-p_1-p_2-\cdots-p_{M-1})}$$

or,

$$p_1 = 1 - p_1 - p_2 - \cdots - p_{M-1}$$

In this way, the $(M-1)$ equations are obtained as:

$$\begin{aligned} 2p_1 &= 1 - p_2 - p_3 - \ldots - p_{M-1} \\ 2p_2 &= 1 - p_1 - p_3 - \ldots - p_{M-1} \\ &\vdots \\ 2p_{M-1} &= 1 - p_1 - p_2 - \ldots - p_{M-2} \end{aligned}$$

Adding all the above equations,

$$2(p_1+p_2\ldots+p_{M-1})=(M-1)-(M-2)(p_1+p_2\ldots+p_{M-1})$$

or

$$2(1-p_M)=(M-1)-(M-2)(1-p_M) \qquad \left[\text{since } \sum_{j=1}^{M} p_j=1\right]$$

or

$$p_M=\frac{1}{M}$$

Thus, $p_M=\frac{1}{M}$ is the condition that produces $\frac{\partial H}{\partial p_j}=0$, for all $j=1, 2, \ldots, M-1$ with p_M being expressed in terms of all other p's. Similarly, it can be proved that H is maximum when all the messages are equiprobable, i.e., $p_1=p_2=\ldots=p_M=\frac{1}{M}$ and $H_{\max}$ is given by

$$H_{\max}=M\times\left(\frac{1}{M}\right)\log_2 M=\log_2 M \text{ bits/message.}$$

2.4 INFORMATION RATE

If a source generates r messages/s, the *rate of information* or the *average information per second* is defined as follows:

$$R=\frac{H}{T}=rH \text{ bits/s} \tag{2.6}$$

where T is the time required to send a single message $\left(=\frac{1}{r}\right)$.

Let there be two sources of equal entropy H, emitting r_1 and r_2 messages/s. The first source emits the information at a rate $R_1=r_1H$ and the second at a rate $R_2=r_2H$. If $r_1>r_2$, then $R_1>R_2$, i.e., the first source emits more information than the second within a given time period even when the entropy is the same. Therefore, a source should be characterized by its entropy as well as its rate of information.

Example 2.5: An event has four possible outcomes with probabilities of occurrence $p_1=\frac{1}{4}$, $p_2=\frac{1}{2}$, $p_3=\frac{1}{8}$, and $p_4=\frac{1}{8}$ respectively. Determine the entropy of the system. Also obtain the rate of information if there are 8 outcomes per second.

Solution: The entropy of the system is given by

$$\begin{aligned}H&=-\sum_{j=1}^{4}p_j\log_2(p_j)\\&=-\frac{1}{4}\log_2\left(\frac{1}{4}\right)-\frac{1}{2}\log_2\left(\frac{1}{2}\right)-\frac{1}{8}\log_2\left(\frac{1}{8}\right)-\frac{1}{8}\log_2\left(\frac{1}{8}\right)\\&=1.75 \text{ bits/message}\end{aligned}$$

Thus, the information rate is given by

$$R=rH=8\times1.75=14 \text{ bits/s}$$

Example 2.6: An analog signal having bandwidth B Hz is sampled at the Nyquist rate and the samples are quantized into four levels Q_1, Q_2, Q_3, and Q_4 with probabilities of occurrence $p_1=p_2=\frac{3}{5}$, and

$p_3 = p_4 = \frac{2}{5}$, respectively. The quantization levels are assumed to be independent. Find the information rate of the source.

Solution: The average information or the entropy is given by

$$H = -\sum_{j=1}^{4} p_j \log_2(p_j)$$
$$= -\frac{3}{5}\log_2\left(\frac{3}{5}\right) - \frac{3}{5}\log_2\left(\frac{3}{5}\right) - \frac{2}{5}\log_2\left(\frac{2}{5}\right) - \frac{2}{5}\log_2\left(\frac{2}{5}\right)$$
$$= 1.94 \text{ bits/message}$$

Thus, the information rate is given by

$$R = rH = 2B(1.94) = 3.88 \text{ bits/s}$$

2.5 CHANNEL MODEL

A *communication channel* is the transmission path or medium through which the symbols flow to the receiver. We begin our discussion on channel model with a *discrete memoryless channel.*

2.5.1 Discrete Memoryless Channel

Figure 2.3 represents a statistical model of a discrete memoryless channel (DMC) with an input X and an output Y. The said channel can accept an input symbol from X, and in response it can deliver an output symbol from Y. Such a channel is 'discrete' because the alphabets of X and Y are both finite. Since the present output of the channel solely depends on the current input and not on the inputs at previous stage(s), it is called 'memoryless'.

The input X of the DMC consists of m input symbols $x_1, x_2, \ldots, x_m$ and the output Y consists of n output symbols $y_1, y_2, \ldots, y_n$. Each possible input-to-output path is related by a conditional probability $P(y_j/x_i)$, where $P(y_j/x_i)$ is the conditional probability of obtaining the output y_j when the input is x_i. $P(y_j/x_i)$ is termed as the *channel transition probability.*

A channel can be completely specified by a matrix of all such transition probabilities as follows:

$$[P(Y/X)] = \begin{bmatrix} P(y_1/x_1) & P(y_2/x_1) & \ldots & P(y_n/x_1) \\ P(y_1/x_2) & P(y_2/x_2) & \ldots & P(y_n/x_2) \\ \vdots & \vdots & \ddots & \vdots \\ P(y_1/x_m) & P(y_2/x_m) & \ldots & P(y_n/x_m) \end{bmatrix} \quad (2.7)$$

The matrix $[P(Y/X)]$ is called the *channel matrix, probability transition matrix* or simply *transition matrix*. As evident from the above matrix, each row contains the conditional probabilities of all possible

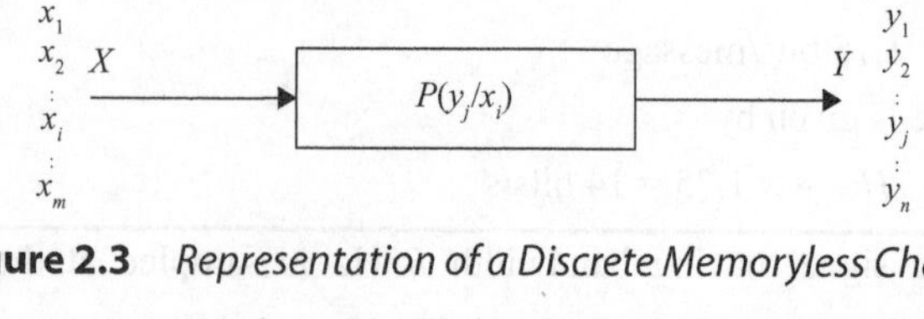

Figure 2.3 *Representation of a Discrete Memoryless Channel*

output symbols for a particular input symbol. As a result, the sum of all elements of each row must be unity, i.e.,

$$\sum_{j=1}^{n} P(y_j/x_i) = 1, \text{ for all } i \tag{2.8}$$

Now, if the input probabilities $P(X)$ are given by the row matrix

$$[P(X)] = [P(x_1)P(x_2)\cdots P(x_m)] \tag{2.9}$$

and the output probabilities $P(Y)$ are represented by

$$[P(Y)] = [P(y_1)P(y_2)\cdots P(y_n)] \tag{2.10}$$

then

$$[P(Y)] = [P(X)][P(Y/X)] \tag{2.11}$$

If $P(X)$ is represented as a diagonal matrix

$$[P(X)]_d = \begin{bmatrix} P(x_1) & 0 & \cdots & 0 \\ 0 & P(x_2) & \cdots & 0 \\ \vdots & \vdots & \ddots & \vdots \\ 0 & 0 & \cdots & P(x_m) \end{bmatrix} \tag{2.12}$$

then

$$[P(X,Y)] = [P(X)]_d[P(Y/X)] \tag{2.13}$$

where the (i, j) element of $[P(X, Y)]$ is of the form $P(x_i, y_j)$. $[P(X, Y)]$ is known as the *joint probability matrix* and $P(x_i, y_j)$ is the joint probability of sending x_i and receiving y_j.

2.5.2 Special Channels

A. Lossless Channel If the channel matrix of a channel contains only one nonzero element in each column, the channel is defined as a *lossless channel*. Figure 2.4 shows an example of a lossless channel and the corresponding channel matrix is shown as follows:

$$[P(Y/X)] = \begin{bmatrix} \frac{1}{6} & \frac{5}{6} & 0 & 0 & 0 \\ 0 & 0 & \frac{1}{4} & \frac{3}{4} & 0 \\ 0 & 0 & 0 & 0 & 1 \end{bmatrix} \tag{2.14}$$

In a lossless channel no source information is lost during transmission.

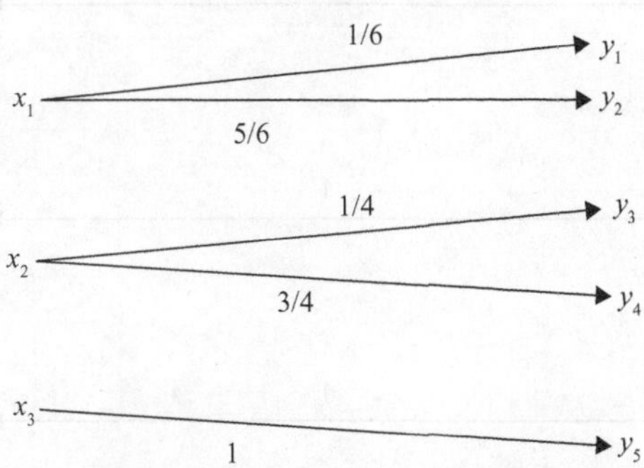

Figure 2.4 *A Lossless Channel*

B. Deterministic Channel For a *deterministic channel*, the channel matrix contains only one nonzero element in each row. The following is an example of a channel matrix of a deterministic channel and the corresponding channel representation is shown in Figure 2.5.

$$[P(Y/X)] = \begin{bmatrix} 1 & 0 & 0 \\ 1 & 0 & 0 \\ 0 & 1 & 0 \\ 0 & 0 & 1 \end{bmatrix}$$

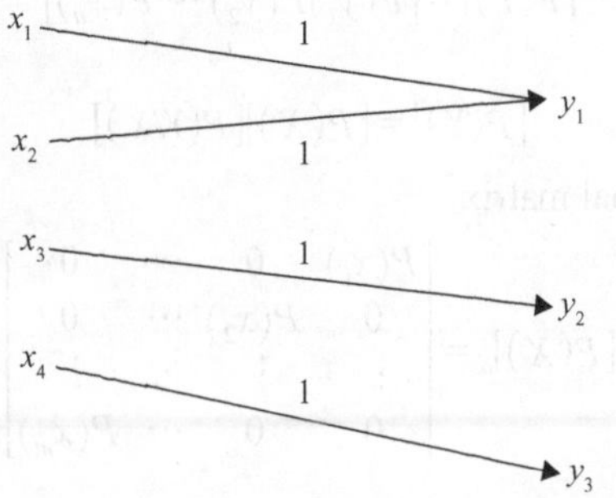

Figure 2.5 *A Deterministic Channel*

Since each row has only one nonzero element, this element must be unity, i.e., when a particular input symbol is transmitted through this channel, it is known which output symbol will be received.

C. Noiseless Channel A channel is known as *noiseless* if it is both lossless and deterministic. The corresponding channel matrix has only one element in each row and in each column, and this element must be equal to unity. As the number of input symbols and output symbols is the same ($m = n$), the channel matrix is a square matrix. Figure 2.6 depicts a typical noiseless channel and corresponding channel matrix is shown in Eq. (2.16).

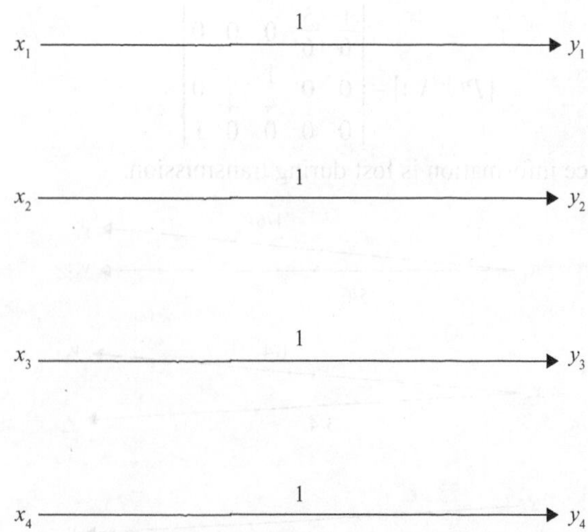

Figure 2.6 *A Noiseless Channel*

$$[P(Y/X)] = \begin{bmatrix} 1 & 0 & 0 & 0 \\ 0 & 1 & 0 & 0 \\ 0 & 0 & 1 & 0 \\ 0 & 0 & 0 & 1 \end{bmatrix} \tag{2.16}$$

D. Binary Symmetric Channel A channel described by a channel matrix as shown below is termed a *binary symmetric channel* (BSC). The corresponding channel diagram is shown in Figure 2.7.

$$[P(Y/X)] = \begin{bmatrix} 1-p & p \\ p & 1-p \end{bmatrix} \tag{2.17}$$

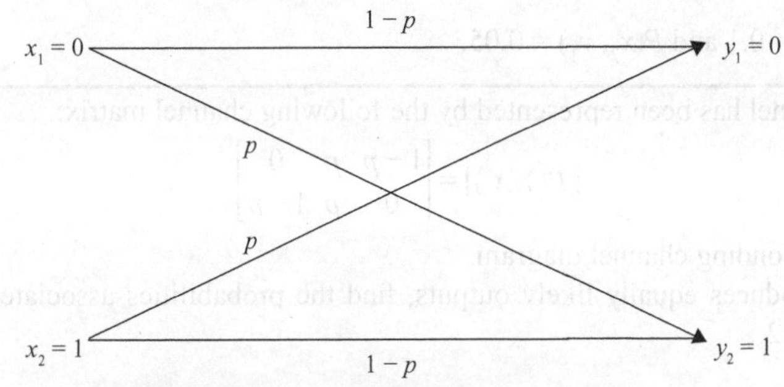

Figure 2.7 *A Binary Symmetric Channel*

It has two inputs ($x_1 = 0, x_2 = 1$) and two outputs ($y_1 = 0, y_2 = 1$). The channel is symmetric as the probability of misinterpreting a transmitted 0 as 1 is the same as that of misinterpreting a transmitted 1 as 0. This common transition probability is denoted by p.

Example 2.7: For the binary channel shown in Figure 2.8, find (a) the channel matrix, (b) $P(y_1)$ and $P(y_2)$ when $P(x_1) = P(x_2) = 0.5$, and (c) the joint probabilities $P(x_1, y_2)$ and $P(x_2, y_1)$ when $P(x_1) = P(x_2) = 0.5$.

Solution:

(a) The channel matrix is given by

$$[P(Y/X)] = \begin{bmatrix} P(y_1/x_1) & P(y_2/x_1) \\ P(y_1/x_2) & P(y_2/x_2) \end{bmatrix} = \begin{bmatrix} 0.8 & 0.2 \\ 0.1 & 0.9 \end{bmatrix}$$

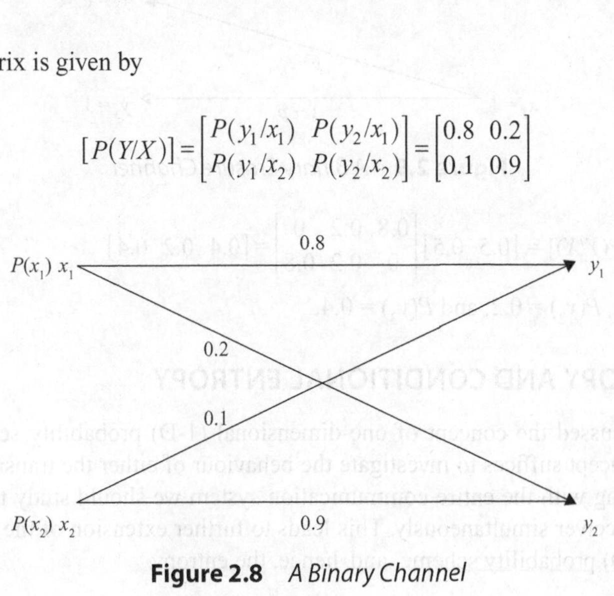

Figure 2.8 *A Binary Channel*

(b) $[P(Y)] = [P(X)][P(Y/X)] = [0.5\ \ 0.5]\begin{bmatrix} 0.8 & 0.2 \\ 0.1 & 0.9 \end{bmatrix}$

$= [0.45\ \ 0.55] = [P(y_1)P(y_2)]$

Hence, $P(y_1) = 0.45$ and $P(y_2) = 0.55$

(c) $[P(X,Y)] = [P(X)]_d[P(Y/X)] = \begin{bmatrix} 0.5 & 0 \\ 0 & 0.5 \end{bmatrix}\begin{bmatrix} 0.8 & 0.2 \\ 0.1 & 0.9 \end{bmatrix}$

$= \begin{bmatrix} 0.4 & 0.1 \\ 0.05 & 0.45 \end{bmatrix} = \begin{bmatrix} P(x_1,y_1) & P(x_1,y_2) \\ P(x_2,y_1) & P(x_2,y_2) \end{bmatrix}$

Hence, $P(x_1, y_2) = 0.1$ and $P(x_2, y_1) = 0.05$.

Example 2.8: A channel has been represented by the following channel matrix:

$$[P(Y/X)] = \begin{bmatrix} 1-p & p & 0 \\ 0 & p & 1-p \end{bmatrix} \tag{2.18}$$

(a) Draw the corresponding channel diagram.
(b) If the source produces equally likely outputs, find the probabilities associated with the channel outputs for $p = 0.2$.

Solution:

(a) The channel diagram is shown in Figure 2.9. The channel represented in Eq. (2.18) is known as the *binary erasure channel*. It has two inputs $x_1 = 0$ and $x_2 = 1$ and three outputs $y_1 = 0$, $y_2 = e$, and $y_3 = 1$, where e indicates an erasure; i.e., the output is in doubt and it should be erased.

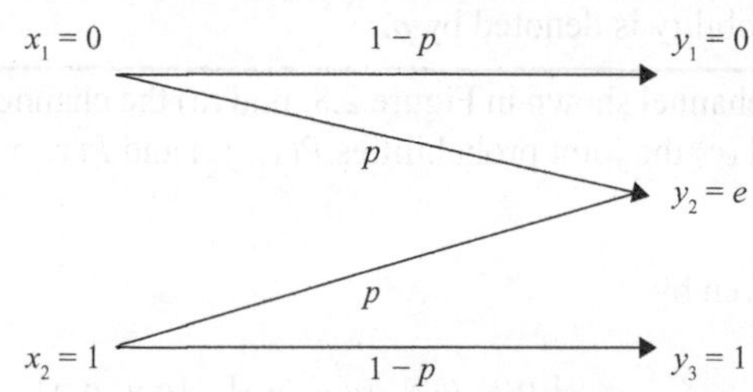

Figure 2.9 *A Binary Erasure Channel*

(b) $[P(Y)] = [P(X)][P(Y/X)] = [0.5\ \ 0.5]\begin{bmatrix} 0.8 & 0.2 & 0 \\ 0 & 0.2 & 0.8 \end{bmatrix} = [0.4\ \ 0.2\ \ 0.4]$

Thus, $P(y_1) = 0.4$, $P(y_2) = 0.2$, and $P(y_3) = 0.4$.

2.6 JOINT ENTROPY AND CONDITIONAL ENTROPY

We have already discussed the concept of one-dimensional (1-D) probability scheme and its associated entropy. This concept suffices to investigate the behaviour of either the transmitter or the receiver. However, while dealing with the entire communication system we should study the behaviour of both the transmitter and receiver simultaneously. This leads to further extension of the probability theory to two-dimensional (2-D) probability scheme, and, hence, the entropy.

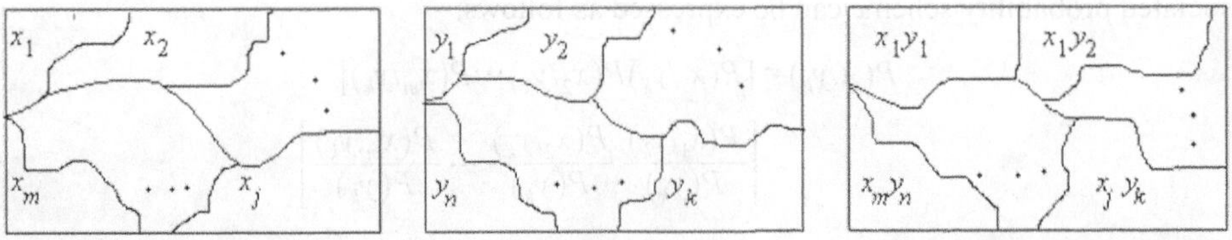

(a) Sample space S_1 (b) Sample space S_2 (c) Sample space $S = S_1S_2$

Figure 2.10 *Sample Spaces for Channel Input and Output and Respective Their Product Space*

Let the channel input and the channel output form two sets of events $[X] = [x_1, x_2, \ldots, x_m]$ and $[Y] = [y_1, y_2, \ldots, y_n]$ with sample spaces S_1 and S_2, respectively, as shown in Figure 2.10. Each event x_j of S_1 produces any event y_k of S_2. Hence, the complete set of events in their product space $S\ (= S_1S_2)$ is (Figure 2.10) given by

$$[XY] = \begin{bmatrix} x_1y_1 & x_1y_2 & \cdots & x_1y_n \\ x_2y_1 & x_2y_2 & \cdots & x_2y_n \\ \vdots & \vdots & \ddots & \vdots \\ x_my_1 & x_my_2 & \cdots & x_my_n \end{bmatrix} \tag{2.19}$$

Therefore, we have three complete probability schemes and naturally there will be three associated entropies.

$$P(X) = [P(x_j)] \tag{2.20}$$

$$P(Y) = [P(y_k)] \tag{2.21}$$

$$P(X, Y) = [P(x_j, y_k)] \tag{2.22}$$

(A probability scheme (x_j) is said to be complete if $\Sigma_j P(x_j) = 1$.)

$$H(X) = -\sum_{j=1}^{m} P(x_j)\log P(x_j) \tag{2.23}$$

where

$$P(x_j) = \sum_{k=1}^{n} P(x_j, y_k) \tag{2.24}$$

$$H(Y) = -\sum_{k=1}^{n} P(y_k)\log P(y_k) \tag{2.25}$$

where

$$P(y_k) = \sum_{j=1}^{m} P(x_j, y_k) \tag{2.26}$$

$$H(X,Y) = -\sum_{j=1}^{m}\sum_{k=1}^{n} P(x_j, y_k)\log P(x_j, y_k) \tag{2.27}$$

Here, $H(X)$ and $H(Y)$ are *marginal entropies* of X and Y, respectively, and $H(X, Y)$ is the *joint entropy* of X and Y. $H(X)$ can be interpreted as the average uncertainty of the channel input and $H(Y)$ the average uncertainty of the channel output. The joint entropy $H(X, Y)$ can be considered as the average uncertainty of the communication channel as a whole.

The conditional probability $P(X/Y)$ is given by

$$P(X/Y) = \frac{P(X,Y)}{P(Y)} \tag{2.28}$$

As y_k can occur in conjunction with $x_1, x_2, \ldots, x_m$, we have

$$[X/y_k] = \left[\frac{x_1}{y_k}\ \frac{x_2}{y_k} \cdots \frac{x_m}{y_k}\right] \tag{2.29}$$

The associated probability scheme can be expressed as follows:

$$P(X/y_k) = [P(x_1/y_k)P(x_2/y_k)\cdots P(x_m/y_k)]$$
$$= \left[\frac{P(x_1,y_k)}{P(y_k)}\frac{P(x_2,y_k)}{P(y_k)}\cdots\frac{P(x_m,y_k)}{P(y_k)}\right] \tag{2.30}$$

Now,

$$P(x_1,y_k)+P(x_2,y_k)+\cdots+P(x_m,y_k)=P(y_k) \tag{2.31}$$

Thus,

$$\sum_{j=1}^{m} P(x_j/y_k)=1 \tag{2.32}$$

Therefore, the sum of elements of the matrix shown in Eq. (2.30) is unity. Hence, the probability scheme defined by Eq. (2.30) is complete. We can then associate entropy with it.

Thus,

$$H(X/y_k) = -\sum_{j=1}^{m}\frac{P(x_j,y_k)}{P(y_k)}\log\frac{P(x_j,y_k)}{P(y_k)}$$
$$= -\sum_{j=1}^{m} P(x_j/y_k)\log P(x_j/y_k) \tag{2.33}$$

Taking the average of this conditional entropy for all admissible values of y_k we can obtain a measure of an average conditional entropy of the system.

$$H(X/Y) = \overline{H(X/y_k)}$$
$$= \sum_{k=1}^{n} P(y_k)H(X/y_k)$$
$$= -\sum_{k=1}^{n} P(y_k)\sum_{j=1}^{m} P(x_j/y_k)\log P(x_j/y_k)$$
$$= -\sum_{j=1}^{m}\sum_{k=1}^{n} P(y_k)P(x_j/y_k)\log P(x_j/y_k)$$
$$= -\sum_{j=1}^{m}\sum_{k=1}^{n} P(x_j,y_k)\log P(x_j/y_k) \tag{2.34}$$

Similarly, it can be shown that

$$H(Y/X) = -\sum_{j=1}^{m}\sum_{k=1}^{n} P(x_j,y_k)\log P(y_k/x_j) \tag{2.35}$$

$H(X/Y)$ and $H(Y/X)$ are the *average conditional entropies* or simply *conditional entropies*. $H(X/Y)$ is a measure of the average uncertainty remaining about the channel input after the channel output has been observed. It describes how well one can recover the transmitted symbols from the received symbols. $H(X/Y)$ is also called the *equivocation* of X with respect to Y. $H(Y/X)$ is the average uncertainty of the channel output when X was transmitted and it describes how well we can recover the received symbols from the transmitted symbols; i.e., it provides a measure of error or noise. Finally, we can conclude that there are five entropies associated with a 2-D probability scheme. They are: $H(X)$, $H(Y)$, $H(X, Y)$, $H(X/Y)$ and $H(Y/X)$.

Example 2.9: Show that $H(X, Y) = H(X/Y) + H(Y)$

Solution:

$$H(X,Y) = -\sum_{j=1}^{m}\sum_{k=1}^{n} P(x_j,y_k)\log P(x_j,y_k)$$
$$= -\sum_{j=1}^{m}\sum_{k=1}^{n} P(x_j,y_k)\log[P(x_j/y_k)P(y_k)]$$

$$= -\sum_{j=1}^{m}\sum_{k=1}^{n} P(x_j,y_k)[\log P(x_j/y_k) + \log P(y_k)]$$
$$= -\sum_{j=1}^{m}\sum_{k=1}^{n} [P(x_j,y_k)\log P(x_j/y_k) + P(x_j,y_k)\log P(y_k)]$$
$$= H(X/Y) - \sum_{j=1}^{m}\sum_{k=1}^{n} [P(x_j,y_k)\log P(y_k)]$$
$$= H(X/Y) - \sum_{k=1}^{n}\left[\sum_{j=1}^{m} P(x_j,y_k)\right]\log P(y_k)$$
$$= H(X/Y) - \sum_{k=1}^{n} P(y_k)\log P(y_k)$$
$$= H(X/Y) + H(Y)$$

Similarly, it can be proved that $H(X, Y) = H(Y/X) + H(X)$.

Example 2.10: For a lossless channel (Figure 2.4), show that $H(X/Y) = 0$.

Solution: For a lossless channel when the output y_j is received, it is clear which x_i was transmitted, i.e.,

$$P(x_i/y_j) = 0 \text{ or } 1$$

Now,

$$H(X/Y) = -\sum_{j=1}^{n}\sum_{i=1}^{m} P(x_i, y_j)\log P(x_i/y_j)$$
$$= -\sum_{j=1}^{n} P(y_j)\sum_{i=1}^{m} P(x_i/y_j)\log P(x_i/y_j)$$

All the terms in the inner summation of the above expression are zero because they are in the form of either $1 \times \log_2 1$ or $0 \times \log_2 0$. Hence, we can conclude that for a lossless channel

$$H(X/Y) = 0$$

Example 2.11: For a noiseless channel (Figure 2.6) with m input symbols and m output symbols show that

(a) $H(X) = H(Y)$.
(b) $H(Y/X) = 0$.

Solution:

(a) For a noiseless channel the transition probabilities are given by

$$P(y_j/x_i) = \begin{cases} 1 & i = j \\ 0 & i \neq j \end{cases}$$

Thus,

$$P(x_i, y_j) = P(y_j/x_i)P(x_i) = \begin{cases} P(x_i) & i = j \\ 0 & i \neq j \end{cases}$$

and

$$P(y_i) = \sum_{i=1}^{m} P(x_i, y_j) = P(x_j)$$

Therefore,

$$H(Y) = -\sum_{j=1}^{m} P(y_j)\log P(y_j)$$
$$= -\sum_{i=1}^{m} P(x_i)\log P(x_i)$$
$$= H(X)$$

(b) We know

$$H(Y/X) = -\sum_{j=1}^{m}\sum_{i=1}^{m} P(x_i, y_j)\log P(y_j/x_i)$$
$$= -\sum_{i=1}^{m} P(x_i)\sum_{j=1}^{m} \log P(y_j/x_i)$$
$$= -\sum_{i=1}^{m} P(x_i)\log_2 1 = 0$$

2.7 MUTUAL INFORMATION

We consider a communication channel with an input X and an output Y. The state of knowledge about a transmitted symbol x_j at the receiver before observing the output is the probability that x_j would be selected for transmission. This is *a priori probability* $P(x_j)$. Thus, the corresponding uncertainty is $-\log P(x_j)$. Once y_k is received at the output, the state of knowledge about x_j is the conditional probability $P(x_j/y_k)$ (also known as *a posteriori probability*). The corresponding uncertainty becomes $-\log P(x_j/y_k)$. Therefore, the information $I(x_j; y_k)$ gathered about x_j after the reception of y_k is the net reduction in the uncertainty, i.e.,

$$\begin{aligned} I(x_j; y_k) &= \text{initial uncertainty} - \text{final uncertainty} \\ &= -\log P(x_j) - [-\log P(x_j/y_k)] \\ &= \log \frac{P(x_j/y_k)}{P(x_j)} \\ &= \log \frac{P(x_j, y_k)}{P(x_j)P(y_k)} = \log \frac{P(y_k/x_j)}{P(y_k)} = I(y_k; x_j) \end{aligned} \tag{2.36}$$

The average of $I(x_j; y_k)$ or the corresponding entropy is given by

$$\begin{aligned} I(X;Y) &= \overline{I(x_j; y_k)} \\ &= \sum_{j=1}^{m}\sum_{k=1}^{n} P(x_j,y_k) I(x_j; y_k) \\ &= \sum_{j=1}^{m}\sum_{k=1}^{n} P(x_j,y_k) \log \frac{P(x_j/y_k)}{P(x_j)} \\ &= \sum_{j=1}^{m}\sum_{k=1}^{n} P(x_j,y_k)[\log P(x_j/y_k) - \log P(x_j)] \\ &= -\sum_{j=1}^{m}\sum_{k=1}^{n} P(x_j,y_k)\log P(x_j) - \left[-\sum_{j=1}^{m}\sum_{k=1}^{n} P(x_j,y_k)\log P(x_j/y_k)\right] \\ &= -\sum_{j=1}^{m}\left[\sum_{k=1}^{n} P(x_j,y_k)\right]\log P(x_j) - H(X/Y) \\ &= -\sum_{j=1}^{m} P(x_j)\log P(x_j) - H(X/Y) \end{aligned}$$

$$= H(X) - H(X/Y) \tag{2.37}$$

$$= H(X) + H(Y) - H(X,Y) \tag{2.38}$$

$$= H(Y) - H(Y/X) \tag{2.39}$$

$I(X; Y)$ is known as the *mutual information* of the channel. It does not depend on the individual symbols x_j or y_k; hence, it is a property of the whole communication channel. The mutual information of a channel can be interpreted as the uncertainty about the channel input that is resolved from the knowledge of the channel output.

The properties of $I(X; Y)$ is summarized as follows:

1. It is non-negative, i.e., $I(X; Y) \geq 0$.
2. Mutual information of a channel is symmetric, i.e., $I(X; Y) = I(Y; X)$.
3. It can also be represented as $I(X; Y) = H(Y) - H(Y/X)$.
4. It is related to the joint entropy $H(X, Y)$ by the following formula:

$$I(X; Y) = H(X) + H(Y) - H(X, Y)$$

Example 2.12: Verify that $I(X; Y) = I(Y; X)$.

Solution: We can express $I(Y; X)$ as follows:

$$I(Y; X) = \sum_{i=1}^{m} \sum_{j=1}^{n} P(y_j, x_i) \log \frac{P(y_j/x_i)}{P(y_j)}$$

As $$P(y_j, x_i) = P(x_i, y_j)$$

and $$\frac{P(y_j/x_i)}{P(y_j)} = \frac{P(x_i/y_j)}{P(x_i)}$$

we conclude that $$I(X; Y) = I(Y; X)$$

Example 2.13: Consider a BSC (Figure 2.11) with $P(x_1) = \alpha$.

(a) Prove that the mutual information $I(X; Y)$ is given by
$I(X; Y) = H(Y) + p \log_2 p + (1 - p) \log_2 (1 - p)$.

(b) Compute $I(X; Y)$ for $\alpha = 0.5$ and $p = 0.1$.

(c) Repeat (b) for $\alpha = 0.5$ and $p = 0.5$ and comment on the result.

Solution:

(a) Using Eqs. (2.12), (2.13), and (2.17), we have

$$[P(X,Y)] = \begin{bmatrix} \alpha & 0 \\ 0 & 1-\alpha \end{bmatrix} \begin{bmatrix} 1-p & p \\ p & 1-p \end{bmatrix}$$

$$= \begin{bmatrix} \alpha(1-p) & \alpha p \\ (1-\alpha)p & (1-\alpha)(1-p) \end{bmatrix} = \begin{bmatrix} P(x_1,y_1) & P(x_1,y_2) \\ P(x_2,y_1) & P(x_2,y_2) \end{bmatrix}$$

Then by Eq. (2.35)

$$H(Y/X) = -P(x_1,y_1)\log_2 P(y_1/x_1) - P(x_1,y_2)\log_2 P(y_2/x_1)$$
$$-P(x_2,y_1)\log_2 P(y_1/x_2) - P(x_2,y_2)P\log_2 P(y_2/x_2)$$
$$= -\alpha(1-p)\log_2(1-p) - \alpha p\log_2 p - (1-\alpha)p\log_2 p - (1-\alpha)(1-p)\log_2(1-p)$$
$$= -p\log_2 p - (1-p)\log_2(1-p)$$

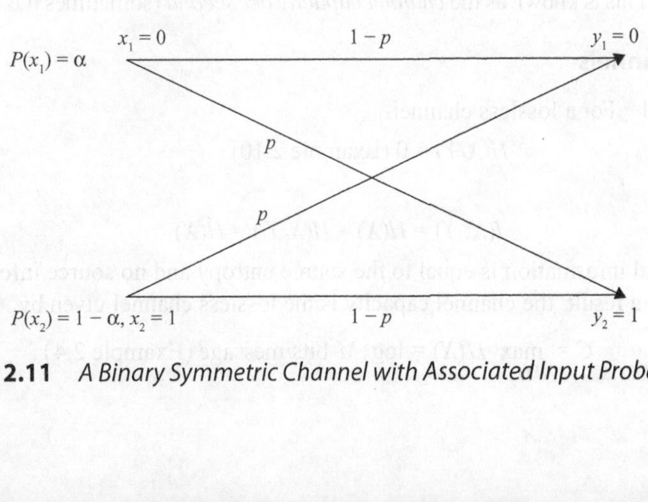

Figure 2.11 *A Binary Symmetric Channel with Associated Input Probabilities*

Hence, $I(X; Y) = H(Y) - H(Y/X)$

$$= H(Y) + p \log_2 p + (1 - p) \log_2 (1 - p)$$

(b) When $\alpha = 0.5$ and $p = 0.1$, using Eq. (2.11) we have

$$[P(Y)] = [0.5\ \ 0.5]\begin{bmatrix} 0.9 & 0.1 \\ 0.1 & 0.9 \end{bmatrix} = [0.5\ \ 0.5]$$

Thus, $$P(y_1) = P(y_2) = 0.5$$

$$H(Y) = -P(y_1)\log_2 P(y_1) - P(y_2)\log_2 P(y_2)$$

$$= -0.5 \log_2 0.5 - 0.5 \log_2 0.5 = 1$$

Also, $$p \log_2 p + (1-p)\log_2(1-p) = 0.1 \log_2 0.1 + 0.9 \log_2 0.9$$

$$= -0.469$$

Thus, $$I(X; Y) = 1 - 0.469 = 0.531$$

(c) When $\alpha = 0.5$ and $p = 0.5$, we have

$$[P(Y)] = [0.5\ \ 0.5]\begin{bmatrix} 0.5 & 0.5 \\ 0.5 & 0.5 \end{bmatrix} = [0.5\ \ 0.5]$$

$$H(Y) = 1$$

and $$p \log_2 p + (1-p)\log_2(1-p) = 0.5 \log_2 0.5 + 0.5 \log_2 0.5$$

$$= -0.1$$

Hence, $$I(X; Y) = 1 - 1 = 0$$

It is to be noted that when $p = 0.5$, no information is being transmitted at all. When $I(X; Y) = 0$, the channel is said to be *useless*.

2.8 CHANNEL CAPACITY

The *channel capacity* of a DMC is defined as the maximum of mutual information. Thus, the channel capacity C is given by

$$C = \max_{\{P(x_j)\}} I(X; Y) \text{ bits/message} \tag{2.40}$$

where the maximization is obtained with respect to $P(x_j)$.

If r messages are being transmitted per second, the maximum rate of transmission of information per second is rC (bits/s). This is known as the *channel capacity per second* (sometimes it is denoted as C bits/s).

2.8.1 Special Channels

A. Lossless Channel For a lossless channel,

$$H(X/Y) = 0 \text{ (Example 2.10)} \tag{2.41}$$

Thus,

$$I(X; Y) = H(X) - H(X/Y) = H(X) \tag{2.42}$$

Therefore, the mutual information is equal to the source entropy and no source information is lost during transmission. As a result, the channel capacity is the lossless channel given by

$$C = \max_{\{P(x_j)\}} H(X) = \log_2 M \text{ bits/message (Example 2.4)} \tag{2.43}$$

B. Deterministic Channel In case of a deterministic channel, $H(Y/X) = 0$ for all input distributions of $P(x_j)$.

Therefore,

$$I(X; Y) = H(Y) \tag{2.44}$$

Hence, it can be concluded that the information transfer is equal to the output entropy. The channel capacity is as follows:

$$C = \max_{\{P(x_j)\}} H(Y) = \log_2 n \text{ bits/message} \tag{2.45}$$

where n is total the number of receiver messages.

C. Noiseless Channel A noise channel is both lossless and deterministic. In this case,

$$I(X; Y) = H(X) = H(Y) \tag{2.46}$$

and the channel capacity is given by

$$C = \log_2 M = \log_2 n \text{ bits/message} \tag{2.47}$$

D. Binary Symmetric Channel For a BSC, the mutual information is given by

$$I(X; Y) = H(Y) + p \log_2 p + (1 - p) \log_2 (1 - p) \text{ (Example 2.13)} \tag{2.48}$$

Since the channel output is binary, $H(Y)$ is maximum when each output has probability of 0.5 and is achieved for equally likely inputs. In this case, $H(Y) = 1$.

Thus, the channel capacity for such a channel is given by

$$C = 1 + p \log_2 p + (1 - p) \log_2 (1 - p) \text{ bits/message} \tag{2.49}$$

2.9 SHANNON'S THEOREM

The performance of a communication system for information transmission from a source to the destination depends on a variety of parameters. These include channel bandwidth, *signal-to-noise ratio* (SNR), probability of bit error, etc. *Shannon's theorem* is concerned with the rate of information transfer through a communication channel. According to this theorem, one can transfer information through a communication channel of capacity C (bits/s) with an arbitrarily small probability of error if the source information rate R is less than or equal to C. The statement of the theorem is as follows:

> Suppose a source of M equally likely messages ($M >> 1$) generating information at a rate R. The messages are to be transmitted over a channel with a channel capacity C (bits/s). If $R \leq C$, then there exists a coding technique such that the transmitted messages can be received in a receiver with an arbitrarily small probability of error.

Thus, the theorem indicates that even in presence of inevitable noise, error-free transmission is possible if $R \leq C$.

2.10 CONTINUOUS CHANNEL

So far we have discussed about the characteristics of discrete channels. However, there are a number of communication systems (amplitude modulation, frequency modulation, etc.) that use continuous sources and *continuous channels.* In this section, we shall extend the concept of information theory developed for discrete channels to continuous channels. We begin our discussion with the concept of *differential entropy.*

2.10.1 Differential Entropy

Let an information source produce a continuous signal $x(t)$ to be transmitted through a continuous channel. The set of all possible signals can be considered to be an ensemble of waveforms generated by some ergodic random process. $x(t)$ is also assumed to have finite bandwidth so that it can be completely described by its periodic sample values. At any sampling instant, the collection of possible sample values constitutes a continuous random variable X. If $f(x)$ be the corresponding probability density function (PDF), then the average information per sample value of $x(t)$ is given by

$$H(X) = -\int_{-\infty}^{\infty} f(x)\log_2 f(x)dx \text{ bits/sample} \tag{2.50}$$

This entropy $H(X)$ is known as the differential entropy of X.

The average mutual information in a continuous channel is given by

$$I(X;Y) = H(X) - H(X/Y) \tag{2.51}$$

$$= H(Y) - H(Y/X) \tag{2.52}$$

where

$$H(Y) = -\int_{-\infty}^{\infty} f(y)\log_2 f(y)dy \tag{2.53}$$

$$H(X/Y) = -\int_{-\infty}^{\infty}\int_{-\infty}^{\infty} f(x,y)\log_2 f(x/y)\,dxdy \tag{2.54}$$

$$H(Y/X) = -\int_{-\infty}^{\infty}\int_{-\infty}^{\infty} f(x,y)\log_2 f(y/x)\,dxdy \tag{2.55}$$

2.10.2 Additive White Gaussian Noise Channel

The channels that possess Gaussian noise characteristics are known as *Gaussian channels*. These channels are often encountered in practice. The results obtained in this case generally provide a lower bound on the performance of a system with non-Gaussian channel. Therefore, if a Gaussian channel with a particular encoder/decoder shows a probability of error p_e, then another encoder/decoder with a non-Gaussian channel can be designed which can yield an error probability less than p_e. Thus, the study of the characteristics of the Gaussian channel is very much essential. The power spectral density of a *white noise* is constant for all frequencies; i.e, it contains all the frequency components in equal amount. If the probability of occurrence of the white noise level is represented by Gaussian distribution function, it is called *white Gaussian noise*. For an *additive white Gaussian noise* (AWGN) channel with input X, the output Y is given by

$$Y = X + n \tag{2.56}$$

where n is an additive band-limited white Gaussian noise with zero mean and variance σ^2.

2.10.3 Shannon–Hartley Law

The PDF of Gaussian distribution with zero mean and variance σ^2 is given by

$$f(x) = \frac{1}{\sqrt{2\pi\sigma^2}} e^{-x^2/(2\sigma^2)} \tag{2.57}$$

We know that

$$H(X) = -\int_{-\infty}^{\infty} f(x)\log_2 f(x)dx$$

Now,

$$-\log_2 f(x) = \log_2 \sqrt{2\pi\sigma^2} + \log_2 e^{x^2/(2\sigma^2)} \tag{2.58}$$

Thus,

$$H(X) = \int_{-\infty}^{\infty} f(x)\log_2 \sqrt{2\pi\sigma^2}\, dx + \int_{-\infty}^{\infty} f(x)\log_2 e^{x^2/(2\sigma^2)} dx \tag{2.59}$$

$$= \log_2 \sqrt{2\pi\sigma^2} \int_{-\infty}^{\infty} f(x)dx + \frac{\log_2 e}{2\sigma^2}\int_{-\infty}^{\infty} x^2 f(x)dx$$

$$= \log_2 \sqrt{2\pi\sigma^2} \times 1 + \frac{\log_2 \sqrt{e}}{\sigma^2} \times \sigma^2$$

$$= \log_2 \sqrt{2\pi e\sigma^2} \text{ bits/message} \tag{2.60}$$

Now according to *sampling theorem*, if a signal is band-limited to B Hz, then it can be completely specified by taking $2B$ samples per second. Hence, the rate of information transfer is given by

$$R' = 2BH(X) \tag{2.61}$$

$$= 2B\log_2 \sqrt{2\pi e\sigma^2} \tag{2.62}$$

$$= B\log_2 (2\pi e\sigma^2) \tag{2.63}$$

Thus, if $f(x)$ be a band-limited Gaussian noise with an average noise power $N\ (= \sigma^2)$, then we have

$$R(n) = B\log_2 (2\pi eN) \tag{2.64}$$

We now consider the information transfer over a noisy channel emitted by a continuous source. If the channel input and the noise are represented by X and n, respectively, then the joint entropy (in bits/s) of the source and noise is given by

$$R(x,n) = R(X) + R(n/X) \tag{2.65}$$

In practical situation, the transmitted signal and noise are found to be independent to each other. Thus,

$$R(X, n) = R(X) + R(n) \tag{2.66}$$

Since, the channel output $Y = X + n$, we equate

$$H(X, Y) = H(X, n) \tag{2.67}$$

or

$$H(Y) + H(X/Y) = H(X) + H(n) \tag{2.68}$$

or

$$R(Y) + R(X/Y) = R(X) + R(n) \tag{2.69}$$

The rate at which the information is received from a noisy channel is given by

$$R = R(X) - R(X/Y) = R(Y) - R(n) \qquad \text{[using Eq. (2.69)]} \tag{2.70}$$

Thus, the channel capacity (in bits/s) is given by

$$C = \max_{\{f(X)\}}[R] = \max_{\{f(X)\}}[R(Y) - R(n)] \tag{2.71}$$

Since $R(n)$ is independent of $x(t)$, maximizing R requires maximizing $R(Y)$.

Let the average power of the transmitted signal be S and that of the white Gaussian noise be N within the bandwidth B of the channel. Then the average power of the received signal will be $(S + N)$. $R(Y)$ is maximum when Y is a Gaussian random process since the noise under consideration is also Gaussian.

Thus,

$$R(Y) = B\log_2[2\pi e(S+N)] \tag{2.72}$$

Hence, the channel capacity of a band-limited white Gaussian channel is given by

$$\begin{aligned} C &= \max_{\{f(X)\}}[R(Y) - R(n)] \\ &= B\log_2[2\pi e(S+N)] - B\log_2(2\pi eN) \\ &= B\log_2\left[\frac{S+N}{N}\right] \\ &= B\log_2\left[1+\frac{S}{N}\right]\text{bits/s} \end{aligned} \tag{2.73}$$

The above expression is known as *Shannon–Hartley law*. S/N is the SNR at the channel output.

If $\eta/2$ be the two-sided power spectral density of the noise in W/Hz, then

$$N = \int_{-B}^{B}\frac{\eta}{2}df = \eta B \tag{2.74}$$

Hence,
$$C = B\log_2\left[1+\frac{S}{\eta B}\right]\text{ bits/s} \tag{2.75}$$

Example 2.14: Find the capacity of a telephone channel with bandwidth $B = 3$ kHz and SNR of 40 dB.

Solution:

Here,
$$\frac{S}{N} = 10^4 = 10000$$

Hence,
$$C = B\log_2\left[1+\frac{S}{N}\right] = 3000\log_2[1+10000] = 39864\text{bits/s}$$

Example 2.15: Prove that the channel capacity of an ideal AWGN channel with infinite bandwidth is given by

$$C_{\max} = \frac{1}{\ln 2}\frac{S}{\eta} = 1.44\frac{S}{\eta}\text{bits/s} \tag{2.76}$$

where S and $\eta/2$ are the average signal power and the power spectral density of the white Gaussian noise respectively.

Solution: From Eq. (2.75)

$$C = B\log_2\left[1+\frac{S}{\eta B}\right]$$

Let
$$\frac{S}{\eta B} = x$$

Then,
$$C = \frac{S}{\eta x}\log_2(1+x) = \frac{1}{\ln 2}\frac{S}{\eta}\frac{\ln(1+x)}{x}$$

As $B \to \infty, x \to 0$

Thus,
$$C_{\max} = \frac{1}{\ln 2}\frac{S}{\eta}\lim_{x\to 0}\frac{\ln(1+x)}{x} = \frac{1}{\ln 2}\frac{S}{\eta} = 1.44\frac{S}{\eta}\text{bits/s}$$

For a fixed signal power and in presence of white Gaussian noise, the channel capacity approaches an upper limit given by expression (2.76) with bandwidth increased to infinity. This is known as *Shannon limit*.

Example 2.16: Determine the differential entropy $H(X)$ of the uniformly distributed random variable X having PDF $f(x) = \begin{cases} \frac{1}{b} & 0 \le x \le b \\ 0 & \text{otherwise} \end{cases}$

Solution:

$$H(X) = -\int_{-\infty}^{\infty} f(x)\log_2 f(x)dx = -\int_0^b \frac{1}{b}\log_2\frac{1}{b}dx = \log_2 b$$

2.11 SOLVED PROBLEMS

Problem 2.1: Show that $0 \le H(X) \le \log_2 m$, where m is the size of the alphabet of X.

Solution:

Proof of the lower bound:

Since, $0 \le P(x_i) \le 1, \frac{1}{P(x_i)} \ge 1$ and $\log_2\frac{1}{P(x_i)} \ge 0$

Thus, $P(x_i)\log_2\frac{1}{P(x_i)} \ge 0$

Also, $H(X) = \sum_{i=1}^{m} P(x_i)\log_2\frac{1}{P(x_i)} \ge 0$

It can be noted that $P(x_i)\log_2\frac{1}{P(x_i)} = 0$, if and only if $P(x_i) = 0$ or 1.

Since $\sum_{i=1}^{m} P(x_i) = 1$

when, $P(x_i) = 1$, then $P(x_j) = 0$ for $j \ne i$. Thus, only in this case, $H(X) = 0$.

Proof of the upper bound:

Let us consider two probability distributions $\{P(x_i) = P_i\}$ and $\{Q(x_i) = Q_i\}$ on the alphabet $\{x_i\}$, $i = 1, 2, \ldots, m$ such that $\sum_{i=1}^{m} P_i = 1$ and $\sum_{i=1}^{m} Q_i = 1$.

We can write $\sum_{i=1}^{m} P_i\log_2\frac{Q_i}{P_i} = \frac{1}{\ln 2}\sum_{i=1}^{m} P_i\ln\frac{Q_i}{P_i}$

Using the inequality $\ln\alpha \le \alpha - 1$, for $\alpha \ge 0$ (the equality holds only if $\alpha = 1$), we get

$$\sum_{i=1}^{m} P_i\log_2\frac{Q_i}{P_i} \le \sum_{i=1}^{m} P_i\left(\frac{Q_i}{P_i} - 1\right) = \sum_{i=1}^{m}(Q_i - P_i) = \sum_{i=1}^{m} Q_i - \sum_{i=1}^{m} P_i = 0$$

Thus,

$$\sum_{i=1}^{m} P_i\log_2\frac{Q_i}{P_i} \le 0 \text{ (the equality holds only if } Q_i = P_i \text{, for all } i)$$

Setting $Q_i = \frac{1}{m}$, $i - 1, 2, \ldots, m$, we obtain

$$\sum_{i=1}^{m} P_i \log_2 \frac{1}{P_i m} = -\sum_{i=1}^{m} P_i \log_2 P_i - \sum_{i=1}^{m} P_i \log_2 m$$
$$= H(X) - \log_2 m \sum_{i=1}^{m} P_i$$
$$= H(X) - \log_2 m \leq 0$$

Hence, $H(X) \leq \log_2 m$

The equality holds only if the symbols in X are equiprobable.

Problem 2.2: A high-resolution B/W TV picture contains 3×10^6 picture elements and 16 different brightness levels. Pictures are repeated at a rate of 24 per second. All levels have equal likelihood of occurrence and all picture elements are assumed to be independent. Find the average rate of information carried by this TV picture source.

Solution:

$$H(X) = -\sum_{j=1}^{16} \frac{1}{16} \log_2 \frac{1}{16} = 4 \text{ bits/element}$$

$$r = 3(10^6)(24) = 72(10^6) \text{ elements/s}$$

Thus, $$R = rH(X) = 72(10^6)(4) = 288(10^6) \text{ bits/s} = 288 \text{ Mbps}$$

Problem 2.3: A telegraph source produces two symbols, dash and dot. The dot duration is 0.2 s. The dash duration is 2 times the dot duration. The probability of the dots occurring is twice that of the dash, and the time between symbols is 0.1 s. Determine the information rate of the telegraph source.

Solution:

$$P(\text{dot}) = 2P(\text{dash})$$

$$P(\text{dot}) + P(\text{dash}) = 3P(\text{dash}) = 1$$

Thus, $$P(\text{dash}) = \frac{1}{3} \text{ and } P(\text{dot}) = \frac{2}{3}$$

Now, $$H(X) = -P(\text{dot})\log_2 P(\text{dot}) - P(\text{dash})\log_2 P(\text{dash})$$
$$= 0.667(0.585) + 0.333(1.585) = 0.92 \text{ bits/symbol}$$

$t_{\text{dot}} = 0.2$ s, $t_{\text{dash}} = 0.4$ s, and $t_{\text{space}} = 0.1$ s

Thus, the average time per symbol is given by

$$T_s = P(\text{dot})t_{\text{dot}} + P(\text{dash})t_{\text{dash}} + t_{\text{space}}$$
$$= \frac{2}{3} \times 0.2 + \frac{1}{3} \times 0.4 + 0.1 = 0.3667 \text{ s/symbol}$$

and the average symbol rate is

$$r = \frac{1}{T_s} = 2.727 \text{symbols/s}$$

Thus, the average information rate of the telegraph source is given by

$$R = rH(X) = 2.727 \times 0.92 = 2.509 \text{ bits/s}$$

Problem 2.4: A Gaussian channel has a bandwidth of 1 MHz. Compute the channel capacity if the signal power to noise spectral density ratio (S/η) is 10^5 Hz. Also calculate the maximum information rate.

Solution:

$$C = B\log_2\left[1+\frac{S}{\eta B}\right] = 10^6\log_2\left[1+\frac{10^5}{10^6}\right] = 137504 \text{ bits/s}$$

$$C_{\max} = \frac{1}{\ln 2}\frac{S}{\eta} = 1.44\frac{S}{\eta} = 1.44 \times 10^5 = 144000 \text{ bits/s}$$

Problem 2.5: An analog signal having 3 kHz bandwidth is sampled at 1.5 times the Nyquist rate. The successive samples are statistically independent. Each sample is quantized into one of 256 equally likely levels.

(a) Find the information rate of the source.

(b) Is error-free transmission of the output of this source is possible over an AWGN channel with a bandwidth of 10 kHz and SNR of 20 dB.

(c) Find the SNR required for error-free transmission for part (b).

(d) Determine the bandwidth required for an AWGN channel for error-free transmission of the output of this source when the SNR is 20 dB.

Solution:

(a) Nyquist rate = $2 \times 3 \times 10^3 = 6 \times 10^3$ samples/s

Hence, $$r = 1.5 \times 6 \times 10^3 = 9 \times 10^3 \text{ samples/s}$$

$$H(X) = \log_2 256 = 8 \text{ bits/sample}$$

Thus, $$R = rH(X) = 9 \times 10^3 \times 8 = 72 \times 10^3 \text{ bits/s} = 72 \text{ Kbps}$$

(b) $\frac{S}{N} = 10^2 = 100$

Hence, $$C = B\log_2\left[1+\frac{S}{N}\right] = 10\log_2[1+100] = 66.6 \text{ Kbps}$$

Since $R > C$, error-free transmission is not possible.

(c) The required SNR can be found by

$$C = 10\log_2\left[1+\frac{S}{N}\right] \geq 72$$

or, $$\log_2\left[1+\frac{S}{N}\right] \geq 7.2$$

or, $$1+\frac{S}{N} \geq 2^{7.2}$$

or, $$\frac{S}{N} \geq 146 \text{ (or equivalently 21.6 dB)}$$

Hence, the required SNR must be greater than or equal to 21.6 dB for error-free transmission.

(d) The required bandwidth can be found as follows:

$$C = B\log_2\left[1+\frac{S}{N}\right] = B\log_2(1+100) \geq 72$$

or, $$B \geq \frac{72}{\log_2(101)}$$

or, $$B \geq 10.8 \text{ kHz}$$

Hence, the required bandwidth of the channel must be greater than or equal to 10.8 KHz for error-free transmission.

MULTIPLE CHOICE QUESTIONS

1. Entropy represents
   (a) amount of information (b) rate of information
   (c) measure of uncertainty (d) probability of message

Ans. **(c)**

2. 1 nat is equal to
   (a) 3.32 bits (b) 1.32 bits (c) 1.44 bits (d) 3.44 bits

Ans. **(c)**

3. Decit is a unit of
   (a) channel capacity (b) information
   (c) rate of information (d) entropy

Ans. **(b)**

4. The entropy of information source is maximum when symbol occurrences are
   (a) equiprobable (b) different probability
   (c) both (a) and (b) (d) none of these

Ans. **(a)**

5. 1 decit equals
   (a) 1 bit (b) 3.32 bits (c) 10 bits (d) none of these

Ans. **(b)**

6. The ideal communication channel is defined for a system which has
   (a) finite C (b) BW = 0 (c) S/N = 0 (d) infinite C.

Ans. **(d)**

7. If a telephone channel has a bandwidth of 3000 Hz and the SNR = 20 dB, then the channel capacity is
   (a) 3 kbps (b) 1.19 kbps (c) 2.19 kbps (d) 19.97 kbps

Ans. **(d)**

8. The channel capacity is a measure of
   (a) entropy rate
   (b) maximum rate of information a channel can handle
   (c) information contents of messages transmitted in a channel
   (d) none of these

Ans. **(b)**

9. Gaussian channel is characterized by a distribution represented by
   (a) $p(x) = \frac{1}{\sqrt{2\pi\sigma}} e^{-x^2/2\sigma^2}$ (b) $p(x) = \frac{1}{\sqrt{2\pi\sigma}} e^{x^2/2\sigma^2}$
   (c) $p(x) = \frac{\sqrt{2\pi}}{\sigma} e^{-x^2/2\sigma^2}$ (d) $p(x) = \sqrt{2\pi\sigma}\, e^{-x^2/2\sigma^2}$

Ans. **(a)**

10. The probability of a message is 1/16. The information in bits is
    (a) 1 bit (b) 2 bits (c) 3 bits (d) 4 bits

Ans. **(d)**

11. As the bandwidth approaches infinity, the channel capacity becomes
    (a) infinite (b) zero (c) $1.44S/\eta$ (d) none of these

Ans. **(c)**

12. Information content in a universally true event is
    (a) infinite (b) positive constant
    (c) negative constant (d) zero

Ans. **(d)**

13. Following is not a unit of information
    (a) Hz (b) nat (c) decit (d) bit

Ans. **(a)**

14. The mutual information of a channel with independent input and output is
    (a) zero (b) constant (c) variable (d) infinite

Ans. **(a)**

15. The channel capacity of a noise free channel having *M* symbols is given by
    (a) *M* (b) log *M* (c) 2^M (d) none of these

Ans. **(b)**

REVIEW QUESTIONS

1. Explain the following terms and their significance:
   (a) entropy
   (b) self information
   (c) mutual information
   (d) conditional entropy
   (e) channel capacity
2. (a) Draw the block diagram of a typical message information communication system.
   (b) Explain source coding and channel coding.
3. (a) Show that the maximum entropy of a binary system occurs when $p = 1/2$.
   (b) Show that $H(X, Y) = H(X/Y) + H(Y)$.
4. (a) State and prove the Shannon-Hartley law of channel capacity.
   (b) A Gaussian channel has a 1 MHz bandwidth. If the signal power-to-noise power spectral density is 10^5 Hz, calculate the channel capacity and the maximum information transfer rate.
5. (a) Write short note on Shannon's theorem in communication.
   (b) State the channel capacity of a white band-limited Gaussian channel. Derive an expression of noisy channel when bandwidth tends to be very long.
6. (a) What do you mean by entropy of a source?
   (b) Consider a source *X* which produces five symbols with probabilities 1/2, 1/4, 1/8, 1/16 and 1/16. Find the source entropy.
   (c) Briefly discuss about the channel capacity of a discrete memoryless channel.
7. For a BSC shown below find the channel capacity for $p = 0.9$. Derive the formula that you have used.

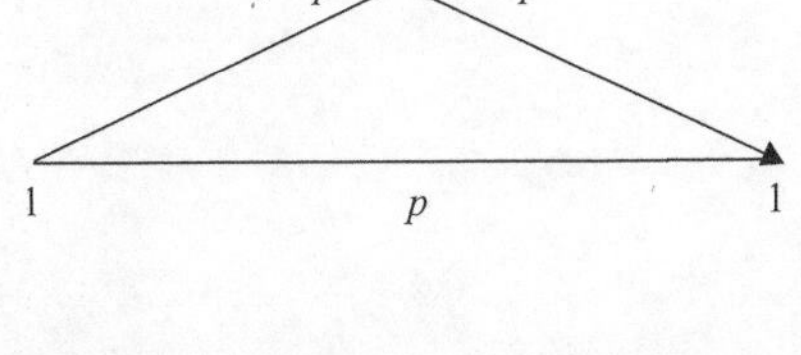

8. A code is composed of dots and dash. Assume that the dash is 3 times as long as the dot and has a one-third the probability of occurrence.
   (i) Calculate the information in a dot and that in dash.
   (ii) Calculate the average information in the dot-dash code.
   (iii) Assume that dot lasts for 10 ms and that this same time interval is allowed between symbols. Calculate the average rate of information transmission.
9. For a binary symmetric channel, compute the channel capacity for $p = 0.7$ and $p = 0.4$.
10. (a) Verify $I(X; Y) \geq 0$.
    (b) What do you mean by differential entropy?
    (c) Determine the capacity of a telephone channel with bandwidth 3000 Hz and SNR 40 dB.

chapter 3

SOURCE CODES

3.1 INTRODUCTION

In Chapter 2, it has been discussed that both source and channel coding are essential for error-free transmission over a communication channel (Figure 2.1). The task of the source encoder is to transform the source output into a sequence of binary digits (bits) called the *information sequence*. If the source is a continuous source, it involves analog-to-digital (A/D) conversion. An ideal source encoder should have the following properties:

1. The average bit rate required for representation of the source output should be minimized by reducing the *redundancy* of the information source.
2. The source output can be reconstructed from the information sequence without any ambiguity.

The channel encoder converts the information sequence into a discrete *encoded sequence* (also called *code word*) to combat the noisy environment. A modulator (not shown in the figure) is then used to transform each output symbol of the channel encoder into a suitable waveform for transmission through the noisy channel. At the other end of the channel, a demodulator processes each received waveform and produces an output called the *received sequence* which can be either discrete or continuous. The channel decoder converts the received sequence into a binary sequence called the *estimated sequence*. Ideally this should be a replica of information source even in presence of the noise in the channel. The source decoder then transforms the estimated sequence into an *estimate* of the source output and transfers the estimate to the destination. If the source is continuous, it involves digital-to-analog (D/A) conversion. For a data storage system, a modulator can be considered as a *writing unit*, a channel as a *storage medium* and a demodulator as a *reading unit*. The process of transmission can be compared to *recording* of data on a storage medium. Efficient representation of symbols leads to compression of data.

In this chapter we will consider various source coding techniques and their possible applications. Source coding is mainly used for compression of data, such as speech, image, video, text, etc.

3.2 CODING PARAMETERS

In Chapter 2, we have seen that the input–output relationship of a channel is specified in terms of either symbols or messages (e.g., the entropy is expressed in terms of bits/message or bits/symbols). In fact, both representations are widely used. In this chapter the following terminology has been used to describe different source coding techniques:

1. *Source Alphabet*—A discrete information source has a finite set of source symbols as possible outputs. This set of source symbols is called the *source alphabet*.
2. *Symbols or Letters*—These are the elements of the source alphabet.
3. *Binary Code Word*—This is a combination of binary digits (bits) assigned to a symbol.
4. *Length of Code Word*—The number of bits in the code word is known as the length of code word.

A. Average Code Length Let us consider a DMS X having finite entropy $H(X)$ and an alphabet $\{x_1, x_2, \ldots, x_m\}$ with corresponding probabilities of occurrence $P(x_j)$, where $j = 1,2,\ldots,m$. If the binary code word assigned to symbol x_j is n_j bits, the *average code word length L* per source symbol is defined as

$$L = \sum_{j=1}^{N} P(x_j) n_j \tag{3.1}$$

It is the average number of bits per source symbol in the source coding process. L should be minimum for efficient transmission.

B. Code Efficiency The *code efficiency* η is given by

$$\eta = \frac{L_{\min}}{L} \tag{3.2}$$

where $L_{\min}$ is the minimum possible value of L. Obviously when $\eta = 1$, the code is the most efficient.

C. Code Redundancy The *redundancy* γ of a code is defined as

$$\gamma = 1 - \eta \tag{3.3}$$

3.3 SOURCE CODING THEOREM

The *source coding theorem* states that if X be a DMS with entropy $H(X)$, the average code word length L per symbol is bounded as

$$L \geq H(X) \tag{3.4}$$

L can be made as close to $H(X)$ as desired for a suitably chosen code.

When $L_{\min} = H(X)$,

$$\eta = \frac{H(X)}{L} \tag{3.5}$$

Example 3.1: A DMS X produces two symbols x_1 and x_2. The corresponding probabilities of occurrence and codes are shown in Table 3.1. Find the code efficiency and code redundancy.

Table 3.1 *Symbols, Their Probabilities, and Codes*

x_j	$P(x_j)$	Code
x_1	0.8	0
x_2	0.2	1

Solution: The average code length per symbol is given by

$$L = \sum_{j=1}^{N} P(x_j) n_j = 0.8 \times 1 + 0.2 \times 1 = 1 \text{ bit}$$

The entropy is

$$H(X) = -\sum_{j=1}^{2} P(x_j) \log_2 P(x_j) = -0.8 \times \log_2 0.8 - 0.2 \times \log_2 0.2 = 0.722 \text{ bits/symbol}$$

The code efficiency is

$$\eta = \frac{H(X)}{L} = 0.722 = 72.2\%$$

The code redundancy is

$$\gamma = 1 - \eta = 1 - 0.722 = .278 = 27.8\%$$

3.4 CLASSIFICATION OF CODES

A. Fixed-length Codes If the code word length for a code is fixed, the code is called *fixed-length code*. A fixed-length code assigns fixed number of bits to the source symbols, irrespective of their statistics of appearance. A typical example of this type of code is the ASCII code for which all source symbols (A to Z, a to z, 0 to 9, punctuation mark, commas etc.) have 7-bit code word.

Let us consider a DMS having source alphabet $\{x_1, x_2, \ldots, x_m\}$. If m is a power of 2, the number of bits required for unique coding is $\log_2 m$. When m is not a power of 2, the bits required will be $[(\log_2 m) + 1]$.

B. Variable-length Codes For a *variable-length code*, the code word length is not fixed. We can consider the example of English alphabet consisting of 26 letters (*a* to *z*). Some letters such as *a*, *e*, etc. appear more frequently in a word or a sentence compared to the letters such as *x*, *q*, *z*, etc. Thus, if we represent the more frequently occurring letters by lesser number of bits and the less frequently occurring letters by larger number of bits, we might require fewer number of bits overall to encode an entire given text than to encode the same with a fixed-length code. When the source symbols are not equiprobable, a variable-length coding technique can be more efficient than a fixed-length coding technique.

C. Distinct Codes A code is called *distinct* if each code word is distinguishable from the other. Table 3.2 is an example of distinct code.

Table 3.2 *Distinct Code*

x_i	Code Word
x_1	00
x_2	01
x_3	10
x_4	11

D. Uniquely Decodable Codes The coded source symbols are transmitted as a stream of bits. The codes must satisfy some properties so that the receiver can identify the possible symbols from the stream of bits. A distinct code is said to be *uniquely decodable* if the original source sequence can be reconstructed perfectly from the received encoded binary sequence. We consider four source symbols A, B, C, and D encoded with two different techniques as shown in Table 3.3.

Table 3.3 *Binary Codes*

Symbol	Code 1	Code 2
A	00	0
B	01	1
C	10	00
D	11	01

Code 1 is a fixed-length code, whereas code 2 is a variable-length code. The message 'A BAD CAB' can be encoded using the above two codes. In code 1 format, it appears as 00 010011 100001, whereas using code 2 format the sequence will be 0 1001 0001. Code 1 requires 14 bits to encode the message, whereas code 2 requires 9 bits. Although code 2 requires lesser number of bits, yet it does not qualify as a valid code as there is a decoding problem with this code. The sequence 0 1001 0001 can be regrouped in different ways, such as [0] [1][0][0][1] [0][0][01] which stands for 'A BAAB AAD' or [0] [1][00][1] [0][0][0][1] which translates to 'A BCB AAAB'. Since in code 2 format we do not know where the code word of one symbol (letter) ends and where the next one begins it creates an ambiguity; it is not a uniquely decodable code. However, there is no such problem associated with code 1 format since it is a fixed-length code and each group must include 2 bits together. Hence, code 1 format is a uniquely decodable code. In should be noted that a uniquely decodable code can be both fixed-length code and variable-length code.

E. Prefix-free Codes A code in which no code word forms the prefix of any other code word is called a *prefix-free code* or *prefix code*. The coding scheme in Table 3.4 is an example of prefix code.

Table 3.4 *Prefix Code*

Symbol	Code Word
A	0
B	10
C	110
D	1110

We consider a symbol being encoded using code 2 in Table 3.3. If a 0 is received, the receiver cannot decide whether it is the entire code word for alphabet 'A' or a partial code word for 'C' or 'D' that it has received. Hence, no code word should be the prefix of any other code word. This is known as the *prefix-free property* or *prefix condition*. The code illustrated in Table 3.4 satisfies this condition.

It is to be mentioned that if no code word forms the prefix of another code word, the code is said to be uniquely decodable. However, the prefix-free condition is not a necessary condition for unique decodability. This is explained in Example 3.2.

F. Instantaneous Codes A uniquely decodable code is said to be an *instantaneous code* if the end of any code is recognizable without checking subsequent code symbols. Since the instantaneous codes also have the property that no code word is a prefix of another code word, prefix codes are also called *instantaneous codes*.

G. Optimal Codes A code is called an *optimal code* if it is instantaneous and has minimum average length L for a given source with a particular probability assignment for the source symbols.

H. Entropy Coding When a variable-length code is designed such that its average code word length approaches the entropy of the DMS, then it is said to be *entropy coding*. *Shannon–Fano coding* and *Huffman coding* (discussed later) are two examples of this type of coding.

Example 3.2: Consider Table 3.5 where a source of size 4 has been encoded in binary codes with 0 and 1. Identify different codes.

Table 3.5 *Different Binary Codes*

x_j	Code 1	Code 2	Code 3	Code 4	Code 5	Code 6
x_1	00	00	0	0	0	1
x_2	01	01	1	10	01	01
x_3	00	10	00	110	011	001
x_4	11	11	11	111	0111	0001

Solution: Code 1 and code 2 are fixed-length codes with length 2.

Codes 3, 4, 5, and 6 are variable-length codes.

All codes except code 1 are distinct codes.

Codes 2, 4, and 6 are prefix (or instantaneous) codes.

Codes 2, 4, and 6 and code 5 are uniquely decodable codes.

(Note that code 5 does not satisfy the prefix-free property, and still it is uniquely decodable since the bit 0 indicates the beginning of each code word.)

Example 3.3: Consider Table 3.6 illustrating two binary codes having four symbols. Compare their efficiency.

Table 3.6 *Two Binary Codes*

x_j	$P(x_j)$	Code 1	Code 2
x_1	0.5	00	0
x_2	0.25	01	10
x_3	0.125	10	110
x_4	0.125	11	111

Solution: Code 1 is a fixed-length code having length 2.

In this case, the average code length per symbol is

$$L = \sum_{j=1}^{4} P(x_j)n_j = 0.5 \times 2 + 0.25 \times 2 + 0.125 \times 2 + 0.125 \times 2 = 2 \text{ bits}$$

The entropy is

$$\begin{aligned} H(X) &= -\sum_{j=1}^{4} P(x_j)\log_2 P(x_j) \\ &= -0.5 \times \log_2 0.5 - 0.25 \times \log_2 0.25 - 0.125 \times \log_2 0.125 - 0.125 \times \log_2 0.125 \\ &= 1.75 \text{ bits/symbol} \end{aligned}$$

The code efficiency is

$$\eta = \frac{H(X)}{L} = \frac{1.75}{2} = 87.5\%$$

Code 2 is a variable-length code.

In this case, the average code length per symbol is

$$L = \sum_{j=1}^{4} P(x_j)n_j = 0.5 \times 1 + 0.25 \times 2 + 0.125 \times 3 + 0.125 \times 3 = 1.75 \text{ bits}$$

The entropy is

$$\begin{aligned} H(X) &= -\sum_{j=1}^{4} P(x_j)\log_2 P(x_j) \\ &= -0.5 \times \log_2 0.5 - 0.25 \times \log_2 0.25 - 0.125 \times \log_2 0.125 - 0.125 \times \log_2 0.125 \\ &= 1.75 \text{ bits/symbol} \end{aligned}$$

The code efficiency is

$$\eta = \frac{H(X)}{L} = \frac{1.75}{1.75} = 100\%$$

Thus, the second coding method is better than the first.

3.5 KRAFT INEQUALITY

Let X be a DMS X having an alphabet $\{x_j\}$ ($j = 1,2,\ldots,m$). If the length of the binary code word corresponding to x_j be n_j, a necessary and sufficient condition for existence of an instantaneous binary code is

$$K = \sum_{j=1}^{m} 2^{-n_j} \leq 1 \tag{3.6}$$

The above expression is known as *Kraft inequality*. It indicates the existence of an instantaneously decodable code with code word lengths that satisfy the inequality. However, it does not show how to obtain these code words, nor does it tell that any code, for which inequality condition is valid, is automatically uniquely decodable.

Example 3.4: Verify that $L \geq H(X)$, where L and $H(X)$ are the average code word length per symbol and the source entropy, respectively.

Solution: In Chapter 2, we have shown that (see Problem 2.1)

$$\sum_{j=1}^{m} p_j \log_2 \frac{Q_j}{P_j} \leq 0$$

where the equality holds only if $Q_j = P_j$.

Let

$$Q_j = \frac{2^{-n_j}}{K}$$

where

$$K = \sum_{j=1}^{m} 2^{-n_j}$$

Thus,

$$\sum_{j=1}^{m} Q_j = \frac{1}{K}\sum_{j=1}^{m} 2^{-n_j} = 1$$

and

$$\sum_{j=1}^{m} P_j \log_2 \frac{2^{-n_j}}{KP_j} = \sum_{j=1}^{m} P_j\left[\log_2 \frac{1}{P_j} - n_j - \log_2 K\right]$$

$$= -\sum_{j=1}^{m} P_j \log_2 P_j - \sum_{j=1}^{m} P_j n_j - (\log_2 K)\sum_{j=1}^{m} P_j$$

$$= H(X) - L - \log_2 K \leq 0$$

From the Kraft inequality, we get

$$\log_2 K \leq 0$$

Thus,

$$H(X) - L \leq \log_2 K \leq 0$$

or

$$L \geq H(x)$$

The equality holds if $Q_j = P_j$ and $K = 1$.

Example 3.5: Consider a DMS with four source symbols encoded with four different binary codes as shown in Table 3.7. Show that

(a) all codes except code 2 satisfy the Kraft inequality
(b) codes 1 and 4 are uniquely decodable but codes 2 and 3 are not uniquely decodable.

Table 3.7 *Different Binary Codes*

x_j	Code 1	Code 2	Code 3	Code 4
x_1	00	0	0	0
x_2	01	10	11	100
x_3	10	11	100	110
x_4	11	110	110	111

Solution:

(a) For code 1: $n_1 = n_2 = n_3 = n_4 = 2$

Thus, $$K = \sum_{j=1}^{4} 2^{-n_j} = 0.25 + 0.25 + 0.25 + 0.25 = 1$$

For code 2: $n_1 = 1, n_2 = n_3 = 2, n_4 = 3$

Thus, $$K = \sum_{j=1}^{4} 2^{-n_j} = 0.5 + 0.25 + 0.25 + 0.125 = 1.125 > 1$$

For code 3: $n_1 = 1, n_2 = 2, n_3 = n_4 = 3$

Thus, $$K = \sum_{j=1} 2^{-n_j} = 0.5 + 0.25 + 0.125 + 0.125 = 1$$

For code 4: $n_1 = 1, n_2 = n_3 = n_4 = 3$

Thus, $$K = \sum_{j=1}^{4} 2^{-n_j} = 0.5 + 0.125 + 0.125 + 0.125 = 0.875 < 1$$

Hence, all codes except code 2 satisfy Kraft inequality.

(b) Codes 1 and 4 are prefix codes; therefore, they are uniquely decodable.

Code 2 does not satisfy the Kraft inequality. Thus, it is not uniquely decodable.

Code 3 satisfies the Kraft inequality; yet it is not uniquely decodable. This can be verified considering the following example:

Let us consider a binary sequence 0110110. Using code 3, this sequence can correspond to $x_1x_2x_1x_4$ or $x_1x_4x_4$.

3.6 IMAGE COMPRESSION

Like an electronic communication system, an image compression system contains two distinct functional components: an encoder and a decoder. The encoder performs compression, while the job of the decoder is to execute the complementary operation of decompression. These operations can be implemented by the using a software or a hardware or a combination of both. A *codec* is a device or a program that performs both coding and decoding operations. In still-image applications, both the encoded input and the decoder output are the functions of two dimensional (2-D) space co-ordinates, whereas video

Table 3.8 *Image Compression Standards, Formats, and Containers*

Still image		Video
Binary	**Continuous tone**	**DV (Digital Video)**
CCITT Group 3 (*Consultative Committee of the International Telephone and Telegraph* standard)	JPEG (*Joint Photographic Experts Group* standard)	H.261
CCITT Group 4	JPEG-LS (Loss less or near loss less JPEG)	H.262
JBIG (or JBIG1) (*Joint Bi-level Image Experts Group* standard)	JPEG-2000	H.263
JBIG2	BMP (Windows Bitmap)	H.264
TIFF (Tagged Image File Format)	GIF (Graphic Interchange Format)	MPEG-1 (*Motion Pictures Expert Group* standard)
	PDF (Portable Document Format)	MPEG-2
	PNG (Portable Network Graphics)	MPEG-4
	TIFF	MPEG-4 AVC (MPEG-4 Part 10 Advanced Video Coding)
		AVS (Audio-Video Standard)
		HDV (High-Definition Video)
		M-JPEG (Motion JPEG)
		Quick Time
		VC-1 (or WMV9)

signals are the functions of space co-ordinates as well as time. In general, decoder output may or may not be an exact replica of the encoded input. If it is an exact replica, the compression system is *error free*, *lossless* or *information preserving*, otherwise, the output image is distorted and the compression system is called *lossy system*.

3.6.1 Image Formats, Containers, and Compression Standards

An *image file format* is a standard way to organize and store image data. It specifies how the data is arranged and which type of compression technique (if any) is used. An *image container* is akin to a file format but deals with multiple types of image data. *Image compression standards* specify the procedures for compressing and decompressing images. Table 3.8 provides a list of the image compression standards, file formats, and containers presently used.

3.7 SPEECH AND AUDIO CODING

Digital audio technology forms an essential part of multimedia standards and technology. The technology has developed rapidly over the last two decades. Digital audio finds applications in multiple domains such as CD/DVD storage, digital telephony, satellite broadcasting, consumer electronics, etc.

Based on their applications, audio signals can be broadly classified into three following subcategories:

1. *Telephone Speech*—This is a low bandwidth application. It covers the frequency range of 300–3400 Hz. Though the intelligibility and naturalness of this type of signal are poor, it is widely used in telephony and some video telephony services.
2. *Wideband Speech*—It covers a bandwidth of 50–7000 Hz for improved speech quality.
3. *Wideband Audio*—Wideband audio includes high fidelity audio (speech as well as music) applications. It requires a bandwidth of at least 20 kHz for digital audio storage and broadcast applications.

The conventional digital format for these signals is the Pulse Code Modulation (PCM). Earlier, the compact disc (CD) quality stereo audio was used as a standard for digital audio representation having sampling frequency 44.1 kHz and 16 bits/sample for each of the two stereo channels. Thus, the stereo net bit rate required is $2 \times 16 \times 44.1 = 1.41$ Mbps. However, the CD needs a significant overhead (extra bits) for synchronization and error correction, resulting in a 49-bit representation of each 16-bit audio sample. Hence, the total stereo bit rate requirement is $1.41 \times 49/16 = 4.32$ Mbps.

Although high bandwidth channels are available, it is necessary to achieve compression for low bit rate applications in cost-effective storage and transmission. In many applications such as mobile radio, channels have limited capacity and efficient bandwidth compression must be employed.

Speech compression is often referred to as *speech coding*, a method for reducing the amount of information needed to represent a speech signal. Most of the speech-coding schemes are usually based on a lossy algorithm. Lossy algorithms are considered acceptable as far as the loss of quality is undetectable to the human ear. Speech coding or compression is usually implemented by the use of *voice coders* or *vocoders*. There are two types of vocoders as follows:

1. *Waveform-following Coders*—Waveform-following coders exactly reproduce the original speech signal if there is no quantization error.
2. *Model-based Coders*—Model-based coders cannot reproduce the original speech signal even in absence of quantization error, because they employ a parametric model of speech production which involves encoding and transmitting the parameters, not the signal.

One of the model-based coders is *Linear Predictive Coding* (LPC) vocoder, which is lossy regardless of the presence of quantization error. All vocoders have the following attributes:

1. *Bit Rate*—It is used to determine the degree of compression that a vocoder achieves. Uncompressed speech is usually transmitted at a rate of 64 kbps using 8 bits/sample and 8 kHz sampling frequency. Any bit rate below 64 kbps is considered compression. The linear predictive coder transmits the signal at a bit rate of 2.4 kbps.
2. *Delay*—It is involved with the transmission of an encoded speech signal. Any delay that is greater than 300 ms is considered unacceptable.
3. *Complexity*—The complexity of algorithm affects both the cost and the power of the vocoder. LPC is very complex as it has high compression rate and involves execution of millions of instructions per second.
4. *Quality*—Quality is a subjective attribute and it depends on how the speech sounds to a given listener.

Any voice coder, regardless of the algorithm it exploits, will have to make trade-offs between these attributes.

3.8 SHANNON–FANO CODING

Shannon–Fano coding, named after Claude Shannon and Robert Fano, is a source coding technique for constructing a prefix code based on a set of symbols and their probabilities. It is suboptimal as it does not achieve the lowest possible expected code word length like Huffman coding.

Shannon–Fano algorithm produces fairly efficient variable-length encoding. However, it does not always produce optimal prefix codes. Hence, the technique is not widely used. It is used in the IMPLODE compression method, which is a part of the ZIP file format, where a simple algorithm with high performance and the minimum requirements for programming is desired.

The steps or algorithm of Shannon–Fano algorithm for generating source code are presented as follows:

Step 1: Arrange the source symbols in order of decreasing probability. The symbols with equal probabilities can be listed in any arbitrary order.
Step 2: Divide the set into two such that the sum of the probabilities in each set is the same or nearly the same.
Step 3: Assign 0 to the upper set and 1 to the lower set.
Step 4: Repeat steps 2 and 3 until each subset contains a single symbol.

Example 3.6: A DMS X has five symbols x_1, x_2, x_3, x_4, and x_5 with $P(x_1) = 0.4$, $P(x_2) = 0.17$, $P(x_3) = 0.18$, $P(x_4) = 0.1$, and $P(x_5) = 0.15$, respectively.
(a) Construct a Shannon–Fano code for X.
(b) Calculate the efficiency of the code.

Solution:

(a) The Shannon–Fano code for X is constructed in Table 3.9.

Table 3.9 *Construction of Shannon-Fano Code*

x_j	$P(x_j)$	Column 1	Column 2	Column 3	Code
x_1	0.4	0	0		00
x_3	0.18	0	1		01
x_2	0.17	1	0		10
x_5	0.15	1	1	0	110
x_4	0.1	1	1	1	111

(b) $L = \sum_{j=1}^{5} P(x_j)n_j = 0.4 \times 2 + 0.17 \times 2 + 0.18 \times 2 + 0.1 \times 3 + 0.15 \times 3 = 2.25$ bits

$$H(X) = -\sum_{j=1}^{5} P(x_j)\log_2 P(x_j)$$

$$= -0.4 \times \log_2 0.4 - 0.17 \times \log_2 0.17 - 0.18 \times \log_2 0.18 - 0.1 \times \log_2 0.1 - 0.15 \times \log_2 0.15$$

$$= 2.15 \text{ bits/symbol}$$

$$\eta = \frac{H(X)}{L} = \frac{2.15}{2.25} = 0.956 = 95.6\%$$

3.9 HUFFMAN CODING

Huffman coding produces prefix codes that always achieve the lowest possible average code word length. Thus, it is an optimal code which has the highest efficiency or the lowest redundancy. Hence, it is also known as the *minimum redundancy code* or *optimum code.*

Huffman codes are used in CCITT, JBIG2, JPEG, MPEG-1/2/4, H.261, H.262, H.263, H.264, etc.

The procedure of the Huffman encoding is as follows:

Step 1: List the source symbols in order of decreasing probability. The symbols with equal probabilities can be arranged in any arbitrary order.

Step 2: Combine the probabilities of the symbols having the smallest probabilities. Now, reorder the resultant probabilities. This process is called reduction 1. The same process is repeated until there are exactly two ordered probabilities remaining. Final step is called the last reduction.

Step 3: Start encoding with the last reduction. Assign 0 as the first digit in the code words for all the source symbols associated with the first probability of the last reduction. Then assign 1 to the second probability.

Step 4: Now go back to the previous reduction step. Assign 0 and 1 to the second digit for the two probabilities that was combined in this reduction step, retaining all assignments made in step 3.

Step 5: Repeat step 4 until the first column is reached.

Example 3.7: Repeat Example 3.6 for the Huffman code and compare their efficiency.

Solution: The Huffman code is constructed in Table 3.10.

Table 3.10 *Construction of Huffman Code*

x_j	$P(x_j)$	Code	Reduction 1	Reduction 2	Reduction 3
x_1	0.4	1	0.4 1	0.4 1	0.6 0
x_3	0.18	000	0.25 01	0.35 00	0.4 1
x_2	0.17	001	0.18 000	0.25 01	
x_5	0.15	010	0.17 001		
x_4	0.1	011			

$$L = \sum_{j=1}^{5} P(x_j)n_j = 0.4 \times 1 + 0.17 \times 3 + 0.18 \times 3 + 0.1 \times 3 + 0.15 \times 3 = 2.2 \text{ bits}$$

$$H(X) = -\sum_{j=1}^{5} P(x_j)\log_2 P(x_j)$$

$$= -0.4 \times \log_2 0.4 - 0.17 \times \log_2 0.17 - 0.18 \times \log_2 0.18 - 0.1 \times \log_2 0.1 - 0.15 \times \log_2 0.15$$

$$= 2.15 \text{ bits/symbol}$$

$$\eta = \frac{H(X)}{L} = \frac{2.15}{2.2} = 0.977 = 97.7\%$$

The average code word length for the Huffman code is shorter than that of the Shannon–Fano code. Hence, the efficiency of Huffman code is higher than that of the Shannon–Fano code.

Example 3.8: A DMS X has seven symbols x_1, x_2, x_3, x_4, x_5, x_6, and x_7 with $P(x_1) = \frac{1}{2}$, $P(x_2) = \frac{1}{2^2}$, $P(x_3) = \frac{1}{2^3}$, $P(x_4) = \frac{1}{2^4}$, $P(x_5) = \frac{1}{2^5}$, $P(x_6) = \frac{1}{2^6}$, and $P(x_7) = \frac{1}{2^6}$, respectively.

(a) Construct a Huffman code for X.
(b) Calculate the efficiency of the code.

Solution: If we proceed similarly as in the previous example, we can obtain the following Huffman code (see Table 3.11).

Table 3.11 *Huffman Code for Example 3.8*

x_j	$P(x_j)$	Self-information	Code	Code Word Length
x_1	$1/2$	1	1	1
x_2	$1/2^2$	2	00	2
x_3	$1/2^3$	3	010	3
x_4	$1/2^4$	4	0110	4
x_5	$1/2^5$	5	01110	5
x_6	$1/2^6$	6	011110	6
x_7	$1/2^6$	6	011111	6

$$L = \sum_{j=1}^{7} P(x_j)n_j = 1.97 \text{ bits}$$

$$H(X) = -\sum_{j=1}^{7} P(x_j)\log_2 P(x_j)$$

$$= 1.97 \text{ bits/symbol}$$

$$\eta = \frac{H(X)}{L} = \frac{1.97}{1.97} = 1 = 100\%$$

In this case, the efficiency of the code is exactly 100%. It is also interesting to note that the code word length for each symbol is equal to its self-information. Therefore, it can be concluded that to achieve optimality ($\eta = 100\%$), the self-information of the symbols must be integer, which in turn, requires that the probabilities must negative powers of 2.

3.10 ARITHMETIC CODING

It has been already been shown that the Huffman codes are optimal only when the probabilities of the source symbols are negative powers of two. This condition of probability is not always valid in practical situations. A more efficient way to match the code word lengths to the symbol probabilities is implemented by using *arithmetic coding*. No one-to-one correspondence between source symbols and code words exists in this coding scheme; instead, an entire sequence of source symbols (message) is assigned a single code word. The arithmetic code word itself defines an interval of real numbers between 0 and 1.

If the number of symbols in the message increases, the interval used to represent it becomes narrower. As a result, the number of information units (say, bits) required to represent the interval becomes larger. Each symbol in the message reduces the interval in accordance with its probability of occurrence. The more likely symbols reduce the range by less, and therefore add fewer bits to the message.

Arithmetic coding finds applications in JBIG1, JBIG2, JPEG-2000, H.264, MPEG-4 AVC, etc.

Example 3.9: Let an alphabet consist of only four symbols *A, B, C,* and *D* with probabilities of occurrence *P*(*A*) = 0.2, *P*(*B*) = 0.2, *P*(*C*) = 0.4, and *P*(*D*) = 0.2, respectively. Find the arithmetic code for the message *ABCCD*.

Solution: Table 3.12 illustrates the arithmetic coding process.

Table 3.12 *Construction of Arithmetic Code*

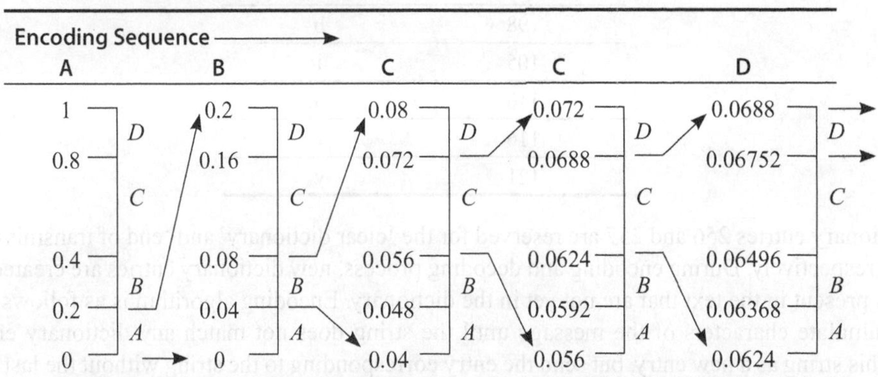

We first divide the interval [0, 1) into four intervals proportional to the probabilities of occurrence of the symbols. The symbol *A* is thus associated with subinterval [0, 0.2). *B*, *C*, and *D* correspond to [0.2, 0.4), [0.4, 0.8), and [0.8, 1.0), respectively. *A* is the first symbol of the message being coded, the interval is narrowed to [0, 0.2). Now, this range is expanded to the full height of the figure with its end points labelled as 0 and 0.2 and subdivided in accordance with the original source symbol probabilities. The next symbol *B* of the message now corresponds to [0.04, 0.08). We repeat the process to find the intervals for the subsequent symbols. The third symbol *C* further narrows the range to [0.056, 0.072). The fourth symbol *C* corresponds to [0.06752, 0.0688). The final message symbol *D* narrows the subinterval to [0.06752, 0.688). Any number within this range (say, 0.0685) can be used to represent the message.

3.11 LEMPEL–ZIV–WELCH CODING

There are many compression algorithms that use a *dictionary* or *code book*, known to the coder and the decoder. This dictionary is generated during the coding and decoding processes. Many of these algorithms are based on the work reported by Abraham Lempel and Jacob Ziv, and are known as *Lempel–Ziv* encoders. In principle, these coders replace repeated occurrences of a string by references to an earlier occurrence. The dictionary is basically the collection of these earlier occurrences. In a written text, groups of letters such as 'th', 'ing', 'qu', etc. appear many times. A *dictionary-based coding* scheme in this case canbe proved effective.

One widely used LZ algorithm is the *Lempel–Ziv–Welch* (LZW) algorithm reported by Terry A. Welch. It is a lossless or *reversible* compression. Unlike Huffman coding, LZW coding requires no a priori knowledge of the probability of occurrences of the symbols to be encoded. It is used in variety of mainstream imaging file formats, including GIFF, TIFF and PDF.

Example 3.10: Encode and decode the following text message using LZW coding:

itty bitty bit bin

Solution: The initial set of dictionary entries is a 8-bit character code having values 0–255, with ASCII as the first 128 characters, including specifically the following which appear in the string.

Table 3.13 *LZW Coding Dictionary*

Value	Character
32	Space
98	b
105	i
110	n
116	t
121	y

Dictionary entries 256 and 257 are reserved for the 'clear dictionary' and 'end of transmission' commands, respectively. During encoding and decoding process, new dictionary entries are created using all *phrases* present in the text that are not yet in the dictionary. Encoding algorithm is as follows.

Accumulate characters of the message until the string does not match any dictionary entry. Then define this string as a new entry, but send the entry corresponding to the string without the last character, which will be used as the first character of the next string to match.

In the given text message, the first character is 'i' and the string consisting of just that character is already present in the dictionary. So the next character is added, and the accumulated string becomes 'it'. This string is not in the dictionary. At this point, 'i' is sent and 'it' is added to the dictionary, at the next available entry, i.e., 258. The accumulated string is reset to be just the last character, which was not sent, so it is 't'. Now, the next character is added; hence, the accumulated string becomes 'tt' which is not in the dictionary. The process repeats.

Initially, the additional dictionary entries are all two-character strings. However, the first time one of these two-character strings is repeated, it is sent (using fewer bits than would be required for two characters) and a new three-character dictionary entry is defined. For the given message, it happens with the string 'itt'. Later, one three-character string gets transmitted, and a four-character dictionary entry is defined.

Decoding algorithm is as follows.

Output the character string whose code is transmitted. For each code transmission, add a new dictionary entry as the previous string plus the first character of the string just received. It is to be noted that the coder and decoder create the dictionary on the fly; the dictionary therefore does not need to be explicitly transmitted, and the coder deals with the text in a single pass.

As seen from Table 3.14, we sent eighteen 8-bit characters (144 bits) in fourteen 9-bit transmissions (126 bits). It is a saving of 12.5% for such a short text message. In practice, larger text files often compress by a factor of 2, and drawings by even more.

Table 3.14 *Transmission Summary Input*

Encoding →				Transmission →		Decoding		
Input		**New Dictionary Entry**		**9-Bit Characters Transmitted**		**New Dictionary Entry**		**Output**
105	i	–	–	256	(start)	–	–	–
116	t	258	it	105	i	–	–	i
116	t	259	tt	116	t	258	it	t
121	y	260	ty	116	t	259	tt	t
32	space	261	y-space	121	y	260	ty	y
98	b	262	space-b	32	space	261	y-space	space
105	i	263	bi	98	b	262	space-b	b
116	t	–	–	–	–	–	–	–
116	t	264	itt	258	it	263	bi	it
121	y	–	–	–	–	–	–	–
32	space	265	ty-space	260	ty	264	itt	ty
98	b	–	–	–	–	–	–	–
105	i	266	space-bi	262	space-b	265	ty-space	space-b
116	t							
32	space	267	it-space	258	it	266	space-bi	it
98	b	–	–	–	–	–	–	–
105	i				–	–		
110	n	268	space-bin	266	space-bi	267	it-space	space-bi
–	–	–	–	110	n	268	space-bin	n
–	–	–	–	257	(stop)	–	–	–

8-bit characters input

3.12 RUN-LENGTH ENCODING

Run-length encoding (RLE) is used to reduce the size of a repeating string of characters. The repeating string is referred to as a *run*. It can compress any type of data regardless of its information content. However, content of data affects the compression ratio. Compression ratio, in this case, is not so high. But it is easy to implement and quick to execute. Typically RLE encodes a run of symbols into two bytes, a count and a symbol.

RLE was developed in the 1950s and became, along with its 2-D extensions, the standard compression technique in facsimile (FAX) coding. FAX is a two-colour (black and white) image which is predominantly white. If these images are sampled for conversion into digital data, many horizontal lines are found to be entirely white (long runs of 0's). Besides, if a given pixel is either black or white, the possibility that the next pixel will match is also very high. The code for a fax machine is actually a combination of a Huffman code and a run-length code. The coding of run-lengths is also used in CCITT, JBIG2, JPEG, M-PEG, MPEG-1/2/4, BMP, etc.

Example 3.11: Consider the following bit stream:

11111111111111110000000000000000000011

Find the run-length code and its compression ratio.

Solution: The stream can be represented as: sixteen 1's, twenty 0's and two 1's, i.e., (16, 1), (20, 0), (2, 1). Since the maximum number of repetitions is 20, which can be represented with 5 bits, we can encode the bit stream as (10000,1), (10100,0), (00010,1).

The compression ratio is 18:38 = 1:2.11.

3.13 MPEG AUDIO AND VIDEO CODING STANDARDS

The Motion Pictures Expert Group (MPEG) of the *International Standards Organization* (ISO) provides the standards for digital audio coding, as a part of multimedia standards. There are three standards discussed as follows.

A. MPEG-1 In the MPEG-1 standard, out of a total bit rate of 1.5 Mbps for CD quality multimedia storage, 1.2 Mbps is provided to video and 256 kbps is allocated to two-channel audio. It finds applications in web movies, MP3 audio, video CD, etc.

B. MPEG-2 MPEG-2 provides standards for high-quality video (including High-Definition TV) at a rate ranging from 3 to 15 Mbps and above. It also supports new audio features including low bit rate digital audio and multichannel audio. In this case, two to five full bandwidth audio channels are accommodated. The standard also provides a collection of tools known as *Advanced Audio Coding* (MPEG-2 AAC).

C. MPEG-4 MPEG-4 addresses standardization of audiovisual coding for various applications ranging from mobile access, low-complexity multimedia terminals to high-quality multichannel sound systems with wide range of quality and bit rate, but improved quality mainly at low bit rate. It provides interactivity, universal accessibility, high degree of flexibility, and extensibility. One of its main applications is found in internet audio–video streaming.

3.14 PSYCHOACOUSTIC MODEL OF HUMAN HEARING

The human auditory system (the inner ear) is fairly complicated. Results of numerous psychoacoustic tests reveal that human auditory response system performs short-term critical band analysis and can be modelled as a bank of band pass filters with overlapping frequencies. The power spectrum is not on linear frequency scale and the bandwidths are in the order of 50 to 100 Hz for signals below 500 Hz and up to 5000 Hz at higher frequencies. Such frequency bands of auditory response system are called *critical bands*. Twenty six critical bands covering frequencies of up to 24 kHz are taken into account.

3.14.1 The Masking Phenomenon

It is observed that the ear is less sensitive to low level sound when there is a higher level sound at a nearby frequency. When this occurs, the low level audio signal becomes either less audible or inaudible. This phenomenon is known as *masking*. The stronger signal that masks the weaker signal is called *masker* and the weaker one that is masked is known as *maskee*. It is also found that the masking is the largest in the critical band within which the masker is present and the masking is also slightly effective in the neighbouring bands.

We can define a *masking threshold*, below which the presence of any audio will be rendered inaudible. It is to be noted that the masking threshold depends upon several factors, such as the *sound pressure level* (SPL), the frequency of the masker, and the characteristics of the maskee and the masker (e.g., whether the masker or maskee is a tone or noise).

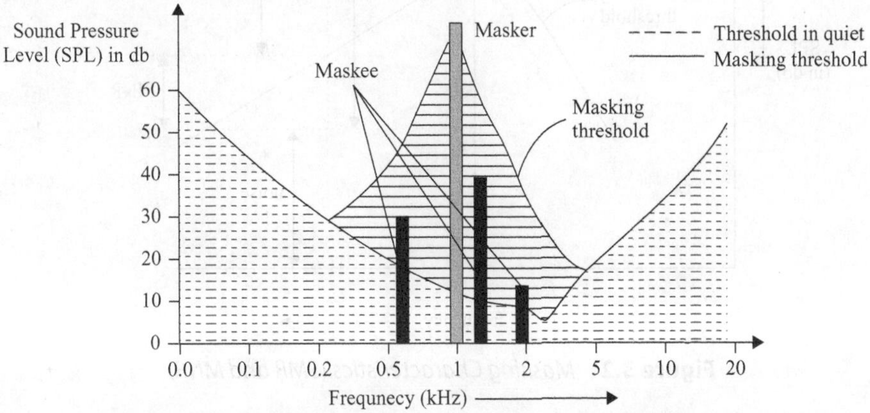

Figure 3.1 *Effects of Masking in Presence of a Masker at 1 kHz*

In Figure 3.1, the 1-kHz signal acts as a masker. The masking threshold (solid line) falls off sharply as we go away from the masker frequency. The slope of the masking threshold is found to be steeper towards the lower frequencies. Hence, it can be concluded that the lower frequencies are not masked to the extent that the higher frequencies are masked. In the above diagram, the three solid bars represent the maskee frequencies and their respective SPLs are well below the masking threshold. The dotted curve represents *quiet threshold* in the absence of any masker. The quiet threshold has a lower value in the frequency range from 500 Hz to 5 kHz of the audio spectrum.

The masking characteristics are specified by the following two parameters:

Signal-to-mask ratio (SMR): The SMR at a given frequency is defined as the difference (in dB) between the SPL of the masker and the masking threshold at that frequency.

Mask-to-noise ratio (MNR): The MNR at a given frequency is the difference (in dB) between the masking threshold at that frequency and the noise level. To make the noise inaudible, its level must be below the masking threshold; i.e., the MNR must be positive.

Figure 3.2 shows a masking threshold curve. The masking signal appears at a frequency f_m. The SMR, the *signal-to-noise ratio* (SNR) and the MNR for a particular frequency f corresponding to a noise level have also been shown in the figure. It is evident that

$$SMR(f) = SNR(f) - MNR(f) \tag{3.7}$$

So far we have considered only one masker. If more than one maskers are present, then each masker has its own masking threshold and a *global masking threshold* is evaluated that describes *just noticeable distortion* as a function of frequency.

3.14.2 Temporal Masking

The masking phenomenon described in the previous subsection is also known as *simultaneous masking*, where both the masker and the maskee appear simultaneously. Masking can also be observed when two

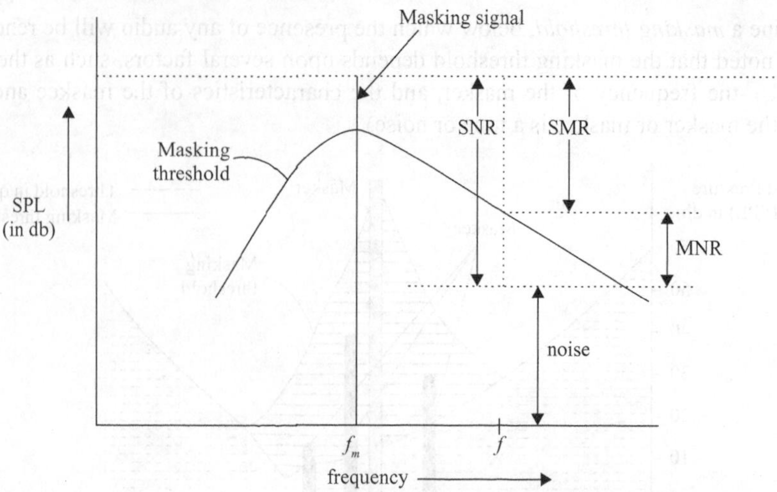

Figure 3.2 *Masking Characteristics (SMR and MNR)*

sounds occur within a small interval of time, the stronger signal being masker and the weaker one being maskee. This phenomenon is referred to as *temporal masking*. Like simultaneous masking, temporal masking plays an important role in human auditory perception. Temporal masking is also possible even when the maskee precedes the masker by a short time interval and is associated with *premasking* and *postmasking*, where the former has less than one-tenth duration of that of the latter. The order of postmasking duration is 50–200 ms. Both premasking and postmasking are being used in MPEG audio coding algorithms.

3.14.3 Perceptual Coding in MPEG Audio

An efficient audio source coding algorithm must satisfy the following two conditions:

1. *Redundancy removal*: It will remove redundant components by exploiting correlations between the adjacent samples.
2. *Irrelevance removal*: It is perceptually motivated since any sound that our ears cannot hear can be removed.

In irrelevance removal, simultaneous and temporal masking phenomena play major roles in MPEG audio coding. It has already been mentioned that the noise level should be below the masking threshold. Since the quantization noise depends on the number of bits to which the samples are quantized, the bit allocation algorithm must take care of this fact. Figure 3.3 shows the block diagram of a perception-based coder that makes use of the masking phenomenon.

As seen from the figure, *Fast Fourier Transform* (FFT) of the incoming PCM audio samples is computed to obtain the complete audio spectrum, from which the tonal components of masking signals can be determined. Using this, a global masking threshold and also the SMR in the entire audio spectrum is evaluated. The dynamic bit allocator uses the SMR information while encoding the bit stream. A coding scheme is called *perceptually transparent* if the quantization noise is below the global masking threshold. The perceptually transparent encoding process will produce the decoded output indistinguishable from the input.

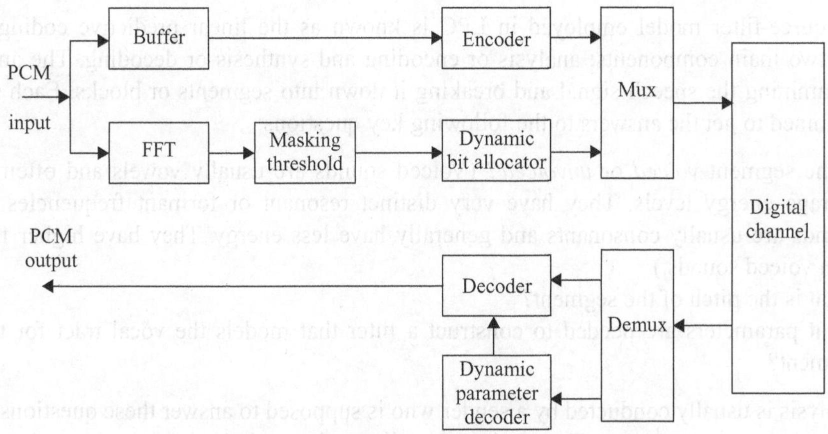

Figure 3.3 *Block Diagram of a Perception Based Coder*

However, our knowledge in computing the global masking threshold is limited as the perceptual model considers only simple and stationary maskers and sometimes it can fail in practical situations. To solve this problem, sufficient safety margin should be maintained.

3.15 DOLBY

Dolby Digital was first developed in 1992 as a means to allow 35-mm theatrical film prints to store multichannel digital audio directly on the film without sacrificing the standard analog optical soundtrack. It is basically a perceptual audio coding system. Since its introduction the system has been adopted for use with laser disc, DVD-audio, DVD-video, DVD-ROM, Internet audio distribution, ATSC high definition and standard definition digital television, digital cable television and digital satellite broadcast. Dolby Digital is used as an emissions coder that encodes audio for distribution to the consumer. It is not a multigenerational coder which is exploited to encode and decode audio multiple times.

Dolby Digital breaks the entire audio spectrum into narrow bands of frequency using mathematical models derived from the characteristics of the ear and then analyzes each band to determine the audibility of those signals. A greater number of bits represent more audible signals, which, in turn, increases data efficiency. In determining the audibility of signals, the system makes use of masking. As mentioned earlier, a low level audio signal becomes inaudible, if there is a simultaneous occurrence of a stronger audio signal having frequency close to the former. This is known as masking. By taking advantage of this phenomenon, audio signals can be encoded much more efficiently than in other coding systems with comparable audio quality, such as linear PCM. Dolby Digital is an excellent choice for those systems where high audio quality is desired, but bandwidth or storage space is limited. This is especially true for multichannel audio. The compact Dolby Digital bit stream allows full 5.1-channel audio to take less space than a single channel of linear PCM audio.

3.16 LINEAR PREDICTIVE CODING MODEL

Linear predictive coding is a digital method for encoding an analog signal (e.g., speech signal) in which a particular value is predicted by a linear function of the past values of the given signal. The particular source-filter model employed in LPC is known as the linear predictive coding model. It consists of two main components: analysis or encoding and synthesis or decoding. The analysis part involves examining the speech signal and breaking it down into segments or blocks. Each segment is further examined to get the answers to the following key questions:

1. Is the segment *voiced* or *unvoiced*? (Voiced sounds are usually vowels and often have high average energy levels. They have very distinct resonant or formant frequencies. Unvoiced sounds are usually consonants and generally have less energy. They have higher frequencies than voiced sounds.)
2. What is the pitch of the segment?
3. What parameters are needed to construct a filter that models the vocal tract for the current segment?

LPC analysis is usually conducted by a sender who is supposed to answer these questions and transmit these answers onto a receiver. The receiver actually performs the task of synthesis. It constructs a filter by using the received answers. When the correct input source is provided, the filter can reproduce the original speech signal.

Essentially, LPC synthesis simulates human speech production. Figure 3.4 illustrates which parts of the receiver correspond to which parts in the human anatomy. In almost all voice coder models, there are two parts: excitation and articulation. Excitation is the type of sound that is transmitted to the filter or vocal tract and articulation is the transformation of the excitation signal into speech.

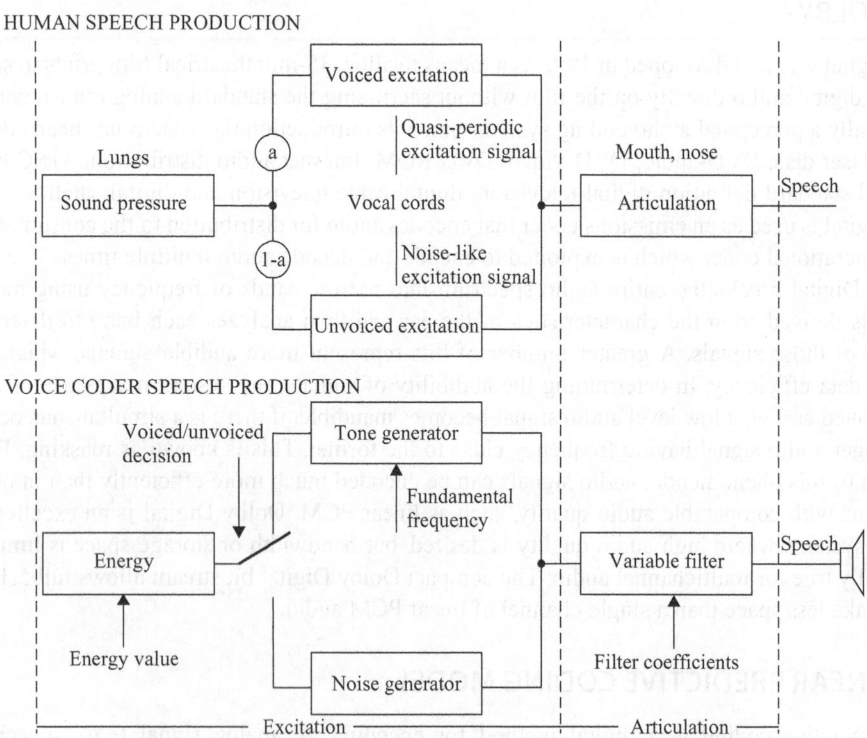

Figure 3.4 *Human vs. Voice Coder Speech Production*

3.17 SOLVED PROBLEMS

Problem 3.1: Consider a DMS X having a symbol x_j with corresponding probabilities of occurrence $P(x_j) = P_j$ where $j = 1,2,\ldots,m$. Let n_j be the length of the code word assigned to symbol x_j such that $\log_2 \frac{1}{P_j} \le n_j \le \log_2 \frac{1}{P_j} + 1$. Prove that this relationship satisfies the Kraft inequality and find the bound on K in the expression of Kraft inequality.

Solution:

$$\log_2 \frac{1}{P_j} \le n_j \le \log_2 \frac{1}{P_j} + 1$$

or

$$-\log_2 P_j \le n_j \le -\log_2 P_j + 1$$

or

$$\log_2 P_j \ge -n_j \ge \log_2 P_j - 1$$

Then

$$2^{\log_2 P_j} \ge 2^{-n_j} \ge 2^{\log_2 P_j} 2^{-1}$$

or

$$P_j \ge 2^{-n_j} \ge \frac{1}{2} P_j$$

or

$$\sum_{j=1}^{m} P_j \ge \sum_{j=1}^{m} 2^{-n_j} \ge \frac{1}{2} \sum_{j=1}^{m} P_j$$

or

$$1 \ge \sum_{j=1}^{m} 2^{-n_j} \ge \frac{1}{2}$$

The result indicates that the Kraft inequality is satisfied. The bound on K is

$$\frac{1}{2} \le K \le 1$$

Problem 3.2: Show that a code constructed with code word length satisfying the condition given in Problem 3.1 will satisfy the following relation:

$$H(X) \le L \le H(X) + 1$$

where $H(X)$ and L are the source entropy and the average code word length, respectively.

Solution: From the previous problem, we have

$$-\log_2 P_j \le n_j \le -\log_2 P_j + 1$$

Multiplying by P_j and summing over j yields

$$-\sum_{j=1}^{m} P_j \log_2 P_j \le \sum_{j=1}^{m} n_j P_j \le \sum_{j=1}^{m} P_j(-\log_2 P_j + 1)$$

or

$$H(X) \le L \le H(X) + 1$$

as

$$\sum_{j=1}^{m} P_j(-\log_2 P_j + 1) = -\sum_{j=1}^{m} P_j \log_2 P_j + \sum_{j=1}^{m} P_j = H(X) + 1$$

Problem 3.3: Apply the Shannon–Fano coding procedure for a DMS with the following source symbols and the given probabilities of occurrence. Calculate its efficiency.

Table 3.15 *Source Symbols and Their Probabilities*

x_j	x_1	x_2	x_3	x_4	x_5	x_6	x_7
$P(x_j)$	0.4	0.2	0.12	0.08	0.08	0.06	0.06

Solution:

Table 3.16 *Construction of Shannon–Fano Code*

x_j	$P(x_j)$	Column 1	Column 2	Column 3	Column 4	Code
x_1	0.4	0	0			00
x_2	0.2	0	1			01
x_3	0.12	1	0	0		100
x_4	0.08	1	0	1		101
x_5	0.08	1	1	0		110
x_6	0.06	1	1	1	0	1110
x_7	0.06	1	1	1	1	1111

$$L = \sum_{j=1}^{7} P(x_j)n_j = 0.4 \times 2 + 0.2 \times 2 + 0.12 \times 3 + 0.08 \times 3 + 0.08 \times 3 + 0.06 \times 4 + 0.06 \times 4$$

$$= 2.52 \text{ bits.}$$

$$H(X) = -\sum_{j=1}^{7} P(x_j)\log_2 P(x_j)$$

$$= -0.4 \times \log_2 0.4 - 0.2 \times \log_2 0.2 - 0.12 \times \log_2 0.12 - 0.08 \times \log_2 0.08 - 0.08 \times \log_2 0.08$$
$$- 0.06 \times \log_2 0.06 - 0.06 \times \log_2 0.06$$

$$= 2.43 \text{ bits/symbol}$$

$$\eta = \frac{H(X)}{L} = \frac{2.43}{2.52} = 0.964 = 96.4\%$$

Another Shannon–Fano code for the same source symbols:

Table 3.17 *Construction of Another Shannon–Fano Code*

x_j	$P(x_j)$	Column 1	Column 2	Column 3	Column 4	Code
x_1	0.4	0				0
x_2	0.2	1	0	0		100
x_3	0.12	1	0	1		101
x_4	0.08	1	1	0	0	1100
x_5	0.08	1	1	0	1	1101
x_6	0.06	1	1	1	0	1110
x_7	0.06	1	1	1	1	1111

$$L = \sum_{j=1}^{7} P(x_j)n_j = 0.4 \times 1 + 0.2 \times 3 + 0.12 \times 3 + 0.08 \times 4 + 0.08 \times 4 + 0.06 \times 4 + 0.06 \times 4$$

$$= 2.48 \text{ bits.}$$

$$\eta = \frac{H(X)}{L} = \frac{2.43}{2.48} = 0.980 = 98.0\%$$

The above two procedures reveal that sometimes Shannon–Fano method is ambiguous. The reason behind this ambiguity is the availability of more than one equally valid schemes of partitioning the symbols.

Problem 3.4: Repeat Problem 3.3 for the Huffman code.

Solution:

Table 3.18 *Construction of Huffman Code*

x_j	$P(x_j)$	Code	Reduction 1	Reduction 2	Reduction 3	Reduction4	Reduction 5
x_1	0.4	1	0.4 1	0.4 1	0.4 1	0.4 1	0.6 0
x_2	0.2	000	0.2 000	0.2 000	0.24 01	0.36 00	0.4 1
x_3	0.12	010	0.12 010	0.16 001	0.2 000	0.24 01	
x_4	0.08	0010	0.12 001	0.12 010	0.16 001		
x_5	0.08	0011	0.08 0010	0.12 011			
x_6	0.06	0110	0.08 0011				
x_7	0.06	0111					

$$L = \sum_{j=1}^{7} P(x_j)n_j = 0.4 \times 1 + 0.2 \times 3 + 0.12 \times 3 + 0.08 \times 4 + 0.08 \times 4 + 0.06 \times 4 + 0.06 \times 4$$

$$= 2.48 \text{ bits.}$$

$$H(X) = -\sum_{j=1}^{7} P(x_j)\log_2 P(x_j)$$

$$= -0.4 \times \log_2 0.4 - 0.2 \times \log_2 0.2 - 0.12 \times \log_2 0.12 - 0.08 \times \log_2 0.08 - 0.08 \times \log_2 0.08$$
$$- 0.06 \times \log_2 0.06 - 0.06 \times \log_2 0.06$$

$$= 2.43 \text{ bits/symbol}$$

$$\eta = \frac{H(X)}{L} = \frac{2.43}{2.48} = 0.980 = 98.0\%$$

MULTIPLE CHOICE QUESTIONS

1. The coding efficiency is expressed as
   (a) 1 + redundancy (b) 1 – redundancy (c) 1/redundancy (d) none of these

   Ans. **(b)**

2. The code efficiency η is given by
   (a) $\eta = \frac{L_{min}}{L}$ (b) $\eta = \frac{L}{L_{min}}$ (c) $\eta = L_{min} \times L$ (d) none of these
   Ans. **(a)**
3. The efficiency of Huffman code is linearly proportional to
   (a) average length of code (b) average entropy
   (c) maximum length of code (d) none of these
   Ans. **(b)**
4. In the expression of Kraft inequality, the value of K is given by
   (a) $K = \sum_{j=1}^{m} 2^{-n_j} = 1$ (b) $K = \sum_{j=1}^{m} 2^{-n_j} \geq 1$
   (c) $K = \sum_{j=1}^{m} 2^{-n_j} \leq 1$ (d) $K = \sum_{j=1}^{m} 2^{-n_j} < 1$
   Ans. **(c)**
5. An example of dictionary based coding is
   (a) Shannon–Fano coding (b) Huffman coding
   (c) arithmetic coding (d) LZW coding
   Ans. **(d)**
6. The run-length code for the bit stream: 11111000011 is
   (a) (101,1), (100,0), (010,1) (b) (101,0), (100,0), (010,1)
   (c) (101,1), (100,1), (010,1) (d) (101,1), (100,0), (010,0)
   Ans. **(a)**
7. The signal-to-mask ratio (SMR), mask to noise ratio (MNR) and signal to noise ratio (SNR) are related by the formula
   (a) $SMR(f) = SNR(f) - MNR(f)$ (b) $SMR(f) = MNR(f) - SNR(f)$
   (c) $SMR(f) = SNR(f) + MNR(f)$ (d) none of these
   Ans. **(a)**
8. Dolby Digital is based on
   (a) multigenerational coding (b) perceptual coding
   (c) Shannon–Fano coding (d) none of these
   Ans. **(b)**
9. The frequency range of telephone speech is
   (a) 4–7 kHz (b) less than 300 Hz
   (c) greater than 20 kHz (d) 300–3400 Hz
   Ans. **(d)**
10. LPC is a
    (a) waveform-following coder (b) model-based coder
    (c) lossless vocoder (d) none of these
    Ans. **(b)**

REVIEW QUESTIONS

1. (a) Define the following terms:
   (i) average code length
   (ii) code efficiency
   (iii) code redundancy.
   (b) State source coding theorem.

2. With suitable example explain the following codes:
   (a) fixed-length code
   (b) variable-length code
   (c) distinct code
   (d) uniquely decodable code
   (e) prefix-free code
   (f) instantaneous code
   (g) optimal code.
3. Write short notes on
   (a) Shanon–Fano algorithm
   (b) Huffman coding
4. (a) Write down the advantages of Huffman coding over Shannon–Fano coding.
   (b) A discrete memoryless source has seven symbols with probabilities of occurrences 0.05, 0.15, 0.2, 0.05, 0.15, 0.3 and 0.1. Construct the Huffman code and determine
      (i) entropy
      (ii) average code length
      (iii) code efficiency.
5. A discrete memoryless source has five symbols with probabilities of occurrences 0.4, 0.19, 0.16, 0.15 and 0.1. Construct both the Shannon–Fano code and Huffman code and compare their code efficiency.
6. With a suitable example explain arithmetic coding. What are the advantages of arithmetic coding scheme over Huffman coding?
7. Encode and decode the following text message using LZW coding:

   DAD DADA DAD
8. With a suitable example describe run-length encoding.
9. (a) What is masking?
   (b) Explain perceptual coding in MPEG audio.
10. Write short notes on
    (a) Dolby digital
    (b) Linear predictive coding.

part

B

ERROR CONTROL CODING

chapter 4

CODING THEORY

4.1 INTRODUCTION

Demand for efficient and reliable data transmission and storage systems is gaining more and more importance in recent years. With the emergence of new and sophisticated electronic gadgets as well as that of large scale, high-speed data networks demand is accelerated. In this sphere, a major concern of the designer is the control of errors so that reliable reproduction of data is obtained. The emergence of coding theory dates back to 1948, when Shannon in his landmark paper 'A mathematical theory of communication' demonstrated that, by proper encoding of the information, errors induced by a noisy channel or storage medium can be reduced to any desired level. Since then, a lot of work has been done for devising efficient encoding and decoding methods for error control in a noisy environment.

A typical transmission (or storage) system is illustrated schematically in Figure 4.1. In fact, transmission and digital data storage system have much in common. The *information source* shown can be a machine or a person. The source output can be a continuous waveform (i.e., analogue in nature) or a sequence of discrete symbols (i.e., digital in nature). *Source encoder* transforms the source output into a sequence of binary digits (bits) known as the *information sequence* **u**. If the source is a continuous one, then analogue-to-digital conversion process is also involved. The process of source coding is already discussed in detail in Chapter 3. The *channel encoder* transforms the information sequence **u** into a

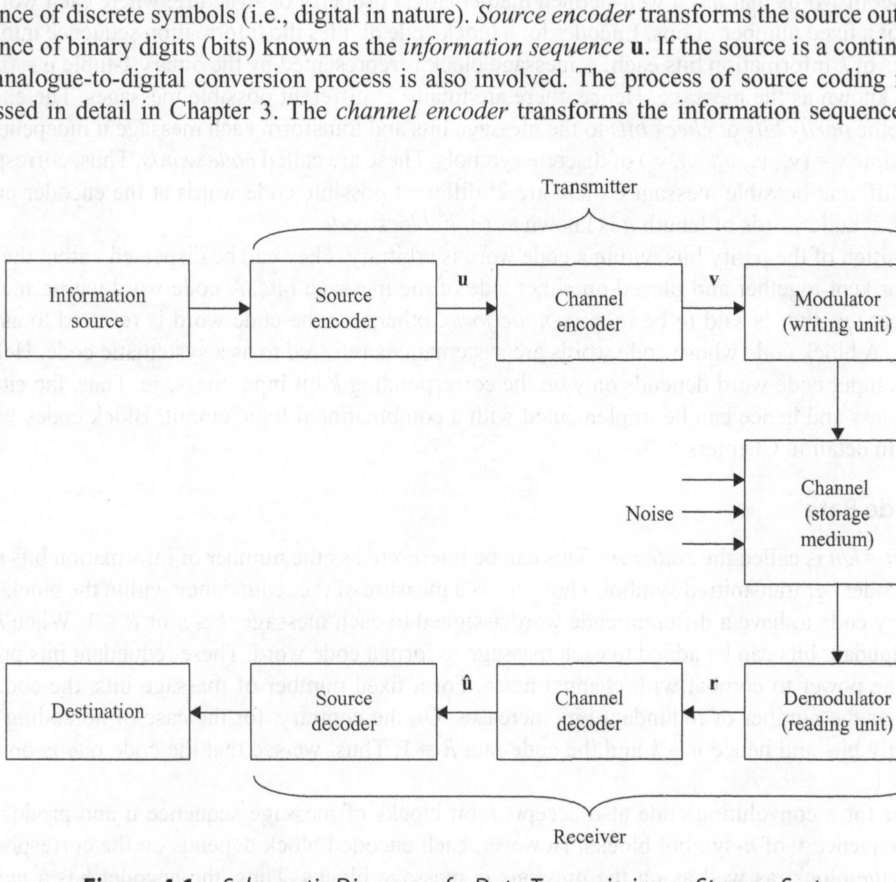

Figure 4.1 *Schematic Diagram of a Data Transmission or Storage System*

discrete encoded sequence **v** known as a code word. Generally **v** is also a binary sequence. But in some instances non-binary code words are also used.

Since discrete symbols are not suitable for transmission over a physical channel or recording on a digital storage medium, usually the *modulator* (or *writing unit*) transforms each output symbol of the channel encoder into a waveform of duration t seconds. These waveforms enter the *channel* (or *storage medium*) and are then corrupted by noise. Then the demodulator (or *reading unit*) processes each received waveform of duration t and produces an output that can be discrete (quantized) or continuous (unquantized). The sequence of demodulator outputs corresponding to the encoded sequence **v** is known as the *received sequence* **r**.

Then the channel decoder transforms the received sequence **r** into a binary sequence $\hat{\mathbf{u}}$ known as the *estimated sequence.* Ideally $\hat{\mathbf{u}}$ should be the replica of **u**, though the noise can cause some *decoding errors.* The *source decoder* transforms $\hat{\mathbf{u}}$ into an estimate of the source output and delivers this estimate to the destination. If the source is continuous, it involves digital-to-analogue conversion.

4.2 TYPES OF CODES

There are two different types of codes commonly used—*block codes* and *convolution codes.* A *block code* is a set of words that has a well-defined mathematical property or structure, where each word is a sequence of a fixed number of bits. Encoder for a block code divides the information sequence into message blocks of k information bits each. A message block is represented by the binary k-tuple $\mathbf{u} = (u_1, u_2, u_3, \ldots, u_k)$ known as the message. Hence, there are totally 2^k different possible messages. The encoder will add some *parity bits* or *check bits* to the message bits and transform each message **u** independently into an n-tuple $\mathbf{v} = (v_1, v_2, v_3, \ldots, v_n)$ of discrete symbols. These are called *code words*. Thus, corresponding to 2^k different possible messages, there are 2^k different possible code words at the encoder output. This set of 2^k code words of length n is known as *(n, k) block code*.

The position of the parity bits within a code word is arbitrary. They can be dispersed within the message bits or kept together and placed on either side of the message bits. A code word whose message bits are kept together is said to be in *systematic form,* otherwise the code word is referred to as *non-systematic*. A block code whose code words are systematic is referred to as a systematic code. Here the n-symbol output code word depends only on the corresponding k-bit input message. Thus, the encoder is memoryless and hence can be implemented with a combinational logic circuit. Block codes will be discussed in detail in Chapters 5–7.

4.2.1 Code Rate

The ratio $R = k/n$ is called the *code rate*. This can be interpreted as the number of information bits entering the encoder per transmitted symbol. Thus, this is a measure of the redundancy within the block code. For a binary code to have a different code word assigned to each message, $k \le n$ or $R \le 1$. When $k < n$, $(n - k)$ redundant bits can be added to each message to form a code word. These redundant bits provide the code the power to combat with channel noise. For a fixed number of message bits, the code rate tends to 0 as the number of redundant bits increases. On the contrary, for the case of no coding there are no parity bits and hence $n = k$ and the code rate $R = 1$. Thus, we see that the code rate is bounded by $0 \le R \le 1$.

Encoder for a convolution code also accepts k-bit blocks of message sequence **u** and produces an encoded sequence **v** of n-symbol blocks. However, each encoded block depends on the corresponding k-bit message block, as well as on the previous m message blocks. Thus, the encoder has a *memory* *order* of m. This set of encoded sequences produced by a k-input, n-output encoder of memory order m is known as (n, k, m) *convolution code*. Since the encoder has memory, it is implemented with sequential logic circuit. Here also the ratio $R = k/n$ is called the *code rate*. In a binary convolution code, redundant bits can be added when $k < n$ or $R < 1$. Generally k and n are small integers and more redundancy is added by increasing m while maintaining k and n and hence code rate R fixed. Convolution code is discussed in detail in Chapter 8.

4.3 TYPES OF ERRORS

In general, errors occurring in channels can be categorized into two types—*random error* and *burst error*. On memoryless channels, noise affects each transmitted symbol independently. Thus, transmission errors occur randomly in the received sequence. Memoryless channels are thus known as *random-error channels*, e.g., deep-space channels, satellite channels, etc. Codes used for correcting random errors are called *random-error-correcting codes*.

On the other hand, on channels with memory, noise is not independent for each transmission. As a consequence, a transmission error occurs in clusters or bursts in these channels called *burst-error channels*, e.g., radio channels, wire and cable transmission, etc. Codes devised for correcting burst errors are called *burst-error-correcting codes*. Finally it is to mention that some channels contain a combination of both random and burst errors. These are known as *compound channels* and the codes used for correcting errors on these channels are called *burst-and-random-error-correcting codes*.

4.4 ERROR CONTROL STRATEGIES

Transmission or storage system can be either a one-way system, where the transmission or recording is strictly in one direction, from transmitter to receiver, or a two-way system, i.e., information can be sent in both directions and the transmitter also acts as a receiver (a transceiver) and vice versa.

For a one-way system, error control is accomplished by using *forward error correction* (FEC). Here error-correcting codes automatically correct errors detected at the receiver. In fact most of the coded systems in use today use some form of FEC, even if the channel is not strictly one way. Examples of such one-way communication are broadcast systems, deep space communication systems, etc.

On the other hand, error control for a two-way system can be accomplished by using *automatic repeat request* (ARQ). In these systems, whenever an error is detected at the receiver, a request is sent for the transmitter to repeat the message, and this will continue until the total message is received correctly. Examples of two-way communication are some satellite communication channels, telephone channels, etc.

ARQ systems are of two types: *continuous* ARQ and *stop-and-wait* ARQ. With the continuous ARQ, the transmitter sends code words to the receiver continuously and receives acknowledgements continuously. If a negative acknowledgement (NAK) is received, the transmitter begins a retransmission. It backs up to the erroneous code word and resends that word plus the following words. This is known as *go-back-N* ARQ. Alternatively, the transmitter can follow *selective-repeat* ARQ, where only those code words which are acknowledged negatively are resent. Selective-repeat ARQ requires more logic and buffering than *go-back-N* ARQ, but at the same time is more efficient.

With the stop-and-wait ARQ, the transmitter sends a code word to the receiver and waits for a positive acknowledgement (ACK) or a NAK from the receiver. If no errors are detected, i.e., ACK is received, the transmitter sends the next code word. Alternatively, if errors are detected and NAK is received, it resends the preceding code word.

Continuous ARQ is more efficient that stop-and-wait ARQ, but it is more expensive. In channels where the transmission rate is high but time taken to receive an acknowledgement is more, generally continuous ARQ is used, e.g., satellite communication system. On the other hand, in channels where the transmission rate is low compared to the time to receive an acknowledgement, stop-and-wait ARQ is used. Generally continuous ARQ is used on full duplex channels, whereas stop-and-wait ARQ is used on half duplex channels.

ARQ is advantageous over FEC, in the sense in the former only error is detected and in the later case error is detected as well as corrected. Since error detection requires much simple decoding circuit than error correction, implementation of ARQ is simpler compared to FEC. The disadvantage of ARQ is that when the channel error rate is high, retransmissions are required too often, and the rate at which newly generated messages are correctly received, i.e., the system throughput is lowered by ARQ. In such a situation, a combination of FEC for the frequent error patterns, together with ARQ for the less likely error patterns, is much efficient.

4.4.1 Throughput Efficiency of ARQ

In ARQ systems, the performance is usually measured using a parameter known as throughput efficiency. The throughput efficiency is defined as the ratio of the average number of information bits per second delivered to the user to the average number of bits per second that have been transmitted in the system. This throughput efficiency is obviously smaller than 100%. For example, using an error-detecting scheme with a code rate $R = 0.97$, an error-free transmission would then correspond to a throughput efficiency of 97%.

A. Stop-and-Wait ARQ For error-free operation using the stop-and-wait ARQ technique, the utilization rate U_R of a link is defined as

$$U_R = \frac{T_S}{T_T} \tag{4.1}$$

where T_s denotes the time required to transmit a single frame, and T_T is the overall time between transmission of two consecutive frames, including processing and ACK/NAK transmissions. The total time T_T can be expressed as follows:

$$T_T = T_p + T_s + T_c + T_p + T_a + T_c \tag{4.2}$$

In above equation, T_p denotes the propagation delay time, i.e., the time needed for a transmitted bit to reach the receiver; T_c is the processing delay time, i.e., the time required for either the sender or the receiver to perform the necessary processing and error checking, whereas T_s and T_a denote the transmission duration of a data frame and of an ACK/NAK frame, respectively.

Assuming the processing time T_c is negligible with respect to T_p and that the sizes of the ACK/NAK frames are very small, leading T_a to negligible value, then from the above equation we can write:

$$T_T = T_S + 2T_p \tag{4.3}$$

Defining the propagation delay ratio as $\alpha = T_p/T_s$, then U_R can be written as follows:

$$U_R = \frac{1}{1+2\alpha} \tag{4.4}$$

The utilization rate expressed in Eq. (4.4) can be used to evaluate the throughput efficiency on a per-frame basis. Due to repetitions caused by transmission errors, the average utilization rate, or throughput efficiency, is defined as follows:

$$\eta = \frac{U_R}{N_t} = \frac{T_S}{N_t T_T} \tag{4.5}$$

where N_t is the expected number of transmissions per frame.

In this definition of the throughput efficiency [i.e., Eq. (4.5)], the coding rate of the error-detecting code, as well as the other overhead bits, is not taken into account. That is, the above equation represents the throughput efficiency on a per-frame performance basis. Some other definitions of the throughput deficiency can be related to the number of information bits actually delivered to the destination. In such a case, the new throughput efficiency is simply:

$$\eta^* = \eta(1 - \rho) \tag{4.6}$$

where ρ represents the fraction of all redundant and overhead bits in the frame.

Assuming error-free transmissions of ACK and NAK frames, and assuming independence for each frame transmission, the probability of requiring exactly k attempts to successfully receive a given frame is $P_k = P^{k-1}(1 - P)$, $k = 1, 2, 3, \ldots$, where P is the frame error probability. The average number of transmissions N_t that are required before a frame is accepted by the receiver is then

$$N_t = \sum_{k=1}^{\infty} kP_k = \sum_{k=1}^{\infty} kP^{k-1}(1-P) = \frac{1}{1-P} \tag{4.7}$$

Using Eqs. (4.4), (4.5), and (4.7) the throughput efficiency can thus be written as follows:

$$\eta = \frac{1-P}{1+2\alpha} \tag{4.8}$$

B. Continuous ARQ For continuous ARQ schemes, the basic expression of the throughput efficiency shown in Eq. (4.8) must be used with the following assumptions: The transmission duration of a data frame is normalized to $T_s = 1$; the transmission time of an ACK/NAK frame, T_a, and the processing delay of any frame, T_c, are negligible. Since $\alpha = T_p/T_s$ and $T_s = 1$, the propagation delay T_p is equal to α. Assuming no transmission errors, the utilization rate of the transmission link for a continuous ARQ using a sliding window protocol of size N is given by:

$$U_R = \begin{cases} 1, & N \geq 2\alpha + 1 \\ \dfrac{N}{1+2\alpha}, & N < 2\alpha + 1 \end{cases} \tag{4.9}$$

Selective-Repeat ARQ: For selective-repeat ARQ scheme, the expression for the throughput efficiency can be obtained by dividing Eq. (4.9) by $N_t = \dfrac{1}{1-P}$ yielding

$$\eta_{SR} = \begin{cases} 1-P, & N \geq 2\alpha + 1 \\ \dfrac{N(1-P)}{1+2\alpha}, & N < 2\alpha + 1 \end{cases} \tag{4.10}$$

Go-back-N ARQ: For the go-back-N ARQ scheme, each frame in error necessitates the retransmission of M frames ($M \leq N$) rather than just one frame, where M depends on the roundtrip propagation delay and the frame size. Let $g(k)$ denote the total number of transmitted frames corresponding to a particular frame being transmitted k times. Since each repetition involves M frames, we can write

$$g(k) = 1 + (k-1)M = (1 - M) + kM$$

Using the same approach as in Eq. (4.7), the average number of transmitted frames N_t to successfully transmit one frame can be expressed as follows:

$$N_t = \sum_{k=1}^{\infty} g(k)P^{k-1}(1-P) = \frac{1-P+PM}{1-P} \tag{4.11}$$

If $N \geq 2\alpha + 1$, the sender transmits continuously and, consequently, M is approximately equal to $2\alpha + 1$. In this case, in accordance with Eq. (4.11), $N_t = (1 + 2\alpha P)/(1 - P)$. Dividing Eq. (4.9) by N_t, the throughput efficiency becomes $\eta = (1 - P)/(1 + 2\alpha P)$.

If $N < 2\alpha + 1$, then $M = N$ and hence $N_t = (1 - P + PN)/(1 - P)$. Dividing Eq. (4.9) again by N_t, we obtain $U = N(1 - P)/(1 + 2\alpha)(1 - P + PN)$.

Summarizing, the throughput efficiency of go-back-N ARQ is given by

$$\eta_{GB} = \begin{cases} \dfrac{1-P}{1+2\alpha p}, & N \geq 2\alpha + 1 \\[2ex] \dfrac{N(1-P)}{(1+2\alpha)(1-P+PN)} & N < 2\alpha + 1 \end{cases} \tag{4.12}$$

4.5 MATHEMATICAL FUNDAMENTALS

To understand the coding theory, it is essential for the reader to have an elementary knowledge of the algebra involved in this. In this section we try to develop a general understanding of the coding algebra. Here, we basically approach in a descriptive way rather than becoming mathematically rigorous.

4.5.1 Modular Arithmetic

Modular arithmetic (sometimes called *clock arithmetic*) is a system of arithmetic of congruences, where numbers 'wrap around' after they reach a certain value, called the *modulus*. If two values x and y have the property that their difference $(x - y)$ is integrally divisible by a value m (i.e., $(x - y)/m$ is an integer), then x and y are said to be 'congruent modulo m.' The value m is called the modulus, and the statement 'x is congruent to y (modulo m)' is written mathematically as $x \equiv y \ (mod\ m)$. On the contrary if $(x - y)$ is *not* integrally divisible by m, then it is said that 'x is not congruent to y (modulo m)'.

It is known that set of integers can be broken up into the following two classes:

- the even numbers (…, −6, −4, −2, 0, 2, 4, 6, …)
- the odd numbers (…, −5, −3, −1, 1, 3, 5, …).

Certain generalizations can be made about the arithmetic of numbers based on which of these two classes come from. For example, we know that the sum of two even numbers is even. The sum of an even number and an odd number is odd. The sum of two odd numbers is even. The product of two even numbers is even, etc.

Modular arithmetic lets us state these results quite precisely, and it also provides a convenient language for similar but slightly more complex statements. In the above example, our *modulus* is the number 2. The modulus can be thought of as the number of classes that we have broken the integers up into. It is also the difference between any two 'consecutive' numbers in a given class.

Now we represent each of our two classes by a single symbol. We assume number '0' means 'the class of all even numbers' and number '1' means 'the class of all odd numbers'. There is no great reason why we have chosen 0 and 1; we could have chosen 2 and 1, or any other numbers, but 0 and 1 are the conventional choices.

The statement 'the sum of two even numbers is even' can be expressed by the following:

$$0 + 0 \equiv 0 \bmod 2$$

where the symbol '≡' is not equality but *congruence*, and the 'mod 2' just signifies that modulus is 2. The above statement is read as 'Zero plus zero is congruent to zero, modulo two'. The statement 'the sum of an even number and an odd number is odd' is represented by

$$0 + 1 \equiv 1 \bmod 2$$

Similarly 'the sum of two odd numbers is even' is written as:

$$1 + 1 \equiv 0 \bmod 2$$

where the symbol '≡' and 'mod 2' are very important. We have analogous statements for multiplication:

$$0 \times 0 \equiv 0 \bmod 2$$

$$0 \times 1 \equiv 0 \bmod 2$$

$$1 \times 1 \equiv 1 \bmod 2$$

In a sense, we have created a number system with addition and multiplication but in which the only numbers that exist are 0 and 1. This number system is the system of *integers modulo* 2, and as a result of the afore-mentioned six properties, *any arithmetic done in the integers translates to arithmetic done in the integers modulo 2.* This means that if we take any equality involving addition and multiplication of integers, say

$$16 \times 41 + 53 \times 88 = 5320$$

and reducing each integer *modulo* 2 (i.e., replacing each integer by its class 'representative' 0 or 1), we will obtain a valid congruence. The above equation reduces to

$$0 \times 1 + 1 \times 0 \equiv 0 \bmod 2$$

or

$$0 + 0 \equiv 0 \bmod 2$$

More useful applications of reduction modulo 2 are found in solving equations. Suppose we want to know which integers might solve the equation

$$5a - 5 = 25$$

Of course, we can solve for a only if we take into account whether a is even or odd, irrespective of other factors, by proceeding with the following. Reducing modulo 2 gives the congruence

$$1a + 1 \equiv 1 \bmod 2$$

or

$$a \equiv 0 \bmod 2$$

so any integer a satisfying the equation $5a - 5 = 25$ must be even.

Since any integer solution of an equation reduces to a solution modulo 2, it follows that *if there is no solution modulo 2 then there is no solution in integers*. For example, assume that a is an integer solution to

$$2a - 1 = 14$$

which reduces to

$$0 \cdot a + 1 \equiv 0 \bmod 2$$

or $1 \equiv 0 \bmod 2$. This is a contradiction because 0 and 1 are different numbers modulo 2 (no even number is an odd number, and vice versa). Therefore, the above congruence has no solution; hence, a is not an integer. This proves that the equation $2a - 1 = 14$ has no integer solution.

Less trivially, consider the system of equations

$$6a - 5b = 4$$

$$2a + 3b = 3$$

Modulo 2: These equations reduce to

$$0 + 1b \equiv 0 \bmod 2$$
$$0 + 1b \equiv 1 \bmod 2$$

This says that b is both even and odd, which is a contradiction. Therefore, we know that the original system of equations has no integer solutions, and to prove this we didn't even need to know anything about a.

As shown by the preceding examples, one of the powers of modular arithmetic is the ability to show, often very simply, that certain equations and systems of equations have no integer solutions. Without modular arithmetic, we would have to find all of the solutions and then see if any turned out to be integers.

In Modulo 2, all of the even numbers are congruent to each other since the difference of any two even numbers is divisible by 2:

$$\ldots \equiv -8 \equiv -6 \equiv -4 \equiv -2 \equiv 0 \equiv 2 \equiv 4 \equiv 6 \equiv 8 \equiv \ldots \bmod 2$$

Also, every odd number is congruent to every other odd number modulo 2 since the difference of any two odd numbers is even:

$$\ldots \equiv -7 \equiv -5 \equiv -3 \equiv -1 \equiv 1 \equiv 3 \equiv 5 \equiv 7 \equiv \ldots \bmod 2$$

Therefore, we can replace '0' by any even number, and similarly '1' by any odd number. For example, instead of writing $0 \times 1 + 1 \times 0 \equiv 0 \bmod 2$, an equally valid statement is

$$10 \times 15 + 29 \times (-8) \equiv -168 \bmod 2$$

Let's now look at other values for the modulus m. For example, let $m = 3$. All multiples of 3 are congruent to each other modulo 3 since the difference of any two is divisible by 3. Similarly, all numbers of the form $3n + 1$ are congruent to each other, and all numbers of the form $3n + 2$ are congruent to each other.

$$\ldots \equiv -9 \equiv -6 \equiv -3 \equiv 0 \equiv 3 \equiv 6 \equiv 9 \equiv \ldots \bmod 3$$
$$\ldots \equiv -8 \equiv -5 \equiv -2 \equiv 1 \equiv 4 \equiv 7 \equiv \ldots \bmod 3$$
$$\ldots \equiv -7 \equiv -4 \equiv -1 \equiv 2 \equiv 5 \equiv 8 \ldots \bmod 3$$

However, when $m = 1$, the difference of *any* two integers is divisible by 1; hence, all integers are congruent to each other modulo 1:

$$\ldots \equiv -3 \equiv -2 \equiv -1 \equiv 0 \equiv 1 \equiv 2 \equiv 3 \ldots \bmod 1$$

For this reason, $m = 1$ is not very interesting, and reducing an equation modulo 1 doesn't give any information about its solutions.

The modulus $m = 12$ comes up quite frequently in everyday life, and its application illustrates a good way to think about modular arithmetic—the 'clock arithmetic' analogy. If it is 5:00, what time will it be in 13 hours? Since $13 \equiv 1 \bmod 12$, we simply add 1 to 5:

$$5 + 13 \equiv 5 + 1 \equiv 6 \bmod 12$$

So the clock will read 6:00. Of course, we don't need the formality of modular arithmetic in order to compute this, but when we do this kind of computation in our heads, this is really what we are doing.

With $m = 12$, there are only 12 numbers ('hours') we ever need to think about. We count them 1, 2, 3, …, 10, 11, 12, 1, 2, …, starting over after 12. The numbers 1, 2, …, 12 represent the twelve equivalence classes modulo 12: Every integer is congruent to exactly one of the numbers 1, 2, …, 12, just as the hour on the clock always reads exactly one of 1, 2, …, 12. These classes are given by

$$12n + 1,\ 12n + 2,\ 12n + 3,\ \ldots,\ 12n + 11,\ 12n$$

as n ranges over the integers.

Of course, the minutes and seconds on a clock are also modular. In these cases the modulus is $m = 60$. If we think of the days of the week as labelled by the numbers 0, 1, 2, 3, 4, 5, 6, then the modulus is $m = 7$. The point is that we measure many things, both in mathematics and in real life, in periodicity, and this can usually be thought of as an application of modular arithmetic.

4.5.2 Sets

Normally we define a set as a '*collection of objects*'. But mathematically we want to define a set such that objects either belong to the set or do not belong to the set. There is no other state possible. Thus, a set with n objects is written as $\{s_1, s_2, s_3, \ldots, s_n\}$. The objects $s_1, s_2, s_3, \ldots, s_n$ are the elements of the set. This set is a *finite set* as there is finite number of elements in the set. If a set is formed taking any m elements from the set of n elements, where $m \le n$, then the new set formed is known as a subset of the original set of n elements. Example of a finite set is set of octal digits $\{0, 1, 2, 3, 4, 5, 6, 7\}$. Similarly, a set of infinite number of elements is referred to as an *infinite set*. Example of such an infinite set is a set of all integers $\{0, \pm 1, \pm 2, \pm 3, \ldots\}$.

We hope the readers are familiar with the idea of different mathematical operations between sets, namely intersection and union of sets that give the set of common elements and set of all elements, respectively. However, here we are more interested in operations between elements within a set, rather than operations between sets. So now we introduce 'higher' mathematical structures known as *group*.

4.5.3 Groups

Let us consider a set of elements G. We define a *binary operation* $*$ on G such that it is a *rule* that assigns to each pair of elements a and b a uniquely defined third element $c = a * b$ in G. If such a binary operation is defined on G, we say that G is closed under $*$.

Let us consider an example, where G is the set of all integers and the binary operation on G is real multiplication $\times$. For any two integers i and j in G, $i \times j$ is a uniquely defined integer in G. Thus, the set of integers is closed under real multiplication. The binary operation $*$ on G is said to be *associative* if, for any a, b and c in G,

$$a * (b * c) = (a * b) * c \tag{4.13}$$

We now introduce a very useful algebraic system called a *group*.

Definition 4.1: A set G on which a binary operation $*$ is defined is called a *group* if the following conditions are satisfied:

1. The binary operation $*$ is associative.
2. G contains an element e, called an *identity element* on G, such that, for any a in G,

$$a * e = e * a = a \tag{4.14}$$

3. For any element a in G, there exists another element a', called an inverse of a in G, such that

$$a * a' = a' * a = e \tag{4.15}$$

A group G is said to be *commutative* if its binary operation $*$ satisfies the following condition: For any a and b in G,

$$a * b = b * a \tag{4.16}$$

We now state two important conditions of groups which are to be satisfied:

1. The inverse of a group element is unique.
2. The identity element in a group G is unique.

Under real addition the set of all integers is a commutative group. In this case, the integer 0 is the identity element and the integer $-i$ is the inverse of integer i. The set of all rational numbers excluding zero is a commutative group under real multiplication. The integer 1 is the identity element with respect to real multiplication, and the rational number b/a is the multiplicative inverse of a/b. The group discussed above contains infinite number of elements. But groups with finite numbers of elements do exist, as we shall see in the next example.

Example 4.1: Show that the set of two integers $G = \{0,1\}$ is a group under the binary operation $\oplus$ on G as follows:

$$0 \oplus 0 = 0, \quad 0 \oplus 1 = 1, \quad 1 \oplus 0 = 1, \quad 1 \oplus 1 = 0$$

Solution: The binary operation $\oplus$ shown in the problem is called *modulo-2* addition. It follows from the definition of modulo-2 addition $\oplus$ that G is closed under $\oplus$ and $\oplus$ is commutative. We can easily check that $\oplus$ is also associative. The element 0 is the identity element. The inverse of 0 is itself and the inverse of 1 is also itself. Thus, the set $G = \{0,1\}$ together with $\oplus$ is a commutative group.

Order of Group: The number of elements in a group is known as the *order* of the group. A group having finite number of elements is called a *finite group*. For any positive integer m, it is possible to construct a group of order m under a binary operation, which is very similar to real addition. We show it in the following example.

Example 4.2: Show that the set of integers $G = \{0,1,2,\ldots, m-1\}$ forms a group under *modulo-m* addition. Here m is a positive integer.

Solution: Let us define *modulo-m* addition by the binary operator [+] on G as follows: For any integers a and b in G,

$$a\,[+]\,b = r$$

where r is the *remainder* resulting from dividing $(a + b)$ by m. By Euclid's division algorithm, the remainder r is an integer between 0 and $(m - 1)$ and is hence in G. Thus, G is closed under the binary operation [+], which is called *modulo-m* addition.

Now we prove that the set $G = \{0,1,2,\ldots,m-1\}$is a group under *modulo-m* addition.

First we see that 0 is the identity element. For $0 < a < m$, a and $(m - 1)$ are both in G. Since

$$a + (m - a) = (m - a) + a = m$$

It can be written from the definition of *modulo-m* addition that

$$a\,[+](m - a) = (m - a)\,[+]\,a = 0$$

Thus, a and $(m - a)$ are inverses to each other with respect to [+]. The inverse of 0 is itself. Since, real addition is commutative, it follows from the definition of *modulo-m* addition that, for any a and b in G, $a\,[+]\,b = b\,[+]\,a$. Hence, *modulo-m* addition is commutative.

Now we show that *modulo-m* addition is associative. We have

$$a + b + c = (a + b) + c = a + (b + c)$$

Dividing $(a + b + c)$ by m, we obtain

$$a + b + c = qm + r \tag{4.17}$$

where q and r are the quotient and the remainder, respectively, and $0 \le r \le m$. Now dividing $(a + b)$ by m, we have

$$a + b = q_1 m + r_1 \tag{4.18}$$

with $0 \le r_1 \le m$. Thus, $a [+]b = r_1$. Dividing $(r_1 + c)$ by m, we have

$$r_1 + c = q_2 m + r_2 \tag{4.19}$$

with $0 \le r_2 \le m$. Thus, $r_1 [+] c = r_2$ and

$$(a[+]b) [+]c = r_2 \tag{4.20}$$

Combining Eqs. (4.18) and (4.19), we have

$$a + b + c = (q_1 + q_2)m + r_2 \tag{4.21}$$

This implies that r_2 is also the remainder when $(a + b + c)$ is divided by m. Since the remainder resulting from dividing an integer by an integer is unique, we must have $r_2 = r$. As a result, we have

$$(a[+]b) [+]c = r \tag{4.22}$$

Similarly, it can be shown that,

$$a[+] (b[+]c) = r \tag{4.23}$$

Therefore, $(a[+]b) [+]c = a[+] (b[+]c)$ and *modulo-m* addition is associative.

Thus, we prove that the set $G = \{0,1,2,\ldots,m - 1\}$ is a group under *modulo-m* addition. We shall call this group an *additive* group. For $m = 2$, we obtain the binary group given in Example 4.1. The additive group under modulo-7 addition is given in Table 4.1.

Table 4.1 *Modulo-7 Addition*

[+]	0	1	2	3	4	5	6
0	0	1	2	3	4	5	6
1	1	2	3	4	5	6	0
2	2	3	4	5	6	0	1
3	3	4	5	6	0	1	2
4	4	5	6	0	1	2	3
5	5	6	0	1	2	3	4
6	6	0	1	2	3	4	5

Finite groups with a binary operation similar to real multiplication can also be constructed.

Example 4.3: Let p be a prime (e.g., $p = 2, 3, 5, 7, 11, 13, 17, \ldots$). Show that the set of integers $G = \{1,2,3,4,\ldots, p - 1\}$ forms a group under *modulo-p* multiplication.

Solution: Let us define *modulo-p* multiplication by the binary operator $[\cdot]$ on G as follows: For any integers a and b in G,

$$a [\cdot] b = r$$

where r is the *remainder* resulting from dividing $(a \cdot b)$ by p. We note that $(a \cdot b)$ is not divisible by p. Hence, $0 < r < p$ and r is an element in G. Thus, G is closed under the binary operation $[\cdot]$, which is called *modulo-p* multiplication. Now we will show that the set $G = \{1,2,3,\ldots, p - 1\}$ is a group under *modulo-p* multiplication.

It can be easily checked that modulo-p multiplication is commutative and associative. The identity element is 1. The only thing to be proved is that every element in G has an inverse. Let a be an element in G. Since $a < p$ and p is a prime, a and p must be relatively prime. By Euclid's theorem, it is well known that there exist two integers i and j such that

$$i \cdot a + j \cdot p = 1 \tag{4.24}$$

where i and p are relatively prime. Rearranging Eq. (4.24), we have

$$i \cdot a = -j \cdot p + 1 \tag{4.25}$$

From Eq. (4.25), we can say that if $(i \cdot a)$ is divided by p, the remainder is 1. If $0 < i < p$, then i is in G and it follows from Eq. (4.25) and the definition of modulo-p multiplication that

$$i\,[\cdot]\,a = a\,[\cdot]\,i = 1$$

Hence, i is the inverse of a. On the contrary, if i is not contained in G, we divide i by p, and get

$$i = q \cdot p + r \tag{4.26}$$

Since, i and p are relatively prime, the remainder r cannot be 0 and it must be between 1 and $(p - 1)$. Hence, r is in G. Now, from Eqs. (4.25) and (4.26), we have

$$r \cdot a = -(j + qa)\,p + 1 \tag{4.27}$$

Therefore, $r\,[\cdot]\,a = a[\cdot]\,r = 1$ and r is the inverse of a. Thus, any element a in G has an inverse with respect to modulo-p multiplication. The group $G = \{1, 2, 3, \ldots, p - 1\}$ under modulo-p multiplication is called a *multiplicative* group. For $p = 2$, we obtain a group $G = \{1\}$ with only one element under modulo-2 multiplication.

Note: If p is not a prime, the set $G = \{1, 2, 3, \ldots, p - 1\}$ is not a group under modulo-p multiplication.

The multiplicative group under modulo-7 multiplication is given in Table 4.4.

Table 4.2 *Modulo-7 Multiplication*

[·]	1	2	3	4	5	6
1	1	2	3	4	5	6
2	2	4	6	1	3	5
3	3	6	2	5	1	4
4	4	1	5	2	6	3
5	5	3	1	6	4	2
6	6	5	4	3	2	1

4.5.4 Fields

We now introduce another very important algebraic system called a *field*. We will use the concepts of group to describe the field. In a rough sense, field is a set of elements in which we can perform addition, subtraction, multiplication and division without leaving the set. Addition and multiplication must satisfy the commutative, associative, and distributive laws. Now we formally define a *field* as follows:

Definition 4.2: Let F be a set of elements in which two binary operations, addition '+' and multiplication '·', are defined. The set F along with the two binary operations (+) and (·) is a field if the following conditions are satisfied:

1. The set of nonzero elements in F is a commutative group under multiplication. The identity element with respect to multiplication is called the *unit* element or the multiplicative identity of F and is denoted by 1.
2. F is a commutative group under addition. The identity element with respect to addition is called the *zero* element or the additive identity of F and is denoted by 0.
3. Multiplication is *distributive* over addition; i.e., for any three elements i, j and k in F,

$$i \cdot (j + k) = i \cdot j + i \cdot k$$

From the definition of field it can be said that a field consists of at least two elements, the multiplicative identity and the additive identity.

Order of Field: The number of elements in a field is known as the *order* of the field. A field having finite number of elements is called a *finite field*.

In a field, the additive inverse of an element i is denoted by $-i$, and the multiplicative inverse of i is denoted by i^{-1}, provided $i \neq 0$. Thus, subtracting a field element j from another field element i is defined as adding the additive inverse $-j$ of j to i. Similarly, if j is a nonzero element, dividing i by j is defined as multiplying i by the multiplicative inverse j^{-1} of j. Some basic properties of fields are now derived from the definition of a field.

Property 1: For every element i in a field, $i \cdot 0 = 0 \cdot i = 0$.

Proof: We have

$$i = 1 \cdot i = (1 + 0) \cdot i = i + 0 \cdot i$$

or

$$-i + i = -i + i + 0 \cdot i$$

or

$$0 = 0 + 0 \cdot i$$

or

$$0 = 0 \cdot i$$

Similarly, we can prove that $i \cdot 0 = 0$. Hence, we obtain $i \cdot 0 = 0 \cdot i = 0$.

Property 2: For any two nonzero elements i and j in a field, $i \cdot j \neq 0$.

Proof: Since nonzero elements of a field are closed under multiplication, the property is proved.

Property 3: For any two elements i and j in a field, $i \cdot j = 0$ and $i \neq 0$ imply that $j = 0$.

Proof: This is a direct consequence of Property 2.

Property 4: For any two elements i and j in a field, $-(i \cdot j) = (-i) \cdot j = i \cdot (-j)$

Proof: We have

$$0 = 0 \cdot j = [\, i + (-i)] \cdot j = i \cdot j + (-i) \cdot j$$

Hence, $(-i) \cdot j$ should be the additive inverse of $i \cdot j$ and $-(i \cdot j) = (-i) \cdot j$.

Similarly, we can prove that $-(i \cdot j) = i \cdot (-j)$.

Property 5: For $i \neq 0$, $i \cdot j = i \cdot k$ implies that $j = k$.

Proof: Since i is a nonzero element in the field, it should have a multiplicative inverse i^{-1}.

Now

$$i \cdot j = i \cdot k$$

or

$$i^{-1} \cdot (i \cdot j) = i^{-1} \cdot (i \cdot k)$$

or

$$(i^{-1} \cdot i) \cdot j = (i^{-1} \cdot i) \cdot k$$

or

$$1 \cdot j = 1 \cdot k$$

or

$$j = k$$

The set of real numbers is a field under real addition and multiplication. This field has infinite number of elements. If the number of elements is finite then the field is called *finite field*.

Example 4.4: Construct a finite field having only two elements $\{0,1\}$.

Solution: Let us consider the set $\{0,1\}$ with modulo-2 addition and multiplication shown in Tables 4.3 and 4.4.

Table 4.3 *Modulo-2 Addition*

+	0	1
0	0	1
1	1	0

Table 4.4 *Modulo-2 Multiplication*

+	0	1
0	0	0
1	0	1

We have already shown that {0,1} is a commutative group under modulo-2 addition in Example 4.1. Also in Example 4.3 we have shown that {1} is a group under modulo-2 multiplication. We can easily check that modulo-2 multiplication is distributive over modulo-2 addition by simply computing $i \cdot (j + k)$ and $i \cdot j + i \cdot k$ for eight possible combinations of i, j and k ($i = 1$ or 0, $j = 1$ or 0 and $k = 1$ or 0). Thus, the set {0,1} is a field of two elements under modulo-2 addition and modulo-2 multiplication.

The field discussed in Example 4.4 is called *binary field* and is denoted by GF(2). This field plays a very important role in coding theory.

Let us consider that p is a prime number. The set of integers $\{0, 1, 2, \ldots, p - 1\}$ forms a commutative group under modulo-p addition (as shown in Example 4.2). We have also shown in Example 4.3 that the nonzero elements $\{1, 2, \ldots, p - 1\}$ forms a commutative group under modulo-p multiplication. We can show that modulo-p multiplication is distributive over modulo-p addition. Hence, the set $\{0, 1, 2, \ldots, p - 1\}$ is a field under modulo-p addition and multiplication. Since the field is constructed from prime p, this field is known as a *prime field* and is denoted as GF(p).

The set of integers {0, 1, 2, 3, 4} is a field of five elements. It is denoted by GF(5), under modulo-5 addition and multiplication. Addition table can also be used for subtraction. Say for example, if we want to subtract 4 from 2, first we should find out the additive inverse of 4 from Table 4.5, which is 1. Then add 1 to 2 to obtain the result 3 [i.e., $2 - 4 = 2 + (-4) = 2 + 1 = 3$]. Similarly in order to perform division, we can use the multiplication table. Suppose that we divide 4 by 3. The multiplicative inverse of 3 is first calculated, which is 2. Then we multiply 4 by 2 to obtain the result 3 [i.e., $4 \div 3 = 4 \times (3^{-1}) = 4 \times 2 = 3$]. Thus, we see that, in a finite field, addition, subtraction, multiplication and division can be carried out in a similar fashion to ordinary arithmetic. Modulo-5 addition and multiplication are shown in Tables 4.5 and 4.6, respectively.

Table 4.5 *Modulo-5 Addition*

[+]	0	1	2	3	4
0	0	1	2	3	4
1	1	2	3	4	0
2	2	3	4	0	1
3	3	4	0	1	2
4	4	0	1	2	3

Table 4.6 *Modulo-5 Multiplication*

[•]	0	1	2	3	4
0	0	0	0	0	0
1	0	1	2	3	4
2	0	2	4	1	3
3	0	3	1	4	2
4	0	4	3	2	1

Thus, we can conclude that, for any prime p, there exists a finite field of p elements. Actually for any positive integer n, it is possible to extend the prime field GF(p) to a field of p^n elements. This is called an *extension field* of GF(p) and is denoted as GF(p^n). It can be proved that the order of any finite field is a power of a prime. Finite fields are also known as *Galois fields* (pronounced as *Galva*). Finite field arithmetic is very similar to ordinary arithmetic and hence most of the rules of ordinary arithmetic apply to finite field arithmetic.

Characteristic of Field: Let us consider a finite field of q elements, GF(q). We form the following sequence of sums of the unit element 1 in GF (q):

$$\sum_{i=1}^{1} 1 = 1, \sum_{i=1}^{2} 1 = 1+1, \sum_{i=1}^{3} 1 = 1+1+1, \cdots, \sum_{i=1}^{4} 1 = 1+1+\cdots+1\,(k \text{ times}), \ldots$$

As the field is closed under addition, these sums should all be the elements of the field. Again since the field is finite, all these sums cannot be distinct. Thus, the sequence of sums should repeat itself at some point of time. Hence, we can say that there exist two positive integers m and n such that $m > n$ and

$$\sum_{i=1}^{m} 1 = \sum_{i=1}^{n} 1$$

This shows that $\sum_{i=1}^{m-n} 1 = 0$. Thus, there must exist a *smallest positive integer* λ such that $\sum_{i=1}^{\lambda} 1 = 0$. This integer λ is called the *characteristic* of the field GF(q). For example, the characteristic of the binary field GF(2) is 2, since $1 + 1 = 0$.

Now we state three relevant theorems. The proofs of these theorems are out of the scope of the current text.

Theorem 4.1: Let b be a nonzero element of a finite field GF(q). Then $b^{q-1} = 1$.

Theorem 4.2: Let b be a nonzero element of a finite field GF(q). Let n be the order of b. Then n divides $(q - 1)$.

Theorem 4.3: The characteristic λ of a finite field is prime.

Primitive Element: In a finite field GF(q), a nonzero element b is called *primitive* if the order of b is $(q - 1)$. Thus, the powers of a primitive element generate all the nonzero elements of GF(q). In fact, every finite field has a primitive element.

Let us consider the prime field GF(5) illustrated in Tables 4.5 and 4.6. The characteristic of this field is 5. If we take the powers of the integer 3 in GF(5) using the multiplication table, we obtain $3^1 = 3$, $3^2 = 3 \times 3 = 4$, $3^3 = 3 \times 3^2 = 2$, $3^4 = 3 \times 3^3 = 1$.

Hence, the order of the integer 3 is 4 and the integer 3 is a *primitive element* of GF(5).

Extension Field: A field K is said to be an extension field, denoted by K/F, of a field F if F is a subfield of K. For example, the complex numbers are an extension field of the real numbers, and the real numbers are an extension field of the rational numbers.

The extension field degree (or relative degree, or index) of an extension field K/F, denoted by $[K : F]$, is the dimension of K as a vector space over F, i.e., $[K : F] = \dim_F K$.

Splitting Field: The extension field K of a field F is called a splitting field for the polynomial $f(x) \in F[x]$ if $f(x)$ factors completely into linear factors in $K[x]$ and $f(x)$ does not factor completely into linear factors over any proper subfield of K containing F. For example, the field extension $Q(\sqrt{3}\,i)$ is the splitting field for $x^2 + 3$ since it is the smallest field containing its roots, $\sqrt{3}\,i$ and $-\sqrt{3}\,i$. Note that it is also the splitting field for $x^3 + 1$.

Example 4.5: Evaluate $((2 - 4) \times 4)/3$ over the prime field modulo-m when (a) $m = 7$ and (b) $m = 5$.

Solution:

(a) In the prime field modulo-7 the additive inverse of 4 is 3 and the multiplicative inverse of 3 is 5. Thus,

$$((2-4)\times 4)/3 = ((2+3)\times 4)\times 5 \text{ modulo-7} =$$
$$= 5\times 4\times 5 \text{ modulo} - 7 = 2 \text{ modulo} - 7 = 2$$

(b) On the other hand, in prime field modulo-5 the additive inverse of 4 is 1 and the multiplicative inverse of 3 is 2. Thus,

$$((2-4)\times 4)/3 = ((2+1)\times 4)\ 2 \text{ modulo-5}$$
$$= 3\times 4\times 2 \text{ modulo} - 5 = 4 \text{ modulo} - 5 = 4$$

4.5.5 Arithmetic of Binary Field

Though codes with symbols from any Galois field GF(q), where q is either a prime p or a power of p, can be constructed, we are mainly concerned with binary codes with symbols from the binary field GF(2) or its extension GF(2^n). So we will discuss arithmetic over the binary field GF(2) in detail.

In binary arithmetic, we use modulo-2 addition and multiplication, which we have already illustrated in Tables 4.3 and 4.4, respectively. The only difference of modulo-2 arithmetic with ordinary arithmetic lies in the fact that in modulo-2 arithmetic we consider $1 + 1 = 2 = 0$. Hence, we can write

$$1 = -1 \tag{4.28}$$

Thus, in binary arithmetic, subtraction is equivalent to addition.

We now consider a polynomial $f(x)$ with one variable x and with coefficients from GF(2). 'A polynomial with coefficients from GF(2)' is also called as 'a polynomial over GF(2)'. Let us consider:

$$f(x) = f_0 + f_1x + f_2x^2 + \ldots + f_mx^m \tag{4.29}$$

where $f_i = 0$ or 1, for $0 \le i \le m$. The *degree* of a polynomial is the largest power of x with a nonzero coefficient. For example in the above polynomial if $f_m = 1$, then the degree $f(x)$ is m. On the other hand, if $f_m = 0$, then the degree $f(x)$ is less than m.

Here there is only one polynomial of degree zero, namely

$$f(x) = 1$$

Again there are two polynomials of degree 1:

$$f(x) = 1 + x \quad \text{and} \quad f(x) = x$$

Similarly, we see that there are four polynomials over GF(2) with degree 2:

$$f(x) = 1 + x + x^2, \quad f(x) = x + x^2, \quad f(x) = 1 + x^2 \quad \text{and} \quad f(x) = x^2.$$

Thus, in general, there are 2^m polynomials over GF(2) with degree m.

Polynomials over GF(2) can be added or subtracted, multiplied and divided in the usual way. We can also verify that the polynomials over GF(2) satisfy the following conditions:

1. *Associative*:

$$a(x) + [b(x) + c(x)] = [a(x) + b(x)] + c(x)$$
$$a(x)\cdot[b(x)\cdot c(x)] = [a(x)\cdot b(x)]\cdot c(x)$$

2. *Commutative*:

$$a(x) + b(x) = b(x) + a(x)$$
$$a(x)\cdot b(x) = b(x)\cdot a(x)$$

3. *Distributive*:

$$a(x)\cdot[b(x) + c(x)] = [a(x)\cdot b(x)] + [a(x)\cdot c(x)] \tag{4.30}$$

where $a(x)$, $b(x)$, and $c(x)$ are three polynomials over GF(2). Now if $s(x)$ is another nonzero polynomial over GF(2), then while dividing $f(x)$ by $s(x)$ we obtain a unique pair of polynomials over GF(2) − $q(x)$, called the quotient, and $r(x)$, called the remainder. Thus, we can write:

$$f(x) = s(x)q(x) + r(x) \tag{4.31}$$

By Euclid's division algorithm, the degree of $r(x)$ is less than that of $s(x)$. If the remainder $r(x)$ is idential to zero, we say that $f(x)$ is divisible by $s(x)$ and $s(x)$ is a factor of $f(x)$.

For real numbers, if a is a *root* of a polynomial $f(x)$ [i.e., $f(a) = 0$], we say that $f(x)$ is divisible by $x - a$. This fact follows from Euclid's division algorithm. This is still true for $f(x)$ over GF(2). For example, let $f(x) = 1 + x + x^3 + x^5$. Substituting $x = 1$, we obtain

$$f(1) = 1 + 1 + 1^3 + 1^5 = 1 + 1 + 1 + 1 = 0$$

Thus, $f(x)$ has 1 as a root and it can be verified that $f(x)$ is divisible by $(x + 1)$.

For a polynomial $f(x)$ over GF(2), if it has an even number of terms, it is divisible by $(x + 1)$. A polynomial $p(x)$ over GF(2) of degree n is *irreducible* over GF(2) if $p(x)$ is not divisible by any polynomial over GF(2) of degree less than n but greater than zero. For example, among the four polynomials of degree 2 over GF(2), three polynomials x^2, $x^2 + 1$ and $x^2 + x$ are not irreducible since they are either divisible by x or $x + 1$. But $x^2 + x + 1$ does not have either '0' or '1' as a root and hence is not divisible by any polynomial of degree 1. Thus, $x^2 + x + 1$ is an irreducible polynomial of degree 2. Similarly it can be verified that $x^3 + x + 1$, $x^4 + x + 1$, and $x^5 + x + 1$ are irreducible polynomials of degree 3, 4, and 5, respectively. It is true that for any $n \geq 1$, there exists an irreducible polynomial of degree n. We state here a condition regarding irreducible polynomials over GF(2).

Any irreducible polynomial over GF(2) of degree n divides $x^{2^n - 1} + 1$.

Eisenstein's Irreducibility Criterion: Eisenstein's irreducibility criterion is a *sufficient* condition assuring that an integer polynomial $p(x)$ is irreducible in the polynomial ring $Q(x)$. The polynomial $p(x) = a_n x^n + a_{n-1} x^{n-1} + \ldots + a_1 x + a_0$, where $a_i \in Z$ for all $i = 0, 1, \ldots, n$ and $a_n \neq 0$ [which means that the degree of $p(x)$ is n], is irreducible if some prime number p divides all coefficients $a_0, \ldots, a_{n-1}$, but not the leading coefficient a_n, and, moreover, p^2 does not divide the constant term a_0.

This is only a sufficient, and by no means a necessary, condition. For example, the polynomial $x^2 + 1$ is irreducible, but does not fulfil the above property, since no prime number divides 1. However, substituting $x + 1$ for x produces the polynomial $x^2 + 2x + 2$, which does fulfil the Eisenstein criterion (with $p = 2$) and shows the polynomial is irreducible.

Primitive Polynomial: An irreducible polynomial $p(x)$ of degree n is called *primitive polynomial* if the smallest positive integer m for which $p(x)$ divides $x^m + 1$ is $m = 2^n - 1$.

We can check that $p(x) = x^3 + x + 1$ divides $x^7 + 1$ but does not divide any $x^m + 1$ for $1 \leq m \leq 7$. Hence, $x^3 + x + 1$ is a primitive polynomial. It is not easy to recognize a primitive polynomial. For a given n, there can be more than one primitive polynomial of degree n. We list some primitive polynomials in Table 4.7. Here we list only one primitive polynomial with the smallest number of terms of each degree n. We now derive an useful property of polynomials over GF(2).

$$\begin{aligned}
f^2(x) &= (f_0 + f_1 x + f_2 x^2 + \ldots + f_m x^m)^2 \\
&= [f_0 + (f_1 x + f_2 x^2 + \ldots + f_m x^m)]^2 \\
&= f_0^2 + f_0 \cdot (f_1 x + f_2 x^2 + \cdots + f_m x^m) + f_0 \cdot (f_1 x + f_2 x^2 + \cdots + f_m x^m) + (f_1 x + f_2 x^2 + \cdots + f_m x^m)^2 \\
&= f_0^2 + (f_1 x + f_2 x^2 + \cdots + f_m x^m)^2
\end{aligned}$$

Table 4.7 *Primitive Polynomials*

n	Polynomial
3	$x^3 + x + 1$
4	$x^4 + x + 1$
5	$x^5 + x^2 + 1$
6	$x^6 + x + 1$
7	$x^7 + x^3 + 1$
8	$x^8 + x^4 + x^3 + x^2 + 1$
9	$x^9 + x^4 + 1$
10	$x^{10} + x^3 + 1$
11	$x^{11} + x^2 + 1$
12	$x^{12} + x^6 + x^4 + x + 1$

Similarly expanding the equation above repeatedly, we eventually obtain

$$f^2(x) = f_0^2 + (f_1x)^2 + (f_2x^2)^2 + \ldots + (f_mx^m)^2$$

As $f_i = 0$ or $1, f_i^2 = f_i$. Thus, we have

$$\begin{aligned} f^2(x) &= f_0 + f_1x^2 + f_2(x^2)^2 + \ldots + f_m(x^2)^m \\ &= f(x^2) \end{aligned} \quad (4.32)$$

It follows from (4.32) that, for any $l \geq 0$,

$$[f(x)]^{2^l} = f(x^{2^l}) \quad (4.33)$$

4.5.6 Roots of Equations

In this section we shall discuss finite fields constructed from roots of equations. We will see that this is the basis of cyclic codes where all code word polynomials $c(x)$ have the generator polynomial $g(x)$ as a factor. We consider an algebraic equation of the form

$$a_mx^m + a_{m-1}x^{m-1} + \ldots + a_2x^2 + a_1x + a_0 = 0 \quad (4.34)$$

where $a_0 \neq 0$. We now consider that the coefficients of Eq. (4.34) are binary. The simplest algebraic equation is the equation of first degree which may be obtained by setting $m = 1$, and is written as follows:

$$a_1x + a_0 = 0$$

There exists one root $x = -a_0/a_1$. The second degree (quadratic) equation is expressed as

$$a_2x^2 + a_1x + a_0 = 0$$

This equation has two roots and is given by the well-known formula for solving quadratic equations

$$x = \frac{-a_1 \pm \sqrt{a_1^2 - 4a_2a_0}}{2a_2} \quad (4.35)$$

The roots of equations of third and fourth degrees can be similarly obtained algebraically, with three and four roots, respectively. However, it has been established that it is not possible to solve the fifth-degree equation using a finite number of algebraic operations. The same is true for equations of degree greater than five also. This does not necessarily mean that roots for fifth and higher degree equations do not exist, rather it can be stated that expressions for giving the roots do not exist. A fifth-degree equation will have five roots. Likewise an equation of degree m will have m roots. However, in some cases there is a slight problem regarding the nature of the roots. For example, in the quadratic equation $a_2x^2 + a_1x + a_0 = 0$, if we substitute $a_2 = a_0 = 1$ and $a_1 = 0$, we have

$$x^2 + 1 = 0 \quad (4.36)$$

In this equation it is not possible to obtain two real numbers. Hence, the only way to obtain two roots for Eq. (4.36) is by defining a new *imaginary* number j (j here should not be confused with j in Section 4.5, where j was an element of the field), which satisfies

$$j^2 + 1 = 0 \tag{4.37}$$

The number j can be combined with two real numbers p and q to give the complex number $p + jq$. Addition and multiplication over the set of all complex numbers obey the rules described in Sec. 4.5 for a set of elements to form a field. The resulting field is known as the *complex field*. Due to the existence of complex fields, all equations of degree m have m roots. The roots of Eq. (4.34) are of the form $p + jq$ with real roots having $q = 0$.

Complex roots, of an equation with real coefficients, always occur in pairs known as *complex conjugates*. Thus, an equation can never have an odd number of complex roots, since that requires a complex root to exist without its conjugate. For example we can say that in an equation of degree three, either all the roots are real, or one of them is real while the other two are complex conjugates.

Complex field includes all the real numbers as they can be considered as field elements with $q = 0$. Basically the real field is referred to as the *base field* and the complex field as an *extension field*. In Eq. (4.34), the coefficients belong to the base field (i.e., the real field) whereas the roots belong to the extension field (i.e., the complex field). The occurrence of complex roots as conjugate pairs is necessary for the coefficients to lie in the real field.

Now we consider roots of equations of the form $p(x) = 0$, where $p(x)$ is a polynomial with binary coefficients. Let us take an example

$$x^3 + x + 1 = 0 \tag{4.38}$$

Since x can have a value of 0 or 1, we can substitute 0 and 1 directly into Eq. (4.38) to see whether 0 or 1 or both are roots. Substituting $x = 0$ or $x = 1$ into Eq. (4.38) gives 1, and so we have a binary polynomial without any binary roots. This is similar to the previous situation where we considered a real quadratic equation without any real roots. So the complex term j was introduced to tackle the problem. Similarly, here we define a new term such that it becomes a root of the polynomial of interest. Instead of using j to denote a root of Eq. (4.38), it is conventional to use α to represent the newly defined root. Substituting $x = \alpha$ into Eq. (4.38) gives

$$\alpha^3 + \alpha + 1 = 0 \tag{4.39}$$

While Eq. (4.39) defines the new root α, it tells us little else about it. Furthermore there are two more roots of Eq. (4.38) that has to be evaluated. We know that α does not belong to the binary field, and to proceed further we need to define the mathematical structure of the field within which α lies. The root α lies within a finite field known as GF(2^3), which can be generated from Eq. (4.39). Once GF(2^3) is established, the other roots can be found. In the next section we will present a method to construct the Galois field of 2^m elements ($m > 1$) from the binary field GF(2).

4.5.7 Galois Field

To construct GF(2^n), we begin with the two elements of GF(2)—0 and 1—and the newly defined symbol α. Now we define a multiplication '·' to introduce a sequence of powers of α as follows:

$$0 \cdot 0 = 0$$
$$0 \cdot 1 = 1 \cdot 0 = 0$$
$$1 \cdot 1 = 1$$
$$0 \cdot \alpha = \alpha \cdot 0 = 0$$

$$
\begin{aligned}
1 \cdot \alpha &= \alpha \cdot 1 = \alpha \\
\alpha^2 &= \alpha \cdot \alpha \\
\alpha^3 &= \alpha \cdot \alpha \cdot \alpha \\
&\vdots \\
\alpha^i &= 0 \cdot \alpha \ldots\ldots \alpha \quad (i \text{ times}) \\
&\vdots
\end{aligned} \tag{4.40}
$$

From the definition of above multiplication, we can say that

$$
\begin{aligned}
0 \cdot \alpha^i &= \alpha^i \cdot 0 = 0 \\
1 \cdot \alpha^i &= \alpha^i \cdot 1 = \alpha^i \\
\alpha^i \cdot \alpha^j &= \alpha^j \cdot \alpha^i = \alpha^{i+j}
\end{aligned} \tag{4.41}
$$

Hence, we have the following set of elements on which the multiplication operation '·' is defined:

$$F = \{0, 1, \alpha, \alpha^2, \ldots, \alpha^i, \ldots\}$$

The element 1 can also be defined as α^0.

Now we put a condition on the element α so that the set F contains only 2^n elements and is closed under the multiplication '·' defined by Eq. (4.40). We assume $p(x)$ to be a primitive polynomial of degree n over GF(2). Let $P(\alpha) = 0$. Since $p(x)$ divides $x^{2^n - 1} + 1$, we have

$$x^{2^n - 1} + 1 = q(x)p(x) \tag{4.42}$$

Substituting x by α in Eq. (4.42), we have

$$\alpha^{2^n - 1} + 1 = q(\alpha)p(\alpha)$$

Since $P(\alpha) = 0$, we get

$$\alpha^{2^n - 1} + 1 = q(a) \cdot 0 = 0 \tag{4.43}$$

Adding 1 to both sides of Eq. (4.43) and using modulo-2 addition results in

$$\alpha^{2^n - 1} = 1 \tag{4.44}$$

Therefore, under the condition that $P(\alpha) = 0$, the set F becomes finite and contains the following elements:

$$F' = \{0, 1, \alpha, \alpha^2, \ldots, \alpha^{2^n - 2}\} \tag{4.45}$$

The nonzero elements of F' are closed under the multiplication operation '·' defined by Eq. (4.40). It is shown that the nonzero elements form a commutative group under '·'. Again the element 1 is the unit element. Moreover from Eqs. (4.40) and (4.41), it is readily obtained that the multiplication operation is both commutative and associative. For any integer j, where $0 < j < 2^n - 1$, $\alpha^{2^n - j - 1}$ is the multiplicative inverse of α^j since

$$\alpha^{2^n - j - 1} \cdot \alpha^j = \alpha^{2^n - 1} = 1$$

Thus, it follows that $1, \alpha, \alpha^2, \ldots, \alpha^{2^n - 2}$ represent $2^n - 1$ distinct elements. Hence, the nonzero elements of F' form a group of order $2^n - 1$ under the multiplication operation '·' defined by Eq. (4.40).

Now we define an addition operation '+' on F' so that F' forms a commutative group under '+'. For $0 < j < 2^n - 1$, we divide the polynomial x^j by $p(x)$ and obtain the following:

$$x^j = q_j(x)p(x) + r_j(x) \tag{4.46}$$

where $q_j(x)$ and $r_j(x)$ are the quotient and the remainder, respectively. Remainder $r_j(x)$ is a polynomial of degree $(n - 1)$ or less over GF(2) and has the following form:

$$r_j(x) = r_{j0} + r_{j1}x + r_{j2}x^2 + r_{j3}x^3 + \ldots + r_{j,n-1}x^{n-1}$$

As x and $p(x)$ are relatively prime, x^j is not divisible by $p(x)$. Thus, for any $j \geq 0$,

$$r_j(x) \neq 0 \tag{4.47}$$

For $0 \leq i, j < 2^n - 1$, and $i \neq j$, it is shown that

$$r_i(x) \neq r_j(x) \tag{4.48}$$

Thus, for $j = 0, 1, 2, \ldots, 2^n - 1$, we have $2^n - 1$ distinct nonzero polynomials $r_j(x)$ of degree $(n - 1)$ or less. Now replacing x by α in Eq. (4.46), we obtain the following polynomial for α^j:

$$\alpha^j = r_j(\alpha) = r_{j0} + r_{j1}\alpha + r_{j2}\alpha^2 + r_{j3}\alpha^3 + \ldots + r_{j,\,n-1}\alpha^{n-1} \tag{4.49}$$

Thus, we see that the $2^n - 1$ nonzero elements, $\alpha^0, \alpha^1, \ldots, \alpha^{2^n-2}$ in F', are represented by $2^n - 1$ *distinct nonzero polynomials* of α over GF(2) with degree $(n - 1)$ or less. The zero element 0 in F' can be represented by the zero polynomial. Hence, the 2^n elements in F' are represented by 2^n *distinct polynomials* of α over GF(2) with degree $(n - 1)$ or less and are regarded as 2^n distinct elements.

Similarly, we can define an addition '+' on F', and it can be shown that the set F' is closed under '+'. It can also be verified that F' is a commutative group under '+'. Using the polynomial representation for the elements in F', it is readily seen that the multiplication on F' is distributive over the addition on F'. Hence, the set $F' = \{0, 1, \alpha, \alpha^2, \ldots, \alpha^{2^n-2}\}$ is a Galois field of 2^n elements, GF(2^n). Here, it can be observed that the multiplication and addition defined on F' = GF(2^n) imply modulo-2 multiplication and addition. The binary field GF(2) is usually known as the *ground field* of GF(2^n). The characteristic of GF(2^n) is 4.

Already we have developed two representations for the nonzero elements of GF(2^n)—the power representation and the polynomial representation. Besides, there is another very useful representation for the field elements of GF(2^n). If $r_0 + r_1\alpha + r_2\alpha^2 + r_3\alpha^3 + \ldots + r_{n-1}\alpha^{n-1}$ is a polynomial representation of a field element β, then we can represent β by an ordered sequence of n components, called an *n-tuple*, as shown:

$$(r_0, r_1, r_2, r_3, \ldots, r_{n-1})$$

where the n components are simply the n coefficients of the polynomial representation of β. There is a one-to-one correspondence between this n-tuple and the polynomial representation of β. The zero element 0 of GF(2^n) is represented by the zero n-tuple $(0, 0, 0, \ldots, 0)$.

Example 4.6: Construct the Galois field for GF(2^3) with $n = 3$. The primitive polynomial here is $P(x) = x^3 + x + 1$.

Solution: We set $P(\alpha) = 1 + \alpha + \alpha^3 = 0$. Thus, $\alpha^3 = 1 + \alpha$. Using this we can construct GF(2^3). The elements of GF(2^3) are shown in Table 4.8. The identity $\alpha^3 = 1 + \alpha$ is used repeatedly to form the polynomial representations for the elements of GF(2^3). For example,

$$\alpha^4 = \alpha \cdot \alpha^3 = \alpha(1 + \alpha) = \alpha + \alpha^2$$
$$\alpha^5 = \alpha \cdot \alpha^4 = \alpha(\alpha + \alpha^2) = \alpha^2 + \alpha^3 = \alpha^2 + \alpha + 1,$$
$$\alpha^6 = \alpha \cdot \alpha^5 = \alpha(\alpha^2 + \alpha + 1) = \alpha^3 + \alpha^2 + \alpha = 1 + \alpha + \alpha^2 + \alpha = \alpha^2 + 1$$

The next power of α is

$$\alpha^7 = \alpha \cdot \alpha^6 = \alpha(\alpha^2 + 1) = \alpha^3 + \alpha = 1 + \alpha + \alpha = 1$$

Hence, the higher powers of α basically generates one of the existing nonzero elements.

Table 4.8 *Three Different Representations for the Elements of GF(2^3)*

Power Representations	Polynomial Representations	3-Tuple Representations		
0	0	0	0	0
1	1	1	0	0
α	α	0	1	0
α^2	α^2	0	0	1
α^3	$1+\alpha$	1	1	0
α^4	$\alpha+\alpha^2$	0	1	1
α^5	$1+\alpha+\alpha^2$	1	1	1
α^6	$1+\alpha^2$	1	0	1

Example 4.7: Find (a) $\alpha^5 + \alpha^2 + 1$ and (b) $\alpha^6 + \alpha^3 + \alpha^2 + \alpha + 1$

Solution:

(a) From Table 4.8, we can write

$$\alpha^5 + \alpha^2 + 1 = (\alpha^2 + \alpha + 1) + \alpha^2 + 1 = \alpha$$

(b) Similarly we can write

$$\alpha^6 + \alpha^3 + \alpha^2 + \alpha + 1 = (\alpha^2 + 1) + (\alpha + 1) + \alpha^2 + \alpha + 1 = 1$$

Example 4.8: Find (a) $\alpha\alpha^4$, (b) $\alpha^6\alpha^4$, and (c) $\alpha^6\alpha^5\alpha^3$

Solution:

(a) $\alpha\alpha^4 = \alpha^5$
(b) $\alpha^6\alpha^4 = \alpha^{10} = \alpha^7\alpha^3 = \alpha^3$
(c) $\alpha^6\alpha^5\alpha^3 = \alpha^{14} = \alpha^7\alpha^7 = 1$

Example 4.9: Find (a) α^4/α^5, (b) $1/\alpha^3$, (c) α^3/α^4, and (d) α/α^6

Solution:

(a) The inverse of α^5 is α^2. Hence, $\alpha^4/\alpha^5 = \alpha^4\alpha^2 = \alpha^6$.
(b) Similarly, $1/\alpha^3 = \alpha^4$.
(c) $\alpha^3/\alpha^4 = \alpha^3\alpha^3 = \alpha^6$.
(d) $\alpha/\alpha^6 = \alpha\alpha = \alpha^2$.

4.6 VECTOR SPACES

A *vector space* V can be defined as a collection of elements, called *vectors*, together with the operations of *vector addition* and *scalar multiplication* which satisfy the following conditions:

1. V is an additive commutative group.
2. For any element a in a field F and any element $\mathbf{v}$ in V, $a \cdot \mathbf{v}$ in an element in V.
3. For any element $\mathbf{v}$ in V and any two elements a and b in a field F, $a \cdot (b \cdot \mathbf{v}) = (a \cdot b) \cdot \mathbf{v}$. This is actually the associative law.
4. For any two elements $\mathbf{u}$ and $\mathbf{v}$ in V and any elements a and b in a field F,

$$(a+b)\cdot\mathbf{v}=a\cdot\mathbf{v}+b\cdot\mathbf{v}$$
$$a\cdot(\mathbf{u}+\mathbf{v})=a\cdot\mathbf{u}+a\cdot\mathbf{v}$$

5. If 1 is an unit element of field F, then for any $\mathbf{v}$ in V, $1\cdot\mathbf{v}=\mathbf{v}$.

Now we state some basic properties of vector space as follows:

Property 1: If 0 is the zero element of field F, then for any vector $\mathbf{v}$ in V, $0\cdot\mathbf{v}=0$.

Property 2: For any scalar c in F, $c\cdot 0=0$.

Property 3: For any scalar c in F and any vector $\mathbf{v}$ in V, $(-c)\cdot\mathbf{v}=c\cdot(-\mathbf{v})=-(c\cdot\mathbf{v})$.

In the definition of a vector space, the vectors and scalars can be abstract objects. In fact, the definition does not specify the nature of the vectors or scalars. Here we are most interested in a vector space over GF(2), since it plays a central role in coding theory. We consider an ordered sequence of n components as $(v_0,v_1,v_2,\ldots,v_{n-1})$. Here each component v_i is an element from GF(2). Hence, v_i should be either 0 or 1. The sequence shown is generally known as n-tuple over GF(2). The delimiting commas in $\mathbf{v}$ can be omitted and we can equally write $(v_0v_1v_2\ldots v_{n-1})$. Since each v_i can have a choice of two values, 2^n distinct n-tuples can be constructed. Now we denote this set of 2^n distinct n-tuples as V_n. We consider any two vectors from V_n as $\mathbf{u}=(u_0,u_1,u_2,\ldots,u_{n-1})$ and $\mathbf{v}=(v_0,v_1,v_2,\ldots,v_{n-1})$. Their sum is given as follows:

$$\begin{aligned}\mathbf{w}=\mathbf{u}+\mathbf{v}&=(u_0,u_1,u_2,\ldots,u_{n-1})+(v_0,v_1,v_2,\ldots,v_{n-1})\\&=(u_0+v_0,u_1+v_1,u_2+v_2,\ldots,u_{n-1}+v_{n-1})\end{aligned}\tag{4.50}$$

where u_i+v_i is carried out in modulo-2 addition and $\mathbf{w}$ is also an n-tuple over GF(2). Thus, V_n is closed under the addition operation defined by Eq. (4.50). It can be verified readily that V_n is a commutative group defined by Eq. (4.50). Now we define scalar multiplication of an n-tuple $\mathbf{v}$ in V_n by an element a from GF(2) as follows:

$$a\cdot(v_0,v_1,v_2,\ldots,v_{n-1})=(a\cdot v_0,a\cdot v_2,\ldots,a\cdot v_{n-1})\tag{4.51}$$

where $a\cdot v_i$ is carried out in modulo-2 multiplication. If $a=1$, we have

$$\begin{aligned}1\cdot(v_0,v_1,v_2,\ldots,v_{n-1})&=(1\cdot v_0,1\cdot v_1,1\cdot v_2,\ldots,1\cdot v_{n-1})\\&=(v_0,v_1,v_2,\ldots,v_{n-1})\end{aligned}$$

It can also be shown that the vector addition and scalar multiplication defined by Eqs. (4.50) and (4.51), respectively, satisfy the distributive and associative laws. Hence, the set V_n of all n-tuples over GF(2) forms a vector space over GF(2).

Example 4.10: Let $n=4$. Construct the vector space V_4 of all 4-tuples over GF(2).

Solution: The vector space V_4 of all 4-tuples over GF(2) consists of 16 vectors, shown as follows:

(0 0 0 0),	(0 0 0 1),	(0 0 1 0),	(0 0 1 1),
(0 1 0 0),	(0 1 0 1),	(0 1 1 0),	(0 1 1 1),
(1 0 0 0),	(1 0 0 1),	(1 0 1 0),	(1 0 1 1),
(1 1 0 0),	(1 1 0 1),	(1 1 1 0),	(1 1 1 1),

Now it can be checked that the vector sum of any two vectors from V_4 will result in another element from the same vector space, which only satisfies the closure property of the vector space. Vector space of all n-tuples over any field F can be constructed similarly.

4.6.1 Subspace

It can happen that a subset S of V is also a vector space over F. Such a subset is known as a *subspace* of V. For any nonempty subspace S of V, the following conditions are satisfied:

1. For any two vectors $\mathbf{u}$ and $\mathbf{v}$ in S, $\mathbf{u} + \mathbf{v}$ is also a vector in S.
2. For any element a in F and any vector $\mathbf{u}$ in S, $a \cdot \mathbf{u}$ is also in S.

4.6.2 Linear Combination

If $\mathbf{v}_1, \mathbf{v}_2, \mathbf{v}_3, \ldots, \mathbf{v}_m$ be m vectors in a vector space V over a field, and $a_1, a_2, a_3, \ldots, a_m$ be m scalars from F, then the sum $a_1\mathbf{v}_1 + a_2\mathbf{v}_2 + a_3\mathbf{v}_3 + \ldots + a_m\mathbf{v}_m$ is known as a *linear combination* of $\mathbf{v}_1, \mathbf{v}_2, \mathbf{v}_3, \ldots, \mathbf{v}_m$. Note that the set of all linear combinations of $\mathbf{v}_1, \mathbf{v}_2, \mathbf{v}_3, \ldots, \mathbf{v}_m$ forms a subspace of V.

A set of vectors $\mathbf{v}_1, \mathbf{v}_2, \mathbf{v}_3, \ldots, \mathbf{v}_m$ in a vector space V over a field F is said to be *linearly dependent* if and only if there exists m scalars $a_1, a_2, a_3, \ldots, a_m$ from F, *not all of them zero*, such that

$$a_1\mathbf{v}_1 + a_2\mathbf{v}_2 + a_3\mathbf{v}_3 + \ldots + a_m\mathbf{v}_m = 0 \tag{4.52}$$

Alternatively, the set of vectors $\mathbf{v}_1, \mathbf{v}_2, \mathbf{v}_3, \ldots, \mathbf{v}_m$ is said to be *linearly independent* if

$$a_1\mathbf{v}_1 + a_2\mathbf{v}_2 + a_3\mathbf{v}_3 + \ldots + a_m\mathbf{v}_m \neq 0 \tag{4.53}$$

unless $a_1 = a_2 = a_3 = \cdots = a_m = 0$.

Example 4.11: For the three sets of vectors determine whether the vectors are linearly dependent or not:

(a) $\mathbf{u}_1 = (4\ \ -9\ \ 5)$, $\mathbf{u}_2 = (-1\ \ 5\ \ 13)$, and $\mathbf{u}_3 = (-3\ \ -4\ \ -18)$

(b) $\mathbf{v}_1 = (14\ \ 7\ \ -9)$, $\mathbf{v}_2 = (-7\ \ -4\ \ 3)$, and $\mathbf{v}_3 = (0\ \ 2\ \ -6)$

Solution:

(a) Taking $a_1 = 1$, $a_2 = 1$, and $a_3 = 1$ gives the linear combination

$$\begin{aligned} a_1\mathbf{u}_1 + a_2\mathbf{u}_2 + a_3\mathbf{u}_3 &= \mathbf{u}_1 + \mathbf{u}_2 + \mathbf{u}_3 \\ &= (4 - 1 - 3\ \ \ -9 + 5 - 4\ \ \ 5 + 13 - 18) \\ &= (0\ \ 0\ \ 0) \end{aligned}$$

Hence, the vectors are linearly dependent

(b) Taking $a_1 = 1$, $a_2 = 1$, and $a_3 = 1$ gives the linear combination

$$\begin{aligned} a_1\mathbf{v}_1 + a_2\mathbf{v}_2 + a_3\mathbf{v}_3 &= \mathbf{v}_1 + \mathbf{v}_2 + \mathbf{v}_3 \\ &= (14 - 7 + 0\ \ \ 7 - 4 + 2\ \ \ -9 + 3 - 6) \\ &= (-7\ \ 5\ \ -12) \end{aligned}$$

The resultant vector is nonzero. This does not necessarily mean that the vectors are independent. There can be other scalars that give a zero linear combination. For example, if we take $a_1 = 1$, $a_2 = 2$, and $a_3 = 1/2$, then

$$\begin{aligned} a_1\mathbf{v}_1 + a_2\mathbf{v}_2 + a_3\mathbf{v}_3 &= \mathbf{v}_1 + 2\mathbf{v}_2 + (1/2)\mathbf{v}_3 \\ &= (14\ \ 7\ \ -9) + 2(-7\ \ -4\ \ 3) + 1/2(0\ \ 2\ \ -6) \\ &= (14\ \ 7\ \ -9) + (-14\ \ -8\ \ 6) + (0\ \ 1\ \ -3) \\ &= (14 - 14 + 0\ \ \ 7 - 8 + 1\ \ \ -9 + 6 - 3) \\ &= (0\ \ 0\ \ 0) \end{aligned}$$

Thus, the vectors are linearly dependent.

Example 4.12: For the three sets of vectors over GF(2), check whether the vectors are linearly dependent or not:

(a) $\mathbf{u}_1 = (1\ \ 0\ \ 1\ \ 1)$, $\mathbf{u}_2 = (0\ \ 1\ \ 0\ \ 0)$, and $\mathbf{u}_3 = (1\ \ 1\ \ 1\ \ 1)$
(b) $\mathbf{v}_1 = (0\ \ 1\ \ 1\ \ 0)$, $\mathbf{v}_2 = (1\ \ 0\ \ 0\ \ 1)$, and $\mathbf{v}_3 = (1\ \ 0\ \ 1\ \ 1)$

Solution:

(a) Taking $a_1 = 1$, $a_2 = 1$, and $a_3 = 1$ gives the linear combination

$$\begin{aligned} a_1\mathbf{u}_1 + a_2\mathbf{u}_2 + a_3\mathbf{u}_3 &= (1\ \ 0\ \ 1\ \ 1) + (0\ \ 1\ \ 0\ \ 0) + (1\ \ 1\ \ 1\ \ 1) \\ &= (1+0+1\ \ \ 0+1+1\ \ \ 1+0+1\ \ \ 1+0+1) \\ &= (0\ \ 0\ \ 0\ \ 0) \end{aligned}$$

Hence, the vectors are linearly dependent

(b) Taking $a_1 = 1$, $a_2 = 1$, and $a_3 = 1$ gives the linear combination

$$\begin{aligned} a_1\mathbf{v}_1 + a_2\mathbf{v}_2 + a_3\mathbf{v}_3 &= (0\ \ 1\ \ 1\ \ 0) + (1\ \ 0\ \ 0\ \ 1) + (1\ \ 0\ \ 1\ \ 1) \\ &= (0+1+1\ \ \ 1+0+0\ \ \ 1+0+1\ \ \ 0+1+1) \\ &= (0\ \ 1\ \ 0\ \ 0) \end{aligned}$$

The resultant vector is nonzero. As shown in the previous example, this does not necessarily mean that the vectors are independent. There can be other scalars that give a zero linear combination. So all of the rest nonzero six linear combinations of these three vectors are checked as follows:

$$\begin{aligned} 0\cdot(0\ \ 1\ \ 1\ \ 0) + 0\cdot(1\ \ 0\ \ 0\ \ 1) + 1\cdot(1\ \ 0\ \ 1\ \ 1) &= (1\ \ 0\ \ 1\ \ 1) \\ 0\cdot(0\ \ 1\ \ 1\ \ 0) + 1\cdot(1\ \ 0\ \ 0\ \ 1) + 0\cdot(1\ \ 0\ \ 1\ \ 1) &= (1\ \ 0\ \ 0\ \ 1) \\ 0\cdot(0\ \ 1\ \ 1\ \ 0) + 1\cdot(1\ \ 0\ \ 0\ \ 1) + 1\cdot(1\ \ 0\ \ 1\ \ 1) &= (0\ \ 0\ \ 1\ \ 0) \\ 1\cdot(0\ \ 1\ \ 1\ \ 0) + 0\cdot(1\ \ 0\ \ 0\ \ 1) + 0\cdot(1\ \ 0\ \ 1\ \ 1) &= (0\ \ 1\ \ 1\ \ 0) \\ 1\cdot(0\ \ 1\ \ 1\ \ 0) + 0\cdot(1\ \ 0\ \ 0\ \ 1) + 1\cdot(1\ \ 0\ \ 1\ \ 1) &= (1\ \ 1\ \ 0\ \ 1) \\ 1\cdot(0\ \ 1\ \ 1\ \ 0) + 1\cdot(1\ \ 0\ \ 0\ \ 1) + 0\cdot(1\ \ 0\ \ 1\ \ 1) &= (1\ \ 1\ \ 1\ \ 1) \end{aligned}$$

Thus, we now find that of all the possible nonzero linear combinations, the resultant vector is nonzero. Hence, the vectors are linearly independent.

4.6.3 Basis (or Base)

In any vector space or subspace, there exists at least one set of linearly independent vectors from which all other vectors can be generated. This set is known as a *basis* (or *base*) of the vector space and the vectors of this space are known as *basis vectors*.

A set of vectors is said to *span* a vector space V if every vector in V is a linear combination of the vectors in the set. Here, each vector within the vector space can be uniquely expressed as a linear combination of the basis vectors. Hence, the basis vectors are said to span the vector space.

4.6.4 Dimension

The number of vectors within the basis is called the *dimension* of the vector space. In an n-dimensional vector space, any set of n linearly independent vectors spans the space and is therefore a basis for the space.

Consider a vector space V_n of all n-tuples over GF(2). The following n n-tuples are formed:

$$\mathbf{x}_0 = (1, 0, 0, 0, \ldots, 0, 0)$$
$$\mathbf{x}_1 = (0, 1, 0, 0, \ldots, 0, 0)$$
$$\mathbf{x}_2 = (0, 0, 1, 0, \ldots, 0, 0)$$
$$\vdots$$
$$\mathbf{x}_{n-1} = (0, 0, 0, 0, \ldots, 0, 1)$$

where the n-tuple x_i has only one nonzero component at the ith position. Then every n-tuple $(a_0, a_1, a_2, \ldots, a_{n-1})$ in V_n can be expressed as linear combinations of $\mathbf{x}_0, \mathbf{x}_1, \mathbf{x}_2, \ldots, \mathbf{x}_{n-1}$ as follows:

$$(a_0, a_1, a_2, \ldots, a_{n-1}) = a_0\mathbf{x}_0 + a_1\mathbf{x}_1 + a_2\mathbf{x}_2 + \ldots + a_{n-1}\mathbf{x}_{n-1}$$

Hence, $\mathbf{x}_0, \mathbf{x}_1, \mathbf{x}_2, \ldots, \mathbf{x}_{n-1}$ span the vector space V_n of all n-tuples over GF(2). We also find that $\mathbf{x}_0, \mathbf{x}_1, \mathbf{x}_2, \ldots, \mathbf{x}_{n-1}$ are linearly independent. Thus, they form a basis for V_n and the dimension of V_n is n. If $m < n$ and $\mathbf{v}_1, \mathbf{v}_2, \mathbf{v}_3, \ldots, \mathbf{v}_m$ are m linearly independent vectors in V_n, then all the linear combinations of $\mathbf{v}_1, \mathbf{v}_2, \mathbf{v}_3, \ldots, \mathbf{v}_m$ of the form

$$\mathbf{u} = c_1\mathbf{v}_1 + c_2\mathbf{v}_2 + c_3\mathbf{v}_3 + \ldots + c_m\mathbf{v}_m$$

form an m-dimensional subspace S of V_n. Since each c_1 has two possible values, 0 or 1, there are 2^m possible distinct linear combinations of $\mathbf{v}_1, \mathbf{v}_2, \mathbf{v}_3, \ldots, \mathbf{v}_m$. Hence, S consists of 2^m vectors and is an m-dimensional subspace of V_n.

Example 4.13: Determine a basis and the dimension of the subspace in V_4 consisting of the vectors:

$$(0\ 0\ 0\ 0) \quad (1\ 1\ 0\ 0) \quad (1\ 0\ 1\ 0) \quad (0\ 0\ 0\ 1)$$
$$(0\ 1\ 1\ 0) \quad (1\ 1\ 0\ 1) \quad (1\ 0\ 1\ 1) \quad (0\ 1\ 1\ 1)$$

Solution: Any two linearly independent nonzero vectors say (1 1 0 0) and (1 0 1 0), can be used as the initial set of vectors. They are linearly independent because if we consider $\mathbf{u} = a_1(1\ 1\ 0\ 0) + a_2(1\ 0\ 1\ 0)$ then the only values that give $\mathbf{u} = 0$ are $a_1 = a_2 = 0$. Of the remaining five nonzero vectors (0 1 1 0) cannot be appended to the set, since (0 1 1 0) = (1 1 0 0) + (1 0 1 0) and is therefore linearly dependent on the two vectors already in the set.

Any one of the vectors (0 0 0 1), (1 1 0 1), (1 0 1 1) or (0 1 1 1) may be appended to the set. Taking, say, (0 1 1 1) as the third basis vector we find that all the vectors within the subspace can be constructed from a linear combination of the vectors (1 1 0 0), (1 0 1 0), and (0 1 1 1) as follows:

$$0\cdot(1\ 1\ 0\ 0) + 0\cdot(1\ 0\ 1\ 0) + 0\cdot(0\ 1\ 1\ 1) = (0\ 0\ 0\ 0)$$
$$0\cdot(1\ 1\ 0\ 0) + 0\cdot(1\ 0\ 1\ 0) + 1\cdot(0\ 1\ 1\ 1) = (0\ 1\ 1\ 1)$$
$$0\cdot(1\ 1\ 0\ 0) + 1\cdot(1\ 0\ 1\ 0) + 0\cdot(0\ 1\ 1\ 1) = (1\ 0\ 1\ 0)$$
$$0\cdot(1\ 1\ 0\ 0) + 1\cdot(1\ 0\ 1\ 0) + 1\cdot(0\ 1\ 1\ 1) = (1\ 1\ 0\ 1)$$
$$1\cdot(1\ 1\ 0\ 0) + 0\cdot(1\ 0\ 1\ 0) + 0\cdot(0\ 1\ 1\ 1) = (1\ 1\ 0\ 0)$$
$$1\cdot(1\ 1\ 0\ 0) + 0\cdot(1\ 0\ 1\ 0) + 1\cdot(0\ 1\ 1\ 1) = (1\ 0\ 1\ 1)$$
$$1\cdot(1\ 1\ 0\ 0) + 1\cdot(1\ 0\ 1\ 0) + 0\cdot(0\ 1\ 1\ 1) = (0\ 1\ 1\ 0)$$
$$1\cdot(1\ 1\ 0\ 0) + 1\cdot(1\ 0\ 1\ 0) + 1\cdot(0\ 1\ 1\ 1) = (0\ 0\ 0\ 1)$$

A basis of the subspace is therefore (1 1 0 0), (1 0 1 0), and (0 1 1 1), and the dimension of the subspace is 3, since there are three basis vectors. A point to be noted is that, the basis is not unique. We could have taken (0 0 0 1), (1 1 0 1), and (1 0 1 1) as the third vector to complete the basis.

4.6.5 Orthogonality

Let $\mathbf{u} = (u_0, u_1, u_2, ..., u_{n-1})$and $\mathbf{v} = (v_0, v_1, v_2, ..., v_{n-1})$ be two n-tuples in V_n. We define the *dot product* (or *inner product*) of $\mathbf{u}$ and $\mathbf{v}$ as follows:

$$\mathbf{u} \cdot \mathbf{v} = u_0v_0 + u_1v_1 + u_2v_2 + ... + u_{m-1}\, v_{m-1} \tag{4.54}$$

where $u_i \cdot v_i$ and $u_i \cdot v_i + u_{i+1} \cdot v_{i+1}$ are carried out in modulo-2 multiplication and addition. Thus, the inner product $\mathbf{u} \cdot \mathbf{v}$ is a scalar in GF(2). Two n-tuples $\mathbf{u}$ and $\mathbf{v}$ are said to be *orthogonal* to each other, if $\mathbf{u} \cdot \mathbf{v} = 0$. Note that orthogonality is a relative property. If $\mathbf{u} \cdot \mathbf{v} = 0$, then $\mathbf{u}$ and $\mathbf{v}$ are orthogonal to each other but not necessarily to other vectors.

It is also possible for a vector in V_n to be orthogonal to itself. For example, let us consider a vector $\mathbf{v} = (1\ 1\ 0\ 1\ 1)$ in V_5. The dot product

$$\mathbf{v} \cdot \mathbf{v} = (1\ 1\ 0\ 1\ 1) \cdot (1\ 1\ 0\ 1\ 1) = 1{\cdot}1 + 1{\cdot}1 + 0{\cdot}0 + 1{\cdot}1 + 1{\cdot}1 = 1 + 1 + 1 + 1 = 0$$

Hence, $(1\ 1\ 0\ 1\ 1)$ is orthogonal to itself.

Inner product has the following properties:

1. $\mathbf{u} \cdot \mathbf{v} = \mathbf{v} \cdot \mathbf{u}$
2. $\mathbf{u} \cdot (\mathbf{v} + \mathbf{w}) = \mathbf{u} \cdot \mathbf{v} + \mathbf{u} \cdot \mathbf{w}$.
3. $(a \cdot \mathbf{u}) \cdot \mathbf{v} = a\,(\mathbf{u} \cdot \mathbf{v})$.

4.6.6 Dual Space

Let S be an m-dimensional subspace in V_n and let S_d be the set of vectors in V_n such that, for any $\mathbf{u}$ in S and $\mathbf{v}$ in S_d, $\mathbf{u} \cdot \mathbf{v} = 0$. Thus, the set of vectors in S_d are orthogonal to the vectors in S and is known as the *dual space* or *null space* of S. Thus, $\mathbf{s} \cdot \mathbf{s}_d = 0$, for all vectors $\mathbf{s}$ and $\mathbf{s}_d$ belonging to S and S_d, respectively. Conversely S is also the dual space of S_d.

If S is m-dimensional space of the vector space V_n of all n-tuples over GF(2), then the dimension of its *dual space* S_d is $n - m$. Alternatively it can be stated that $\dim(S) + \dim(S_d) = n$.

Example 4.14: Show that the three-dimensional subspace S of the vector space V_4 consisting of the vectors:

$$(0\ \ 0\ \ 0\ \ 0) \qquad (1\ \ 1\ \ 0\ \ 0) \qquad (1\ \ 0\ \ 1\ \ 1) \qquad (0\ \ 1\ \ 1\ \ 1)$$

and the space S_d consisting of

$$(0\ \ 0\ \ 0\ \ 0) \qquad (1\ \ 1\ \ 0\ \ 1) \qquad (1\ \ 1\ \ 1\ \ 0) \qquad (0\ \ 0\ \ 1\ \ 1)$$

form dual subspace of V_4. Also determine the dimension of S_d.

Solution: Taking the dot product of first nonzero vector in S with the nonzero vectors in S_d gives:

$$(1\ \ 1\ \ 0\ \ 0) \cdot (1\ \ 1\ \ 0\ \ 1) = 1{\cdot}1 + 1{\cdot}1 + 0{\cdot}0 + 0{\cdot}1 = 0$$
$$(1\ \ 1\ \ 0\ \ 0) \cdot (1\ \ 1\ \ 1\ \ 0) = 1{\cdot}1 + 1{\cdot}1 + 0{\cdot}1 + 0{\cdot}0 = 0$$
$$(1\ \ 1\ \ 0\ \ 0) \cdot (0\ \ 0\ \ 1\ \ 1) = 1{\cdot}0 + 1{\cdot}0 + 0{\cdot}1 + 0{\cdot}1 = 0$$

Taking the dot product of second nonzero vector in S with the nonzero vectors in S_d gives:

$$(1\ \ 0\ \ 1\ \ 1) \cdot (1\ \ 1\ \ 0\ \ 1) = 1{\cdot}1 + 0{\cdot}1 + 1{\cdot}0 + 1{\cdot}1 = 0$$
$$(1\ \ 0\ \ 1\ \ 1) \cdot (1\ \ 1\ \ 1\ \ 0) = 1{\cdot}1 + 0{\cdot}1 + 1{\cdot}1 + 1{\cdot}0 = 0$$
$$(1\ \ 0\ \ 1\ \ 1) \cdot (0\ \ 0\ \ 1\ \ 1) = 1{\cdot}0 + 0{\cdot}0 + 1{\cdot}1 + 1{\cdot}1 = 0$$

Taking the dot product of third nonzero vector in S with the nonzero vectors in S_d gives:

$$(0\,1\,1\,1)\cdot(1\,1\,0\,1) = 0{\cdot}1 + 1{\cdot}1 + 1{\cdot}0 + 1{\cdot}1 = 0$$
$$(0\,1\,1\,1)\cdot(1\,1\,1\,0) = 0{\cdot}1 + 1{\cdot}1 + 1{\cdot}1 + 1{\cdot}0 = 0$$
$$(0\,1\,1\,1)\cdot(0\,0\,1\,1) = 0{\cdot}0 + 1{\cdot}0 + 1{\cdot}1 + 1{\cdot}1 = 0$$

Thus, we see that all the vectors of S are orthogonal to the vectors in S_d, and therefore S and S_d are dual subspaces of V_4.

In S, the vectors (1 0 1 1) and (0 1 1 1) are linearly independent but the vector (1 1 0 0) = (1 0 1 1) + (0 1 1 1) and hence the dimension of S is 2.

Similarly the vectors (1 1 0 1) and (1 1 1 0) are linearly independent but the vector (0 0 1 1) = (1 1 0 1) + (1 1 1 0) and thus the dimension of the dual space S_d is also 2.

4.7 MATRICES

An $m \times n$ matrix over GF(2) (or over any other field) is a rectangular array with m rows and n columns can be written as follows:

$$\mathbf{G} = \begin{bmatrix} g_{00} & g_{01} & g_{02} & \cdots & g_{0,n-1} \\ g_{10} & g_{11} & g_{12} & \cdots & g_{1,n-1} \\ \vdots & \vdots & \vdots & \ddots & \vdots \\ g_{m-1,0} & g_{m-1,1} & g_{m-1,2} & \cdots & g_{m-1,n-1} \end{bmatrix} \tag{4.55}$$

where each entry g_{ij} with $0 \le i < m$ and $0 \le j < n$ is an element from the binary field GF(2). The first index i indicates the row containing g_{ij} and the second index j tells the column having g_{ij}. Often the matrix shown in Eq. (4.55) is written as $[g_{ij}]$. We find that each row of **G** is an n-tuple over GF(2) and each column is a m-tuple over GF(2). The matrix **G** can be expressed in terms of its m row vectors as follows:

$$\mathbf{G} = \begin{bmatrix} g_0 \\ g_1 \\ \vdots \\ g_{m-1} \end{bmatrix}$$

4.7.1 Row Space

If the m ($m \le n$) rows of **G** are linearly independent, then the 2^m linear combinations of these rows from an m-dimensional subspace of the vector space V_n of all the n-tuples over GF(2). This subspace is called the *row space* of **G**.

Example 4.15: Determine the row space of the matrix:

$$\mathbf{G} = \begin{bmatrix} 1 & 0 & 0 & 1 & 0 & 1 \\ 0 & 1 & 0 & 0 & 1 & 1 \\ 0 & 0 & 1 & 1 & 1 & 0 \end{bmatrix}$$

Solution: The row vectors are:

$$\mathbf{g}_0 = (1\ \ 0\ \ 0\ 1\ \ 0\ \ 1),\ \mathbf{g}_1 = (0\ \ 1\ \ 0\ \ 0\ \ 1\ \ 1),\ \text{and}\ \mathbf{g}_2 = (0\ \ 0\ \ 1\ \ 1\ \ 1\ \ 0)$$

Taking all the 2^3 linear combinations of $\mathbf{g}_1$, $\mathbf{g}_2$, and $\mathbf{g}_3$ gives:

$$0 \cdot \mathbf{g}_0 + 0 \cdot \mathbf{g}_1 + 0 \cdot \mathbf{g}_2 = (0\,0\,0\,0\,0\,0)$$
$$0 \cdot \mathbf{g}_0 + 0 \cdot \mathbf{g}_1 + 1 \cdot \mathbf{g}_2 = \mathbf{g}_2 = (0\,0\,1\,1\,1\,0)$$
$$0 \cdot \mathbf{g}_0 + 1 \cdot \mathbf{g}_1 + 0 \cdot \mathbf{g}_2 = \mathbf{g}_1 = (0\,1\,0\,0\,1\,1)$$
$$0 \cdot \mathbf{g}_0 + 1 \cdot \mathbf{g}_1 + 1 \cdot \mathbf{g}_2 = \mathbf{g}_1 + \mathbf{g}_2 = (0\,1\,1\,1\,0\,1)$$
$$1 \cdot \mathbf{g}_0 + 0 \cdot \mathbf{g}_1 + 0 \cdot \mathbf{g}_2 = \mathbf{g}_0 = (1\,0\,0\,1\,0\,1)$$
$$1 \cdot \mathbf{g}_0 + 0 \cdot \mathbf{g}_1 + 1 \cdot \mathbf{g}_2 = \mathbf{g}_0 + \mathbf{g}_2 = (1\,0\,1\,0\,1\,1)$$
$$1 \cdot \mathbf{g}_0 + 1 \cdot \mathbf{g}_1 + 0 \cdot \mathbf{g}_2 = \mathbf{g}_0 + \mathbf{g}_1 = (1\,1\,0\,1\,1\,0)$$
$$1 \cdot \mathbf{g}_0 + 1 \cdot \mathbf{g}_1 + 1 \cdot \mathbf{g}_2 = \mathbf{g}_0 + \mathbf{g}_1 + \mathbf{g}_2 = (1\,1\,1\,0\,0\,0)$$

The row space of **G** therefore contains the vectors:

(0 0 0 0 0 0), (0 0 1 1 1 0), (0 1 0 0 1 1), (0 1 1 1 0 1), (1 0 0 1 0 1), (1 0 1 0 1 1), (1 1 0 1 1 0) and (1 1 1 0 0 0).

We may also express a matrix in terms of *column vectors* constructed from columns of the matrix, and taking all the linear combinations of the column vectors gives the *column space* of a matrix. Such a matrix is known as the *transpose* of **G** and is usually denoted by $\mathbf{G}^T$. Thus, if **G** is an $m \times n$ matrix over GF(2), then $\mathbf{G}^T$ will be an $n \times m$ matrix over GF(2). Thus, any matrix **G** determines two vector spaces—the row vector space and column vector space of **G**. The dimensions of the column and row vector spaces are known as the *column* and *row rank*, respectively. They are the same and referred to as the *rank* of the matrix.

We can interchange any two rows of **G** or multiply a row by a nonzero scalar or simply add one row or a multiple of one row to another. These are called *elementary row operations*. By performing elementary row operations on **G**, we obtain another matrix **G′** over GF(2). Both **G** and **G′** have the same row space.

Example 4.16: Consider the matrix **G** in Example 4.15. Adding row 3 to row 1 and then interchanging rows 2 and 3 gives:

$$\mathbf{G}' = \begin{bmatrix} 1 & 0 & 1 & 0 & 1 & 1 \\ 0 & 0 & 1 & 1 & 1 & 0 \\ 0 & 1 & 0 & 0 & 1 & 1 \end{bmatrix}$$

Show that the row space generated by **G′** is the same as that generated by **G**.

Solution: The row vectors are now (1 0 1 0 1 1), (0 0 1 1 1 0), and (0 1 0 0 1 1). Taking all the eight combinations of these three vectors gives the vectors:

(0 0 0 0 0 0), (0 0 1 1 1 0), (0 1 0 0 1 1), (0 1 1 1 0 1), (1 0 0 1 0 1), (1 0 1 0 1 1), (1 1 0 1 1 0), and (1 1 1 0 0 0).

This is the same set of vectors obtained in Example 4.15 and hence the row spaces generated by **G** and **G′** are the same.

Let S be the row space of an $m \times n$ matrix **G** over GF(2) whose m rows $\mathbf{g}_0, \mathbf{g}_1, \mathbf{g}_2, \ldots, \mathbf{g}_{m-1}$ are linearly independent. Let S_d be the null space of S. In such a case, the dimension of S_d is $n - m$. Let $\mathbf{h}_0, \mathbf{h}_1, \mathbf{h}_2, \ldots, \mathbf{h}_{n-m-1}$ be $n - m$ linearly independent vectors in S_d. Obviously these rows span S_d. We can form an $(n - m) \times n$ matrix **H** using $\mathbf{h}_0, \mathbf{h}_1, \mathbf{h}_2, \ldots, \mathbf{h}_{n-m-1}$ as rows:

$$\mathbf{H} = \begin{bmatrix} \mathbf{h}_0 \\ \mathbf{h}_1 \\ \vdots \\ \mathbf{h}_{n-m-1} \end{bmatrix} = \begin{bmatrix} h_{00} & h_{01} & h_{02} & \cdots & h_{0,n-1} \\ h_{10} & h_{11} & h_{12} & \cdots & h_{1,n-1} \\ \vdots & \vdots & \vdots & \ddots & \vdots \\ h_{n-m-1,0} & h_{n-m-1,1} & h_{n-m-1,2} & \cdots & h_{n-m-1,n-1} \end{bmatrix}$$

The row space of H is S_d. Since each row $\mathbf{g}_i$ of $\mathbf{G}$ is a vector in S and each row $\mathbf{h}_j$ of $\mathbf{H}$ is a vector in S_d, the dot product of $\mathbf{g}_i$ and $\mathbf{h}_j$ must be zero (i.e., $\mathbf{g}_i \cdot \mathbf{h}_j = 0$). Since the row space S of $\mathbf{G}$ is the null space of the row space S_d of $\mathbf{H}$, we call S the null (or dual) space of $\mathbf{H}$.

Two matrices can be added if they have the same number of rows and the same number of columns. Similarly two matrices can be multiplied if the number of columns in the first matrix is equal to the number of rows in the second matrix. An $m \times m$ matrix is called an *identity* matrix if it has 1's on the main diagonal and 0's elsewhere. This matrix is denoted by $\mathbf{I}_m$. A *submatrix* of a matrix $\mathbf{G}$ is a matrix that can be obtained by striking out given rows or columns of $\mathbf{G}$.

4.8 SOLVED PROBLEMS

Problem 4.1: Show that $p(x) = x^3 + 9x + 6$ is irreducible in $Q(x)$. Let θ be a root of $p(x)$. Find the inverse of $1 + \theta$ in $Q(\theta)$.

Solution: Irreducibility follows from Eisenstein's criterion with $p = 3$. To evaluate $1/(1 + \theta)$, note that we must have $1/(1 + \theta) = a + b\theta + c\theta^2$ for some $a, b, c \in Q$.

Multiplying this out, we find that

$$a + (a + b)\theta + (b + c)\theta^2 + c\theta^3 = 1$$

but we also have $\theta^3 = -9\theta - 6$, so this simplifies to

$$(a - 6c) + (a + b - 9c)\theta + (b + c)\theta^2 = 1$$

Solving for a, b, c gives $a = 5/2$, $b = -1/4$, and $c = 1/4$. Thus,

$$\frac{1}{1+\theta} = \frac{5}{2} - \frac{\theta}{4} + \frac{\theta^2}{4}$$

Problem 4.2: Show that $x^3 - 2x - 2$ is irreducible over Q and let θ be a root. Compute $(1 + \theta)(1 + \theta + \theta^2)$ and $(1+ \theta)/(1 + \theta + \theta^2)$ in $Q(\theta)$.

Solution: This polynomial is irreducible by Eisenstein with $p = 2$. We perform the multiplication and division just as in the previous problem to get

$$(1 + \theta)(1 + \theta + \theta^2) = 3 + 4\theta + 2\theta^2$$

and

$$\frac{1+\theta}{1+\theta+\theta^2} = \frac{1}{3} + \frac{2\theta}{3} - \frac{\theta^2}{3}$$

Problem 4.3 Show that $x^3 + x + 1$ is irreducible over GF(2) and let θ be a root. Compute the powers of θ in GF (2).

Solution: If a cubic polynomial factors, then one of its factors must be linear. Hence, to check that $x^3 + x + 1$ is irreducible over GF(2), it suffices to show that it has no roots in GF(2). Since GF(2) = {0, 1} has only two elements, it is easy to check that this polynomial has no roots. Hence, it is irreducible. For the powers, we have

$$\theta^0 = 1$$

$$\theta^1 = \theta$$

$$\theta^2 = \theta^2$$

$$\theta^3 = \theta + 1$$

$$\theta^4 = \theta^2 + \theta$$
$$\theta^5 = \theta^2 + \theta + 1$$
$$\theta^6 = \theta^2 + 1$$
$$\theta^7 = 1$$

Problem 4.4: Determine the degree of the extension $\sqrt{3+2\sqrt{2}}$ over Q.

Solution: Since $(1+\sqrt{2})^2 = 3+2\sqrt{2}$, we have

$$Q(\sqrt{3+2\sqrt{2}}) = Q(\sqrt{2})$$

which has degree 2 over Q.

Problem 4.5: Let $F \subset E$ be an extension of finite fields. Prove that $|E| = |F|^{(E/F)}$.

Solution: Let $m = (E/F)$. Choose a basis $\alpha_1, \ldots, \alpha_m$ in E over F. Every element $\alpha \in E$ can be written uniquely as $\alpha = b_1\alpha_1 + \ldots + b_m\alpha_m$ with $b_1, \ldots, b_m \in F$. Hence, $|E| = |F|^m$.

MULTIPLE CHOICE QUESTIONS

1. A (7, 4) linear block code has a rate of
   (a) 7 (b) 4 (c) 1.75 (d) 0.571

   Ans. (**d**)

2. A polynomial is called monic if
   (a) odd terms are unity (b) even terms are unity
   (c) leading coefficient is unity (d) leading coefficient is zero

   Ans. (**c**)

3. For $GF(2^3)$, the elements in the set are
   (a) {1 2 3 4 5 6 7} (b) {0 1 2 3 4 5 6}
   (c) {0 1 2 3 4} (d) {0 1 2 3 4 5 6 7}

   Ans. (**d**)

4. What is $5 \times 3 - 4 \times 2$ in $Z(6) = \{0,1,2,3,4,5\}$?
   (a) 1 (b) 2 (c) 3 (d) 4

   Ans. (**a**)

5. How many solutions are there in $Z6 = \{0,1,2,3,4,5\}$ of the equation $2x = 0$?
   (a) 2 (b) 1 (c) 3 (d) 4

   Ans. (**a**)

6. In a go-back-N ARQ, if the window size is 63, what is the range of sequence numbers?
   (a) 0 to 63 (b) 0 to 64 (c) 1 to 63 (d) 1 to 64

   Ans. (**a**)

7. ARQ stands for ________.
   (a) automatic repeat quantization (b) automatic repeat request
   (c) automatic retransmission request (d) acknowledge repeat request

   Ans. (**b**)

8. In stop-and-wait ARQ, for 10 data packets sent, ________ acknowledgments are needed.
   (a) exactly 10 (b) less than 10 (c) more than 10 (d) none of the above

   Ans. (**a**)

9. The stop-and-wait ARQ, the go-back-N ARQ, and the selective-repeat ARQ are for ______ channels.
(a) noisy (b) noiseless (c) either (a) or (b) (d) neither (a) nor (b)
Ans. **(a)**

10. $A = \{\text{set of odd integers}\}$ and $B = \{\text{set of even integers}\}$. Find the intersection of A and B.
(a) {1,2,3,4,5,7,9} (b) What the sets have in common
(c) { } (d) {2,4}
Ans. **(c)**

11. A burst error means that two or more bits in the data unit have changed
(a) double-bit (b) burst (c) single-bit (d) none of the above
Ans. **(b)**

12. In ________ error correction, the receiver corrects errors without requesting retransmission.
(a) backward (b) onward (c) forward (d) none of the above
Ans. **(c)**

13. We can divide coding schemes into two broad categories, ______ and ______ coding.
(a) block; linear (b) linear; nonlinear
(c) block; convolution (d) none of the above
Ans. **(c)**

14. In modulo-2 arithmetic, __________ give the same results.
(a) addition and multiplication (b) addition and division
(c) addition and subtraction (d) none of the above
Ans. **(c)**

15. In modulo-2 arithmetic, we use the ______ operation for both addition and subtraction.
(a) XOR (b) OR (c) AND (d) none of the above
Ans. **(a)**

16. In modulo-11 arithmetic, we use only the integers in the range ______, inclusive.
(a) 1 to 10 (b) 1 to 11 (c) 0 to 10 (d) 0 to 1
Ans. **(c)**

17. The _______ of a polynomial is the highest power in the polynomial.
(a) range (b) degree (c) power (d) none of these
Ans. **(b)**

18. $100110 \oplus 011011$, when $\oplus$ represents modulo-2 addition for binary number, yields
(a) 100111 (b) 111101 (c) 000001 (d) 011010
Ans. **(b)**

Review Questions

1. Compare ARQ and FEC schemes of error control strategies.
2. Calculate the throughput efficiency of the stop-and-wait ARQ system.
3. Draw the block diagram of a typical data transmission system and explain the function of each block.
4. Find the roots of $x^3 + \alpha^8 x^2 + \alpha^{12} x + \alpha = 0$ defined over $GF(2^4)$.
5. Determine whether the following polynomials over $GF(2)$ are (a) irreducible and (b) primitive:

$$p_1(x) = x^3 + x^2 + 1$$
$$p_2(x) = x^4 + x^3 + x + 1$$
$$p_3(x) = x^2 + x + 1$$

6. Prove that GF(2^m) is a vector space over GF(2).
7. Find all the irreducible polynomials of degree 4 over GF(2).
8. Consider the primitive polynomial $p(Z) = Z^4 + Z + 1$ over GF(2). Use this to construct the expansion field GF(16).
9. Given the matrices

$$\mathbf{G} = \begin{vmatrix} 1 & 1 & 0 & 1 & 1 & 0 & 0 \\ 1 & 1 & 1 & 0 & 0 & 1 & 0 \\ 0 & 1 & 1 & 1 & 0 & 0 & 1 \end{vmatrix} \qquad \mathbf{H} = \begin{vmatrix} 1 & 0 & 0 & 0 & 1 & 1 & 0 \\ 0 & 1 & 0 & 0 & 1 & 1 & 1 \\ 0 & 0 & 1 & 0 & 0 & 1 & 1 \\ 0 & 0 & 0 & 1 & 1 & 0 & 1 \end{vmatrix}$$

show that the row space of **G** is the null space of **H**, and vice versa.
10. Prove that $x^5 + x^3 + 1$ is irreducible over GF(2).
11. Let S_1 and S_2 be two subspaces of a vector V. Show that the intersection of S_1 and S_2 is also a subspaces in V.
12. Let V be a vector space over a field F. For any element c in F, prove that $c \cdot 0 = 0$.
13. Let m be a positive integer. If m is not prime, prove that the set $\{0, 1, 2, \ldots, m-1\}$ is not a field under modulo-m addition and multiplication.
14. Construct the prime field GF(13) with modulo-13 addition and multiplication. Find all the primitive elements and determine the orders of other elements.
15. Construct the vector space V_5 of all 5-tuples over GF(2). Find a three-dimensional subspace and determine its null space.
16. Prove that if β is an element of order n in GF(2^m), all its conjugates have the same order n.

chapter 5

LINEAR BLOCK CODES

5.1 INTRODUCTION

With the advent of digital computers and digital data communication systems, information is coded in binary digits '0' or '1'. This binary information sequence is segmented into *message* blocks of fixed length in block coding. Each message block consists of k-information bits and is denoted by $\mathbf{u}$. Thus, there may be 2^k distinct messages. According to certain rules, this message $\mathbf{u}$ is then transformed into a binary n-tuple $\mathbf{v}$, with $n > k$. The binary n-tuple $\mathbf{v}$ is referred to as the *code* vector (or *code* word) of the message $\mathbf{u}$. Thus, there may be 2^k distinct code vectors corresponding to 2^k distinct possible message vectors. The set of these 2^k distinct code vectors is known as *block* code. A desirable property for block codes is linearity, which means that its code words satisfy the condition that the sum of any two code words gives another code word.

Definition 5.1: A block code c of length n consisting of 2^k code words is known as a *linear* (n, k) code if and only if the 2^k code words form a k-dimensional subspace of the vector space V_n of all the n-tuples over the field GF(2).

It may be seen that in a binary linear code, the modulo-2 sum of any pair of code words gives another code word. Another very desirable property for a linear block code is to possess the *systematic structure* of the code as illustrated in Figure 5.1. Here the code word is divided into parts—the message part and the redundant checking part. The message part consists of k unaltered message digits, while the redundant checking part consists of $(n - k)$ digits. A linear block code with this type of structure is referred to as a *linear systematic block code*. The structure may be altered; i.e., the message part of k digits can come first followed by $(n - k)$ digits of redundant checking part.

Redundant checking part ($n - k$ digits)	Message part (k digits)

Figure 5.1 *Systematic Form of a Code Word*

5.2 GENERATOR MATRICES

From the definition of the linear code, we see that it is possible to find k linearly independent code words, $\mathbf{g}_0, \mathbf{g}_1, \mathbf{g}_2, \ldots, \mathbf{g}_{k-1}$, in c such that every code word $\mathbf{v}$ in c is a linear combination of these k code words. Thus, it may be said that

$$\mathbf{v} = u_0\mathbf{g}_0 + u_1\mathbf{g}_1 + u_2\mathbf{g}_2 + \ldots + u_{k-1}\mathbf{g}_{k-1} \tag{5.1}$$

where $u_i = 0$ or 1 for $0 \le i \le k$. These k linearly independent code words may be arranged as the rows of a $k \times n$ matrix as follows:

$$\mathbf{G} = \begin{bmatrix} \mathbf{g}_0 \\ \mathbf{g}_1 \\ \vdots \\ \mathbf{g}_{k-1} \end{bmatrix} = \begin{bmatrix} g_{00} & g_{01} & g_{02} & \cdots & g_{0,n-1} \\ g_{10} & g_{11} & g_{12} & \cdots & g_{1,n-1} \\ \vdots & \vdots & \vdots & \ddots & \vdots \\ g_{k-1,0} & g_{k-1,1} & g_{k-1,2} & \cdots & g_{k-1,n-1} \end{bmatrix} \tag{5.2}$$

where $\mathbf{g}_i = (g_{i0}, g_{i1}, g_{i2}, ..., g_{i,n-1})$ for $0 \le i \le k$. Let us consider the message to be encoded is $\mathbf{u} = (u_0, u_1, u_2, ..., u_{k-1})$. Thus, the corresponding code word is given as follows:

$$\begin{aligned}\mathbf{v} &= \mathbf{u} \cdot \mathbf{G} \\ &= (u_0, u_1, u_2, ..., u_{k-1}) \cdot \begin{bmatrix} \mathbf{g}_0 \\ \mathbf{g}_1 \\ \mathbf{g}_2 \\ \vdots \\ \mathbf{g}_{k-1} \end{bmatrix} \\ &= u_0\mathbf{g}_0 + u_1\mathbf{g}_1 + u_2\mathbf{g}_2 + \dots + u_{k-1}\mathbf{g}_{k-1}\end{aligned} \tag{5.3}$$

Thus, the rows of **G** *generate* the (n, k) linear code c. Hence, the matrix **G** is known as *generator matrix* for c. A point to be remembered is that any k linearly independent code words of c can be used to form a generator matrix.

Example 5.1: Determine the set of code words for the (7, 4) code with the generator matrix

$$\mathbf{G} = \begin{bmatrix} \mathbf{g}_0 \\ \mathbf{g}_1 \\ \mathbf{g}_2 \\ \mathbf{g}_3 \end{bmatrix} = \begin{bmatrix} 1 & 1 & 0 & 1 & 0 & 0 & 0 \\ 0 & 1 & 1 & 0 & 1 & 0 & 0 \\ 1 & 1 & 1 & 0 & 0 & 1 & 0 \\ 1 & 0 & 1 & 0 & 0 & 0 & 1 \end{bmatrix}$$

Solution: First we consider all the 16 possible message words (0 0 0 0), (1 0 0 0), (0 1 0 0), ..., (1 1 1 1). Substituting **G** and u = (1 0 0 0) into Eq. (5.3) gives the code word as follows:

$$c = (1\ 0\ 0\ 0) \cdot \begin{bmatrix} 1 & 1 & 0 & 1 & 0 & 0 & 0 \\ 0 & 1 & 1 & 0 & 1 & 0 & 0 \\ 1 & 1 & 1 & 0 & 0 & 1 & 0 \\ 1 & 0 & 1 & 0 & 0 & 0 & 1 \end{bmatrix} = (1\ 1\ 0\ 1\ 0\ 0\ 0)$$

Similarly, substituting all other values of u, we may find out the other code words. Just to illustrate the process, we find out another code word by substituting u = (1 1 1 1) which gives

$$c = (1\ 1\ 1\ 1) \cdot \begin{bmatrix} 1 & 1 & 0 & 1 & 0 & 0 & 0 \\ 0 & 1 & 1 & 0 & 1 & 0 & 0 \\ 1 & 1 & 1 & 0 & 0 & 1 & 0 \\ 1 & 0 & 1 & 0 & 0 & 0 & 1 \end{bmatrix} = (1\ 1\ 1\ 1\ 1\ 1\ 1)$$

The total linear block code for the given generator matrix is shown in Table 5.1.

Table 5.1 *The (7, 4) Linear Block Code*

Messages (u)	Code Words (c)
(0 0 0 0)	(0 0 0 0 0 0 0)
(1 0 0 0)	(1 1 0 1 0 0 0)
(0 1 0 0)	(0 1 1 0 1 0 0)
(1 1 0 0)	(1 0 1 1 1 0 0)
(0 0 1 0)	(1 1 1 0 0 1 0)

Messages (u)	Code Words (c)
(1 0 1 0)	(0 0 1 1 0 1 0)
(0 1 1 0)	(1 0 0 0 1 1 0)
(1 1 1 0)	(0 1 0 1 1 1 0)
(0 0 0 1)	(1 0 1 0 0 0 1)
(1 0 0 1)	(0 1 1 1 0 0 1)
(0 1 0 1)	(1 1 0 0 1 0 1)
(1 1 0 1)	(0 0 0 1 1 0 1)
(0 0 1 1)	(0 1 0 0 0 1 1)
(1 0 1 1)	(1 0 0 1 0 1 1)
(0 1 1 1)	(0 0 1 0 1 1 1)
(1 1 1 1)	(1 1 1 1 1 1 1)

From Example 5.1, it is clear that the resultant code words are in systematic form, as the last four digits of each code word are actually the four unaltered message digits. This is possible since the generator matrix is in the form of **G** = [**P** $\;$ **I**$_4$], where **I**$_4$ is an 4 × 4 identity matrix. Thus, a linear systematic (n, k) code may be completely specified by a $k \times n$ matrix **G** of the following form:

$$\mathbf{G} = \begin{bmatrix} \mathbf{g}_0 \\ \mathbf{g}_1 \\ \vdots \\ \mathbf{g}_{k-1} \end{bmatrix} = \left[\underbrace{\begin{matrix} p_{00} & p_{01} & p_{02} & \cdots & p_{0,n-k-1} \\ p_{10} & p_{11} & p_{12} & \cdots & p_{1,n-k-1} \\ \vdots & \vdots & \vdots & \ddots & \vdots \\ p_{k-1,0} & p_{k-1,1} & p_{k-1,2} & \cdots & p_{k-1,n-k-1} \end{matrix}}_{\mathbf{P}\text{ matrix}} \middle| \underbrace{\begin{matrix} 1 & 0 & 0 & \cdots & 0 \\ 0 & 1 & 0 & \cdots & 0 \\ \vdots & \vdots & \vdots & \ddots & \vdots \\ 0 & 0 & 0 & \cdots & 1 \end{matrix}}_{k \times k \text{ identity matrix } (\mathbf{I}_k)} \right] \tag{5.4}$$

where $p_{ij} = 0$ or 1. Thus, **G** = [**P** $\;$ **I**$_k$] , where **I**$_k$ denote the $k \times k$ identity matrix.

However, a generator matrix **G** may not necessarily be in a systematic form. In such a case, it generates a nonsystematic code. If two generator matrices differ only by elementary row operations, i.e., by swapping any two rows or by adding any row to another row, then the matrices generate the same set of code words and hence the same code. Alternatively if two matrices differ by column permutations then the code words generated by the matrices will differ by the order of the occurrence of the bits. Two codes differing only by a permutation of bits are said to be *equivalent*. It may be shown that every linear code is equivalent to a systematic linear code and hence every nonsystematic generator matrix can be put into a systematic form by column permutations and elementary row operations.

Example 5.2: A generator matrix the (5, 3) linear code is given by

$$\mathbf{G} = \begin{bmatrix} \mathbf{g}_0 \\ \mathbf{g}_1 \\ \mathbf{g}_2 \end{bmatrix} = \begin{bmatrix} 1 & 0 & 1 & 0 & 0 \\ 0 & 1 & 0 & 0 & 1 \\ 0 & 1 & 1 & 1 & 0 \end{bmatrix}$$

Determine both the systematic and nonsystematic forms of the code words.

Solution: Here **G** is not of the systematic form (i.e., **G** ≠ [**P** $\;$ **I**$_k$]). To express **G** in systematic form, some elementary row operations have to be performed. It means we have to express **G** as **G** = [**P** $\;$ **I**$_3$], where $\mathbf{I}_3$ is a 3 × 3 identity matrix and **P** is a 3 × 2 matrix. It is helpful to include a line in **G** showing where the matrix is augmented. To reduce **G** in systematic form, we first need to swap the positions of row 2 and row 3. This gives

$$\mathbf{G} = \begin{bmatrix} 1 & 0 & 1 & 0 & 0 \\ 0 & 1 & 1 & 1 & 0 \\ 0 & 1 & 0 & 0 & 1 \end{bmatrix}$$

Then we add row 1 to row 2 to give

$$\mathbf{G} = \begin{bmatrix} 1 & 0 & 1 & 0 & 0 \\ 1 & 1 & 0 & 1 & 0 \\ 0 & 1 & 0 & 0 & 1 \end{bmatrix}$$

This is the required systematic form. Table 5.2 shows the resulting nonsystematic and systematic code words.

Table 5.2 *The (5, 3) Linear Block Code*

Nonsystematic Code Words		Systematic Code Words	
Messages (u)	Code Words (c)	Messages (u)	Code Words (c)
(0 0 0)	(0 0 0 0 0)	(0 0 0)	(0 0 0 0 0)
(1 0 0)	(1 0 1 0 0)	(1 0 0)	(1 0 1 0 0)
(0 1 0)	(0 1 0 0 1)	(0 1 0)	(1 1 0 1 0)
(1 1 0)	(1 1 1 0 1)	(1 1 0)	(0 1 1 1 0)
(0 0 1)	(0 1 1 1 0)	(0 0 1)	(0 1 0 0 1)
(1 0 1)	(1 1 0 1 0)	(1 0 1)	(1 1 1 0 1)
(0 1 1)	(0 0 1 1 1)	(0 1 1)	(1 0 0 1 1)
(1 1 1)	(1 0 0 1 1)	(1 1 1)	(0 0 1 1 1)

The code words generated by a systematic and a nonsystematic generator matrix of a linear code differ only in the mapping or correspondence between message words and code words. For example, the (5, 3) linear code with nonsystematic and systematic code words shown in Table 5.2 have the same set of code words but arranged in a different order. In both the cases, the mapping between the message words and code words is unique and hence either set of code words can be used to represent the message words. Thus, we can clearly see that a linear code does not have a unique generator matrix. Rather many generator matrices exist, all of which are equivalent and generate equivalent codes.

5.3 PARITY-CHECK MATRICES

There is another very important matrix associated with every linear block code. We have already discussed in Chapter 4 that for any $m \times n$ matrix **G**, there exists an $(n - m) \times n$ matrix **H** such that any vector in the row space of **G** is orthogonal to the rows of **H**. This is similarly true for the $k \times n$ generator matrix **G** discussed in this chapter. Thus, there exists an $(n - k) \times n$ matrix **H** with vectors orthogonal to the vectors in **G**. This matrix **H** is known as the *parity-check matrix* of the code. Parity-check matrix is used at the decoding stage to determine the error syndrome of the code. This will be discussed in detail in the following section.

5.3.1 Dual Code

Since **H** is an $(n-k) \times n$ matrix, the 2^{n-k} linear combinations of the rows can form an $(n, n-k)$ linear code c_d. This code is the null space of the (n, k) linear code c generated by the matrix **G**. The code c_d is known as the *dual code* of c. Thus, it may be said that a parity-check matrix for a linear code c is the generator matrix for its dual code c_d.

If **G** of an (n, k) linear code is expressed in systematic form, the parity-check matrix **H** will be of the form:

$$\mathbf{H} = [\mathbf{I}_{n-k} \quad \mathbf{P}^T] \tag{5.5}$$

Here $\mathbf{P}^T$ is the transpose of **P** and is hence an $(n-k) \times k$ matrix and $\mathbf{I}_{n-k}$ is an $(n-k) \times (n-k)$ identity matrix. Thus, **H** may be represented in the following form:

$$\mathbf{H} = \left[\begin{array}{ccccc|ccccc} 1 & 0 & 0 & \cdots & 0 & p_{00} & p_{01} & p_{20} & \cdots & p_{k-1,0} \\ 0 & 1 & 0 & \cdots & 0 & p_{01} & p_{11} & p_{21} & \cdots & p_{k-1,1} \\ \vdots & \vdots & \vdots & \ddots & \vdots & \vdots & \vdots & \vdots & \ddots & \vdots \\ 0 & 0 & 0 & \cdots & 1 & p_{0,n-k-1} & p_{1,n-k-1} & p_{2,n-k-1} & \cdots & p_{k-1,n-k-1} \end{array}\right] \tag{5.6}$$

These $(n-k)$ rows of **H** are linearly independent.

Example 5.3: Determine the parity-check matrix of the (7, 4) code with the generator matrix

$$\mathbf{G} = \begin{bmatrix} 1 & 1 & 0 & 1 & 0 & 0 & 0 \\ 0 & 1 & 1 & 0 & 1 & 0 & 0 \\ 1 & 1 & 1 & 0 & 0 & 1 & 0 \\ 1 & 0 & 1 & 0 & 0 & 0 & 1 \end{bmatrix}$$

Solution: The given generator matrix **G** for the (7, 4) code may be expressed as $\mathbf{G} = [\mathbf{P} \quad \mathbf{I}_4]$, where $\mathbf{I}_4$ is a 4×4 identity matrix and

$$\mathbf{P} = \begin{bmatrix} 1 & 1 & 0 \\ 0 & 1 & 1 \\ 1 & 1 & 1 \\ 1 & 0 & 1 \end{bmatrix}$$

The transpose of **P** is given by

$$\mathbf{P}^T = \begin{bmatrix} 1 & 0 & 1 & 1 \\ 1 & 1 & 1 & 0 \\ 0 & 1 & 1 & 1 \end{bmatrix}$$

The parity-check matrix is expressed as $\mathbf{H} = [\mathbf{I}_3 \quad \mathbf{P}^T]$, where $\mathbf{I}_3$ is an 3×3 identity matrix.

Thus, **H** is given by

$$\mathbf{H} = \begin{bmatrix} 1 & 0 & 0 & 1 & 0 & 1 & 1 \\ 0 & 1 & 0 & 1 & 1 & 1 & 0 \\ 0 & 0 & 1 & 0 & 1 & 1 & 1 \end{bmatrix}$$

Since $\mathbf{G} = [\mathbf{P} \quad \mathbf{I}_k]$ and $\mathbf{H} = [\mathbf{I}_{n-k} \quad \mathbf{P}^T]$, the product of **G** and the transpose of **H** of an (n, k) linear code is given by:

$$\mathbf{G} \cdot \mathbf{H}^T = [\mathbf{P} \quad \mathbf{I}_k] \cdot [\mathbf{I}_{n-k} \quad \mathbf{P}^T]^T \tag{5.7}$$

It is seen that $[\mathbf{P} \quad \mathbf{I}_k] = \mathbf{P}$, where the order is $[k \times (n-k)] \times (k \times k) = k \times (n-k)$. Similarly, $[\mathbf{I}_{n-k} \quad \mathbf{P}^T] = \mathbf{P}$ with order $[(n-k) \times (n-k)] \times [k \times (n-k)] = k \times (n-k)$. Hence, from Eq. (5.7) we have

$$\begin{aligned}\mathbf{G} \cdot \mathbf{H}^T &= \mathbf{P}\mathbf{I}_k + \mathbf{I}_{n-k}\mathbf{P} \\ &= \mathbf{P} + \mathbf{P} \\ &= 0\end{aligned} \tag{5.8}$$

If there is an n-tuple $\mathbf{v}$, which is a code word in c, we know $\mathbf{v} = \mathbf{u} \cdot \mathbf{G}$ and multiplying this by $\mathbf{H}^T$ gives:

$$\mathbf{v} \cdot \mathbf{H}^T = (\mathbf{u} \cdot \mathbf{G}) \cdot \mathbf{H}^T = \mathbf{u} \cdot (\mathbf{G} \cdot \mathbf{H}^T)$$

However, from Eq. (5.8), $\mathbf{G} \cdot \mathbf{H}^T = 0$ and hence $\mathbf{v} \cdot \mathbf{H}^T = 0$. Thus, for any linear code and parity-check matrix $\mathbf{H}$, we have

$$\mathbf{v} \cdot \mathbf{H}^T = 0 \tag{5.9}$$

Example 5.4: Determine the parity-check matrix $\mathbf{H}$ for the (5, 3) code. Show that $\mathbf{G} \cdot \mathbf{H}^T = 0$ and $\mathbf{v} \cdot \mathbf{H}^T = 0$ for $\mathbf{v} = (1\ 1\ 0\ 1\ 0)$

$$\mathbf{G} = \begin{bmatrix} 1 & 0 & 1 & 0 & 0 \\ 1 & 1 & 0 & 1 & 0 \\ 0 & 1 & 0 & 0 & 1 \end{bmatrix}$$

Solution: From the given generator matrix $\mathbf{G}$, we get the parity matrix $\mathbf{P}$ as follows:

$$\mathbf{P} = \begin{bmatrix} 1 & 0 \\ 1 & 1 \\ 0 & 1 \end{bmatrix}$$

The parity-check matrix is given by $\mathbf{H} = [\mathbf{I}_{n-k} \quad \mathbf{P}^T]$, and hence

$$\mathbf{H} = \begin{bmatrix} 1 & 0 & 1 & 1 & 0 \\ 0 & 1 & 0 & 1 & 1 \end{bmatrix}$$

The product $\mathbf{G} \cdot \mathbf{H}^T$ gives

$$\mathbf{G} \cdot \mathbf{H}^T = \begin{bmatrix} 1 & 0 & 1 & 0 & 0 \\ 1 & 1 & 0 & 1 & 0 \\ 0 & 1 & 0 & 0 & 1 \end{bmatrix} \begin{bmatrix} 1 & 0 \\ 0 & 1 \\ 1 & 0 \\ 1 & 1 \\ 0 & 1 \end{bmatrix}$$

$$= \begin{bmatrix} 1+1 & 0 \\ 1+1 & 1+1 \\ 0 & 1+1 \end{bmatrix}$$

$$= \begin{bmatrix} 0 & 0 \\ 0 & 0 \\ 0 & 0 \end{bmatrix}$$

Thus, $\mathbf{G} \cdot \mathbf{H}^T = 0$ as required.

Given $\mathbf{v} = (1\ 1\ 0\ 1\ 0)$. Hence,

$$\mathbf{v} \cdot \mathbf{H}^T = (1\ \ 1\ \ 0\ \ 1\ \ 0) \cdot \begin{bmatrix} 1 & 0 \\ 0 & 1 \\ 1 & 0 \\ 1 & 1 \\ 0 & 1 \end{bmatrix}$$

$$= [1{\cdot}1 + 1{\cdot}0 + 0{\cdot}1 + 1{\cdot}1 + 0{\cdot}0 \quad 1{\cdot}0 + 1{\cdot}1 + 0{\cdot}0 + 1{\cdot}1 + 0{\cdot}1]$$

$$= [1 + 1 \quad 1 + 1]$$

$$= [0 \quad 0]$$

Hence, $\mathbf{v} \cdot \mathbf{H}^T = 0$ as required.

5.4 ERROR SYNDROME

We consider an (n, k) linear code generated by the generator matrix **G** and having parity-check matrix **H**. Let us consider that **v** is a transmitted (n, k) code word over a channel and **r** is the corresponding received code word at the receiver end of the channel. If the channel is noisy then the received code word **r** may be different form the transmitted code word **v**. If we denote the received erroneous code word by the vector **e**, then it may be said that

$$\mathbf{e} = \mathbf{v} + \mathbf{r} \tag{5.10}$$

Here **e** is also an n-tuple where $e_i = 0$ for $r_i = v_i$, and $e_i = 1$ for $r_i \neq v_i$. This n-tuple vector **e** is also known as the *error vector* (or *error pattern*). The 1's in **e** are the *transmitted errors* caused by the channel noise. From Eq. (5.10) it follows:

$$\mathbf{r} = \mathbf{v} + \mathbf{e} \tag{5.11}$$

The receiver is unaware of either **v** or **e**. Hence, after receiving **r**, the decoder must first determine whether there is any transmission error within **r**. To do this, the decoder computes the $(n - k)$ tuple as follows:

$$\mathbf{s} = \mathbf{r} \cdot \mathbf{H}^T \tag{5.12}$$

$$= (\, s_0\, s_1\, s_2 \ldots s_{n-k-1})$$

The vector **s** is called the *syndrome* of **r**. If there is no error (i.e., $\mathbf{e} = 0$), then $\mathbf{r} = \mathbf{v}$ (i.e., a valid code word) and $\mathbf{s} = 0$ (since $\mathbf{v} \cdot \mathbf{H}^T = 0$). On the other hand, if an error is detected (i.e., $\mathbf{e} \neq 0$), then $\mathbf{r} \neq \mathbf{v}$. In such a case, $\mathbf{s} \neq 0$.

5.4.1 Undetectable Error Pattern

It may happen that the errors in certain vectors are not detectable. This happens if the error pattern **e** is identical to a nonzero code word. In such a case, **r** is the sum of two code words which is also another code word, and thus $\mathbf{r} \cdot \mathbf{H}^T = 0$. This type of error patterns are known as *undetectable error patterns*. Thus, all valid nonzero code words become undetectable error patterns. Since there are $2^k - 1$ valid nonzero code words, there are $2^k - 1$ undetectable error patterns. Hence, when an undetectable error pattern occurs, the decoder makes a *decoding error*.

The syndrome digits may be computed from Eqs. (5.6) and (5.12) as follows:

$$s_0 = r_0 + r_{n-k}p_{00} + r_{n-k+1}p_{10} + r_{n-k+2}p_{20} + \ldots + r_{n-1}p_{k-1,0}$$

$$s_1 = r_1 + r_{n-k}p_{01} + r_{n-k+1}p_{11} + r_{n-k+2}p_{21} + \ldots + r_{n-1}p_{k-1,1}$$

$$s_2 = r_2 + r_{n-k}p_{02} + r_{n-k+1}p_{12} + r_{n-k+2}p_{22} + \ldots + r_{n-1}p_{k-1,2} \tag{5.13}$$

$$\vdots$$

$$s_{n-k-1} = r_{n-k-1} + r_{n-k}p_{0,n-k-1} + r_{n-k+1}p_{1,n-k-1} + \ldots + r_{n-1}p_{k-1,n-k-1}$$

Thus, from Eq. (5.13), we find that the syndrome **s** is simply the vector sum of the received parity digits $(r_0, r_1, r_2, \ldots, r_{n-k-1})$ and the parity-check digits recomputed from the received message digits $(r_{n-k}, r_{n-k+1}, r_{n-k+2}, \ldots, r_{n-1})$.

Example 5.5: Compute the error syndrome for the (7, 4) linear code whose parity-check matrix is similar to that computed in Example 5.3. Also design the syndrome circuit for the code.

Solution: Let us consider that **r** is the received 7-tuple vector. Then the syndrome **s** will be a 7 – 4 or 3-tuple vector. Let us denote $\mathbf{s} = (s_0, s_1, s_2)$. Hence, we have

$$\begin{aligned}\mathbf{s} &= (s_0, s_1, s_2)\\ &= \mathbf{r}\cdot\mathbf{H}^T\\ &= (r_0, r_1, r_2, r_3, r_4, r_5, r_6)\begin{bmatrix}1&0&0\\0&1&0\\0&0&1\\1&1&0\\0&1&1\\1&1&1\\1&0&1\end{bmatrix}\end{aligned}$$

Thus, the syndrome digits are

$$\begin{aligned}s_0 &= r_0 + r_3 + r_5 + r_6\\ s_1 &= r_1 + r_3 + r_4 + r_5\\ s_2 &= r_2 + r_4 + r_5 + r_6\end{aligned}$$

The syndrome circuit for the code is illustrated in Figure 5.2.

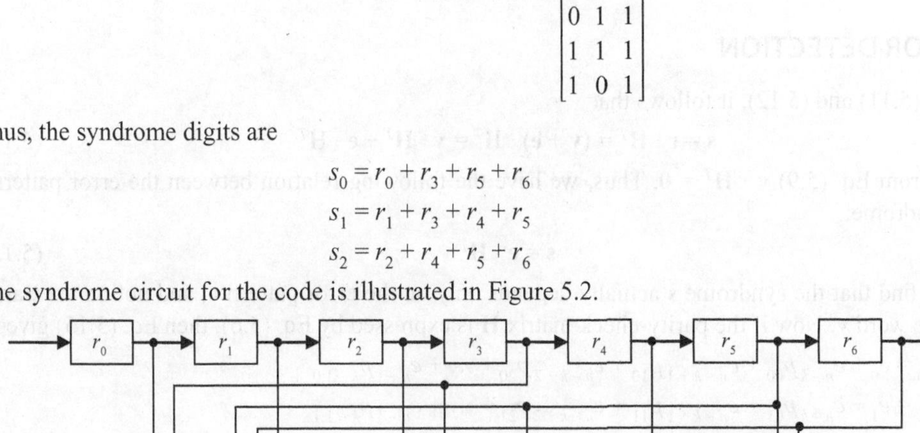

Figure 5.2 *Syndrome Circuit for the (7, 4) Linear Code of Example 5.5*

Example 5.6: Assume that $\mathbf{r}_1$ and $\mathbf{r}_2$ represent two received code words of the (7, 4) linear code that have incurred errors. Compute the error syndromes of $\mathbf{r}_1 = (1\ 0\ 1\ 0\ 0\ 1\ 1)$ and $\mathbf{r}_2 = (1\ 1\ 1\ 1\ 0\ 0\ 0)$. The parity-check matrix is similar to that computed in Example 5.3.

Solution: Using the parity-check matrix for (7, 4) linear code similar to that computed in Example 5.3, we have the syndrome for the first received code word $\mathbf{r}_1$ as follows:

$$\mathbf{s}_1 = \mathbf{r}_1 \cdot \mathbf{H}^T$$

$$= (1\ \ 0\ \ 1\ \ 0\ \ 0\ \ 1\ \ 1)\begin{bmatrix} 1 & 0 & 0 \\ 0 & 1 & 0 \\ 0 & 0 & 1 \\ 1 & 1 & 0 \\ 0 & 1 & 1 \\ 1 & 1 & 1 \\ 1 & 0 & 1 \end{bmatrix}$$

$$= (1\ \ \ 1\ \ \ 1)$$

Similarly for $\mathbf{r}_2$, we may compute the error syndromes as follows:

$$\mathbf{s}_2 = \mathbf{r}_2 \cdot \mathbf{H}^T = (0\ 0\ 1)$$

5.5 ERROR DETECTION

From Eqs. (5.11) and (5.12), it follows that

$$\mathbf{s} = \mathbf{r} \cdot \mathbf{H}^T = (\mathbf{v} + \mathbf{e}) \cdot \mathbf{H}^T = \mathbf{v} \cdot \mathbf{H}^T + \mathbf{e} \cdot \mathbf{H}^T \tag{5.14}$$

However, from Eq. (5.9) $\mathbf{v} \cdot \mathbf{H}^T = 0$. Thus, we have the following relation between the error patterns and the syndrome:

$$\mathbf{s} = \mathbf{e} \cdot \mathbf{H}^T \tag{5.15}$$

Hence, we find that the syndrome **s** actually depends only on the error pattern **e**, and not on the transmitted code word **v**. Now if the parity-check matrix **H** is expressed by Eq. (5.6), then Eq. (5.15) gives

$$\begin{aligned}
s_0 &= e_0 + e_{n-k}p_{00} + e_{n-k+1}p_{10} + e_{n-k+2}p_{20} + \ldots + e_{n-1}p_{k-1,0} \\
s_1 &= e_1 + e_{n-k}p_{01} + e_{n-k+1}p_{11} + e_{n-k+2}p_{21} + \ldots + e_{n-1}p_{k-1,1} \\
s_2 &= e_2 + e_{n-k}p_{02} + e_{n-k+1}p_{12} + e_{n-k+2}p_{22} + \ldots + e_{n-1}p_{k-1,2} \\
&\vdots \\
s_{n-k-1} &= e_{n-k-1} + e_{n-k}p_{0,n-k-1} + e_{n-k+1}p_{1,n-k-1} + e_{n-k+2}p_{2,n-k-1} + \ldots + e_{n-1}p_{k-1,n-k-1}
\end{aligned} \tag{5.16}$$

It may seem that by solving the $(n-k)$ linear equations of (5.16), the error pattern **e** can be found out and therefore the vector $(\mathbf{r} + \mathbf{e})$ will be the actual transmitted code word **v**. The problem that arises in the $(n-k)$ linear equations of (5.16) is that they do not have a unique solution but have 2^k solutions. Hence, there are 2^k error patterns which will result in the same syndrome. However, the true error patterns **e** is just one among them. Hence, the decoder has to determine the true error pattern from a set of 2^k error patterns. However, it is seen that if the channel is a BSC, the *most probable error pattern* is that which has the least number of 1's. Thus, the decoder makes a choice of that error pattern which has smallest number of nonzero digits. Let us clarify it with an example.

Example 5.7: Assume that the actual code word sent over a BSC is **v** = (1 0 1 0 0 0 1). While received code word is **r** which is same as $\mathbf{r}_1$ in Example 5.6. Correct the error occurred in the transmitted code word. The parity-check matrix is similar to that computed in Example 5.3.

Solution: From Example 5.6, we know that the computed syndrome for the received code word is **s** = (1 1 1). Now the receiver has to determine the true error pattern that may produce the computed syndrome. From Eqs. (5.15) and (5.16), we may write the equations relating the syndrome and error digits as follows:

$$1 = e_0 + e_3 + e_5 + e_6$$
$$1 = e_1 + e_3 + e_4 + e_5$$
$$1 = e_2 + e_4 + e_5 + e_6$$

Now there are $2^4 = 16$ error patterns that satisfy the above equations. They are as follows:

$$\mathbf{e}_1 = (0\ \ 0\ \ 0\ \ 0\ \ 0\ \ 1\ \ 0) \qquad \mathbf{e}_2 = (1\ \ 1\ \ 1\ \ 0\ \ 0\ \ 0\ \ 0)$$
$$\mathbf{e}_3 = (1\ \ 1\ \ 0\ \ 1\ \ 0\ \ 1\ \ 0) \qquad \mathbf{e}_4 = (0\ \ 0\ \ 1\ \ 1\ \ 0\ \ 0\ \ 0)$$
$$\mathbf{e}_5 = (0\ \ 1\ \ 0\ \ 0\ \ 0\ \ 0\ \ 1) \qquad \mathbf{e}_6 = (1\ \ 0\ \ 0\ \ 0\ \ 1\ \ 0\ \ 0)$$
$$\mathbf{e}_7 = (1\ \ 0\ \ 0\ \ 1\ \ 0\ \ 0\ \ 1) \qquad \mathbf{e}_8 = (0\ \ 1\ \ 0\ \ 1\ \ 1\ \ 0\ \ 0)$$
$$\mathbf{e}_9 = (0\ \ 1\ \ 1\ \ 1\ \ 0\ \ 1\ \ 1) \qquad \mathbf{e}_{10} = (1\ \ 0\ \ 1\ \ 1\ \ 1\ \ 1\ \ 0)$$
$$\mathbf{e}_{11} = (1\ \ 1\ \ 1\ \ 1\ \ 1\ \ 0\ \ 1) \qquad \mathbf{e}_{12} = (0\ \ 0\ \ 1\ \ 0\ \ 1\ \ 0\ \ 1)$$
$$\mathbf{e}_{13} = (1\ \ 0\ \ 1\ \ 0\ \ 0\ \ 1\ \ 1) \qquad \mathbf{e}_{14} = (0\ \ 0\ \ 0\ \ 1\ \ 1\ \ 1\ \ 1)$$
$$\mathbf{e}_{15} = (1\ \ 1\ \ 0\ \ 0\ \ 1\ \ 1\ \ 1) \qquad \mathbf{e}_{16} = (0\ \ 1\ \ 1\ \ 0\ \ 1\ \ 1\ \ 0)$$

Since the channel is a BSC, the most probable error pattern is that which has the least number of 1's. Hence, from the above 16 error patterns, we see that the most probable error pattern that satisfies the above equations is $\mathbf{e}_1$ = (0 0 0 0 0 1 0). Thus, the receiver decodes the received vector $\mathbf{r}_1$ as

$$\begin{aligned}\mathbf{v}' &= \mathbf{r} + \mathbf{e}\\ &= (1\,0\,1\,0\,0\,1\,1) + (0\,0\,0\,0\,0\,1\,0)\\ &= (1\,0\,1\,0\,0\,0\,1)\end{aligned}$$

We find that **v**′ is same as the transmitted code word **v**. Thus, the error has been corrected by the receiver.

5.6 MINIMUM DISTANCE

In a block code, parity bits added with the message bits increase the separation or distance between the code words. The concept of distance between code words, and in particular the *minimum distance* within a code, is fundamental to error-control codes. This parameter determines the random-error-detecting and random-error-correcting capabilities of a code. The *Hamming weight* (or simply weight) of a binary *n*-tuple **v** is defined as the number of nonzero components of **v** and is denoted by *w*(**v**). For example, the Hamming weight of **v** = (1 1 0 0 1 1 1) is 5. The Hamming distance between two words $\mathbf{v}_1$ and $\mathbf{v}_2$, having same number of bits, is defined as the number of places in which they differ and is denoted by $d(\mathbf{v}_1, \mathbf{v}_2)$.

For example, the code words $\mathbf{v}_1$ = (1 0 1 0 0 0 1) and $\mathbf{v}_2$ = (0 1 1 1 0 0 1) are separated in the zeroth, first, and third places and thus have Hamming distance of 3. Now the Hamming weight of the sum of $\mathbf{v}_1$ and $\mathbf{v}_2$ is as follows:

$$
\begin{aligned}
w(\mathbf{v}_1 + \mathbf{v}_2) &= w[(1\ \ 0\ \ 1\ \ 0\ \ 0\ \ 0\ \ 1) + (0\ \ 1\ \ 1\ \ 1\ \ 0\ \ 0\ \ 1)] \\
&= w(1\ \ 1\ \ 0\ \ 1\ \ 0\ \ 0\ \ 0) \\
&= 3
\end{aligned}
$$

Thus, it may be written as follows:

$$d(\mathbf{v}_1, \mathbf{v}_2) = w(\mathbf{v}_1, + \mathbf{v}_2) \tag{5.17}$$

It may be proved that the Hamming distance satisfies the *triangle inequality*. If $\mathbf{v}_1$, $\mathbf{v}_2$, and $\mathbf{v}_3$ are the n-tuples in c, then

$$d(\mathbf{v}_1, \mathbf{v}_2) + d(\mathbf{v}_2, \mathbf{v}_3) \geq d(\mathbf{v}_1, \mathbf{v}_3) \tag{5.18}$$

Definition 5.2: The *minimum distance* $d_{\min}$ of a block code c is the smallest distance between code words. Mathematically it is expressed as follows:

$$d_{\min} = \min\{d(\mathbf{v}_1, \mathbf{v}_2): \mathbf{v}_1, \mathbf{v}_2 \in c, \mathbf{v}_1 \neq \mathbf{v}_2\} \tag{5.19}$$

The minimum distance of a block code has the following property:

Property 1: The minimum distance of a linear block code is equal to the minimum weight of its nonzero code words. Mathematically it may be expressed as follows:

$$d_{\min} = w_{\min} \tag{5.20}$$

5.7 ERROR-DETECTING CAPABILITY

For a block code c with minimum distance $d_{\min}$, it is obvious from Eq. (5.20) that there cannot remain any code word with weight less than $d_{\min}$. Let a code vector $\mathbf{v}$ be transmitted over a noisy channel and be received as a vector $\mathbf{r}$. Due to some error pattern within the channel, $\mathbf{r}$ is different from the transmitted vector $\mathbf{v}$. If the error pattern is less than or equal to $d_{\min} - 1$, then it cannot change one code vector to another, and hence the received vector $\mathbf{r}$ can in no way resemble a valid code word within c. Hence, the error will be definitely detected. Thus, it may be said that a block code c with minimum distance $d_{\min}$ is capable of detecting all error patterns of $d_{\min} - 1$ or fewer errors. However, if the error pattern is of $d_{\min}$ errors, then this error pattern will change the transmitted code vector $\mathbf{v}$ into another valid code vector within c, since at least one pair of code vectors will exist which differs in $d_{\min}$ places. Hence, the error cannot be detected. The same argument applies for error patterns of more than $d_{\min}$ errors. Hence, it may be said that *the random-error-detecting capability of a block code with minimum distance $d_{\min}$ is $d_{\min} - 1$*.

At the same time, it may be seen that the block code with minimum distance $d_{\min}$ is also capable of detecting a large fraction of error patterns with $d_{\min}$ or more errors. For an (n, k) block code there are $2^n - 1$ possible error patterns. Among them there will be $2^k - 1$ error patterns identical to $2^k - 1$ nonzero code words. If any of these $2^k - 1$ error patterns occurs, it alters the transmitted code word $\mathbf{v}$ into another valid code word $\mathbf{w}$ within the block. When $\mathbf{w}$ is received, the computed syndrome is zero, and the decoder accepts $\mathbf{w}$ as the transmitted code word. Hence, the decoder commits an incorrect decoding. Thus, these $2^k - 1$ error patterns are *undetectable*. On the contrary, if the error pattern is not identical to any nonzero code word, then the received vector $\mathbf{r}$ cannot be a code word and hence the computed syndrome is nonzero. Thus, the error gets detected. Therefore, there will be $2^n - 2^k$ error patterns which will not be identical to any of the code words of that (n, k) block code. These $2^n - 2^k$ error patterns are *detectable*. In fact, an (n, k) linear code is capable of detecting $2^n - 2^k$ error patterns of length n.

5.8 ERROR-CORRECTING CAPABILITY

The error correction capability of a block code c is determined by its minimum distance d_{min}. The minimum distance may either be even or odd. We consider that the code c can correct all error patterns of t or fewer bits. The relation between t and the minimum distance d_{min} is given as follows:

$$2t + 1 \leq d_{min} \leq 2t + 2 \tag{5.21}$$

It may be proved that a block code with minimum distance d_{min} corrects all error patterns of $t = (d_{min} - 1)/2$ or fewer errors. The parameter $(d_{min} - 1)/2$ is known as *random-error-correcting capability* of the code. Hence, the code is referred as t error-correcting code.

At the same time t error-correcting code is usually capable of correcting many error patterns of $t + 1$ or more errors. In fact it may be shown that a t error-correcting (n, k) linear code is capable of correcting a total 2^{n-k} error patterns, which includes those with t or fewer errors.

5.9 STANDARD ARRAY AND SYNDROME DECODING

Let $\mathbf{v}_1, \mathbf{v}_2, \mathbf{v}_3, \ldots, \mathbf{v}_{2^k}$ be the 2^k code vectors of the (n, k) linear code c. Irrespective of the code vector transmitted over a noisy channel, the received vector should be any of the 2^n n-tuples. To develop a decoding scheme, all the possible 2^n received vectors are partitioned into 2^k disjoint subsets $d_1, d_2, d_3, \ldots, d_{2^k}$. The code vector $\mathbf{v}_i$ is contained in the subset d_i for $1 \leq i \leq 2^k$. Now if the received vector $\mathbf{r}$ is found in the subset d_i, $\mathbf{r}$ is automatically decoded into $\mathbf{v}_i$.

Let us develop the method to partition all the possible 2^n received vectors into 2^k disjoint subsets. This is done as follows:

1. Place all the 2^k code vectors of c in a row with the all-zero code vector $\mathbf{v}_1 = (0,0,0,\ldots,0)$ as the first element.
2. From the remaining $2^n - 2^k$ n-tuples, choose an n-tuple $\mathbf{e}_1$ and place it under the zero code vector $\mathbf{v}_1$.
3. Now fill in the second row by adding $\mathbf{e}_1$ to each code vector $\mathbf{v}_i$ in the first row and place the sum $\mathbf{v}_i + \mathbf{e}_1$ under $\mathbf{v}_i$.
4. Then another unused n-tuple $\mathbf{e}_2$ is chosen from the remaining n-tuples and is placed under $\mathbf{v}_1$.
5. Form the third row, by adding $\mathbf{e}_2$ to each code vector $\mathbf{v}_i$ in the first row and placing the sum $\mathbf{v}_i + \mathbf{e}_2$ under $\mathbf{v}_i$.
6. Continue this process until all the n-tuples are used.

Thus, an array of rows and columns is constructed as shown in Table 5.3. This array is known as a *standard array*. A very important property of standard array to remember is that two n-tuples in the

Table 5.3 *Standard Array for an (n, k) Linear Code*

$\mathbf{v}_1$	$\mathbf{v}_2$	$\mathbf{v}_3$	…	$\mathbf{v}_i$	…	$\mathbf{v}_{2^k}$
$\mathbf{e}_1$	$\mathbf{v}_2 + \mathbf{e}_1$	$\mathbf{v}_3 + \mathbf{e}_1$	…	$\mathbf{v}_i + \mathbf{e}_1$	…	$\mathbf{v}_{2^k} + \mathbf{e}_1$
$\mathbf{e}_2$	$\mathbf{v}_2 + \mathbf{e}_2$	$\mathbf{v}_3 + \mathbf{e}_2$	…	$\mathbf{v}_i + \mathbf{e}_2$	…	$\mathbf{v}_{2^k} + \mathbf{e}_2$
⋮	⋮	⋮		⋮	⋮	⋮
$\mathbf{e}_l$	$\mathbf{v}_2 + \mathbf{e}_l$	$\mathbf{v}_3 + \mathbf{e}_l$	…	$\mathbf{v}_i + \mathbf{e}_l$	…	$\mathbf{v}_{2^k} + \mathbf{e}_l$
⋮	⋮	⋮		⋮	⋮	⋮
$\mathbf{e}_{2^{n-k}-1}$	$\mathbf{v}_2 + \mathbf{e}_{2^{n-k}-1}$	$\mathbf{v}_3 + \mathbf{e}_{2^{n-k}-1}$	…	$\mathbf{v}_i + \mathbf{e}_{2^{n-k}-1}$	…	$\mathbf{v}_{2^k} + \mathbf{e}_{2^{n-k}-1}$

same row of a standard array cannot be identical and every n-tuple appears in one and only one row. Hence, from the construction of the standard array it is obvious that there are $2^n/2^k = 2^{n-k}$ disjoint rows, where each row consists of 2^k distinct elements.

5.9.1 Coset and Coset Leader

Each row in the standard array is known as the *coset* of the code c and the first element of each coset is called the *coset leader*. Any element of a coset may be used as a coset leader.

Due to the noise over the channel, if the error pattern caused is identical to the coset leader, then the received vector **r** is correctly decoded to the transmitted vector **v**. But if the error pattern caused is not identical to a coset leader, then the decoding will be erroneous. Thus, it may be concluded that the 2^{n-k} coset leaders (including the all zero vector) are the *correctable error* patterns.

Hence, to minimize the probability of an error in decoding, the coset leaders should be chosen in such a way that they happen to be the most probable error patterns. For a BSC, error patterns with lower weight are more probable than those with higher weight. Hence, when a standard array is formed, each coset leader chosen is a vector of least weight from the remaining available vectors. This is illustrated in Example 5.8. Thus, a coset leader has the minimum weight in a coset. In effect, the decoding based on the standard array is the maximum likelihood decoding (or, minimum distance decoding).

In fact, it may be said that for an (n, k) linear code c with minimum distance d_{min}, all the n-tuples of weight $t = (d_{min} - 1)/2$ or less may be used as coset leaders of a standard array of c.

Example 5.8: Construct a standard array for the (5, 2) single-error-correcting code with the following generator matrix.

$$\mathbf{G} = \begin{bmatrix} 1 & 1 & 1 & 1 & 0 \\ 1 & 0 & 1 & 0 & 1 \end{bmatrix}$$

Solution: The four code words will be (0 0 0 0 0), (1 0 1 0 1), (1 1 1 1 0), and (0 1 0 1 1). These code words form the first row of the standard array (as shown in Table 5.4). The second row is formed by taking (1 0 0 0 0) as the coset leader. The row is completed by adding (1 0 0 0 0) to each code word.

Table 5.4 *Standard Array for an (5, 2) Linear Code*

Coset Leader			
0 0 0 0 0	1 0 1 0 1	1 1 1 1 0	0 1 0 1 1
1 0 0 0 0	0 0 1 0 1	0 1 1 1 0	1 1 0 1 1
0 1 0 0 0	1 1 1 0 1	1 0 1 1 0	0 0 0 1 1
0 0 1 0 0	1 0 0 0 1	1 1 0 1 0	0 1 1 1 1
0 0 0 1 0	1 0 1 1 1	1 1 1 0 0	0 1 0 0 1
0 0 0 0 1	1 0 1 0 0	1 1 1 1 1	0 1 0 1 0
1 1 0 0 0	0 1 1 0 1	0 0 1 1 0	1 0 0 1 1
1 0 0 1 0	0 0 1 1 1	0 1 1 0 0	1 1 0 0 1

Rows 3, 4, 5, and 6 are constructed using (0 1 0 0 0), (0 0 1 0 0), (0 0 0 1 0), and (0 0 0 0 1), respectively, as the coset leaders. Till row 6, we find that six words of weight 2 have already been used. Hence, there are four words left with weight 2, namely (1 1 0 0 0), (1 0 0 1 0), (0 1 1 0 0), and (0 0 1 1 0). Any of these may be used to construct the seventh row. We have used (1 1 0 0 0). Finally, (1 0 0 1 0) is used to construct the last row.

We have discussed that the syndrome of an n-tuple is an $(n-k)$-tuple. There are 2^{n-k} distinct $(n-k)$-tuples. There is a one-to-one correspondence between a coset and an $(n-k)$-tuple syndrome. It may be said there is a one-to-one correspondence between a coset leader and a syndrome. If we use this one-to-one correspondence relationship, a much simpler decoding table compared to a standard array may be formed. The table will consist of 2^{n-k} distinct coset leaders and their corresponding syndromes. Such a table is known as *lookup table.* In principle, this technique can be applied to any (n, k) linear code. This method results in minimum decoding delay and minimum error probability.

Using the lookup table, the decoding of a received vector follows the below-mentioned steps:

1. The syndrome of $\mathbf{r}$ is computed as $\mathbf{r} \cdot \mathbf{H}^T$.
2. The coset leader $\mathbf{e}_i$ whose syndrome equals $\mathbf{r} \cdot \mathbf{H}^T$ is located. Then $\mathbf{e}_i$ is assumed to be the error pattern of the channel.
3. Finally, the received vector $\mathbf{r}$ is decoded as $\mathbf{v} = \mathbf{e}_i + \mathbf{r}$.

However, it is to be noted that for large $n-k$, this scheme of decoding becomes impractical. In such case, different other practical decoding schemes are used.

Example 5.9: Construct the lookup table for the (7, 4) linear code as given in Table 5.1. The parity-check matrix is determined in Example 5.3 and is given as follows:

$$\mathbf{H} = \begin{bmatrix} 1 & 0 & 0 & 1 & 0 & 1 & 1 \\ 0 & 1 & 0 & 1 & 1 & 1 & 0 \\ 0 & 0 & 1 & 0 & 1 & 1 & 1 \end{bmatrix}$$

Solution: The code will have $2^3 = 8$ cosets. Thus, there are 8 correctable error patterns which include the all zero vector.

The minimum distance of the code is 3. Hence, it is capable of correcting all error patterns of weight 1 or 0. Thus, all the 7-tuples of weight 1 or 0 can be used as coset leaders. Hence, the lookup table may be constructed as shown in Table 5.5.

Table 5.5 *Lookup Table*

Coset Leaders	Syndromes
(1 0 0 0 0 0 0)	(1 0 0)
(0 1 0 0 0 0 0)	(0 1 0)
(0 0 1 0 0 0 0)	(0 0 1)
(0 0 0 1 0 0 0)	(1 1 0)
(0 0 0 0 1 0 0)	(0 1 1)
(0 0 0 0 0 1 0)	(1 1 1)
(0 0 0 0 0 0 1)	(1 0 1)

5.10 PROBABILITY OF UNDETECTED ERRORS OVER A BSC

For an (n, k) linear code c, if n is large, then undetectable error patterns $2^k - 1$ is much smaller compared to 2^n. Thus, only a small fraction of error patterns remain undetected. We can find the probability of undetected errors from the weight distribution of c. Let there be A_i number of code vectors having weight i in c. Let the weight distribution of c be $\{A_0, A_1, A_2, \dots A_n\}$ Let us denote the probability of an undetected error pattern as $P_u(E)$. We know that an error pattern remains undetected when the error pattern is identical to a nonzero code vector of c. Hence,

$$P_u(E) = \sum_{i=1}^{n} A_i p^i (1-p)^{n-i} \tag{5.22}$$

where p is the transition probability of the BSC. There exists an interesting relationship between the weight distribution of a linear code c and its dual code c_d.

Let us assume that $\{B_0, B_1, B_2, \dots, B_n\}$ be the weight distribution of the dual code c_d, which is represented in the polynomial form as follows:

$$A(x) = A_0 + A_1 x + A_2 x^2 + \dots + A_n x^n,$$

$$B(x) = B_0 + B_1 x + B_2 x^2 + \dots + B_n x^n \tag{5.23}$$

where $A(x)$ and $B(x)$ are related by an identity known as *MacWilliams identity*, and is given as follows:

$$A(x) = 2^{-(n-k)}(1+x)^n B\left(\frac{1-x}{1+x}\right) \tag{5.24}$$

The polynomials $A(x)$ and $B(x)$ are known as the *weight enumerators* for the (n, k) linear code c and its dual code c_d. Hence, using MacWilliams identity, the probability of an undetected error for an (n, k) linear code c can be computed from the weight distribution of its dual code c_d also. Eq. (5.22) may be written as follows:

$$P_u(E) = \sum_{i=1}^{n} A_i p^i (1-p)^{n-i}$$

$$= (1-p)^n \sum_{i=1}^{n} A_i \left(\frac{p}{1-p}\right)^i \tag{5.25}$$

Putting $x = p/(1-p)$ in $A(x)$ of Eq. (5.23) and using the fact that $A_0 = 1$ (since, there is only one all zero code), we obtain:

$$A\left(\frac{p}{1-p}\right) - 1 = \sum_{i=1}^{n} A_i \left(\frac{p}{1-p}\right)^i \tag{5.26}$$

Combining Eqs. (5.25) and (5.26), we have:

$$P_u(E) = (1-p)^n \left[A\left(\frac{p}{1-p}\right) - 1\right] \tag{5.27}$$

Using Eqs. (5.27) and (5.24), we finally have:

$$P_u(E) = (1-p)^n A\left(\frac{p}{1-p}\right) - (1-p)^n$$

$$= 2^{-(n-k)}(1-p)^n \left(1 + \frac{p}{1-p}\right)^n B\left(\frac{1 - \frac{p}{1-p}}{1 + \frac{p}{1-p}}\right) - (1-p)^n$$

$$= 2^{-(n-k)} B(1-2p) - (1-p)^n \tag{5.28}$$

Therefore, we have two ways to calculate the probability of an undetected error for a linear code over a BSC. Generally if k is smaller than $(n - k)$, it is easier to compute $P_u(E)$ from Eq. (5.27); otherwise it is easier to use Eq. (5.28).

5.11 HAMMING CODE

Hamming codes have an important position in the history of error control codes. In fact, Hamming codes were the first class of linear codes devised for error control. The simplest Hamming code is the (7, 4) code that takes 4-bit information words and encodes them into 7-bit code words. Three parity bits are required, which are determined from the information bits.

For any positive integer $m \geq 3$, there exists a Hamming code with the following parameters:

Code length: $n = 2^m - 1$

Information length: $k = 2^m - 1 - m$

Number of parity bits: $m = n - k$

Error correcting capability: $t = 1$ (for $d_{min} = 3$)

All the nonzero m-tuples will construct columns of the parity-check matrix $\mathbf{H}$ of this code. In systematic form, it may be written as follows:

$$\mathbf{H} = [\mathbf{I}_m \quad \mathbf{Q}] \tag{5.29}$$

where the submatrix $\mathbf{Q}$ consists of k columns which are the m-tuples of weight 2 or more and $\mathbf{I}_m$ is an $m \times m$ identity matrix.

Here let us consider that $m = 3$. Then the parity-check matrix of the Hamming code of length 7 can be written as follows:

$$\mathbf{H} = \begin{bmatrix} 1 & 0 & 0 & 1 & 0 & 1 & 1 \\ 0 & 1 & 0 & 1 & 1 & 1 & 0 \\ 0 & 0 & 1 & 0 & 1 & 1 & 1 \end{bmatrix} \tag{5.30}$$

The parity-check matrix of the (7, 4) linear code is the same as given in Table 5.1. Thus, we conclude that the code shown in Table 5.1 is a Hamming code. Without affecting the weight distribution and the distance property of the code, the columns of $\mathbf{Q}$ may be arranged in any other order. Thus, the generator matrix of the code may be written in systematic form as follows:

$$\mathbf{G} = [\mathbf{Q}^T \quad \mathbf{I}_k] \tag{5.31}$$

Here $\mathbf{Q}^T$ is the transpose of $\mathbf{Q}$ and $\mathbf{I}_k$ is a $k \times k$ identity matrix.

The columns of $\mathbf{H}$ are nonzero and distinct. Thus, no two columns of $\mathbf{H}$ can add up to zero. Hence, the minimum distance of a Hamming code is at least 3. Again as all the nonzero m-tuples form the columns of $\mathbf{H}$, the vector sum of any two columns, say $\mathbf{h}_i$ and $\mathbf{h}_j$, will be another column of $\mathbf{H}$, say $\mathbf{h}_l$. Hence,

$$\mathbf{h}_i + \mathbf{h}_j + \mathbf{h}_l = \mathbf{0} \tag{5.32}$$

This code can correct all the error patterns with a single error and can detect all the error patterns of two or fewer errors.

5.12 SOLVED PROBLEMS

Problem 5.1: Consider a (6, 3) linear block code defined by the generator matrix

$$\mathbf{G} = \begin{vmatrix} 1 & 1 & 0 & 1 & 0 & 0 \\ 0 & 1 & 1 & 0 & 1 & 0 \\ 1 & 0 & 1 & 0 & 0 & 1 \end{vmatrix}$$

(a) Determine if the code is a Hamming code. Find the parity-check matrix **H** of the code in systematic form.
(b) Find the encoding table for the linear block code.
(c) What is the minimum distance d_{min} of the code? How many errors can the code detect? How many errors can the code correct?
(d) Find the decoding table for the linear block code.
(e) Suppose **c** = [0 0 0 1 1 1] is sent and **r** = [0 0 0 1 0 1] is received. Show how the code can correct this error.

Solution:

(a) Testing for hamming code, we have

$$m = n - k = 6 - 3 = 3$$

$$k = 2^m - m - 1 = 2^3 - 3 - 1 = 4 \neq 3$$

$$n = 2^m - 1 = 2^3 - 1 = 7 \neq 6$$

Hence, (6, 3) is not a Hamming code.

We have

$$\mathbf{G} = \begin{vmatrix} 1 & 1 & 0 & 1 & 0 & 0 \\ 0 & 1 & 1 & 0 & 1 & 0 \\ 1 & 0 & 1 & 0 & 0 & 1 \end{vmatrix}$$

$$\mathbf{P} = \begin{vmatrix} 1 & 1 & 0 \\ 0 & 1 & 1 \\ 1 & 0 & 1 \end{vmatrix}$$

$$\mathbf{P}^T = \begin{vmatrix} 1 & 0 & 1 \\ 1 & 1 & 0 \\ 0 & 1 & 1 \end{vmatrix}$$

$$\mathbf{I}_3 = \begin{vmatrix} 1 & 0 & 0 \\ 0 & 1 & 0 \\ 0 & 0 & 1 \end{vmatrix}$$

$$\mathbf{H} = [\mathbf{I}_{n-k} \vdots \mathbf{P}^T]$$

$$\mathbf{H} = \begin{vmatrix} 1 & 0 & 0 & 1 & 0 & 1 \\ 0 & 1 & 0 & 1 & 1 & 0 \\ 0 & 0 & 1 & 0 & 1 & 1 \end{vmatrix}$$

(b) The encoding table for (6, 3) linear block code is

Message	Code Word	Weight of Code Word
000	000000	0
001	101001	3
010	011010	3
011	110011	4
100	110100	3
101	011101	4
110	101110	4
111	000111	3

(c) From encoding table, we have

$$d_{\min} = 3$$

$$e = d_{\min} - 1 = 2$$

$$t \leq \frac{(d_{\min} - 1)}{2} \leq 1$$

Hence, the (6, 3) linear block code can detect two bit errors and correct one bit error in a 6-bit output code word.

(d) We have

$$\mathbf{H} = \begin{vmatrix} 1 & 0 & 0 & 1 & 0 & 1 \\ 0 & 1 & 0 & 1 & 1 & 0 \\ 0 & 0 & 1 & 0 & 1 & 1 \end{vmatrix}$$

$$\mathbf{H}^T = \begin{vmatrix} 1 & 0 & 0 \\ 0 & 1 & 0 \\ 0 & 0 & 1 \\ 1 & 1 & 0 \\ 0 & 1 & 1 \\ 1 & 0 & 1 \end{vmatrix}$$

The decoding table is

Error Pattern	Syndrome	Comment
000000	000	all 0's
100000	100	1st row of $\mathbf{H}^T$
010000	010	2nd row of $\mathbf{H}^T$
001000	001	3rd row of $\mathbf{H}^T$
000100	110	4th row of $\mathbf{H}^T$
000010	011	5th row of $\mathbf{H}^T$
000001	101	6th row of $\mathbf{H}^T$

(e) Given that $\mathbf{c} = [0\ 0\ 0\ 1\ 1\ 1]$ is sent and $\mathbf{r} = [0\ 0\ 0\ 1\ 0\ 1]$ is received.

$$\mathbf{s} = \mathbf{r}\mathbf{H}^T = \begin{vmatrix}0 & 0 & 0 & 1 & 0 & 1\end{vmatrix}\begin{vmatrix}1 & 0 & 0\\ 0 & 1 & 0\\ 0 & 0 & 1\\ 1 & 1 & 0\\ 0 & 1 & 1\\ 1 & 0 & 1\end{vmatrix}$$

$$= \begin{vmatrix}0 & 1 & 0\end{vmatrix}$$

From decoding table, this syndrome corresponds to error pattern $\mathbf{e} = [0\ 0\ 0\ 0\ 1\ 0]$. Hence, the corrected code word is

$$\begin{aligned}\mathbf{y} &= \mathbf{r} + \mathbf{e}\\ &= [0\ \ 0\ \ 0\ \ 1\ \ 0\ \ 1] + [0\ \ 0\ \ 0\ \ 0\ \ 1\ \ 0]\\ &= [0\ \ 0\ \ 0\ \ 1\ \ 1\ \ 1]\end{aligned}$$

Problem 5.2: Consider a (5, 1) linear block code defined by the generator matrix

$$\mathbf{G} = [1\ \ 1\ \ 1\ \ 1\ \ 1]$$

(a) Find the parity-check matrix $\mathbf{H}$ of the code in systematic form.
(b) Find the encoding table for the linear block code.
(c) What is the minimum distance $d_{\min}$ of the code? How many errors can the code detect? How many errors can the code correct?
(d) Find the decoding table for the linear block code (consider single bit errors only).
(e) Suppose $\mathbf{c} = [1\ 1\ 1\ 1\ 1]$ is sent and $\mathbf{r} = [0\ 1\ 1\ 1\ 1]$ is received. Show how the code can correct this error.

Solution:

(a) We have: $\mathbf{G} = [\mathbf{P} \vdots \mathbf{I}_k]$

$$\mathbf{G} = [1\ \ 1\ \ 1\ \ 1\ \ 1]$$

$$\mathbf{H} = [\mathbf{I}_{n-k} \vdots \mathbf{P}^T]$$

$$\mathbf{H} = \begin{vmatrix}1 & 0 & 0 & 0 & 1\\ 0 & 1 & 0 & 0 & 1\\ 0 & 0 & 1 & 0 & 1\\ 0 & 0 & 0 & 1 & 1\end{vmatrix}$$

(b) The encoding table for (5, 1) linear block code is

Message	Code Word	Weight of Code Word
0	00000	0
1	11111	5

(c) From encoding table, we have

$$d_{\min} = 5$$

$$e = d_{\min} - 1 = 4$$

$$t \leq \frac{(d_{\min} - 1)}{2} \leq 2$$

Hence, the (5, 1) linear block code can detect four bit errors and correct two bit errors in a 5-bit output code word.

(d) We have

$$\mathbf{H}^T = \begin{vmatrix} 1 & 0 & 0 & 0 \\ 0 & 1 & 0 & 0 \\ 0 & 0 & 1 & 0 \\ 0 & 0 & 0 & 1 \\ 1 & 1 & 1 & 1 \end{vmatrix}$$

The decoding table is

Error Pattern	Syndrome
00000	0000
10000	1000
01000	0100
00100	0010
00010	0001
00001	1111

(e) Given that $\mathbf{c} = [1\ 1\ 1\ 1\ 1]$ is sent and $\mathbf{r} = [0\ 1\ 1\ 1\ 1]$ is received.

$$\mathbf{s} = \mathbf{r}\mathbf{H}^T = \begin{vmatrix} 0 & 1 & 1 & 1 & 1 \end{vmatrix} \begin{vmatrix} 1 & 0 & 0 & 0 \\ 0 & 1 & 0 & 0 \\ 0 & 0 & 1 & 0 \\ 0 & 0 & 0 & 1 \\ 1 & 1 & 1 & 1 \end{vmatrix}$$
$$= \begin{vmatrix} 1 & 0 & 0 & 0 \end{vmatrix}$$

From decoding table, this syndrome corresponds to the error pattern $\mathbf{e} = [1\ 0\ 0\ 0]$. Hence, the corrected code word is

$$\begin{aligned} \mathbf{y} &= \mathbf{r} + \mathbf{e} \\ &= [0\ 1\ 1\ 1\ 1] + [1\ 0\ 0\ 0\ 0] \\ &= [1\ 1\ 1\ 1\ 1] \end{aligned}$$

Problem 5.3: Construct the syndrome table for the (6, 3) single-error-correcting code, whose parity-check matrix is given by

$$\mathbf{H} = \begin{vmatrix} 1 & 0 & 0 & 0 & 1 & 1 \\ 0 & 1 & 0 & 1 & 0 & 1 \\ 0 & 0 & 1 & 1 & 1 & 0 \end{vmatrix}$$

Solution: Block length of the code = 6.

The transpose of **H** is

$$\mathbf{H}^T = \begin{vmatrix} 1 & 0 & 0 \\ 0 & 1 & 0 \\ 0 & 0 & 1 \\ 0 & 1 & 1 \\ 1 & 0 & 1 \\ 1 & 1 & 0 \end{vmatrix}$$

Hence, the error syndrome table is

Error Pattern	Syndrome
000000	000
100000	100
010000	010
001000	001
000100	011
000010	101
000001	110

Problem 5.4: Consider the following code vectors:

$\mathbf{c}_1 = [1\ 0\ 0\ 1\ 0]$
$\mathbf{c}_2 = [0\ 1\ 1\ 0\ 1]$
$\mathbf{c}_3 = [1\ 1\ 0\ 0\ 1]$

(a) Find $d(\mathbf{c}_1,\mathbf{c}_2)$, $d(\mathbf{c}_2,\mathbf{c}_3)$, and $d(\mathbf{c}_1,\mathbf{c}_3)$.
(b) Show that $d(\mathbf{c}_1,\mathbf{c}_2) + d(\mathbf{c}_2,\mathbf{c}_3) \geq d(\mathbf{c}_1,\mathbf{c}_3)$.

Solution:
(a) We know:

$$d(\mathbf{c}_1, \mathbf{c}_2) = w(\mathbf{c}_1 \oplus \mathbf{c}_2) = w[1\ 1\ 1\ 1\ 1] = 5$$
$$d(\mathbf{c}_2, \mathbf{c}_3) = w(\mathbf{c}_2 \oplus \mathbf{c}_3) = w[1\ 0\ 1\ 0\ 0] = 2$$
$$d(\mathbf{c}_1, \mathbf{c}_3) = w(\mathbf{c}_1 \oplus \mathbf{c}_3) = w[0\ 1\ 0\ 1\ 1] = 3$$

(b) Now, $d(\mathbf{c}_1, \mathbf{c}_2) + d(\mathbf{c}_2, \mathbf{c}_3) = 5 + 2 \geq 3 = d(\mathbf{c}_1, \mathbf{c}_3)$

Problem 5.5: Construct the eight code words in the dual code for the (7, 4) Hamming code and also find the minimum distance of this dual code. The parity matrix is

$$\mathbf{P} = \begin{vmatrix} 1 & 1 & 0 \\ 0 & 1 & 1 \\ 1 & 1 & 1 \\ 1 & 0 & 1 \end{vmatrix}$$

Solution: Parity-check matrix is

Number of message bits $(k) = 4$;
Block length $(n) = 7$;
Number of parity bits $(n - k) = 3$

$$\mathbf{H} = \begin{vmatrix} 1 & 0 & 0 & 1 & 0 & 1 & 1 \\ 0 & 1 & 0 & 1 & 1 & 1 & 0 \\ 0 & 0 & 1 & 0 & 1 & 1 & 1 \end{vmatrix}$$

For a (7, 4) dual code **H** is used as a generator matrix.
Hence, code vector $\mathbf{C}_\mathbf{D} = m\mathbf{H}$

Message	Code Word	Hamming Weight
000	0000000	0
001	0010111	4
010	0101110	4
011	0111001	4
100	1001011	4
101	1011100	4
110	1100101	4
111	1110010	5

The minimum value of the Hamming weight defines the Hamming distance of the dual code as follows:

$$d_{\min} = 4$$

MULTIPLE CHOICE QUESTIONS

1. The Hamming distance between **v** = 1100001011 and **w** = 1001101001 is
   (a) 1 (b) 5 (c) 3 (d) 4

   Ans. **(d)**

2. Consider the parity-check matrix $H = \begin{vmatrix} 1 & 0 & 0 & 1 & 0 & 1 \\ 0 & 1 & 0 & 1 & 1 & 0 \\ 0 & 0 & 1 & 0 & 1 & 1 \end{vmatrix}$ and the received vector **r** = (001110).

   Then the syndrome is given by
   (a) (110) (b) (100) (c) (111) (d) (101)

   Ans. **(b)**

3. The number of undetectable errors for an (n, k) linear code is
   (a) 2^{n-k} (b) 2^n (c) $2^n - 2^k$ (d) 2^k

   Ans. **(d)**

4. (7, 4) Hamming codes are
   (a) single-error-correcting codes (b) double-error-correcting codes
   (c) burst-error-correcting codes (d) triple-error-correcting codes

   Ans. **(a)**

5. The condition of a dual code in case of linear block code is
   (a) $GH^T = 0$ (b) $(GH)^T = 0$ (c) $G^T H^T = 0$ (d) $HG^T = 0$

   Ans. **(a)**

6. A code is with minimum distance $d_{\min} = 5$. How many errors can it correct?
   (a) 3 (b) 2 (c) 4 (d) 1

   Ans. **(b)**

7. Check which code is a linear block code over GF(2).
   (a) {111, 100, 001, 010} (b) {00000, 01111, 10100, 11011}
   (c) {110, 101, 001, 010} (d) {0000, 0111, 1000, 1101}

   Ans. **(b)**

8. The ________ between two words is the number of differences between corresponding bits
   (a) Hamming code (b) Hamming distance
   (c) Hamming rule (d) none of the above

   Ans. **(b)**

9. To guarantee the detection of up to five errors in all cases, the minimum Hamming distance in a block code must be ________
   (a) 5 (b) 6 (c) 11 (d) 12

   Ans. (b)

10. To guarantee correction of up to five errors in all cases, the minimum Hamming distance in a block code must be ________.
    (a) 5 (b) 6 (c) 11 (d) 12

    Ans. (c)

11. In a linear block code, the ________ of any two valid code words creates another valid code word.
    (a) XORing (b) ORing (c) ANDing (d) none of these

    Ans. (a)

12. In block coding, if $k = 2$ and $n = 3$, we have ________ invalid code words.
    (a) 8 (b) 4 (c) 2 (d) 6

    Ans. (b)

13. The Hamming distance between equal code words is ________.
    (a) 1 (b) n (c) 0 (d) none of these

    Ans. (c)

14. In block coding, if $n = 5$, the maximum Hamming distance between the two code words is ____.
    (a) 2 (b) 3 (c) 5 (d) 4

    Ans. (c)

15. If the Hamming distance between a dataword and the corresponding code word is three, there are _____ bits in the error.
    (a) 3 (b) 4 (c) 5 (d) 2

    Ans. (a)

16. The binary Hamming codes have the property that
    (a) $(n, k) = (2^m + 1, 2^m - 1 - m)$ (b) $(n, k) = (2^m + 1, 2^m - 1 + m)$
    (c) $(n, k) = (2^m - 1, 2^m - 1 - m)$ (d) $(n, k) = (2^{m-1}, 2^{m-1} - m)$

    Ans. (c)

17. A (7, 4) linear block code with minimum distance guarantees error detection of
    (a) ≤ 4 bits (b) ≤ 3 bits (c) ≤ 2 bits (d) ≤ 6 bits

    Ans. (c)

Review Questions

1. What is the systematic structure of a code word?
2. Show that $C = \{0000, 1100, 0011, 1111\}$ is a linear code. What is its minimum distance?
3. What is standard array? Explain how the standard array can be used to make correct decoding.
4. What is syndrome and what is its significance? Draw the syndrome circuit for a (7, 4) linear block code with parity-check matrix $H = \begin{vmatrix} 1 & 0 & 0 & 1 & 0 & 1 & 1 \\ 0 & 1 & 0 & 1 & 1 & 1 & 0 \\ 0 & 0 & 1 & 0 & 1 & 1 & 1 \end{vmatrix}$.
5. Consider a systematic (8, 4) code with the following parity-check equations

$$V_0 = U_0 + U_1 + U_2$$
$$V_1 = U_1 + U_2 + U_3$$

$$V_2 = U_0 + U_1 + U_3$$
$$V_3 = U_0 + U_2 + U_3$$

where U_0, U_1, U_2, and U_3 are messages, V_0, V_1, V_2, and V_3 are parity-check digits.

(a) Find the generator matrix and the parity-check matrix for this code.
(b) Find the minimum weight for this code.
(c) Find the error-detecting and the error-correcting capability of this code.
(d) Show with an example that the code can detect three errors in a code word.

6. A (7, 3) linear code has the following generator matrix:

$$G = \begin{vmatrix} 1 & 1 & 1 & 0 & 1 & 0 & 0 \\ 0 & 1 & 1 & 1 & 0 & 1 & 0 \\ 1 & 1 & 0 & 1 & 0 & 0 & 1 \end{vmatrix}$$

Determine a systematic form of G. Hence, find the parity-check matrix **H** for the code. Design the encoder circuit for the above code.

7. A code has the parity-check matrix

$$\mathbf{H} = \begin{vmatrix} 1 & 1 & 0 & 1 & 0 & 0 \\ 0 & 1 & 1 & 0 & 1 & 0 \\ 1 & 0 & 1 & 0 & 0 & 1 \end{vmatrix}$$

Assuming that a vector (111011) is received, determine whether the received vector is a valid code. If 'not' determine what is the probable code vector originally transmitted. If 'yes' conform.

8. The generator matrix for a (7, 4) block code is given:

$$G = \begin{vmatrix} 1 & 0 & 0 & 0 & 1 & 0 & 1 \\ 0 & 1 & 0 & 0 & 1 & 1 & 1 \\ 0 & 0 & 1 & 0 & 1 & 1 & 0 \\ 0 & 0 & 0 & 1 & 0 & 1 & 1 \end{vmatrix}$$

(a) Find the parity-check matrix of this code.
(b) If the received code word is (0001110), then find the transmitted code word.

9. Consider the (7, 4) linear block code whose decoding table is given as follows:

Syndrome	Coset Leader
100	1000000
010	0100000
001	0010000
110	0001000
011	0000100
111	0000010
101	0000001

Show with an example that this code can correct any single error but makes a decoding error when two or more errors occur.

10. A (7, 3) code C has the following parity-check matrix with two missing columns.

$$H = \begin{vmatrix} 1 & - & - & 1 & 0 & 0 & 0 \\ 0 & - & - & 0 & 1 & 0 & 0 \\ 1 & - & - & 0 & 0 & 1 & 0 \\ 1 & - & - & 0 & 0 & 0 & 1 \end{vmatrix}$$

Provide possible bits in the missing columns given that [0110011] is a code word of C and the minimum distance of C is 4.

11. A code C has generator matrix

$$G = \begin{vmatrix} 1 & 0 & 0 & 0 & 1 & 1 & 0 & 0 & 0 & 1 & 1 & 0 \\ 0 & 1 & 0 & 0 & 1 & 0 & 1 & 0 & 0 & 0 & 1 & 1 \\ 0 & 0 & 1 & 0 & 1 & 0 & 0 & 1 & 0 & 1 & 0 & 1 \\ 0 & 0 & 0 & 1 & 1 & 0 & 0 & 0 & 1 & 1 & 1 & 1 \end{vmatrix}$$

(a) What is the minimum distance of C?
(b) Decode the received word [111111111111].

12. A code C has only odd-weight code words. Say 'possible' or 'impossible' for the following with reasons.
(a) C is linear.
(b) Minimum distance of C is 5.

13. Show that, in each of the following cases, the generator matrices **G** and **G′** generate equivalent codes.

(a) $G = \begin{vmatrix} 1 & 1 & 0 & 0 \\ 0 & 1 & 1 & 0 \\ 0 & 0 & 1 & 1 \end{vmatrix}, \; G' = \begin{vmatrix} 1 & 0 & 0 & 1 \\ 0 & 1 & 0 & 1 \\ 0 & 0 & 1 & 1 \end{vmatrix}$

(b) $G = \begin{vmatrix} 1 & 1 & 0 & 0 & 0 & 0 \\ 0 & 0 & 1 & 1 & 0 & 0 \\ 0 & 0 & 0 & 0 & 1 & 1 \end{vmatrix}, \; G' = \begin{vmatrix} 1 & 1 & 1 & 1 & 1 & 1 \\ 0 & 1 & 1 & 0 & 1 & 1 \\ 0 & 0 & 1 & 0 & 0 & 1 \end{vmatrix}$

14. If C is a linear code with both even and odd-weight code words, show that the number of even-weight code words is equal to the number of odd-weight code words. Show that the even-weight code words form a linear code.

15. Consider two codes with parity-check matrices

$$H = \begin{vmatrix} 1 & 0 & 1 & 0 \\ 1 & 1 & 0 & 1 \end{vmatrix} \text{ and } H = \begin{vmatrix} 0 & 1 & 1 & 1 \\ 1 & 1 & 0 & 1 \end{vmatrix}$$

respectively.
(a) List all code words of the two codes.
(b) Provide **G** and **H** in systematic form for both codes.

16. Suppose that all the rows in the generator matrix **G** of a binary linear code C have even weight. Prove that all code words in C have even weight.

17. Let C be the binary [9, 5] code with parity-check matrix

$$\mathbf{H} = \begin{bmatrix} 0 & 0 & 0 & 1 & 1 & 0 & 1 & 1 & 0 \\ 1 & 1 & 0 & 1 & 1 & 0 & 0 & 0 & 0 \\ 0 & 1 & 1 & 0 & 1 & 1 & 0 & 0 & 0 \\ 0 & 0 & 0 & 0 & 1 & 1 & 0 & 1 & 1 \end{bmatrix}$$

Find the coset leader(s) of the cosets containing the following words:

(a) 1 1 1 1 0 1 0 0 0

(b) 1 1 0 1 0 1 0 1 1

(c) 0 1 0 0 1 0 0 1 0.

chapter 6

CYCLIC CODES

6.1 INTRODUCTION

Cyclic code is a subclass of linear codes. Any cyclic shift of a code word results in another valid code. This feature allows easy implementation of encoding as well as syndrome computation with linear sequential circuits by employing shift registers and feedback connections. Since it possesses considerable amount of algebra inherently, there are many practical methods of decoding. Random error correction and burst error correction are possible to the large extent due to involvement of algebra. The theory of Galois field can be used effectively to study and analyze new cyclic codes.

6.2 GENERATION

If a set of n-components $\mathbf{v} = (v_0,v_1,v_2,\ldots,v_{n-1})$ is cyclically shifted one place to right, another set of n-components is obtained as $\mathbf{v}_1 = (v_{n-1}, v_0, v_1, v_2, \ldots, v_{n-2})$. This is called cyclic shift of $\mathbf{v}$. If components of $\mathbf{v}$ are shifted by i places, we obtain

$$\mathbf{v}_i = (v_{n-i}, v_{n-i+1}, v_{n-i+2}, \ldots, v_0, v_1, v_2, \ldots, v_{n-i-1})$$

Clearly, cyclic shift of right is equivalent to cyclic shift of left.

Definition 6.1: An (n, k) linear code in C is called cyclic code, if cyclic shift of a code vector in C is also a code vector in C. This means that if the code word $(v_0,v_1,v_2,\ldots,v_{n-1})$ is in C then $(v_{n-1},v_0,v_1,v_2,\ldots,v_{n-2})$ is also in C.

Method of Cyclic Codes Generation—The following steps can be used to generate a cyclic code:

1. Consider a polynomial $f(x)$ in C_n. The block length of the code is n.
2. Obtain a set of polynomials by multiplying $f(x)$ to all the possible polynomials of message $\mathbf{u}(x)$.
3. A set of polynomials obtained in the above steps are the set of code words belonging to a cyclic code.

Following is an example to generate the cyclic code from 4-bit message codes with the polynomial $f(x) = 1 + x + x^3$. As the maximum degree of the message polynomial is 3, the maximum degree of code polynomial will be 6, i.e., block length is 7.

To examine the algebraic properties of a cyclic code, let us consider the components of a code vector $\mathbf{v} = (v_0,v_1,v_2,\ldots,v_{n-1})$ as the coefficients of a polynomial as follows:

$$\mathbf{v}(x) = v_0 + v_1x + v_2x^2 + \ldots + v_{n-1}x^{n-1} \tag{6.1}$$

where symbol x is called the indeterminate and coefficients of $\mathbf{v}(x)$. If $v_{n-1} \neq 0$, the degree of $\mathbf{v}(x)$ is $(n - 1)$. Each code vector corresponds to a polynomial of degree $(n - 1)$ or less. Similarly, the code polynomial corresponding to $\mathbf{v}_i(x)$ (with ith shift) is

$$\mathbf{v}_i(x) = v_{n-i} + v_{n-i+1}x + v_{n-i+2}x^2 + \ldots + v_{n-1}x^{i-1} + v_0x^i + v_1x^{i+1} + \ldots + v_{n-i-1}x^{n-1} \tag{6.2}$$

Table 6.1 *(7, 4) Cyclic Code Generated by the Polynomial f(x) = 1 + x + x³*

Messages	Message Polynomial $\mathbf{u}(x)$	Code Polynomial $c(x) = \mathbf{u}(x) \cdot f(x)$	Code Vector
0 0 0 0	0	$0 \cdot (1+x+x^3) = 0$	0 0 0 0 0 0 0
0 0 0 1	x^3	$x^3 \cdot (1+x+x^3) = x^3 + x^4 + x^6$	0 0 0 1 1 0 1
0 0 1 0	x^2	$x^2 \cdot (1+x+x^3) = x^2 + x^3 + x^5$	0 0 1 1 0 1 0
0 0 1 1	$x^2 + x^3$	$(x^2+x^3) \cdot (1+x+x^3) = x^2 + x^4 + x^5 + x^6$	0 0 1 0 1 1 1
0 1 0 0	x	$x \cdot (1+x+x^3) = x + x^2 + x^4$	0 1 1 0 1 0 0
0 1 0 1	$x + x^3$	$(x+x^3) \cdot (1+x+x^3) = x + x^2 + x^3 + x^6$	0 1 1 1 0 0 1
0 1 1 0	$x + x^2$	$(x+x^2) \cdot (1+x+x^3) = x + x^3 + x^4 + x^5$	0 1 0 1 1 1 0
0 1 1 1	$x + x^2 + x^3$	$(x+x^2+x^3) \cdot (1+x+x^3) = x + x^5 + x^6$	0 1 0 0 0 1 1
1 0 0 0	1	$1 \cdot (1+x+x^3) = 1 + x + x^3$	1 1 0 1 0 0 0
1 0 0 1	$1 + x^3$	$(1+x^3) \cdot (1+x+x^3) = 1 + x + x^4 + x^6$	1 1 0 0 1 0 1
1 0 1 0	$1 + x^2$	$(1+x^2) \cdot (1+x+x^3) = 1 + x + x^2 + x^5$	1 1 1 0 0 1 0
1 0 1 1	$1 + x^2 + x^3$	$(1+x^2+x^3) \cdot (1+x+x^3) = 1 + x + x^2 + x^3 + x^4 + x^5 + x^6$	1 1 1 1 1 1 1
1 1 0 0	$1 + x$	$(1+x) \cdot (1+x+x^3) = 1 + x^2 + x^3 + x^4$	1 0 1 1 1 0 0
1 1 0 1	$1 + x + x^3$	$(1+x+x^3) \cdot (1+x+x^3) = 1 + x^2 + x^6$	1 0 1 0 0 0 1
1 1 1 0	$1 + x + x^2$	$(1+x+x^2) \cdot (1+x+x^3) = 1 + x^4 + x^5$	1 0 0 0 1 1 0
1 1 1 1	$1 + x + x^2 + x^3$	$(1+x+x^2+x^3) \cdot (1+x+x^3) = 1 + x^3 + x^5 + x^6$	1 0 0 1 0 1 1

There exists an interesting algebraic property between $\mathbf{v}(x)$ and $\mathbf{v}_i(x)$. Multiplying Eq. (6.1) by x^i, we obtain

$$\begin{aligned} x^i\mathbf{v}(x) &= v_0x^i + v_1x^{i+1} + \ldots + v_{n-i+1}x^{n-1} + \ldots + v_{n-1}x^{n+i-1} \\ &= v_{n-i} + v_{n-i+1}x + v_{n-i+2}x^2 + \ldots + v_{n-1}x^{i-1} + v_0x^i + v_1x^{i+1} + \ldots + v_{n-i-1}x^{n-1} \\ &\quad + v_{n-i}(x^n+1) + v_{n-i+1}x(x^n+1) + \ldots + v_{n-i}x^{i-1}(x^n+1) \\ &= \mathbf{Q}(x)(x^n+1) + \mathbf{v}_i(x) \end{aligned} \tag{6.3}$$

where

$$\mathbf{Q}(x) = v_{n-i} + v_{n-i+1}x + v_{n-i+2}x^2 + \ldots + v_{n-1}x^{i-1} \tag{6.4}$$

This means the code polynomial $\mathbf{v}_i(x)$ is the remainder part when polynomial $x^i\mathbf{v}(x)$ is divided by $(x^n + 1)$.

There are some important properties of cyclic code which help to implement the encoding and syndrome computation in a simple manner.

Theorem 6.1: The nonzero code polynomial of minimum degree in a cyclic code C is unique.

Proof: Let us consider a nonzero code polynomial $P(x) = p_0 + p_1x + p_2x^2 + \ldots + p_{r-1}x^{r-1} + x^r$ of minimum degree in c. It is assumed that $P(x)$ is not unique. Then there exists another code polynomial of minimum degree r in C, say $P'(x) = p_0' + p_1'x + p_2'x^2 + \ldots + p_{r-1}'x^{r-1} + x^r$. Since C is linear, $P(x) + P'(x) = (p_0 + p_0') + (p_1 + p_1')x + (p_2 + p_2')x^2 + \ldots + (p_{r-1} + p_{r-1}')x^{r-1}$ is also a code polynomial of degree $(r - 1)$ (since $x^r + x^r = 0$). If $P(x) + P'(x) \neq 0$, then $P(x) + P'(x)$ is a nonzero code polynomial of minimum degree less than r. This is not possible. Therefore $P(x) + P'(x) = 0$. This means $P(x) = P'(x)$, or $P(x)$ is unique.

Theorem 6.2: If $P(x) = p_0 + p_1x + p_2x^2 + \ldots + p_{r-1}x^{r-1} + x^r$ is nonzero code polynomial of minimum degree in an (n, k) cyclic code in C, then the constant term p_0 must be equal to 1.

Proof: If $p_0 = 0$, then $$P(x) = p_1x + p_2x^2 + \dots + p_{r-1}x^{r-1} + x^r$$
$$= x(p_1 + p_2x + \dots + p_{r-1}x^{r-2} + x^{r-1})$$

Now, if $P(x)$ is shifted cyclically to right by $n - 1$ places (or one place to left), a nonzero code polynomial $p_1 + p_2x + \dots + p_{r-1}x^{r-2} + x^{r-1}$ is obtained which has the degree less than r. This contradicts the assumption of nonzero code polynomial with a minimum degree. Hence, it is concluded that, $p_0 \neq 0$.

From Theorem 6.1, it may be considered that the nonzero code polynomial of minimum degree in an (n, k) cyclic code C is of the following form:

$$f(x) = 1 + f_1x + f_2x^2 + \dots + f_{r-1}x^{r-1} + x^r \tag{6.5}$$

Consider the (7, 4) cyclic code as shown in Table 6.1. The nonzero code polynomial of minimum degree is $f(x) = 1 + x + x^3$. Therefore, the polynomials $xf(x), x^2f(x), x^3f(x), \dots, x^{n-r-1}f(x)$ have the minimum degrees as $r + 1, r + 2, r + 3, \dots, n - 1$. Now from Theorem 6.1, $xf(x), x^2f(x), x^3f(x), \dots, x^{n-r-1}f(x)$ are the cyclic shifts of $f(x)$. Hence, they are the code polynomials in C. As C is linear, $\mathbf{v}(x)$, the linear combination of $f(x), xf(x), x^2f(x), x^3f(x), \dots, x^{n-r-1}f(x)$, is also a code polynomial in C, i.e.,

$$\mathbf{v}(x) = u_0f(x) + u_1xf(x) + u_2x^2f(x) + u_3x^3f(x) + \dots + u_{n-r-1}x^{n-r-1}f(x)$$
$$= (u_0 + u_1x + u_2x^2 + u_3x^3 + \dots + u_{n-r-1}x^{n-r-1})f(x)$$

where $u_i = 0$ or 1 for $i = 0, 1, 2, \dots, n - r - 1$.

Theorem 6.3: If $f(x) = 1 + f_1x + f_2x^2 + \dots + f_{r-1}x^{r-1} + x^r$ is the nonzero code polynomial of minimum degree in (n, k) cyclic code C, then a binary polynomial of degree $n - 1$ or less is a code polynomial, if and only if, it is the multiple of $f(x)$.

Proof: Let $\mathbf{v}(x)$ is a binary code polynomial of degree $n - 1$or less, and is a multiple of $f(x)$, such that

$$\mathbf{v}(x) = (a_0 + a_1x + a_2x^2 + a_3x^3 + \dots + a_{n-r-1}x^{n-r-1})f(x)$$
$$= a_0f(x) + a_1xf(x) + a_2x^2f(x) + a_3x^3f(x) + \dots + a_{n-r-1}x^{n-r-1}f(x)$$

Since $\mathbf{v}(x)$ is the linear combination of $f(x), xf(x), x^2f(x), x^3f(x), \dots, x^{n-r-1}f(x)$, it is also a code polynomial in C. Now let us consider that

$$\mathbf{v}(x) = \mathbf{a}(x)f(x) + \mathbf{b}(x) \tag{6.6}$$

where $\mathbf{b}(x)$ is identical to 0, or it has the degree less than that of $f(x)$. Rearranging Eq. (6.6), we obtain

$$\mathbf{b}(x) = \mathbf{v}(x) + \mathbf{a}(x)f(x) \tag{6.7}$$

Since both $\mathbf{v}(x)$ and $\mathbf{a}(x)f(x)$ are the code polynomials, $\mathbf{b}(x)$ must be a code polynomial. If $\mathbf{b}(x) \neq 0$, then it is a nonzero code polynomial of degree less than $f(x)$. This contradicts the assumption that $f(x)$ is a nonzero code polynomial of minimum degree. Hence, $\mathbf{b}(x)$ must be identical to 0. This proves that $\mathbf{v}(x)$ is the multiple of $f(x)$.

The number of binary polynomials of degree $n - 1$ or less that are multiples of $f(x)$ is 2^{n-r}. They are the code polynomials of (n, k) cyclic code in C. Since there are 2^k polynomials in (n, k) cyclic code C, 2^{n-r} must be equal to 2^k. So, $(n - k) = r$. Hence, an (n, k) cyclic code has the following form:

$$f(x) = 1 + f_1x + f_2x^2 + \dots + f_{n-r-1}x^{n-k-1} + x^{n-k} \tag{6.8}$$

Theorem 6.4: In an (n, k) cyclic code, there exists one and only one code polynomial of degree $n - k$.

$$f(x) = 1 + f_1x + f_2x^2 + \dots + f_{n-r-1}x^{n-k-1} + x^{n-k}$$

Proof: Every code polynomial is a multiple of $f(x)$ and every binary polynomial of degree $n - 1$ or less that is a multiple of $f(x)$ is a code polynomial.

Hence every code polynomial $\mathbf{v}(x)$ in an (n, k) cyclic code may be expressed as

$$\begin{aligned}\mathbf{v}(x) &= \mathbf{u}(x)f(x) \\ &= (u_0 + u_1x + u_2x^2 + \ldots + u_{k-1}x^{k-1})f(x) \qquad (6.9)\end{aligned}$$

Above equation implies that if $u_0, u_1, u_2, \ldots, u_{k-1}$ are the coefficient of message digits to be encoded, the corresponding code polynomial is $\mathbf{v}(x)$. Therefore, the encoding can be achieved by multiplying message polynomial $\mathbf{u}(x)$ by $f(x)$, and an (n, k) cyclic code can be completely specified by its nonzero code polynomial $f(x)$ of minimum degree. The polynomial $f(x)$ is called *generator polynomial.* The degree of $f(x)$ is equal to the number of parity checks. Table 6.1 is the example of generation of an (7, 4) cyclic code, where $f(x) = 1 + x + x^3$ is the generator polynomial.

Theorem 6.5: The generator polynomial $f(x)$ of an (n, k) cyclic code is a factor of $1 + x^n$.

Proof: As the generator polynomial $f(x)$ is of degree of $n - k$, $x^kf(x)$ has the degree of n. Dividing $x^kf(x)$ by $1 + x^n$, we find

$$x^kf(x) = 1 + x^n + f_k(x) \qquad (6.10)$$

where $f_k(x)$ is the remainder, which is the kth cyclically right shift of $f(x)$ as follows from Eq. (6.3). Again from Theorem 6.3, $f_k(x)$ is the multiple $f(x)$. Let us consider $f_k(x) = \mathbf{a}(x)f(x)$. Hence, Eq. (6.10) may be written as follows:

$$x^kf(x) = 1 + x^n + \mathbf{a}(x)f(x)$$

or

$$1 + x^n = [x^k + \mathbf{a}(x)]f(x)$$

Thus $f(x)$ is the factor of $1 + x^n$.

Theorem 6.6: If $f(x)$ is a polynomial of degree $n - k$, and is a factor of $1 + x^n$, then $f(x)$ generates (n, k) cyclic code.

Proof: Consider k number of polynomials as $f(x), xf(x), x^2f(x), \ldots, x^{k-1}f(x)$, all of which have the degree of $n - 1$ or less. A linear combination of these polynomials may be considered as follows:

$$\begin{aligned}\mathbf{v}(x) &= a_0f(x) + a_1xf(x) + a_2x^2f(x) + a_3x^3f(x) + \ldots + a_{k-1}x^{k-1}f(x) \\ &= [a_0 + a_1x + a_2x^2 + a_3x^3 + \ldots + a_{k-1}x^{k-1}]f(x)\end{aligned}$$

$\mathbf{v}(x)$ is also a polynomial of degree $n - 1$ or less and multiple of $f(x)$. There are 2^k number of code polynomials to form (n, k) cyclic code.

Now let us consider the code polynomial $\mathbf{v}(x) = v_0 + v_1x + v_2x^2 + \ldots + v_{n-1}x^{n-1}$, then

$$\begin{aligned}x\mathbf{v}(x) &= v_0x + v_1x^2 + v_2x^3 + \ldots + v_{n-1}x^n \\ &= v_{n-1}(1 + x^n) + (v_{n-1} + v_0x + v_1x^2 + v_2x^3 + \ldots + v_{n-2}x^{n-1}) \\ &= v_{n-1}(1 + x^n) + v_1(x)\end{aligned}$$

$v_1(x)$ is the cyclic shift of $v(x)$. As both $xv_1(x)$ and $1 + x^n$ are divisible by $f(x)$, $v_1(x)$ is also divisible by $f(x)$, and is linear combination of $f(x), xf(x), x^2f(x), \ldots, x^{k-1}f(x)$. Hence, $v_1(x)$ is a code polynomial. Therefore, linear code generated by $f(x), xf(x), x^2f(x), \ldots, x^{k-1}f(x)$ is the (n, k) cyclic code.

This theorem implies that any factor of $1 + x^n$ with degree $n - k$ generates an (n, k) cyclic code. For large values of n, there exist several numbers of codes consisting both good codes and bad codes. Selection of polynomials to generate good codes is difficult job. However, several classes of good codes have been discovered and successfully implemented.

Example 6.1: Let us consider a polynomial $1 + x^7$, which can be factorized as follows:

$$1 + x^7 = (1 + x)(1 + x + x^3)(1 + x^2 + x^3)$$

There are two polynomials of degree 3, each of which can generate a (7, 4) cyclic code. Table 6.1 shows the generation of cyclic code with the generator polynomial $f(x) = 1 + x + x^3$. Each code has been generated from the product of message polynomial and generator polynomial. Suppose message bits are 1100, then its message polynomial $\mathbf{u}(x)$ is $1 + x$. Multiplying $\mathbf{u}(x)$ and $f(x)$, the code polynomial $\mathbf{v}(x)$ is

$$\begin{aligned}\mathbf{v}(x) &= \mathbf{u}(x)f(x) = (1 + x)(1 + x + x^3)\\ &= 1 + x^2 + x^3 + x^4\end{aligned}$$

The encoded code vector is 1011100. Thus encoded cyclic code as shown in Table 6.1 has minimum distance of 3 and is a single-error-correcting code.

It may be noted that the code is not of systematic form. With the generator polynomial $f(x)$ in a cyclic code, the code can be put into a systematic form, i.e., the rightmost k digits of code vector are unaltered information bits and leftmost $n - k$ digits are parity-check bits. Suppose message polynomial $\mathbf{u}(x)$ is given as follows:

$$\mathbf{u}(x) = u_0 + u_1x + u_2x^2 + \ldots + u_{k-1}x^{k-1}$$

Multiplying $\mathbf{u}(x)$ by x^{n-k}, a polynomial of degree $n - 1$ is obtained as follows:

$$x^{n-k}\mathbf{u}(x) = u_0x^{n-k} + u_1x^{n-k+1} + u_2x^{n-k+2} + \ldots + u_{k-1}x^{n-1}$$

Dividing $x^{n-k}\mathbf{u}(x)$ by the generator polynomial $f(x)$, we may write

$$x^{n-k}\mathbf{u}(x) = \mathbf{a}(x)f(x) + \mathbf{b}(x) \tag{6.11}$$

where $\mathbf{a}(x)$ and $\mathbf{b}(x)$ are the quotient and remainder, respectively. Since degree of $f(x)$ is $n - k$, then degree of $\mathbf{b}(x)$ is $n - k - 1$ or less. This means

$$\mathbf{b}(x) = b_0 + b_1x + b_2x^2 + \ldots + b_{n-k-1}x^{n-k-1}$$

Eq. (6.11) may be rearranged as follows:

$$\begin{aligned}\mathbf{b}(x) + x^{n-k}\,\mathbf{u}(x) &= \mathbf{a}(x)f(x)\\ &= b_0 + b_1x + b_2x^2 + \ldots + b_{n-k-1}x^{n-k-1} + u_0x^{n-k} + u_1x^{n-k+1} + u_2x^{n-k+2} + \ldots + u_{k-1}x^{n-1}\end{aligned} \tag{6.12}$$

The above polynomial is a multiple of generator polynomial $f(x)$ and therefore it is a code polynomial of cyclic code. The corresponding code vector is $(b_0, b_1, b_2, \ldots, b_{n-k-1}, u_0, u_1, u_2, \ldots, u_{k-1})$. It may be noted that the code vector consists of k-unaltered message bits $(u_0, u_1, u_2, \ldots, u_{k-1})$ at rightmost part and $n - k$ parity-check bits $(b_0, b_1, b_2, \ldots, b_{n-k-1})$ at leftmost part, yielding a systematic form. Parity digits are generated from remainder part. To encode a systematic cyclic code, the following steps are to be followed.

- Multiply the message polynomial $\mathbf{u}(x)$ by x^{n-k}.
- Obtain the remainder $\mathbf{b}(x)$ as parity digits from dividing $x^{n-k}\,\mathbf{u}(x)$ by a generator polynomial $f(x)$.
- Combine $\mathbf{b}(x)$ and $x^{n-k}\mathbf{u}(x)$ to obtain code polynomial $\mathbf{b}(x) + x^{n-k}\mathbf{u}(x)$.

Example 6.2: Let us consider a (7, 4) cyclic code with the generator polynomial $f(x) = 1 + x + x^3$. Let the message be 1001, i.e., the message polynomial is $\mathbf{u}(x) = 1 + x^3$. Obtain the systematic encoded form.

Solution: Systematic form may be obtained if $\mathbf{b}(x)$ is taken as remainder part of $x^{n-k}\mathbf{u}(x)/f(x)$.

$$\mathbf{b}(x) = x^3(1 + x^3)/(1 + x + x^3) = x + x^2$$

Therefore, the code vector $\mathbf{v}(x) = \mathbf{b}(x) + x^{n-k}\mathbf{u}(x) = x + x^2 + x^3 + x^6$, and thus the encoded form will be 0111001. It may be noted that first three digits are parity digits and rest four digits are unaltered information bits. Hence, the 16 code vectors in systematic form may be listed as in Table 6.2.

Table 6.2 *(7, 4) Cyclic Code Generated by f(x) = 1 + x + x³*

Messages	Message Polynomial u(x)	Code Polynomial v(x) = b(x) + x³ u(x)	Code Vector
0000	0	0	0000000
0001	x^3	$1+x^2+x^6$	1010001
0010	x^2	$1+x+x^2+x^5$	1110010
0011	x^2+x^3	$x+x^5+x^6$	0100011
0100	x	$x+x^2+x^4$	0110100
0101	$x+x^3$	$1+x+x^4+x^6$	1100101
0110	$x+x^2$	$1+x^4+x^5$	1000110
0111	$x+x^2+x^3$	$x^2+x^4+x^5+x^6$	0010111
1000	1	$1+x+x^3$	1101000
1001	$1+x^3$	$x+x^2+x^3+x^6$	0111001
1010	$1+x^2$	$x^2+x^3+x^6$	0011010
1011	$1+x^2+x^3$	$1+x^3+x^5+x^6$	1001011
1100	$1+x$	$1+x^2+x^3+x^4$	1011100
1101	$1+x+x^3$	$x^3+x^4+x^6$	0001101
1110	$1+x+x^2$	$x+x^3+x^4+x^5$	0101110
1111	$1+x+x^2+x^3$	$1+x+x^2+x^3+x^4+x^5+x^6$	1111111

6.2.1 Generation and Parity-check Matrices

Consider an (n, k) cyclic code with the generator polynomial $f(x) = 1 + f_1x + f_2x^2 + \ldots + f_{r-1}x^{n-k-1} + x^{n-k}$. We have observed that k code polynomials $f(x), xf(x), x^2f(x), \ldots, x^{k-1}f(x)$ are attributed to cyclic code C, and polynomials $xf(x), x^2f(x), \ldots, x^{k-}f(x)$ correspond to cyclic shifts. Hence, the coefficients of these polynomials may be arranged in $k \times n$ matrix form as follows:

$$\mathbf{F} = \begin{bmatrix} f_0 & f_1 & f_2 & \cdots & f_{n-k} & 0 & 0 & 0 & \cdots & 0 \\ 0 & f_0 & f_1 & f_2 & \cdots & f_{n-k} & 0 & 0 & \cdots & 0 \\ 0 & 0 & f_0 & f_1 & f_2 & \cdots & f_{n-k} & 0 & \cdots & 0 \\ \vdots & \vdots & \vdots & \vdots & \vdots & \vdots & \vdots & \vdots & \ddots & \vdots \\ 0 & 0 & 0 & \cdots & 0 & f_0 & f_1 & f_2 & \cdots & f_{n-k} \end{bmatrix} \quad (6.13)$$

It may be noted that $f_0 = f_{n-k} = 1$. However, this is not in the systematic form. To get the systematic form, some operations on the matrix may be performed. It may be recalled that $f(x)$ is one of the factor of $1 + x^n$, say

$$1 + x^n = f(x)\mathbf{h}(x) \quad (6.14)$$

where $\mathbf{h}(x)$ is the polynomial of degree of k which may be expressed as follows:

$$\mathbf{h}(x) = h_0 + h_1x + h_2x^2 + \ldots + h_{k-1}x^{k-1} + h_kx^k$$

$h_0 = h_k = 1$. It may be shown that parity-check matrix of c can be obtained from $\mathbf{h}(x)$. If $\mathbf{v}(x)$ is the code vector in C of degree n, then $\mathbf{v}(x) = \mathbf{a}(x)f(x)$. Multiplying $\mathbf{v}(x)$ by $\mathbf{h}(x)$, we obtain

$$\begin{aligned}\mathbf{v}(x)\mathbf{h}(x) &= \mathbf{a}(x)f(x)\mathbf{h}(x)\\ &= \mathbf{a}(x)(1 + x^n)\\ &= \mathbf{a}(x) + x^n\mathbf{a}(x)\end{aligned} \tag{6.15}$$

Since $\mathbf{a}(x)$ has the degree of $k - 1$ or less, powers of $x^k, x^{k+1}, \ldots, x^{n-1}$ do not exist in the polynomial $\mathbf{a}(x) + x^n\mathbf{a}(x)$. This means the coefficients of $x^k, x^{k+1}, \ldots, x^{n-1}$ in the polynomial $\mathbf{v}(x)\mathbf{h}(x)$ are zero. We may write that

$$\sum_{i=0}^{k} h_i v_{n-i-j} = 0 \quad \text{for } 1 \le i \le n - k \tag{6.16}$$

Now we consider the polynomial $x^k\,\mathbf{h}(x^{-1})$ that may be expressed as follows:

$$x^k\,\mathbf{h}(x^{-1}) = h_k + h_{k-1}x + h_{k-2}x^2 + \ldots + h_1x^{k-1} + h_0x^k \tag{6.17}$$

It may be clearly seen that $x^k\mathbf{h}(x^{-1})$ is also a factor of $1 + x^n$. This polynomial generates an $(n, n - k)$ cyclic code in c, with $(n - k) \times n$ generator matrix as follows:

$$\mathbf{H} = \begin{bmatrix} h_k & h_{k-1} & h_{k-2} & \cdots & h_0 & 0 & 0 & 0 & \cdots & 0\\ 0 & h_k & h_{k-1} & h_{k-2} & \cdots & h_0 & 0 & 0 & \cdots & 0\\ 0 & 0 & h_k & h_{k-1} & h_{k-2} & \cdots & h_0 & 0 & \cdots & 0\\ \vdots & \vdots & \vdots & \vdots & \vdots & \vdots & \vdots & \vdots & \ddots & \vdots\\ 0 & 0 & 0 & \cdots & 0 & h_k & h_{k-1} & h_{k-2} & \cdots & h_0 \end{bmatrix} \tag{6.18}$$

It may be observed that to satisfy Eq. (6.16) any code vector $\mathbf{v}$ in C must be orthogonal to every row of $\mathbf{H}$. Therefore, $\mathbf{H}$ is the parity-check matrix in cyclic code C and row space of $\mathbf{H}$ is the dual code of C. As parity-check matrix is obtained from $\mathbf{h}(x)$, it is called the *parity polynomial* in C and hence a cyclic code is uniquely specified by its parity polynomial. The above derivation leads to an important property which is stated in the following theorem.

Theorem 6.7: If an (n, k) cyclic code is generated with the generator polynomial $f(x)$, the dual code of C is cyclic and can be generated using by the polynomial $x^k\,\mathbf{h}(x^{-1})$, where $\mathbf{h}(x) = (1 + x^n)/f(x)$.

Example 6.3: Consider the (7, 4) cyclic code with the generator polynomial $f(x) = 1 + x + x^3$. The parity polynomial is

$$\begin{aligned}\mathbf{h}(x) &= (1 + x^n)/f(x)\\ &= 1 + x + x^2 + x^4\end{aligned}$$

Hence,

$$\begin{aligned}x^4\mathbf{h}(x^{-1}) &= x^4(1 + x^{-1} + x^{-2} + x^{-4})\\ &= 1 + x^2 + x^4 + x^4\end{aligned}$$

Code vectors generated by $x^4\mathbf{h}(x^{-1}) = 1 + x^2 + x^4 + x^4$ have the minimum distance of 4 and is capable of correcting any single error as well as detecting combinations of double error.

The generator matrix in systematic form can be obtained from dividing x^{n-k-i} by generator polynomial $f(x)$ for $i = 0, 1, 2, \ldots, k - 1$, such that

$$x^{n-k-i} = \mathbf{a}_i(x)f(x) + \mathbf{b}_i(x)$$

where $\mathbf{b}_i(x)$ is remainder of the form of

$$\mathbf{b}_i(x) = b_{i,0} + b_{i,1}x + b_{i,2}x^2 + \ldots + b_{i,n-k-1}x^{n-k-1}$$

Since $x^{n-k-i} + \mathbf{b}_i(x)$ is the multiple of $f(x)$ for $i = 0, 1, 2, \ldots, k-1$, they are code polynomials and generator matrix for systematic form may be arranged in $k \times n$ matrix form as

$$\mathbf{G} = \begin{bmatrix} b_{0,0} & b_{0,1} & b_{0,2} & \cdots & b_{0,n-k-1} & 1 & 0 & 0 & \cdots & 0 \\ b_{1,0} & b_{1,1} & b_{1,2} & \cdots & b_{1,n-k-1} & 0 & 1 & 0 & \cdots & 0 \\ b_{2,0} & b_{2,1} & b_{2,2} & \cdots & b_{2,n-k-1} & 0 & 0 & 1 & \cdots & 0 \\ \vdots & \vdots & \vdots & \ddots & \vdots & \vdots & \vdots & \vdots & \ddots & \vdots \\ b_{k-1,0} & b_{k-1,1} & b_{k-1,2} & \cdots & b_{k-1,n-k-1} & 0 & 0 & 0 & \cdots & 1 \end{bmatrix} \tag{6.19}$$

and corresponding parity matrix is

$$\mathbf{H} = \begin{bmatrix} 1 & 0 & 0 & \cdots & 0 & b_{0,0} & b_{1,0} & b_{2,0} & \cdots & b_{k-1,0} \\ 0 & 1 & 0 & \cdots & 0 & b_{0,1} & b_{1,1} & b_{2,1} & \cdots & b_{k-1,1} \\ 0 & 0 & 1 & \cdots & 0 & b_{0,2} & b_{1,2} & b_{2,2} & \cdots & b_{k-1,2} \\ \vdots & \vdots & \vdots & \ddots & \vdots & \vdots & \vdots & \vdots & \ddots & \vdots \\ 0 & 0 & 0 & \cdots & 1 & b_{0,n-k-1} & b_{1,n-k-1} & b_{2,n-k-1} & \cdots & b_{k-1,n-k-1} \end{bmatrix} \tag{6.20}$$

6.2.2 Realization of Cyclic Code

We have seen that systematic form of cyclic code may be obtained by the following steps:

- Multiply the message polynomial $u(x)$ by x^{n-k}.
- Obtain the remainder $\mathbf{b}(x)$ as parity digits from dividing $x^{n-k}u(x)$ by a generator polynomial $f(x)$.
- Combine $\mathbf{b}(x)$ and $x^{n-k}u(x)$ to obtain code polynomial $\mathbf{b}(x) + x^{n-k}u(x)$.

All three steps can be realized by shift registers of $n - k$ stages with the feedback connections based on the polynomial $f(x) = 1 + f_1x + f_2x^2 + \quad + f_{n-r-1}x^{n-k-1} + x^{n-k}$. The schematic diagram of realization of encoded form of cyclic code is shown in Figure 6.1.

First, message bits are shifted into the communication channel as well as to the gate. This is equivalent to the message polynomial of k bits, $u(x) = u_0 + u_1x + u_2x^2 + \ldots + u_{k-1}x^{k-1}$. While all the information bits are fed to the communication channel, the parity bits are simultaneously generated in the shift registers. Now the switch is turned to parity side and parity bits are shifted for $n - k$ times to

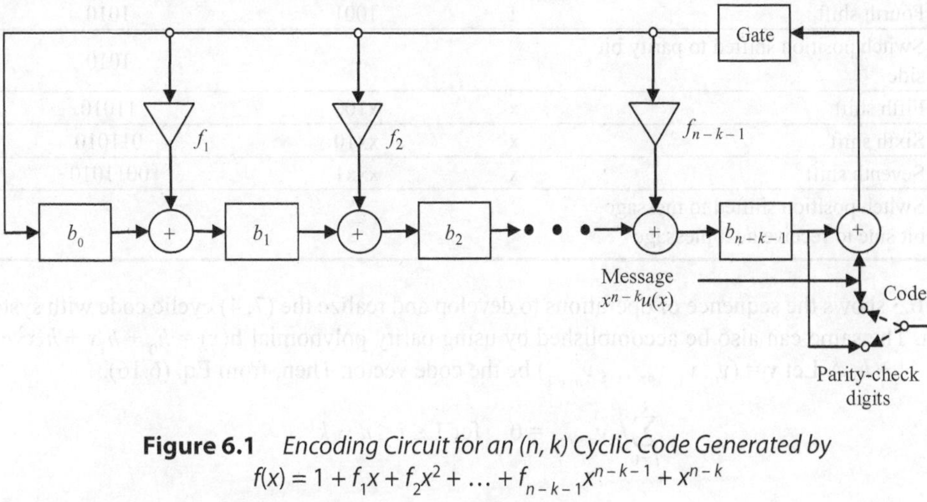

Figure 6.1 *Encoding Circuit for an (n, k) Cyclic Code Generated by* $f(x) = 1 + f_1x + f_2x^2 + \ldots + f_{n-k-1}x^{n-k-1} + x^{n-k}$

communication channel. Thus the message bits are also shifted $n - k$ times, which is equivalent to $\mathbf{b}(x) + x^{n-k}u(x)$. Next the switch is again turned to gate/message input side. Let us take the example encoding of 4-bit information to an (7, 4) cyclic code.

Example 6.4: Consider the (7, 4) cyclic code with the generator polynomial $f(x) = 1 + x + x^3$. The message is 1010 and the circuit schematic is shown in Figure 6.2. Let us consider all the shift registers are reset to 0.

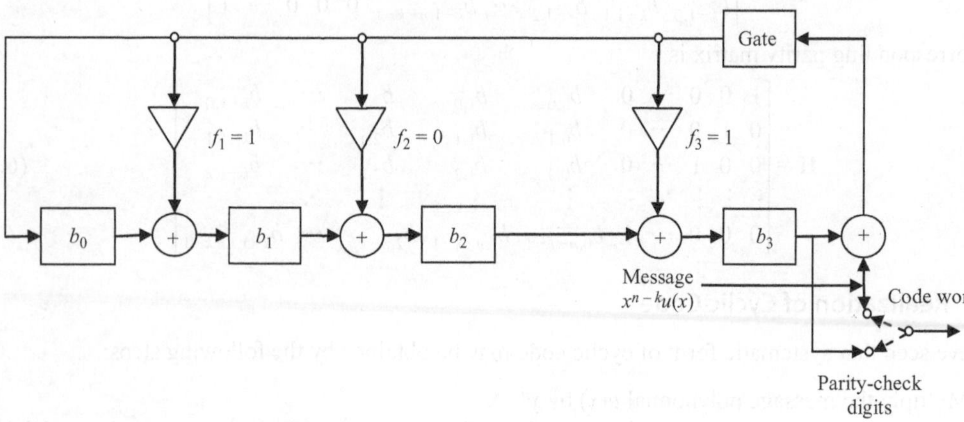

Figure 6.2 *Encoding Circuit for an (7, 4) Cyclic Code Generated by $f(x) = 1 + x + x^3$*

Table 6.3 *Sequence of Operations to Develop and Realize the (7, 4) Cyclic Code for Message 1010*

Step	Operations	Input	Contents of Shift Registers	Contents of Communication Channel
1	–	–	0000	x
2	First shift	0	0000	0
3	Second shift	1	1101	10
4	Third shift	0	0110	010
5	Fourth shift	1	1001	1010
6	Switch position shifted to parity bit side	–	–	1010
7	Fifth shift	x	x100	11010
8	Sixth shift	x	xx10	011010
9	Seventh shift	x	xxx1	0011010
10	Switch position shifted to message bit side to receive next message	–	–	–

Table 6.3 shows the sequence of operations to develop and realize the (7, 4) cyclic code with systematic form. The same can also be accomplished by using parity polynomial $\mathbf{h}(x) = h_0 + h_1x + h_2x^2 + \ldots + h_{k-1}x^{k-1} + h_kx^k$. Let $\mathbf{v} = (v_0, v_1, v_2, \ldots, v_{n-1})$ be the code vector. Then, from Eq. (6.16),

$$\sum_{i=0}^{k} h_i v_{n-i-j} = 0 \quad \text{for } 1 \le i \le n-k$$

As $h_k = 1$, it may be written that

$$v_{n-k-j} = \sum_{i=0}^{k-1} h_i v_{n-i-j} \quad \text{for } 1 \le j \le n-k \tag{6.21}$$

The above equation is also termed as *difference equation*. In code vector $v_{n-k}, v_{n-k+1}, v_{n-k+2}, \ldots, v_{n-1}$ are the information digits and $v_0, v_1, v_2, \ldots, v_{n-k-1}$ are the parity digits. The encoded information may be realized by the schematic as shown in Figure 6.3. The feedback connections are made so that $h_0 = h_k = 1$. Initially the message bits are fed through gate1 as well as to the registers of k-stages, keeping gate2 as turned off. These information bits go to the communication channel also. Once all the k-bits information is entered, gate1 is turned off and gate2 is turned on. The first parity digit has been generated as follows:

$$\begin{aligned} v_{n-k-1} &= h_0 v_{n-1} + h_1 v_{n-2} + h_2 v_{n-3} + \ldots + h_{k-1} v_{n-k} \\ &= u_{k-1} + h_1 u_{k-2} + h_2 u_{k-3} + \ldots + h_{k-1} u_0 \end{aligned}$$

It is fed to the communication channel and also to the shift register. At the next shift, the second parity bit is generated and enters the communication channel, which is given by

$$\begin{aligned} v_{n-k-2} &= h_0 v_{n-2} + h_1 v_{n-3} + h_2 v_{n-4} + \ldots + h_{k-1} v_{n-k-1} \\ &= u_{k-2} + h_1 u_{k-3} + h_2 u_{k-4} + \ldots + h_{k-2} u_0 + h_{k-1} v_{n-k-1} \end{aligned}$$

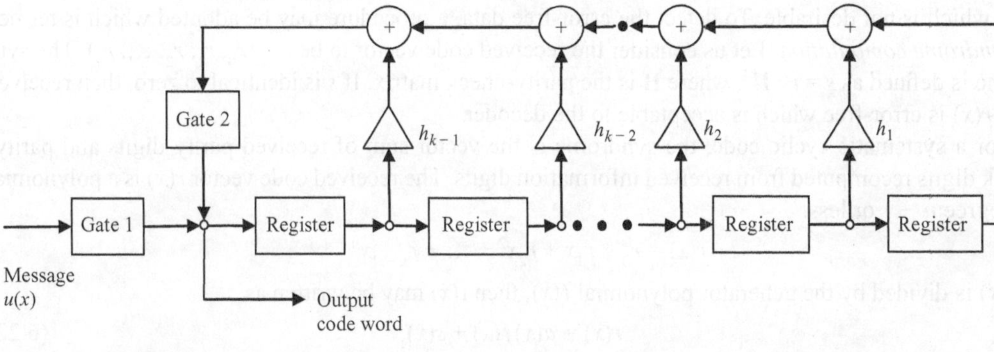

Figure 6.3 *Encoding Circuit for an (n, k) Cyclic Code using Parity Polynomial h(x)*

It is also fed to the shift register. This process of generation of parity bits and feeding to communication channel is continued for $n - k$ number of shifts. Thereafter, gate2 is turned off and gate1 is turned on to accept the next information block.

Example 6.5: Let us consider previous example of (7, 4) cyclic code with the generator polynomial $f(x) = 1 + x + x^3$. The message is 1010. The parity polynomial $h(x)$ will be

$$h(x) = (1 + x^7)/(1 + x + x^3) = 1 + x + x^2 + x^4$$

From Eq. (6.21), the parity bits are

$$\begin{aligned} v_{n-k-j} &= v_{7-4-j} = v_{3-j} = h_0 v_{7-j} + h_1 v_{6-j} + h_2 v_{5-j} + h_3 v_{4-j} \\ &= 1 \cdot v_{7-j} + 1 \cdot v_{6-j} + 1 \cdot v_{5-j} + 0 \cdot v_{4-j} && \text{for } 1 \le j \le 3 \\ &= v_{7-j} + v_{6-j} + v_{5-j} && \text{for } 1 \le j \le 3 \end{aligned}$$

For the message 1010, $v_3 = 1$, $v_4 = 0$, $v_5 = 1$, $v_6 = 0$. The parity bits are

For $j = 1$, $v_2 = v_6 + v_5 + v_4 = 0 + 1 + 0 = 1$

For $j = 2$, $v_1 = v_5 + v_4 + v_3 = 1 + 0 + 1 = 0$

For $j = 3$, $v_0 = v_4 + v_3 + v_2 = 0 + 1 + 1 = 0$

Thus the corresponding code vector is (0 0 1 1 0 1 0) and can be realized by the circuit schematic as shown in Figure 6.4.

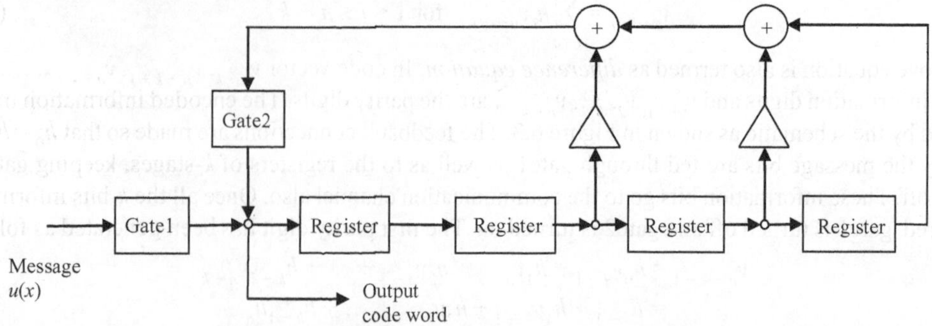

Figure 6.4 *Generation of Code Vector for Message 1010*

6.3 SYNDROME COMPUTATION AND ERROR DETECTION

Due to various factors, noises, and interferences, the received data may not be same as the transmitted data which is not desirable. To detect the error-free data, a procedure may be adopted which is termed as *syndrome computation*. Let us consider the received code vector to be $\mathbf{r} = (r_0, r_1, r_2, \ldots, r_n)$. The syndrome is defined as $s = r \cdot \mathbf{H}^T$, where $\mathbf{H}$ is the parity-check matrix. If s is identical to zero, then received data $r(x)$ is error-free which is acceptable to the decoder.

For a systematic cyclic code, the syndrome is the vector sum of received parity digits and parity-check digits recomputed from received information digits. The received code vector $r(x)$ is a polynomial of degree $n - 1$ or less.

$$r(x) = r_0 + r_1x + r_2x^2 + \ldots + r_{n-1}x^{n-1}$$

If $r(x)$ is divided by the generator polynomial $f(x)$, then r(x) may be written as

$$r(x) = a(x)f(x) + s(x) \tag{6.22}$$

The remainder $s(x)$ is a polynomial of degree $n - k - 1$ or less. The $n - k$ coefficients of $s(x)$ form the syndrome. It is obvious from Theorem 6.4 that $s(x)$ is identical to zero if and only if the received polynomial $r(x)$ is a code polynomial.

The syndrome polynomial can be realized by the circuit schematic as shown in Figure 6.5. Initially all the registers are set to 0. The received vector $r(x)$ is shifted to the registers. As soon as the full block length is received, the register contents will be equivalent to syndrome of the received message block.

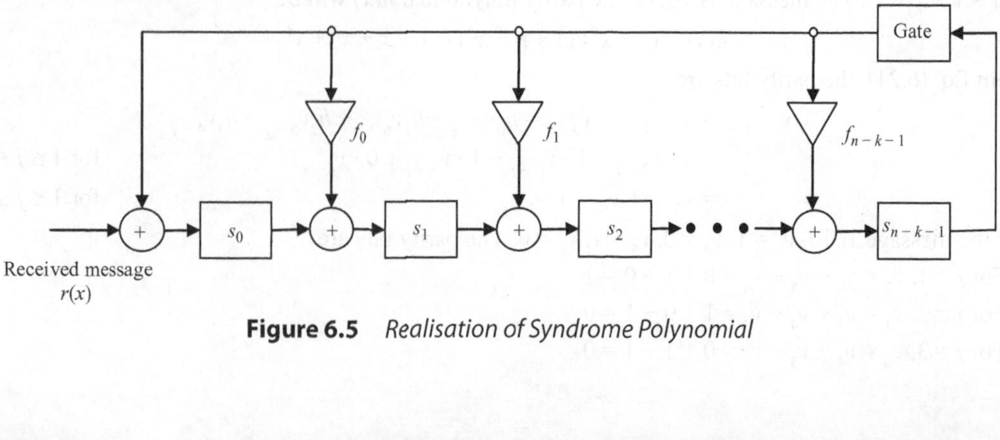

Figure 6.5 *Realisation of Syndrome Polynomial*

Theorem 6.8: If $s(x)$ is the syndrome of a received polynomial $r(x) = r_0 + r_1x + r_2x^2 + \ldots + r_{n-1}x^{n-1}$, then remainder $s_1(x)$ resulting from dividing $xs(x)$ by generator polynomial $f(x)$ is the syndrome of $r_1(x)$ which is the cyclic shift of $r(x)$.

Proof:

As shown in Eq. (6.3), $\quad xr(x) = r_{n-1}(1 + x^n) + r_1(x)$

or $\quad r_1(x) = r_{n-1}(1 + x^n) + xr(x)$

As $\quad (1 + x^n) = f(x)h(x), \; r_1(x) = r_{n-1}f(x)h(x) + xr(x)$

Considering $f(x)$ as divisor polynomial,

$$b(x)f(x) + c(x) = r_{n-1}f(x)h(x) + x[a(x)f(x) + s(x)] \tag{6.23}$$

where $c(x)$ is the remainder resulting from dividing $r_1(x)$ by $f(x)$ and it is equivalent to syndrome of $r_1(x)$. Eq. (6.23) may be rewritten as follows:

$$xs(x) = [b(x) + r_{n-1}h(x) + xa(x)]f(x) + c(x) \tag{6.24}$$

It is seen from above equation that $c(x)$ is the remainder if $xs(x)$ is divided by $f(x)$. Therefore $c(x)$ is the syndrome of $xs(x)$ or $s_1(x)$. This leads to an important property of syndrome that $s_i(x)$ is the syndrome of $r_i(x)$, which can be realized simply by ith shift. Furthermore this property helps to detect and correct errors from received messages.

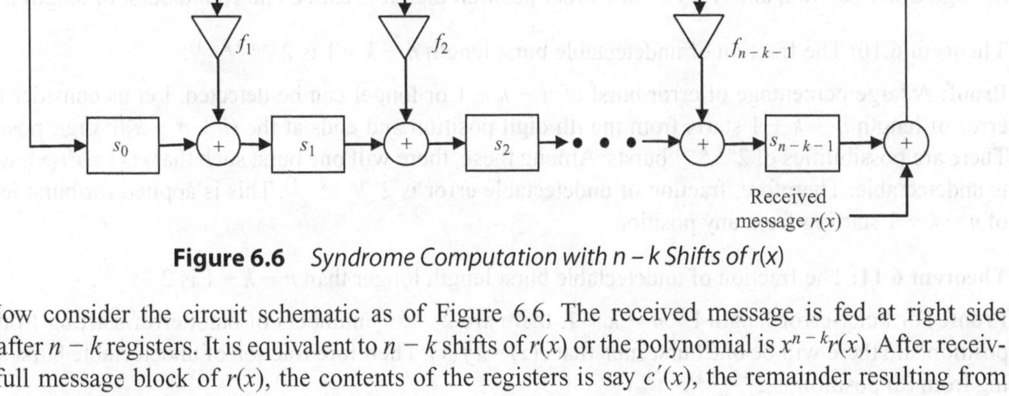

Figure 6.6 *Syndrome Computation with n – k Shifts of r(x)*

Now consider the circuit schematic as of Figure 6.6. The received message is fed at right side i.e., after $n - k$ registers. It is equivalent to $n - k$ shifts of $r(x)$ or the polynomial is $x^{n-k}r(x)$. After receiving full message block of $r(x)$, the contents of the registers is say $c'(x)$, the remainder resulting from dividing $x^{n-k}r(x)$ by $f(x)$.

$$x^{n-k}r(x) = a(x)f(x) + c'(x)$$

As shown in Eq. (6.3), $\quad x^{n-k}r(x) = b(x)(1 + x^n) + r_{n-k}(x)$

Again as $(1 + x^n) = f(x)h(x)$, $\quad a(x)f(x) + c'(x) = b(x)f(x)h(x) + r_{n-k}(x)$

or

$$r_{n-k}(x) = [a(x) + b(x)h(x)]f(x) + c'(x) \tag{6.25}$$

Eq. (6.25) implies that $r_{n-k}(x)$ is divided by $f(x)$ resulting in the remainder as $c'(x)$. This means $c'(x)$ is the syndrome of $r_{n-k}(x)$, i.e., $n - k$ times cyclic shift of $r(x)$.

Now let us consider that $v(x)$, $r(x)$, and $e(x)$ are the transmitted vector, received vector, and error, respectively, introduced in the channel. Then following relation can be written:

$$r(x) = v(x) + e(x) \tag{6.26}$$

So,
$$a(x)f(x) + s(x) = b(x)f(x) + e(x)$$
or
$$e(x) = [a(x) + b(x)]f(x) + s(x) \tag{6.27}$$

This shows that the syndrome is actually the remainder resulting from dividing the error polynomial by the generator polynomial $f(x)$. Syndrome can be computed by shift registers as shown, but error pattern $e(x)$ is unknown. Hence, decoder has to estimate $e(x)$ based on $s(x)$. However $e(x)$ can be correctly determined, using decoder lookup table, if $e(x)$ is a coset leader in standard array.

From Eq. (6.27), it may be noticed that $s(x)$ is identical to zero, if and only if $e(x)$ is either identical to zero or equivalent to code vector. If $e(x)$ is identical to code vector, it is undetectable to estimate the error. Cyclic codes are very effective to detect any errors—random or burst. Multiple errors in small segment of message is termed as burst error. Error detection may be made simply by feeding all the syndrome register digits to an OR gate. If any of the syndrome digits is not 0, which is in case of presence of error, output of the OR gate is 1.

Theorem 6.9: An (n, k) cyclic code is capable of detecting any burst error of length of $n - k$ or less, including end-round burst.

Proof: Let us consider that the error pattern $e(x)$ is burst type of length $n - k$ or less. Then $e(x)$ can be expressed as $e(x) = x^j q(x)$, for $0 \leq j \leq n - 1$ and $q(x)$ is a polynomial of degree $n - k - 1$. Since $q(x)$ has the degree less than $n - k - 1$, it is not divisible by generator polynomial $f(x)$. Also x^j is not a factor or $f(x)$; hence, $x^j q(x)$ is not divisible by $f(x)$. Therefore $e(x)$ is not equal to zero. This implies that (n, k) cyclic code is capable of detecting any error length $n - k$ or less. In cyclic code, if error occurs within ith high order position and $(1 - i)$th low order position then it is called end-round burst of length 1.

Theorem 6.10: The fraction of undetectable burst length $n - k + 1$ is $2^{-(n-k-1)}$.

Proof: A large percentage of error burst of $n - k + 1$ or longer can be detected. Let us consider burst error of length $n - k + 1$ starts from the ith digit position and ends at the $(i + n - k)$th digit position. There are possibilities of 2^{n-k-1} bursts. Among these, there will one burst such that $e(x) = x^1 f(x)$, which is undetectable. Therefore, fraction of undetectable error is $2^{-(n-k-1)}$. This is applied for burst length of $n - k + 1$ starting from any position.

Theorem 6.11: The fraction of undetectable burst length longer than $n - k + 1$ is $2^{-(n-k)}$.

Proof: For burst-error length $1 > n - k + 1$, there are 2^{n-k-1} numbers of burst error starting from ith position and there will be one burst such that $e(x) = x^1 f(x)$. Therefore fraction of undetectable burst starting from ith position is $2^{-(n-k)}$.

This shows that cyclic codes are very effective to detect burst errors. As example, (7, 4) cyclic code generated by the polynomial $f(x) = 1 + x + x^3$ has the minimum distance of 3 and capable of detecting any combination of two or fewer random errors as well as burst error of length 3 or less. It is also capable of detecting many error burst of length greater than 3.

6.4 DECODING

There are three basic steps to decode a cyclic code—(i) syndrome computation, (ii) obtaining error pattern, and (iii) error correction. Figure 6.7 represents the basic schematic of error detection and correction from the received data of cyclic code. The decoding operation is described as follows:

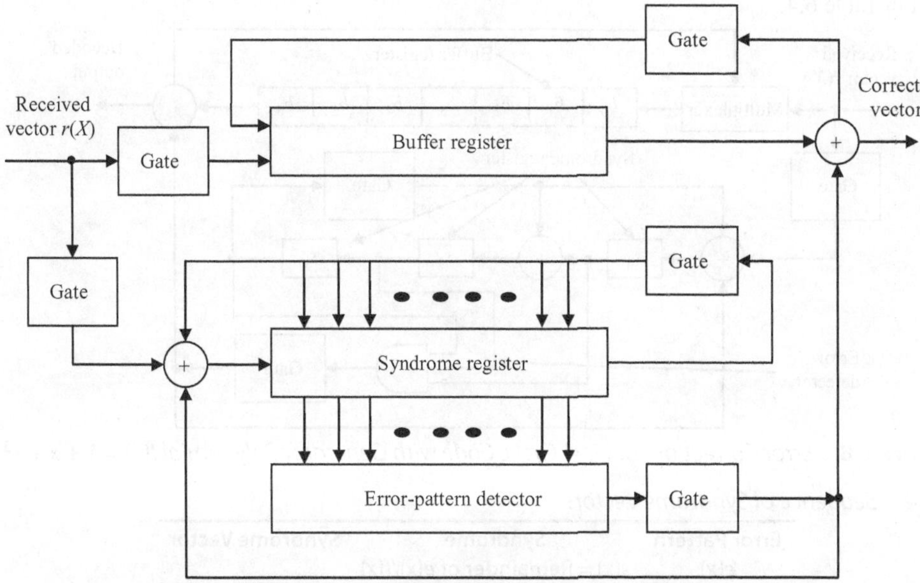

Figure 6.7 *Basic Schematic of Error Detection and Correction*

1. The received polynomial is shifted into syndrome register from the left end. At the same time it is fed into buffer register.
2. The syndrome is checked against corresponding error pattern. The error-pattern detector is a combinational circuit that is designed in such a way that its output is 1, if and only if the syndrome register contents correspond to a correctable error pattern with the error at the highest order position x^{n-1}. This means if the rightmost digit of received polynomial is erroneous, 1 will appear at error detector. If 0 appears at error detector, the rightmost stage of received polynomial is correct and no correction is necessary. The output of error detector is the estimated error value of the buffer.
3. The first received symbol is read out of the buffer and at the same time the syndrome register is shifted once. If the first received symbol is erroneous, it is corrected by the output of the detector. The output of the detector is also fed to the syndrome register to form new syndrome shifted once to right which is free from error effect.
4. The new syndrome is now compared for any error effect in similar manner which is for the second rightmost digit. Second rightmost digit is corrected and read out from buffer, and error-detector output is fed to syndrome register to form a new syndrome vector for next digit.
5. This process is continued till the leftmost digit of received vector is read out with correction.

The above decoder is known as *Meggitt decoder*, which is applicable to any cyclic code. Its performance depends on the error-pattern detection circuit. Meggitt decoder can also be designed with the detection and correction from leftmost digit.

Example 6.6: Considering a (7, 4) cyclic code with generator polynomial $f(x) = 1 + x + x^3$, the decoding circuit is shown in Figure 6.8. This code is capable of removing any of the single error over a block of seven digits. Suppose the received polynomial is $r(x) = r_0 + r_1x + r_2x^2 + r_3x^3 + r_4x^4 + r_5x^5 + r_6x^6$ from the left end of syndrome register. The seven single-error patterns and their corresponding syndromes are listed in Table 6.4.

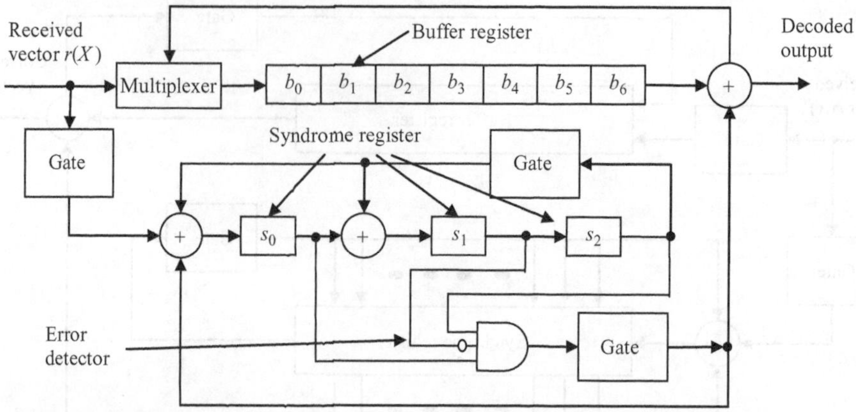

Figure 6.8 *Error Correction for (7, 4) Cyclic Code with Generator Polynomial f(x) = 1 + x + x³*

Table 6.4 *Sequence of Syndrome Vectors*

Error Pattern $e(x)$	Syndrome $s(x)$ = Remainder of $e(x)/f(x)$	Syndrome Vector
$e(x) = x^6$	$s(x) = 1 + x^2$	1 0 1
$e(x) = x^5$	$s(x) = 1 + x + x^2$	1 1 1
$e(x) = x^4$	$s(x) = x + x^2$	0 1 1
$e(x) = x^3$	$s(x) = 1 + x$	1 1 0
$e(x) = x^2$	$s(x) = x^2$	0 0 1
$e(x) = x^1$	$s(x) = x$	0 1 0
$e(x) = x^0$	$s(x) = 1$	1 0 0

Example 6.7: Consider the transmitted code vector to be $\mathbf{v}$ = 1001011 [$\mathbf{v}(x) = 1 + x^3 + x^5 + x^6$] and received vector $\mathbf{r}$ = 1011011 [$\mathbf{r}(x) = 1 + x^2 + x^3 + x^5 + x^6$]. There is an error of single digit at location x^2. When the entire received digits are loaded into buffer register, the syndrome register will contain 001. In Figure 6.9, the contents of syndrome register and buffer register are shown after every shift. Also error location has been shown for each shift. It may be noticed that after four shifts the error comes out of buffer and after seven shift the buffer contains the corrected data. Thus it is observed that the cyclic code makes decoding and error-correction circuit simple. However, it is slow due to the correction made in serial manner. In general, speed and simplicity cannot be achieved at the same time and a trade-off must be made.

Decoding of cyclic code may be achieved by feeding the received vector from the right end to syndrome register. When $r(x)$ is shifted from the right end as shown in Figure 6.10, the syndrome register contains $s_{n-k}(x)$ which is the syndrome of $r_{n-k}(x)$, the $n - k$ cyclic shift of $r(x)$. If $s_{n-k}(x)$ corresponds to error pattern $e(x)$ with $e_{n-1} = 1$, the highest digit r_{n-1} of $r(x)$ is erroneous and is to be corrected. In $r_{n-k}(x)$, r_{n-1} is at the location x^{n-k-1}. When r_{n-1} is corrected, the error effect of $s_{n-k}(x)$ will be removed. The new syndrome is the sum of $s_{n-k}(x)$ and the remainder $p(x)$ resulting from dividing x^{n-k-1} by generator polynomial $f(x)$. Since the degree of x^{n-k-1} is less than the degree of $f(x)$, $p(x) = x^{n-k-1}$. This implies that the error effect at the location x^{n-1} can be removed by feeding the error digit from right end to the syndrome register through the exclusive OR gate as shown in Figure 6.10. The error correction and decoding process is identical to Figure 6.8. The schematic circuit for error correction and decoding of (7, 4) cyclic code for the generator polynomial $f(x) = 1 + x + x^3$ is shown in Figure 6.11.

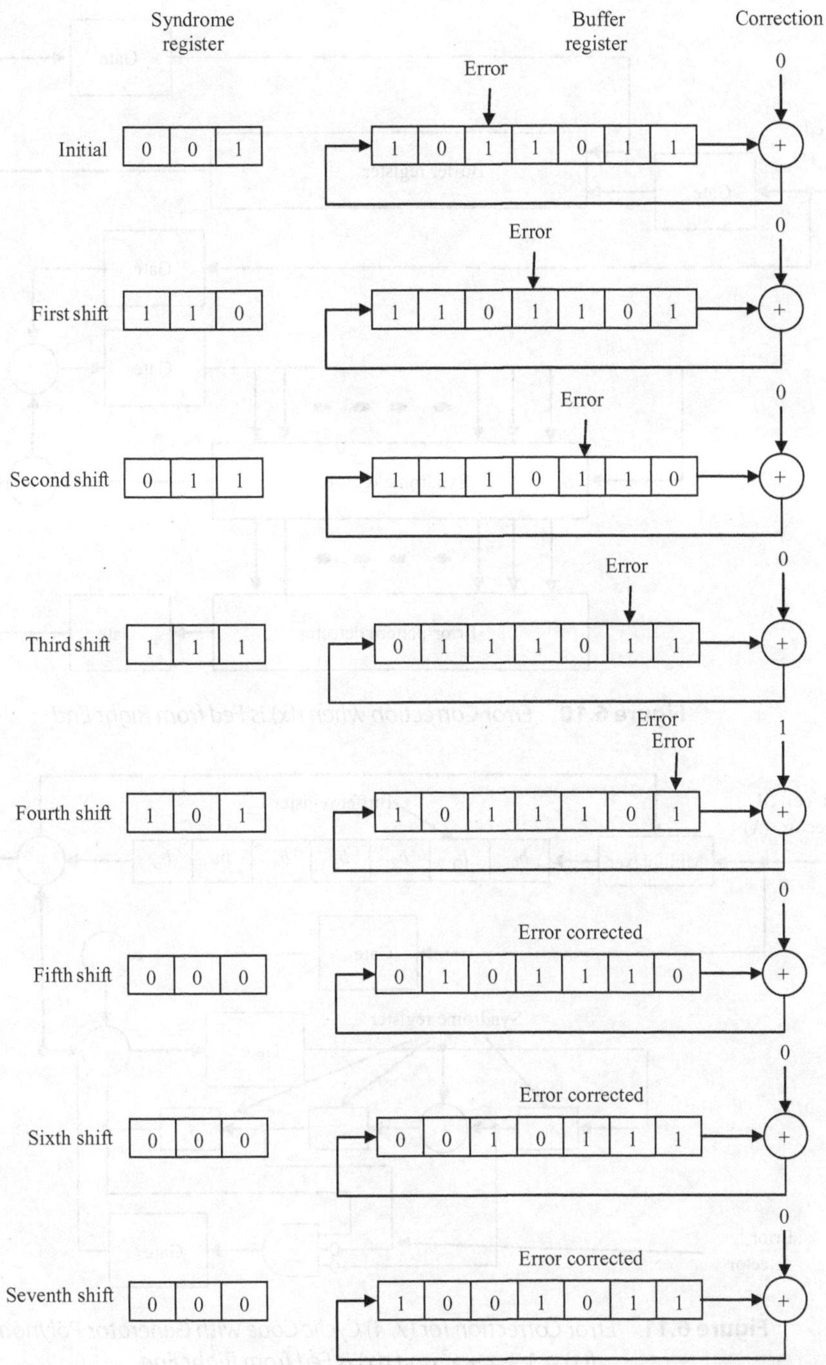

Figure 6.9 *Sequence of Operation of Registers for Received Code 1011011 with Error*

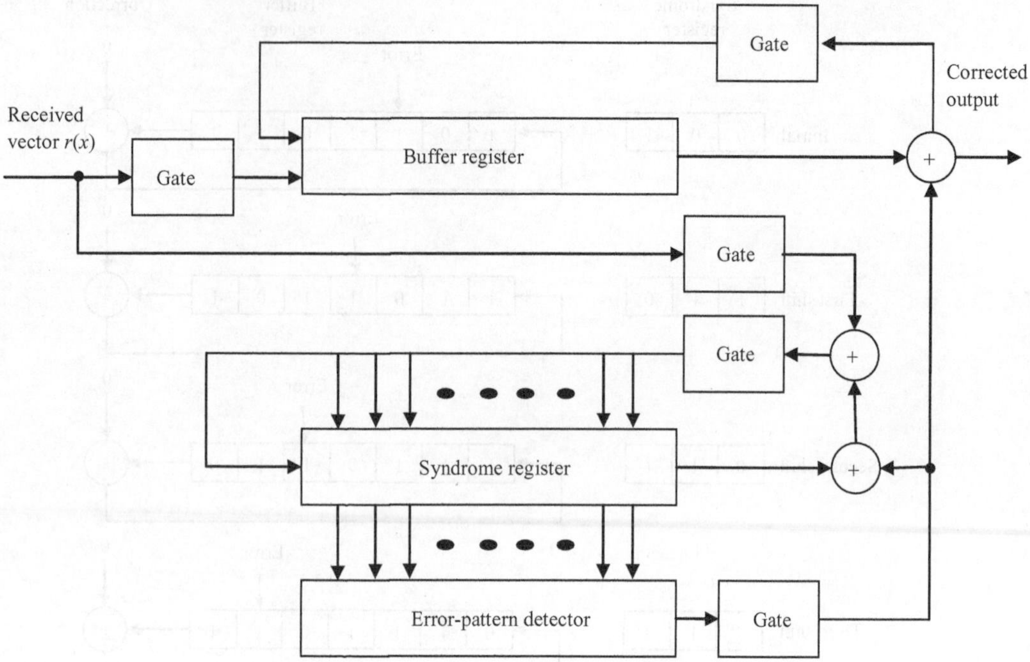

Figure 6.10 *Error Correction when r(x) is Fed from Right End*

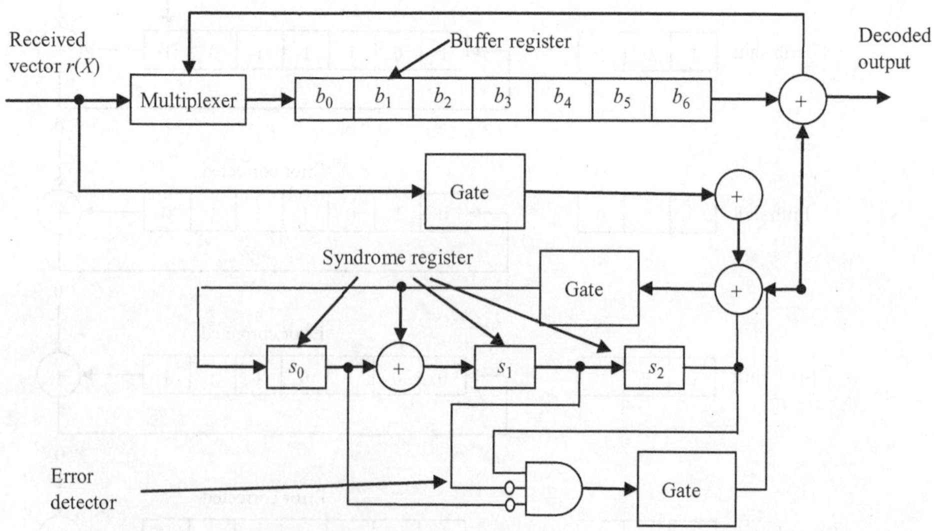

Figure 6.11 *Error Correction for (7, 4) Cyclic Code with Generator Polynomial $f(x) = 1 + x + x^3$ and r(x) is Fed from Right End*

The error pattern and the syndrome register contents are shown in Table 6.5 when received data is fed through right end of syndrome register for generator polynomial $f(x) = 1 + x + x^3$.

Table 6.5 *Error Pattern and Syndrome Register for Generation Polynomial f(x) = 1+ x + x³*

Error Pattern e(x)	Syndrome s(x) = Remainder of e(x)/f(x) $s_3(x)$ is three shifts of s(x)	Syndrome Vector
$e(x) = x^6$	$s_3(x) = 1$	0 0 1
$e(x) = x^5$	$s_3(x) = x$	0 1 0
$e(x) = x^4$	$s_3(x) = 1$	1 0 0
$e(x) = x^3$	$s_3(x) = 1 + x^2$	1 0 1
$e(x) = x^2$	$s_3(x) = 1 + x + x^2$	1 1 1
$e(x) = x^1$	$s_3(x) = x + x^2$	0 1 1
$e(x) = x^0$	$s_3(x) = 1 + x$	1 1 0

6.5 CYCLIC HAMMING CODE

A cyclic Hamming code of length $2^m - 1$ with $m \geq 3$ can be generated in a cyclic form using the primitive polynomial $p(x)$ of degree m. Dividing x^{m+i} by generator polynomial $p(x)$ for $0 \leq i \leq 2^m - m - 1$, we obtain

$$x^{m+i} = a_i(x)p(x) + b_i(x)$$

where $$b_i(x) = b_{i,0} + b_{i,1}x + b_{i,2}x^2 + \dots + b_{i,m-1}x^{m-1}$$

x^{m+i} and $p(x)$ are relatively prime as x is not a factor of $p(x)$. Therefore, $b_i(x) \neq 0$ and consists of at least two terms. If $b_i(x)$ has one term say x^j with $0 \leq j \leq m$, then

$$x^{m+i} = a_i(x)p(x) + x^j$$

or $$x^j(x^{m+i-j} + 1) = a_i(x)p(x)$$

This implies that $x^{m+i-j} + 1$ is completely divisible by $p(x)$ which is impossible as $m + i - j < 2^m - 1$ and $p(x)$ is a primitive polynomial of degree m. Therefore, $b_i(x)$ consists of at least two terms. Other characteristic is that for $i \neq j$, $b_i(x) \neq b_j(x)$.

$$b_i(x) + x^{m+i} = a_i(x)p(x)$$

and $$b_j(x) + x^{m+j} = a_j(x)p(x)$$

If $b_i(x) = b_j(x)$, then combining the above two equations, we obtain

$$x^{m+i}(x^{j-i} + 1) = [a_i(x) + a_j(x)]p(x) \quad \text{for } i < j$$

This implies that $(x^{j-i} + 1)$ is divisible by $p(x)$, which is impossible. Hence, $b_i(x) \neq b_j(x)$. Therefore, cyclic Hamming code may be generated by the polynomial $p(x)$. The matrix $\mathbf{H} = [\mathbf{I_m}\ \mathbf{Q}]$ forms the parity-check matrix of the cyclic Hamming code as referred in Eq. (6.20). $\mathbf{I_m}$ is an $m \times m$ identity matrix and $\mathbf{Q}$ is an $m \times (2^m - m - 1)$ matrix formed with $b_i(x)$. The columns of $\mathbf{Q}$ has $2^m - m - 1$ elements of b_i's with $0 \leq i \leq 2^m - m - 1$. From above discussion, it is found that no two columns are similar and each column has at least two 1's. Thus, $\mathbf{H}$ is the parity-check matrix of a Hamming code.

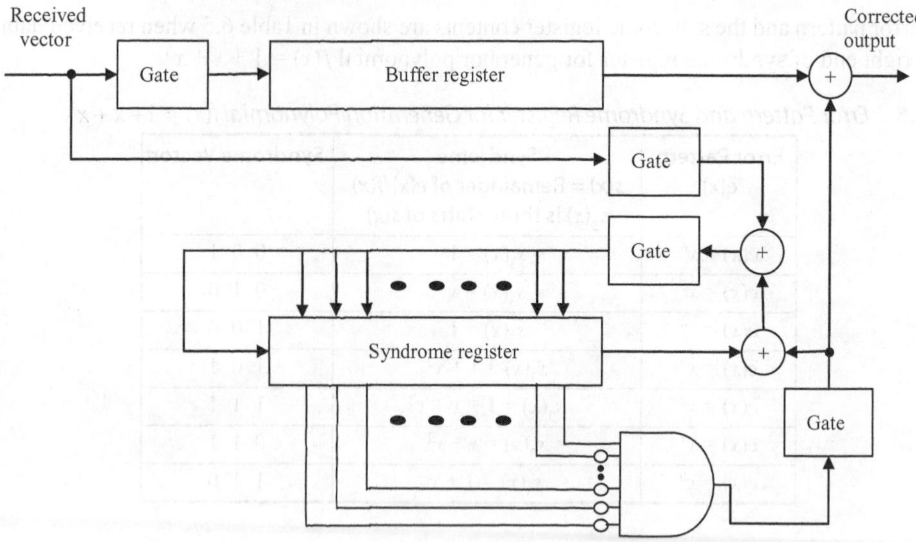

Figure 6.12 *Decoding Scheme of Hamming Code*

Decoding of Hamming code can be devised with schematic circuit shown in Figure 6.12. The received vector is fed to the syndrome register from right end. When all the data of a block is received, the syndrome register contents is equivalent to the remainder resulting from dividing $x^m x^{n-2}$ ($n = 2^m$) by generator polynomial $p(x)$. The syndrome will be of the form of $s(x) = x^{m-1}$. Therefore, if any single error occurs at highest position, the syndrome will be (0000...01). For any single error at any other position, syndrome will be different from (0000...01). Hence, only a single multi-input AND gate is needed to detect the syndrome, where the highest location content of the AND gate is connected directly whereas rest of the contents are complemented.

6.6 SHORTENED CYCLIC CODE

In a system, if a code of suitable natural length or of suitable number of information digits is not found, it may be desired to shorten a code to meet the requirements. Consider that in an (n, k) cyclic code C there is set of code vectors for which l numbers of leading locations are identical to zeros. There are 2^{k-l} code vectors that form a part of the linear subcode of C. If l numbers of zero information digits are deleted from each of these code vectors, we obtain 2^{k-l} set of vectors of length $n - l$. These 2^{k-l} shortened vectors form an $(n - l, k - l)$ linear code. This code is called *shortened cyclic code* or *polynomial code*. It is not cyclic. The shortened cyclic code has at least the same error-correction capability as the code from which it is derived.

The encoding and decoding with shortened cyclic code can be accomplished with the similar circuits as those of original cyclic code. However, at decoding end, the contents of syndrome register is critically shifted l times to generate proper syndrome. For large l, these extra l shifts of syndrome register cause unnecessary delay which can be eliminated by modifying either the connections of syndrome register or error-pattern circuit. Figure 6.13 exhibits a typical circuit schematic for decoding of (31, 26) shortened cyclic code shortened to (28, 23) with generator polynomial $f(x) = 1 + x^2 + x^5$.

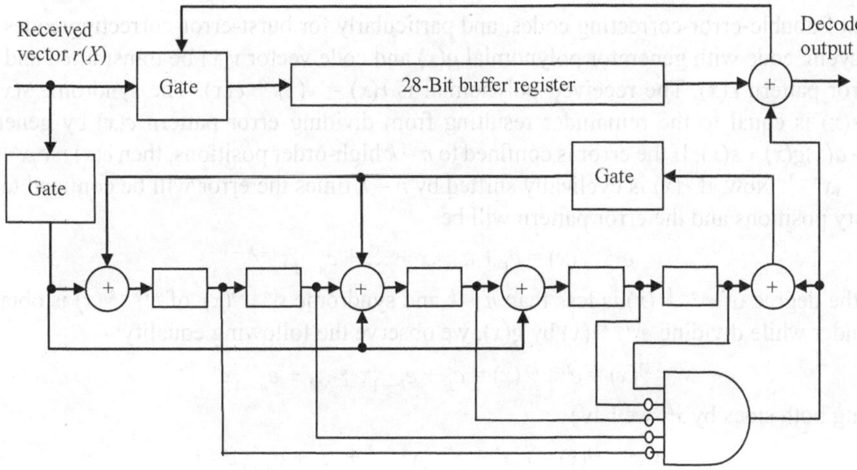

Figure 6.13 *Decoding of Shortened Cyclic Code*

6.7 GOLAY CODE

The binary form of the Golay code is one of the most important types of linear binary block codes. It is of particular significance since it is one of only a few examples of a nontrivial perfect code. A t-error-correcting code can correct a maximum of t errors. A perfect t-error-correcting code has the property that every word lies within a distance of t to exactly one code word. Equivalently, the code has minimum distance of $2t + 1$. If there is an (n, k) code with an alphabet of q elements and a minimum distance of $2t + 1$, then for M codewords,

$$M\left[\sum_{i=0}^{t}\binom{n}{i}(q-1)^i\right] \le q^n$$

The above inequality is known as the Hamming bound. Clearly, a code is perfect precisely when it attains equality in the Hamming bound. Two Golay codes do attain equality, making them perfect codes: The (23, 12) binary code with minimum distance of 7, and the (11, 6) ternary code with minimum distance of 5. The (23, 12) binary Golay code can correct up to three errors.

This (23, 12) Golay code can be generated either by

$$f_1(x) = 1 + x^2 + x^4 + x^5 + x^6 + x^{10} + x^{11}$$

or

$$f_2(x) = 1 + x + x^5 + x^6 + x^7 + x^9 + x^{11}$$

Both polynomials $f_1(x)$ and $f_2(x)$ are factors of $x^{23} + 1$ and $x^{23} + 1 = (1 + x)f_1(x)f_2(x)$. Several different ways are available to decode the (23, 12) binary Golay code that maximizes its error-correcting capability.

Extended Golay Code—Codes can be easily extended by adding an overall parity-check to the end of each code word. The (23, 12) Golay code can be extended by adding an overall parity check to each code word to form the (24, 12) extended Golay code.

6.8 ERROR-TRAPPING DECODING

Error-trapping decoding is a practical variation of Meggitt decoding devised by Kasami, Mitchell, and Rudolph. This decoding technique is most effective for decoding single-error-correcting codes, for some sort of double-error-correcting codes, and particularly for burst-error-correcting codes. Consider an (n, k) cyclic code with generator polynomial $g(x)$ and code vector $v(x)$ be transmitted and corrupted by the error pattern $e(x)$. The received polynomial is $r(x) = v(x) + e(x)$. The syndrome $s(x)$ computed from $r(x)$ is equal to the remainder resulting from dividing error pattern $e(x)$ by generator $g(x)$, i.e., $e(x) = a(x)g(x) + s(x)$. If the error is confined to $n - k$ high-order positions, then $e(x) = e_k x^k + e_{k+1}x^{k+1} + \ldots + e_{n-1}x^{n-1}$. Now, if $r(x)$ is cyclically shifted by $n - k$ times the error will be confined to $n - k$ low order parity positions and the error pattern will be

$$e^{(n-k)}(x) = e_k + e_{k+1}x + \ldots + e_{n-1}x^{n-k-1} \tag{6.28}$$

Since the degree of $e^{(n-k)}(x)$ is less than $n - k$ and syndrome $s^{(n-k)}(x)$ of $r^{(n-k)}(x)$ is obtained from the remainder while dividing $e^{(n-k)}(x)$ by $g(x)$, we observe the following equality:

$$s^{(n-k)}(x) = e^{(n-k)}(x) = e_k + e_{k+1}x + \ldots + e_{n-1}x^{n-k-1} \tag{6.29}$$

Multiplying both sides by x^k, we have

$$x^k s^{(n-k)}(x) = e_k x^k + e_{k+1}x^{k+1} + \ldots + e_{n-1}x^{n-1} \tag{6.30}$$

This means, if errors are confined to the $n - k$ high order positions of received polynomial $r(x)$, the error pattern $e(x)$ is identical to $x^k s^{(n-k)}(x)$, where $s^{(n-k)}(x)$ is the syndrome of $r^{(n-k)}(x)$, the $(n - k)$th cyclic shift of $r(x)$. Therefore, the transmitted code vector can be obtained by computing $s^{(n-k)}(x)$ and addition of $x^k s^{(n-k)}(x)$ to $r(x)$.

Now consider that burst error has occurred at $(n - k)$ consecutive positions of $r(x)$, starting from ith position, but not confined to $(n - k)$ high-order positions. If $r(x)$ is cyclically shifted to right by $(n - i)$ times, the errors will be confined to $(n - k)$ lower order position of $r^{(n-i)}(x)$, i.e., $r(x)$ with $(n - i)$ right shifts, and the error pattern is identical to $x^i s^{(n-i)}(x)$, where $s^{(n-i)}(x)$ is the syndrome of $r^{(n-i)}(x)$.

If polynomial $r(x)$ is received through syndrome register from right end and shifted, it makes equivalent to pre-multiplication of $r(x)$ by $x^{(n-k)}$. The contents of syndrome register form the syndrome $s^{(n-k)}(x)$ of $r^{(n-k)}(x)$ after entire $r(x)$ is shifted into syndrome register. If errors occur at $(n - k)$ high-order positions, they are identical to $s^{(n-i)}(x)$. However, if errors are confined to$(n - k)$ consecutive positions other than $(n - k)$ high-order positions, the syndrome register must be further shifted for certain number of times before its contents are identical to the error digits. This shifting of syndrome register is called *error trapping*. Now the error correction can be accomplished by simply adding the contents of syndrome register to the received vector. For t-error-correcting code, the weight of the syndrome register may be tested after each shift. As soon as the weight of the syndrome becomes t or less, it may be assumed that errors are trapped in the syndrome register. For t or fewer errors confined to $(n - k)$ consecutive positions, the error pattern will be of the form $e(x) = x^j B(x)$, where $B(x)$ has t or fewer terms and has degree $n - k - 1$ or less. For end-around case, same form may be obtained after certain cyclic shift of $e(x)$. Dividing $e(x)$ by generator polynomial $g(x)$, we have

$$x^j B(x) = a(x)g(x) + s(x)$$

where $s(x)$ is the syndrome of $x^j B(x)$. As $s(x) + x^j B(x)$ is a multiple of $g(x)$, it is a code polynomial. If the weight of $s(x)$ is t or less and $s(x) \neq x^j B(x)$, then $s(x) + x^j B(x)$ is a nonzero code vector with weight less than $2t + 1$. But t-error-correcting code must have the minimum weight of $2t + 1$. Therefore, it may be concluded that errors are trapped in syndrome register only when the weight of the syndrome becomes t or less and $s(x) = x^j B(x)$.

Based on the discussions above, the error-trapping decoder may be implemented as shown in the schematic diagram of Figure 6.14. The polynomial $r(x)$ is received in syndrome register shifting through right end, as well as in k-bit buffer register, as only k bits of information are required to be analyzed. After receiving entire $r(x)$ in the syndrome register, the weights of its contents are tested by an $(n - k)$

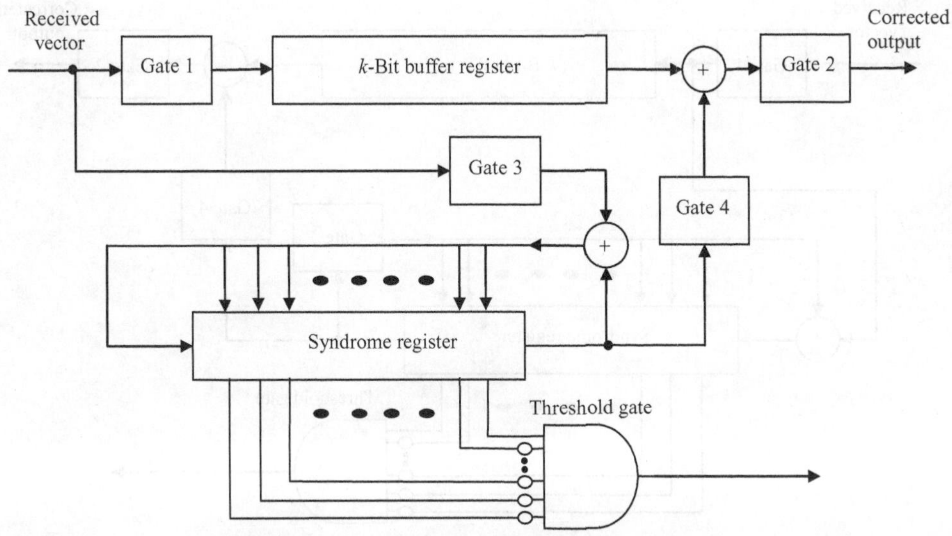

Figure 6.14 *Schematic of Error Trapping Decoder*

input threshold gate. The output of threshold gate is 1 when t or fewer inputs are 1. If the weight of the syndrome is t or less, the contents of syndrome register are identical to the error digits at $(n - k)$ high-order positions of $r(x)$.

In case of the error not confined to $(n - k)$ high-order positions, cyclically shift the syndrome register once, keeping gate3 on and all other gates at off condition. If weight of the new syndrome is tested to be t or less, the errors are confined to the locations $x^{k-1}, x^k, \ldots, x^{n-2}$ of $r(x)$ and contents of syndrome register are identical to errors at these locations. Therefore, the received digit r_{n-1} is error-free and read out from buffer register. If the weight of the syndrome is greater than t, the syndrome register is shifted once more and tested as described previously.

Thus, syndrome register is shifted continuously until the weights of its contents go down to t or less. If the weight becomes t or less after ith shift, the contents of buffer register are error-free and read out of the buffer register, the contents of syndrome register are shifted out and used to correct next $n - k$ received digits. Any nonzero digits left in the syndrome register are ignored as they are the parity parts.

Implementation of error-trapping decoder is possible in a different manner as shown in schematic diagram of Figure 6.15. In this scheme the error patterns confined to $n - k$ consecutive end-around locations can be corrected in a faster way. Here the received vector is shifted from left into the syndrome register. If the errors are confined to $n - k$ low-order parity positions of $r(x)$, then, after entire $r(x)$ is entered in the syndrome register, the contents of syndrome register are identical to error digits of similar positions of $r(x)$. And if errors are not confined to $n - k$ low-order parity positions of $r(x)$, but are confined to $n - k$ consecutive locations, after $n - i$ cyclic shifts of $r(x)$, errors will be shifted to the $n - k$ low-order positions of $r^{(n-i)}(x)$. The syndrome of $r^{(n-i)}(x)$ will be identical to the errors confined to the positions $x^i, x^{i+1}, \ldots, x^{(n-k)+i-1}$ of $r(x)$.

The decoding of cyclic Hamming code as described earlier is actually an error-trapping decoding. Error-trapping decoding is most effective for single or burst error correction. However, this decoding technique is ineffective for long and high rate codes with large error-correcting capability.

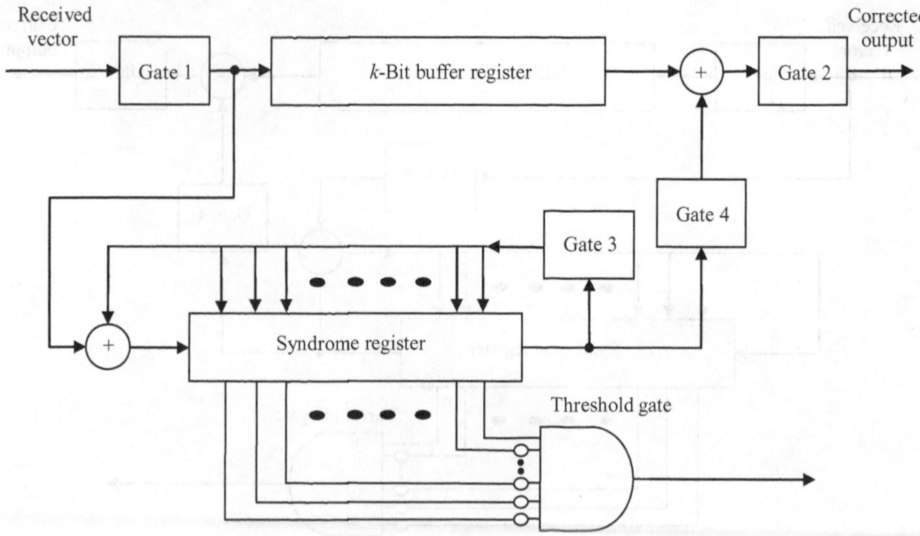

Figure 6.15 *Error Trapping Decoder*

6.8.1 Improved Error-trapping

The error-trapping decoding as described above may be further improved with additional circuitry if most errors are confined to $n - k$ consecutive locations and fewer errors are outside the $n - k$ digits span. An improvement proposed by Kasami is discussed here.

The error pattern $e(x)$ of received vector $r(x)$ may be divided into two parts: $e_P(x)$, errors at parity section, and $e_I(x)$, errors at information section.

$$e_P(x) = e_0 + e_1 x + e_2 x^2 + \dots + e_{n-k-1} x^{n-k-1} \tag{6.31}$$

$$e_I(x) = e_{n-k} x^{n-k} + \dots + e_{n-1} x^{n-1} \tag{6.32}$$

Dividing $e_I(x)$ by generator polynomial $g(x)$, we have

$$e_I(x) = q(x)g(x) + p(x) \tag{6.33}$$

The remainder $p(x)$ is of the degree of $n - k - 1$ or less. Therefore,

$$e(x) = e_P(x) + e_T(x) = q(x)g(x) + p(x) + e_P(x) \tag{6.34}$$

As $e_I(x)$ has the degree of $n - k - 1$ or less, $p(x) + e_P(x)$ must be the remainder resulting from dividing the error pattern $e(x)$ by the generator polynomial. Hence, $p(x) + e_P(x)$ is equal to the syndrome of received vector $r(x)$.

$$s(x) = p(x) + e_P(x)$$

or

$$e_P(x) = s(x) + p(x) \tag{6.35}$$

Thus, if error pattern of information part $e_I(x)$ is known, the error pattern of parity part $e_P(x)$ can be found.

The improved error-trapping decoding technique as devised by Kasami requires searching a set of polynomials $[\Phi_j(x)]_{j=1}^{N}$ of degree $k - 1$, such that, for any correctable error pattern $e(x)$ there exists one polynomial $\Phi_j(x)$. This implies that $x^{n-k}\Phi_j(x)$ matches the information part of $e(x)$ or cyclic shift of $e(x)$.

The polynomials $\Phi_j(x)$'s are called *covering polynomials*. The decoding procedure is described as follows:

1. The received vector is entirely shifted into syndrome register.
2. Weight of $s(x) + p_j(x)$ is calculated for each $j = 1, 2, \ldots, N$, where $p_j(x)$ is the remainder resulting from dividing $x^{n-k}\Phi_j(x)$ by the generator polynomial $g(x)$.
3. If, for some m, [the weight of $s(x) + p_m(x)$] $\le$ [t – weight of $\Phi_m(x)$], then $x^{n-k}\Phi_j(x)$ matches the error pattern in the information part of $e(x)$ and $s(x) + p_m(x)$ matches the error pattern in parity part. Hence, $e(x) = s(x) + p_m(x) + x^{n-k}\Phi_m(x)$. Correction may be done by taking modulo-2 sum of $r(x) + e(x)$. In this step, $N(n-k)$-input threshold gates are required to test the weights of $s(x) + p_j(x)$ for $j = 1, 2, \ldots, N$.
4. If [the weight of $s(x) + p_j(x)$] > [t – weight of $\Phi_j(x)$] for all $j = 1, 2, \ldots, N$, both the buffer and syndrome registers are shifted cyclically once. The weights of new contents of syndrome register and $p_j(x)$ is again tested as above.
5. The syndrome and buffer registers are continuously and cyclically shifted till the condition [the weight of $s^{(i)}(x) + p_m(x)$] $\le$ [t – weight of $\Phi_m(x)$] is not fulfilled, $s^{(i)}(x)$ being the ith shift of $s(x)$.
6. If the above condition never arises, the error pattern is uncorrectable.

This error-trapping method is applicable to many double-error-correcting and triple-error-correcting codes. It is applicable to relatively short and low rate codes. For longer code length, its complexity increases, as the number of covering polynomials N is required to be more, as well as $N(n - k)$-input threshold gate is required.

6.9 MAJORITY LOGIC DECODING

Majority logic decoding scheme is an effective method of decoding certain classes of block codes especially certain cyclic codes. It was first devised by Reed for a class of multiple-error-correcting codes and its algorithm is later extended and generalized by many investigators. First such generalization was performed by Massey.

Let us consider an (n, k) cyclic code c with parity-check matrix $\mathbf{H}$. The row space of $\mathbf{H}$ is an $(n, n-k)$ cyclic code denoted by C_d which is a dual code of C. For any vector $\mathbf{V}$ in C and $\mathbf{W}$ in C_d, the inner product of $\mathbf{V}$ and $\mathbf{W}$ is zero, i.e.,

$$\mathbf{W} \cdot \mathbf{V} = W_0V_0 + W_1V_1 + W_2V_2 + \ldots + W_{n-1}V_{n-1} = 0 \tag{6.36}$$

In fact there exists a code vector in c, if and only if $\mathbf{W} \cdot \mathbf{V} = 0$, where $\mathbf{V}$ is the vector in C_d. The equality of Eq. (6.36) is called *parity-check equation* and there are 2^{n-k} such parity-check equations.

If code vector $\mathbf{V}$ is transmitted and received vector is $\mathbf{R}$ with error vector $\mathbf{E}$, then $\mathbf{R} = \mathbf{V} + \mathbf{E}$. For any vector $\mathbf{W}$ in dual code C_d, the *parity-check sum* or *check sum* may be formed with linear sum of the received digits as follows:

$$A = \mathbf{W} \cdot \mathbf{R} = W_0R_0 + W_1R_1 + W_2R_2 + \ldots + W_{n-1}R_{n-1} \tag{6.37}$$

If $\mathbf{R}$ is a code vector, A must be zero. In case of error,

$$A = \mathbf{W} \cdot \mathbf{R} = \mathbf{W} \cdot (\mathbf{V} + \mathbf{E}) = \mathbf{W} \cdot \mathbf{V} + \mathbf{W} \cdot \mathbf{E}.$$

As $\mathbf{W} \cdot \mathbf{V} = 0$, $A = \mathbf{W} \cdot \mathbf{E}$,

or

$$A = W_0E_0 + W_1E_1 + W_2E_2 + \ldots + W_{n-1}E_{n-1} \tag{6.38}$$

An error digit E_i is assumed to be checked by check sum A, if $W_i = 1$. Suppose there exists J numbers of vectors in the dual code C_d. Then we have the following sets of relations:

$$\mathbf{W}_1 = (W_{10}, W_{11}, W_{12}, \ldots, W_{1,n-1}),$$
$$\mathbf{W}_2 = (W_{20}, W_{21}, W_{22}, \ldots, W_{2,n-1}),$$
$$\mathbf{W}_3 = (W_{30}, W_{31}, W_{32}, \ldots, W_{3,n-1}),$$
$$\vdots$$
$$\mathbf{W}_J = (W_{J0}, W_{J1}, W_{J2}, \ldots, W_{J,n-1})$$

These J vector are orthogonal on the $(n-1)$th position and said to be orthogonal vectors. This set of equations has the following properties:

1. The $(n-1)$th component of each vector is '1', i.e.,

$$W_{1,n-1} = W_{2,n-1} = W_{3,n-1} = \ldots = W_{J,n-1} = 1$$

2. For $i \neq n-1$, there exists at most one vector whose ith component is "1", i.e., if $W_{1,i} = 1$, then

$$W_{2,i} = W_{3,i} = \cdots = W_{J,i} = 0$$

Using these properties, the following equations may be formed with J orthogonal vectors and Eq. (6.38).

$$A_1 = W_{10}E_0 + W_{11}E_1 + W_{12}E_2 + \ldots + W_{1,n-2}E_{n-2} + E_{n-1}$$
$$A_2 = W_{20}E_0 + W_{21}E_1 + W_{22}E_2 + \ldots + W_{2,n-2}E_{n-2} + E_{n-1}$$
$$\vdots$$
$$A_J = W_{J,0}E_0 + W_{J,1}E_1 + W_{J,2}E_2 + \ldots + W_{J,,n-2}E_{n-2} + E_{n-1}$$

These J check sums are said to be orthogonal on error digit E_{n-1}. Since $W_{i,j} = 0$ or 1, the check sum equations can be generalized in the form:

$$A_j = E_{n-1} + \sum_{i \neq n-1} E_i \tag{6.39}$$

If all error digits in check sum A_J are zero for $i \neq n-1$, then $A_J = E_{n-1}$. Based on this fact, E_{n-1} or the received digit R_{n-1} can be estimated. Suppose there are at most $[J/2]$ errors in the error vector E, i.e., $[J/2]$ or fewer components of E are 1. If E_{n-1} is 1, the other nonzero errors are distributed among at most $[J/2] - 1$ check sums orthogonal on E_{n-1}. Hence, at least $[J/2] + 1$, or more than one-half of the check sums orthogonal on E_{n-1} have $E_{n-1} = 1$. On the other hand, if E_{n-1} is 0, the other nonzero errors are distributed among at most $[J/2]$ check sums. Therefore, at least $[J/2]$ or one-half of the check sums orthogonal on E_{n-1} have $E_{n-1} = 0$. Hence, the value of E_{n-1} is equal to the value assumed by *clear majority* of the parity-check sums orthogonal on E_{n-1}. If no value is assumed by clear majority of the parity-check sum, i.e., in case of tie, the error digit $E_{n-1} = 0$. Hence, an algorithm for decoding E_{n-1} may be formulated as: The error digit E_{n-1} is decoded as 1, if a clear majority of the check sums orthogonal on E_{n-1} is 1, otherwise E_{n-1} is decoded as 0.

If there are $[J/2]$ or fewer errors are present in error vector E, correct decoding of E_{n-1} is guaranteed and it is possible to form J parity-check sums orthogonal on any error digit because of the symmetry in cyclic code, which is identical to decoding of E_{n-1}. It may further be noted that a cyclic code with minimum distance $d_{\min}$ is said to be completely orthogonalizable in one step, if and only if it is possible to form $J = d_{\min} - 1$ parity-check sums orthogonal on an error digit. A general schematic diagram of majority logic decoding is shown in Figure 6.16.

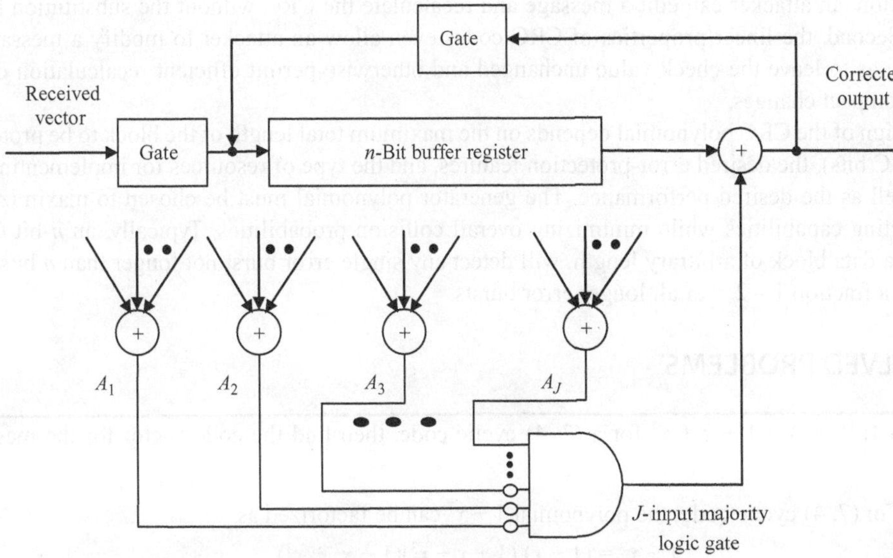

Figure 6.16 *Majority Logic Decoder*

6.10 CYCLIC REDUNDANCY CHECK

A cyclic redundancy check (CRC) is an error-detecting code whose algorithm is based on cyclic codes. It designed to detect accidental changes to raw computer data, and is commonly used in digital networks and storage devices such as hard disk drives. Blocks of data entering these systems get a short check value attached, derived from the remainder of a polynomial division of their contents; on retrieval the calculation is repeated, and corrective action can be taken against presumed data corruption if the check values do not match.

If $m(x)$ is the message polynomial and $g(x)$ is generator polynomial, then $m(x) = q(x)g(x) + r(x)$, where $q(x)$ and $r(x)$ are the quotient and remainder, respectively. Transmitted data will be $m(x) + r(x)$. If $g(x)$ is chosen to be of k bits, the remainder must be of $k - 1$ bits. Message polynomial $m(x)$ is initially formed with original message followed by $k - 1$ numbers of zeros. The cyclic redundancy check is formed by the remainder polynomial $r(x)$. The receiver repeats the calculation, verifying the received and computed $r(x)$. If they are equal, then the receiver assumes the received message bits are correct.

Example 6.8: Suppose there is the message data 11010011101100 is to be transmitted, where $g(x) =$ 1011. As $g(x)$ is of four bits, the remainder must be of three bits.

The message polynomial is formed by inserting three 0s at the end, as $m(x) =$ 11010011101100 000. Now with the long division operation we have the remainder as $r(x) = 100$. Therefore, the transmitted coded message will be $m(x) + r(x)$, i.e., 11010011101100 000 + 100 = 11010011101100100.

The validity of a received message can easily be verified by performing the above calculation again. The received data 11010011101100100 is divided by $g(x)$, i.e., 1011. The remainder should be equal to zero if there are no detectable errors.

CRCs are specifically designed to protect against common types of errors on communication channels, where they can provide quick and reasonable assurance of the integrity of messages delivered. However, they are not suitable for protecting against intentional alteration of data. First, as there is no authentication, an attacker can edit a message and recalculate the CRC without the substitution being detected. Second, the linear properties of CRC codes even allow an attacker to modify a message in such a way as to leave the check value unchanged and otherwise permit efficient recalculation of the CRC for compact changes.

The design of the CRC polynomial depends on the maximum total length of the block to be protected (data + CRC bits), the desired error-protection features, and the type of resources for implementing the CRC as well as the desired performance. The generator polynomial must be chosen to maximize the error-detecting capabilities while minimizing overall collision probabilities. Typically, an n-bit CRC, applied to a data block of arbitrary length, will detect any single error burst not longer than n bits, and will detect a fraction $1 - 2^{-n}$ of all longer error bursts.

6.11 SOLVED PROBLEMS

Problem 6.1: If $g(x) = 1 + x + x^3$ for a (7, 4) cyclic code, then find the code vector for the message $\mathbf{u} = (1010)$.

Solution: For (7, 4) cyclic code, the polynomial $1 + x^7$ can be factorized as

$$1 + x^7 = (1 + x)(1 + x + x^3)(1 + x^2 + x^3)$$

For generator polynomial $g(x) = 1 + x + x^3$, the minimum distance is 3 of single-error-correction capability. The message word $\mathbf{u} = (1010)$ is equivalent to $\mathbf{u}(x) = 1 + x^2$. The code vector is $g(x) \cdot \mathbf{u}(x) = (1 + x + x^3)(1 + x^2) = 1 + x + x^2 + x^5$ or (1110010).

Problem 6.2: Consider $g(x) = 1 + x + x^3$ for a (7, 4) cyclic code. Find the generator matrix of systematic form.

Solution: Dividing x^3, x^4, x^5 and x^6 by $g(x)$, we have

$$x^3 = g(x) + 1 + x$$
$$x^4 = xg(x) + x + x^2$$
$$x^5 = (1 + x^2)g(x) + 1 + x + x^2$$
$$x^6 = (1 + x + x^3)g(x) + 1 + x^2$$

Rearranging the above equations, we have

$$v_0(x) = 1 + x + x^3$$
$$v_1(x) = x + x^2 + x^4$$
$$v_2(x) = 1 + x + x^2 + x^5$$
$$v_3(x) = 1 + x^2 + x^6$$

Considering above equations in matrix form, we obtain the generator matrix of order of (4 × 7) in systematic form in cyclic code.

$$G = \begin{bmatrix} 1 & 1 & 0 & 1 & 0 & 0 & 0 \\ 0 & 1 & 1 & 0 & 1 & 0 & 0 \\ 1 & 1 & 1 & 0 & 0 & 1 & 0 \\ 1 & 0 & 1 & 0 & 0 & 0 & 1 \end{bmatrix}$$

Problem 6.3: Let the generator polynomial is $g(x) = 1 + x + x^2 + x^4 + x^5 + x^8 + x^{10}$ of cyclic code over GF(2) with block length of 15. Find the parity-check matrix H. How many errors can be detected by this code? How many errors can be corrected by this code? Write the generator matrix in systematic form. Find the generator polynomial of its dual code.

Solution: The parity polynomial $h(x) = (1 + x^{15})/g(x)$

$$= 1 + x + x^3 + x^5$$

Hence, $$x^5h(x^{-1}) = x^5 (1 + x^{-1} + x^{-3} + x^{-5})$$

$$= 1 + x^2 + x^4 + x^5$$

Code vectors generated by $x^5h(x^{-1}) = 1 + x^2 + x^4 + x^5$ have the minimum distance of 5 and are capable of correcting any single error as well as detecting combinations of double error.

The generator matrix in systematic form can be obtained from dividing x^{n-k-i} by generator polynomial $g(x)$ for $i = 0, 1, 2, \ldots, k - 1$, such that

$$x^{n-k-i} = a_i(x)g(x) + b_i(x)$$

where $b_i(x)$ is remainder of the form of

$$b_i(x) = b_{i,0} + b_{i,1}x + b_{i,2}x^2 + \ldots + b_{i,n-k-1}x^{n-k-1}$$

Since $x^{n-k-i} + b_i(x)$ is the multiple of $g(x)$ for $i = 0, 1, 2, \ldots, k - 1$, they are code polynomials and generator matrix for systematic form may be arranged in $k \times n$ matrix form as

$$\mathbf{G} = \begin{bmatrix} b_{0,0} & b_{0,1} & b_{0,2} & \cdots & b_{0,n-k-1} & 1 & 0 & 0 & \cdots & 0 \\ b_{1,0} & b_{1,1} & b_{1,2} & \cdots & b_{1,n-k-1} & 0 & 1 & 0 & \cdots & 0 \\ b_{2,0} & b_{2,1} & b_{2,2} & \cdots & b_{2,n-k-1} & 0 & 0 & 1 & \cdots & 0 \\ \vdots & \vdots & \vdots & \cdots & \vdots & \vdots & \vdots & \vdots & \cdots & 0 \\ \vdots & \vdots & \vdots & \cdots & \vdots & \vdots & \vdots & \vdots & \cdots & 0 \\ b_{k-1,0} & b_{k-1,1} & b_{k-1,2} & \cdots & b_{k-1,n-k-1} & 0 & 0 & 0 & \cdots & 1 \end{bmatrix}$$

and corresponding parity matrix is

$$\mathbf{H} = \begin{bmatrix} 1 & 0 & 0 & \cdots & 0 & b_{0,0} & b_{1,0} & b_{2,0} & \cdots & b_{k-1,0} \\ 0 & 1 & 0 & \cdots & 0 & b_{0,1} & b_{1,1} & b_{2,1} & \cdots & b_{k-1,1} \\ 0 & 0 & 1 & \cdots & 0 & b_{0,2} & b_{1,2} & b_{2,2} & \cdots & b_{k-1,2} \\ \vdots & \vdots & \vdots & \ddots & \vdots & \vdots & \vdots & \vdots & \ddots & \vdots \\ 0 & 0 & 0 & \cdots & 1 & b_{0,n-k-1} & b_{1,n-k-1} & b_{2,n-k-1} & \cdots & b_{k-1,n-k-1} \end{bmatrix}$$

Problem 6.4: Consider the decoding of a (7, 4) cyclic code generated by $g(x) = 1 + x + x^3$. The code has minimum distance of 3 and capable of correcting any single error over the block length of 7. Draw the schematic diagram of the syndrome circuit and find out the register contents after seventh shift for a received vector of 0010110.

Solution: The schematic of syndrome circuit is given in Figure 6.17. The syndrome register contents for each shift are given in Table 6.6.

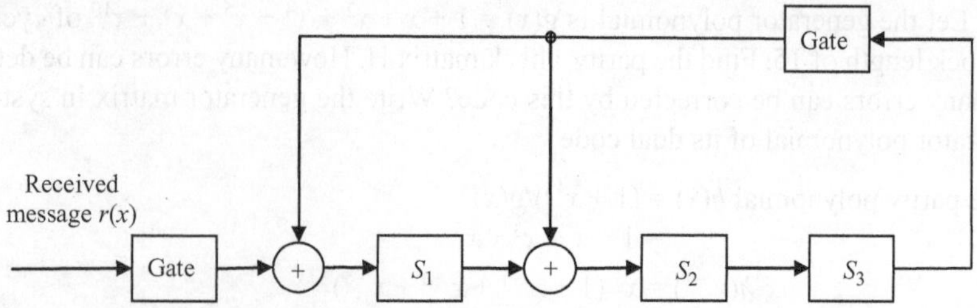

Figure 6.17 *Syndrome Computing Circuit*

Table 6.6 *Syndrome Register Contents*

Shift	Input	Register Contents	
		0 0 0	Initial state
1	0	0 0 0	
2	1	1 0 0	
3	1	1 1 0	
4	0	0 1 1	
5	1	0 1 1	
6	0	1 1 1	
7	0	1 0 1	s_0
8	–	1 0 0	s_1
9	–	0 1 0	s_2

MULTIPLE CHOICE QUESTIONS

1. For a (7, 4) cyclic code generated by $g(x) = 1 + x + x^3$ the syndrome of error pattern $e(x) = x^3$ is
   (a) 101 (b) 110 (c) 111 (d) 011
   Ans. **(b)**
2. For generator polynomial $g(x) = 1 + x^2 + x^3$ of a (7, 4) cyclic code the message word **u** = (1010). The code vector is
   (a) 1010101 (b) 1001001 (c) 1001110 (d) 1100011
   Ans. **(c)**
3. The generator polynomial of cyclic code of block length n is a factor of
   (a) $1 + x^n$ (b) $1 + x^{n+1}$ (c) $1 + x^{n+2}$ (d) $1 + x^{n-1}$
   Ans. **(a)**
4. The generator polynomial of a (7, 4) cyclic code has the degree of
   (a) 2 (b) 3 (c) 4 (d) 5
   Ans. **(b)**
5. If C is a code word and H is the parity-check matrix, then for a valid and correctly received code word
   (a) $CH = 0$ (b) $C^TH = 0$ (c) $C^TH^T = 0$ (d) $CH^T = 0$
   Ans. **(d)**

6. The syndrome polynomial in a cyclic code solely depends on
   (a) generator polynomial (b) parity polynomial
   (c) error polynomial (d) code word

Ans. (c)

7. What is the minimum distance for a (31, 21) code?
   (a) 3 (b) 4 (c) 5 (d) 6

Ans. (c)

REVIEW QUESTIONS

1. What do you mean by Cyclic Burst?
2. What are the degree of polynomials for (7, 4), (15, 8) and (31,16) cyclic codes?
3. Show that the generator polynomial $g(x) = 1 + x^2 + x^4 + x^6 + x^7 + x^{10}$ generates a (21, 11) cyclic code. Develop a decoder circuit for it. If the received polynomial is $r(x) = 1 + x^5 + x^{17}$, compute the syndrome for it.
4. Consider g(x) is the generator polynomial of binary cyclic code of block length n.
   (i) Show that, if $1 + x$ is one of the factors of g(x), the code contains the code vectors of all even weights.
   (ii) If n is odd and $1 + x$ is not the factor of $g(x)$, show that one of the code vector contains all 1's.
   (iii) If n is the smallest integer such that g(x) divides $x^n + 1$, show that the code has the minimum weight of at least 3.
5 Consider generator polynomial $g(x) = 1 + x + x^3$. Find the encoding circuit and complete the code vector for the massage vector $u(x) = c$
6. Consider a systematic (8, 4) code whose parity-check equations are $v_0 = u_1 + u_2 + u_3$, $v_1 = u_0 + u_1 + u_2$, $v_2 = u_0 + u_1 + u_3$ and $v_3 = u_0 + u_2 + u_3$. Find the generator matrix and parity-check matrix for the code. Show that the minimum distance of the code is 4.
7. Determine whether the received code (111011) is a valid code when the parity-check matrix is
$$\mathbf{H} = \begin{bmatrix} 1 & 1 & 0 & 1 & 0 & 0 \\ 0 & 1 & 1 & 0 & 1 & 0 \\ 1 & 0 & 1 & 0 & 0 & 1 \end{bmatrix}$$
8. Shorten the (31, 26) cyclic Hamming code by deleting 11 high order message digits to form (20, 15) shorten cyclic code. Devise a decoder circuit for this.
9. Devise an encoder and a decoder circuits for (15, 11) cyclic code generated by the generator polynomial $g(x) = 1 + x + x^4$.
10. Consider two cyclic codes c_1 and c_2 of block length n generated by generators $g_1(x)$ and $g_2(x)$, respectively. Show that the code polynomials common to both c_1 and c_2 also forms a cyclic code c_3. Determine the generator polynomial for c_3. If d_1 and d_2 are the minimum distances of c_1 and c_2, respectively, find the minimum distance of c_3.

chapter 7

BCH CODES

7.1 INTRODUCTION

A large class of powerful random-error-correcting cyclic codes had been formed by BCH codes that made remarkable generalization of the Hamming codes for multiple error correction. BCH codes were invented in 1959 by Alexis Hocquenghem, and independently in 1960 by Raj Chandra Bose and Dwijendra Kumar Ray-Chaudhuri. Thus the code has been named as BCH (Bose Chaudhuri Hocquenghem) code. The cyclic structure of this code was observed and subsequently generalization of binary BCH codes to codes of p^m symbols (p is a prime) was done. However, in this chapter, the discussion will be confined to mainly binary BCH codes.

7.2 PRIMITIVE ELEMENTS

For any positive integers m ($m \geq 3$) and t ($t < 2^m - 1$), there exist a BCH code with following parameters.

Block length:	$n = 2^m - 1$
Number of parity-check digits:	$n - k \leq mt$
Minimum distance:	$d_{min} \geq 2t + 1$

These features imply that this code is capable of correcting any combination of t or few numbers of errors in a block code $n = 2^m - 1$ digits and hence it is called t-error-correcting BCH code. The generator polynomial of this code is specified in terms of its roots from Galois field GF(2^m). If α is the *primitive element* of GF(2^m), then the generator polynomial $g(x)$ of t-error-correcting BCH code of length $2^m - 1$ is the lowest degree polynomial with the roots as $\alpha, \alpha^2, \alpha^3, \ldots, \alpha^{2t}$ and also the conjugates of them [i.e., $g(\alpha^i) = 0$, for $1 \leq i \leq 2t$]. If $\Phi_i(x)$ has the root as α^i, $g(x)$ is least common multiple of $\Phi_1(x), \Phi_2(x), \ldots, \Phi_{2t}(x)$, i.e.,

$$g(x) = \text{LCM}\,\{\Phi_1(x) \cdot \Phi_2(x) \cdot \Phi_3(x) \cdot \ldots \cdot \Phi_{2t}(x)\} \tag{7.1}$$

If i is even integer, this can be expressed as $i = k2^l$, where k is odd integer and $l \geq 1$. Then α^i has a conjugate α^k, and hence α^i and α^k have same polynomial. Therefore, $g(x)$ may be expressed as follows:

$$g(x) = \text{LCM}\,\{\Phi_1(x) \cdot \Phi_3(x) \cdot \Phi_5(x) \cdot \ldots \cdot \Phi_{2t-1}(x)\} \tag{7.2}$$

As the degree of each polynomial is m or less, the degree of $g(x)$ is at most mt. From Eq. (7.2), the single-error-correcting code may be generated by $g(x) = \Phi_1(x)$.

Example 7.1: For $n = 7$ and $k = 4$, $t = 1$, this means single-error-correcting code may be generated. Similarly, for $n = 15$ and $k = 11$, $t = 1$ or this is also a single-error-correcting code. For $n = 15$, double error correction and 3-error correction can be achieved with $k = 7$ and $k = 5$, respectively.

7.3 MINIMAL POLYNOMIALS

If $\Phi(x)$ is the polynomial with the coefficients from Galois field GF(2^m), which is irreducible, it is called *minimal polynomial*. It has the degree $\leq m$ and it divides $x^{2m} + x$. For example, the minimal polynomials of $\gamma = \alpha^7$ in GF(2^4) is $\phi(x) = 1 + x^3 + x^4$.

Minimal polynomials are obtained by solving the equation

$$\phi(x) = a_0 + a_1x + a_2x^2 + a_3x^3 + x^4$$

where x is substituted by $\gamma = \alpha^7$ and $m = 4$ for GF(2^4). The minimal polynomials generated by $p(x) = x^4 + x + 1$ are given at Table 7.1.

Table 7.1 *Minimal Polynomials in GF (2^4) Generated by $p(x) = x^3 + x + 1$*

Conjugate Roots	Minimal Polynomials
0	x
1	$x + 1$
$\alpha, \alpha^2, \alpha^4, \alpha^8$	$x^4 + x + 1$
$\alpha^3, \alpha^6, \alpha^9, \alpha^{12}$	$x^4 + x^3 + x^2 + x + 1$
α^5, α^{10}	$x^2 + x + 1$
$\alpha^7, \alpha^{11}, \alpha^{13}, \alpha^{14}$	$x^4 + x^3 + 1$

7.4 GENERATOR POLYNOMIALS

Using the minimal polynomials, Galois field of any order may be constructed and generator polynomials may be selected according to error-correction capability. A t-error-correcting BCH code, polynomial of code length of $n = 2^m - 1$ may be generated where each code polynomial has the roots $\alpha, \alpha^2, \alpha^3, \ldots, \alpha^{2t}$ and their conjugates. Now if $\mathbf{v}(x)$ is the code polynomial from GF(2), it is divisible by the minimal polynomials $\Phi_1(x), \Phi_2(x), \ldots, \Phi_{2t}(x)$. Therefore, $\mathbf{v}(x)$ is also divisible by their least common multiple or generator polynomial $g(x)$, where $g(x) = \text{LCM}\,\{\Phi_1(x) \cdot \Phi_2(x) \cdot \Phi_3(x) \ldots \Phi_{2t}(x)\}$. A list of generator polynomial of binary BCH codes of block length up to $2^5 - 1$ is given in Table 7.2.

Table 7.2 *Generator Polynomials of BCH Code*

n	k	t	Generator Polynomials
7	4	1	$1 + x + x^3$
15	11	1	$1 + x + x^4$
15	7	2	$1 + x^4 + x^6 + x^7 + x^8$
15	5	3	$1 + x + x^2 + x^4 + x^5 + x^8 + x^{10}$
31	26	1	$1 + x^2 + x^5$
31	21	2	$1 + x^3 + x^5 + x^6 + x^8 + x^9 + x^{10}$
31	16	3	$1 + x + x^2 + x^3 + x^5 + x^7 + x^8 + x^9 + x^{10} + x^{11} + x^{15}$
31	11	5	$1 + x^2 + x^4 + x^6 + x^7 + x^9 + x^{10} + x^{13} + x^{17} + x^{18} + x^{20}$
31	6	7	$1 + x + x^2 + x^5 + x^9 + x^{11} + x^{13} + x^{13} + x^{14} + x^{15} + x^{16} + x^{18} + x^{19} + x^{21} + x^{24} + x^{25}$

If t-error-correcting code polynomial $\mathbf{v}(x) = v_0 + v_1x + v_2x^2 + \ldots + v_{n-1}x^{n-1}$ of code length $2^m - 1$ has the root α^i, then

$$v(\alpha^i) = v_0 + v_1\alpha^i + v_1\alpha^{2i} + \ldots + v_{n-1}\alpha^{(n-1)i} = 0 \qquad (7.3)$$

If we consider a matrix **H** consisting of the primitive elements that are the roots of the code vector as follows:

$$\mathbf{H} = \begin{bmatrix} 1 & \alpha & \alpha^2 & \alpha^3 & \cdots & \alpha^{n-1} \\ 1 & (\alpha^2) & (\alpha^2)^2 & (\alpha^2)^3 & \cdots & (\alpha^2)^{n-1} \\ 1 & (\alpha^3) & (\alpha^3)^2 & (\alpha^3)^3 & \cdots & (\alpha^3)^{n-1} \\ \cdot & & & & & \cdot \\ \cdot & & & & & \cdot \\ 1 & (\alpha^{2i}) & (\alpha^{2i}) & (\alpha^{2i})^3 & \cdots & (\alpha^{2i})^{n-1} \end{bmatrix} \tag{7.4}$$

As **v** is a code vector, then $\mathbf{v} \cdot \mathbf{H}^T = 0.$ (7.5)

The BCH code with minimum distance at least d_0 has no more than $m(d_0 - 1)$ parity-check digits and capable of correcting $(d_0 - 1)/2$ or fewer errors. The lower bound on minimum distance is called the BCH bound.

A list of primitive elements for minimal polynomials for $1 < m \leq 6$ is given in Table 7.3.

Table 7.3 *Primitive Elements of Minimal Polynomials*

m	Primitive elements	m	Primitive elements
$m = 2$	1 (0 1 2)	$m = 6$	1 (0 1 6)
$m = 3$	1 (0 1 3)		3 (0 1 2 4 6)
	3 (0 2 3)		5 (0 1 2 5 6)
$m = 4$	1 (0 1 4)		7 (0 3 6)
	3 (0 1 2 3 4)		9 (0 2 3)
	5 (0 1 2)		11 (0 2 3 5 6)
	7 (0 3 4)		13 (0 1 3 4 6)
$m = 5$	1 (0 2 5)		15 (0 2 4 5 6)
	3 (0 2 3 4 5)		21 (0 1 2)
	5 (0 1 2 4 5)		23 (0 1 4 5 6)
	7 (0 1 2 3 5)		27 (0 1 3)
	11 (0 3 4 5)		31 (0 5 6)
	15 (0 3 5)		

Example 7.2: If α be the primitive element of Galois field GF(2^4), with $1 + \alpha + \alpha^4 = 0$, the minimal polynomials are

$$\Phi_1(x) = 1 + x + x^4$$
$$\Phi_3(x) = 1 + x + x^2 + x^3 + x^4$$
$$\Phi_5(x) = 1 + x + x^2$$

Double-error-correction BCH code of length $n = 2^4 - 1 = 15$ is generated by

$$\begin{aligned} f(x) &= \text{LCM}\,\{\Phi_1(x) \cdot \Phi_3(x)\} \\ &= (1 + x + x^4)\,(1 + x + x^2 + x^3 + x^4) \\ &= 1 + x^4 + x^6 + x^7 + x^8 \end{aligned}$$

Thus, this code is (15, 7) cyclic code of $d_{\min} = 5$.

Similarly, triple-error-correcting (15, 5) code with $d_{\min} = 7$ may be generated by the generator polynomial

$$\begin{aligned} f(x) &= \text{LCM}\,\{\Phi_1(x) \cdot \Phi_3(x) \cdot \Phi_5(x)\} \\ &= (1 + x + x^4)\,(1 + x + x^2 + x^3 + x^4)\,(1 + x + x^2) \\ &= 1 + x + x^2 + x^4 + x^5 + x^8 + x^{10} \end{aligned}$$

7.5 DECODING OF BCH CODES

Let us consider that the transmitted code vector $\mathbf{v}(x) = v_0 + v_1x + v_2x^2 + \ldots + v_{n-1}x^{n-1}$ is received as $\mathbf{r}(x) = r_0 + r_1x + r_2x^2 + \ldots + r_{n-1}x^{n-1}$. If $\mathbf{e}(x)$ is error introduced then

$$\mathbf{r}(x) = v(x) + e(x) \tag{7.6}$$

Syndrome vector can be calculated as $\mathbf{S} = \mathbf{r} \cdot \mathbf{H}^T$ (7.7)

where $\mathbf{H}$ is given in Eq. (7.4). The ith component of syndrome is $\mathbf{S}_i = r(\alpha^i)$, i.e., for $1 \le i \le 2t$

$$\mathbf{S}_i = r_0 + r_1\alpha^i + r_2\alpha^{2i} + \ldots + r_{n-1}\alpha^{(n-1)i} \tag{7.8}$$

It may be noticed that syndrome components are the elements in the field GF(2^m). Dividing $\mathbf{r}(x)$ by the minimal polynomial $\Phi_i(x)$ of α^i, we have $\mathbf{r}(x) = a_i(x)\Phi_i(x) + b_i(x)$, where $b_i(x)$ is the remainder with degree less than that of $\Phi_i(x)$. Now $\Phi_i(\alpha^i) = 0$, therefore

$$\mathbf{S}_i = r(\alpha^i) = b_i(\alpha^i) \tag{7.9}$$

Thus the syndrome components may be obtained by evaluating $b_i(x)$ with $x = \alpha^i$. Since α^i is the root of each code polynomial and $v(\alpha^i) = 0$, from Eqs. (7.6) and (7.9), for $1 \le i \le 2t$, we may relate the syndrome components with the error pattern as follows:

$$\mathbf{S}_i = r(\alpha^i) = b_i(\alpha^i) = e(\alpha^i) \tag{7.10}$$

It may be noticed that syndrome components $\mathbf{S}_i$ depend on error pattern. Suppose there exists p number of errors in error pattern $e(x)$ at locations $x^{j1}, x^{j2}, \ldots, x^{jp}$, we may write

$$e(x) = x^{j1} + x^{j2} + x^{j3} + \cdots + x^{jp} \tag{7.11}$$

where $0 < j1 < j2 < \cdots < jp < n$. From Eq. (7.10), we may derive the following set of equations for $\mathbf{S}_i$.

$$\begin{aligned}
S_1 &= \alpha^{j1} + \alpha^{j2} + \alpha^{j3} + \ldots + \alpha^{jp} \\
S_2 &= (\alpha^{j1})^2 + (\alpha^{j2})^2 + (\alpha^{j3})^2 + \cdots + (\alpha^{jp})^2 \\
S_3 &= (\alpha^{j1})^3 + (\alpha^{j2})^3 + (\alpha^{j3})^3 + \cdots + (\alpha^{jp})^3 \\
&\vdots \\
S_{2t} &= (\alpha^{j1})^{2t} + (\alpha^{j2})^{2t} + (\alpha^{j3})^{2t} + \cdots + (\alpha^{jp})^{2t}
\end{aligned} \tag{7.12}$$

In the above set of equations, the roots $\alpha^{j1}, \alpha^{j2}, \alpha^{j3}, \ldots, \alpha^{jp}$ are unknown. Solving these equations we may find the error locations. Any method for solving these equations is a decoding algorithm for BCH codes.

For convenience, α^{jl} is substituted by β_l, such that $\alpha^{jl} = \beta_l$ for $0 < l < n$. The elements β_l are called the *error location numbers*. Eq. (7.12) may be rewritten as follows:

$$\begin{aligned}
S_1 &= \beta_1 + \beta_2 + \beta_3 + \ldots + \beta_p \\
S_2 &= \beta_1^{\,2} + \beta_2^{\,2} + \beta_2^{\,2} + \ldots + \beta_p^{\,2} \\
S_3 &= \beta_1^{\,3} + \beta_2^{\,3} + \beta_2^{\,3} + \ldots + \beta_p^{\,3} \\
&\vdots \\
S_{2t} &= \beta_1^{\,2t} + \beta_2^{\,2t} + \beta_2^{\,2t} + \ldots + \beta_p^{\,2t}
\end{aligned} \tag{7.13}$$

The above set of equations are symmetric functions of $\beta_1, \beta_2, \beta_3, \ldots, \beta_p$, which are known as *power-sum symmetric functions*. Let us consider the following polynomial.

$$\begin{aligned}
\sigma(X) &= (1+\beta_1x)(1+\beta_2x)(1+\beta_3x)\ldots(1+\beta_px) \\
&= \sigma_0 + \sigma_1x + \sigma_2x^2 + \ldots + \sigma_px^p
\end{aligned} \tag{7.14}$$

The roots of $\sigma(x)$ are $\beta_1^{-1}, \beta_2^{-1}, \beta_3^{-1}, \dots, \beta_p^{-1}$, which are the inverse of the error location numbers, and therefore $\sigma(x)$ is called as *error location polynomial.* $\sigma_0, \sigma_1, \sigma_2, \dots, \sigma_p$ are the elementary symmetric functions of $\beta_1, \beta_2, \beta_3, \dots, \beta_p$. The coefficients of $\sigma(x)$ can be computed as per following relations.

$$\begin{aligned}
\sigma_0 &= 1 \\
\sigma_1 &= \beta_1 + \beta_2 + \beta_3 + \dots + \beta_p \\
\sigma_1 &= \beta_1\beta_2 + \beta_2\beta_3 + \beta_3\beta_4 + \dots + \beta_{p-1}\beta_p \\
\sigma_p &= \beta_1\beta_2\beta_3 \dots \beta_p
\end{aligned} \tag{7.15}$$

The $\sigma_0, \sigma_1, \sigma_2, \dots, \sigma_p$ are known as the *elementary symmetric functions* of $\beta_1, \beta_2, \beta_3, \dots, \beta_p$. From Eqs. (7.13) and (7.15), we can relate the syndrome components by following Newton's identities.

$$\begin{aligned}
S_1 + \sigma_1 &= 0 \\
S_2 + \sigma_1 S_1 + 2\sigma_2 &= 0 \\
S_3 + \sigma_1 S_2 + \sigma_2 S_2 + 3\sigma_3 &= 0 \\
&\vdots \\
S_p + \sigma_1 S_{p-1} + \sigma_2 S_{p-2} + \dots + \sigma_{p-1} S_1 + p\sigma_1 &= 0 \\
S_{p+1} + \sigma_1 S_p + \sigma_2 S_{p-1} + \dots + \sigma_{p-1} S_2 + \sigma_1 S_1 &= 0
\end{aligned} \tag{7.16}$$

Solving the above equations for the elementary functions $\sigma_0, \sigma_1, \sigma_2, \dots, \sigma_p$, we may find out the error locations $\beta_1, \beta_2, \beta_3, \dots, \beta_p$. Eq. (7.16) may have many solutions. However, the solution that yields $\sigma(x)$ of minimal degree is to be considered for determining the error pattern. If $p \le t$, $\sigma(x)$ will give the actual error pattern $e(x)$. Therefore, the error correction procedure for BCH codes may be described as follows:

- Computation of syndromes from the received polynomial $r(x)$.
- Determining of error location polynomial $\sigma(x)$ from syndrome components $S_1, S_2, S_3, \dots, S_{2t}$.
- Finding the roots of $\sigma(x)$ to determine the error location numbers $\beta_1, \beta_2, \beta_3, \dots, \beta_p$ and correction of errors in $r(x)$.

Finding the error location polynomial $\sigma(x)$ is most complicated and can be achieved by iterative process. The first step is to search a minimum degree polynomial $\sigma^{(1)}(x)$ whose coefficients satisfy the first Newton's identity of Eq. (7.16). In the next step, coefficients of $\sigma^{(1)}(x)$ are tested to satisfy the second Newton's identity of Eq. (7.16). If this satisfies, then $\sigma^{(2)}(x) = \sigma^{(1)}(x)$. If the coefficients of $\sigma^{(1)}(x)$ do not satisfy the second Newton's identity, a correction term is added to $\sigma^{(1)}(x)$ to form $\sigma^{(2)}(x)$ such that $\sigma^{(2)}(x)$ has minimum degree and satisfies second Newton's identity. Next $\sigma^{(2)}(x)$ is to be tested for third Newton's identity equation. This iteration process is to be continued till all the Newton's identity equations are tested and finally the error location polynomial will be obtained after 2tth iteration such that $\sigma(x) = \sigma^{(2t)}(x)$.

Let the minimal degree polynomial at the μth step of iteration whose coefficients satisfy the first μ Newton's identity equations be

$$\sigma^{(\mu)}(x) = 1 + \sigma_1^{(\mu)}x + \sigma_2^{(\mu)}x^2 + \dots + \sigma_{l_\mu}^{(\mu)}x^{l_\mu} \tag{7.17}$$

To determine $\sigma^{(\mu+1)}(x)$, we compute the following.

$$d_\mu = S_{\mu+1} + \sigma_1^{(\mu)}S_\mu + \sigma_2^{(\mu)}S_{\mu-1} + \dots + \sigma_{l_\mu}^{(\mu)}S_{\mu+1-l_\mu} \tag{7.18}$$

The quantity d_μ is called μth discrepancy. If $d_\mu = 0$, the coefficients of $\sigma^{(\mu)}(x)$ satisfy the $(\mu + 1)$th Newton's identity and $\sigma^{(\mu+1)}(x) = \sigma^{(\mu)}(x)$. If $d_\mu \ne 0$, a correction term is to be added as stated earlier. To find the correction term, we have to consider the step prior to μth step, say ρth step, where ρth discrepancy $d_\rho \ne 0$. If l_ρ is the degree of the polynomial $\sigma^{(\rho)}(x)$, where $\rho - l\rho$ has the largest value, then

$$\sigma^{(\mu+1)}(x) = \sigma^{(\mu)}(x) + d_\mu d_\rho^{-1} x^{(\mu-\rho)} \sigma^{(\rho)}(x) \tag{7.19}$$

After completion of iterative method, the final error location polynomial $\sigma(x)$ is determined. Now the error location numbers can be found simply by substituting $1, \alpha, \alpha^2, \ldots, \alpha^{n-1}$ $(n = 2^m - 1)$ into $\sigma(x)$ and subsequently the error pattern $e(x)$ may be obtained. Therefore, the decoding process is to be performed on a bit-by-bit basis.

Example 7.3: Consider the (15, 5) triple-error-correcting BCH code in Galois field GF(2^4) such that $1 + \alpha + \alpha^4 = 0$. Assume that the code vector $\mathbf{v}$ = (000000000000000) has been received as $\mathbf{r}$ = (000101000000100).

Therefore,
$$r(x) = x^3 + x^5 + x^{12}$$
The minimal polynomials of α, α^2, and α^4 are identical and
$$\Phi_1(x) = \Phi_2(x) = \Phi_4(x) = 1 + x + x^4$$
The minimal polynomials for α^3 and α^6 are
$$\Phi_3(x) = \Phi_6(x) = 1 + x + x^2 + x^3 + x^4$$
The minimal polynomial for α^5 is $\Phi_5(x) = 1 + x + x^2$

Dividing $r(x)$ by above minimal polynomials, we obtain the remainders as follows:
$$b_1(x) = 1,\ b_3(x) = 1 + x^2 + x^3, \text{ and } b_5(x) = x^2$$
Substituting $\alpha, \alpha^2, \alpha^4$ in $b_1(x)$, α^3, α^4 in $b_3(x)$, and α^5 in $b_5(x)$, we obtain the syndrome components as $S_1 = S_2 = S_4 = 1$, $S_3 = 1 + \alpha^6 + \alpha^9 = \alpha^{10}$, $S_6 = 1 + \alpha^{12} + \alpha^{18} = \alpha^5$, and $S_5 = \alpha^{10}$. These results are obtained from the polynomial representations of the elements of GF(2^4) as in Table 7.4.

Table 7.4 *Polynomial Representation of Elements of GF(2^4)*

Power Representation	Polynomial Representation	Power Representation	Polynomial Representation
0	0	α^7	$1 + \alpha + \alpha^3$
1	1	α^8	$1 + \alpha^2$
α	α	α^9	$\alpha + \alpha^3$
α^2	α^2	α^{10}	$1 + \alpha + \alpha^2$
α^3	α^3	α^{11}	$\alpha + \alpha^2 + \alpha^3$
α^4	$1 + \alpha$	α^{12}	$1 + \alpha + \alpha^2 + \alpha^3$
α^5	$\alpha + \alpha^2$	α^{13}	$1 + \alpha^2 + \alpha^3$
α^6	$\alpha^2 + \alpha^3$	α^{14}	$1 + \alpha^3$

To find the error location polynomial, the iterative method as described above is used. The steps and results of iterative process are indicated in Table 7.5. To begin the iterative process, for the first row, we assume $\mu = -1$. Therefore, from Eqs. (7.17) and (7.18), $\sigma^{(\mu=-1)}(x) = 1$, $d_{\mu=-1} = 1$ and l_μ is the degree of $\sigma^{(\mu)}(x)$.

For the next row $\mu = 0$, $\sigma^{(\mu=0)}(x) = \sigma^{(\mu=-1)}(x) = 1$ as $d_{\mu=-1} = 0$. Now $d_{\mu=0} = S_1 = 1$ from Eq. (7.18). Thus, the iterative process continues to develop till $\mu = 2t$. The algorithm maintained is as follows:

- If $d_\mu = 0$, $\sigma^{(\mu+1)}(x) = \sigma^{(\mu)}(x)$ and $l_{\mu+1} = l_\mu$.
- If $d_\mu \neq 0$, another row to be found prior to μth, say ρth, such that $\rho - 1_\rho$ is maximum and $d_\rho \neq 0$. Then, $\sigma^{(\mu+1)}(x)$ is computed as from Eq. (7.19). In either case
$$I_{\mu+1} = \max(l_\mu, l_\rho + \rho - \mu). \quad (7.20)$$
and
$$d_{\mu+1} = S_{\mu+2} + \sigma_1^{\mu+1} S_{\mu+1} + \cdots + \sigma_{l_{\mu+1}}^{\mu+1} S_{\mu+2-l_{\mu+1}} \quad (7.21)$$
- If polynomial $\sigma^{2t}(x)$ in the last row has the degree greater than t, there are more than t errors that cannot be located.

Table 7.5 *Iterative Process to Find the Error Location*

μ	$\sigma^{(\mu)}(x)$	d_μ	l_μ	$\mu - l_\mu$
−1	1	1	0	−1
0	1	$S_1 = 1$	0	0
1	$1+x$	0	1	$0\ (\rho = -1)$
2	$1+x$	$S_3 + S_2S_1 = \alpha^5$	1	1
3	$1+x+\alpha^5x^2$	0	2	$1\ (\rho = 0)$
4	$1+x+\alpha^5x^2$	α^{10}	2	2
5	$1+x+\alpha^5x^3$	0	3	$2\ (\rho = 2)$
6	$1+x+\alpha^5x^3$	–	–	–

Thus, we obtain the error location polynomial

$$\sigma(x) = 1 + x + \alpha^5 x^3$$

We can verify that α^3, α^{10}, and α^{12} are the roots of above error location polynomial $\sigma(x)$. The inverse of these roots are α^{12}, α^5, and α^3. Hence, the error pattern is $e(x) = x^3 + x^5 + x^{12}$. Adding $e(x)$ with $r(x)$ we can recover errorless code vector.

7.6 IMPLEMENTATION OF GALOIS FIELD

As discussed above, decoding of BCH codes requires computation using Galois field arithmetic that consists of mainly two operations—addition and multiplication. For addition operation, the resultant vector is the vector representation of the sum of the two field elements. The addition operation can be accomplished with circuit diagram shown in Figure 7.1.

Two elements are loaded in registers $A(a_0, a_1, a_2, a_3)$ and $B(b_0, b_1, b_2, b_3)$. Register A also serves as accumulator. The sum of two elements is available at the accumulator after applying triggering pulse to the adders.

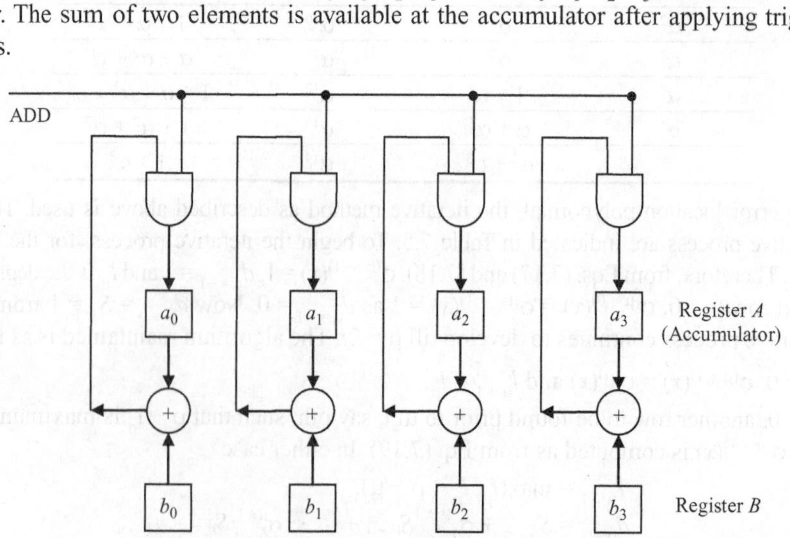

Figure 7.1 *Schematic for Addition Operation*

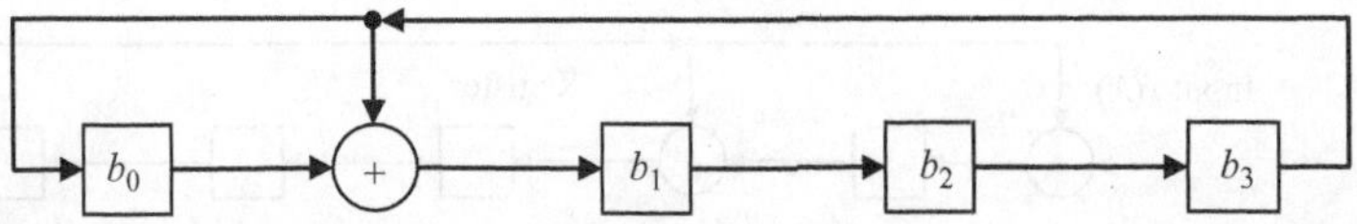

Figure 7.2 *Multiplication Scheme of a Field Element with a Fixed Element*

Multiplication of field element by a fixed element may be carried out using shift registers as shown at Figure 7.2. Let us consider the multiplication of field element B in GF(2^4) by primitive element α whose minimal polynomial is $\Phi(x) = 1 + x + x^4$. The element B can be expressed as a polynomial with respect to α as $B = b_0 + b_1\alpha + b_2\alpha^2 + b_3\alpha^3$. Using the fact $\alpha^4 = 1 + \alpha$, we obtain the equality, $\alpha B = b_3 + (b_0 + b_3)\alpha + b_1\alpha^2 + b_2\alpha^3$, which can be realized by the circuit as shown in Figure 7.2.

Successive shifts of the shift register will generate the vector representation of successive powers of α according to the order in Galois field. If initially register is loaded with 1000, after 15th shift the register will contain 1000 again.

Now, let us consider the multiplication of two arbitrary field elements B and C, such that

$$B = b_0 + b_1\alpha + b_2\alpha^2 + b_3\alpha^3$$
$$C = c_0 + c_1\alpha + c_2\alpha^2 + c_3\alpha^3$$

The product BC may be written in the following form.

$$BC = (\{[(c_3B)\alpha + c_2B]\alpha + c_3B\}\alpha + c_0B)$$

The steps of multiplication may be described as follows:

- Multiply c_3B by α and add to c_2B.
- Multiply $(c_3B)\alpha + c_2B$ by α and add to c_1B.
- Multiply $[(c_3B)\alpha + c_2B)\alpha + c_1B$ by α and add to c_0B.

Multiplication by α can be performed by the circuit as shown in Figure (7.2). Overall computation for the multiplication of two field elements B and C can be carried out by the schematic circuit diagram as shown in Figure (7.3). Here, the field elements B and C are loaded in the register B and register C, respectively. Register A is initially empty. After four simultaneous shifts of registers A and C, the desired product is available in register A.

The received vector $r(x)$ may be computed in similar way. Figure 7.4 demonstrate the computation of $r(\alpha^i)$, where α is the primitive element of GF(2^4).

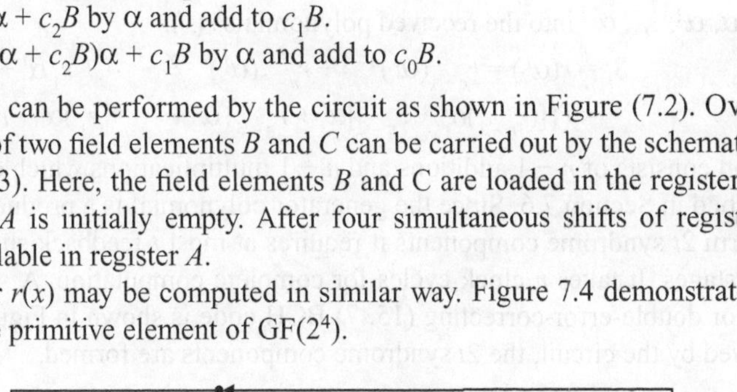

Figure 7.3 *Multiplication Scheme for Two Field Elements*

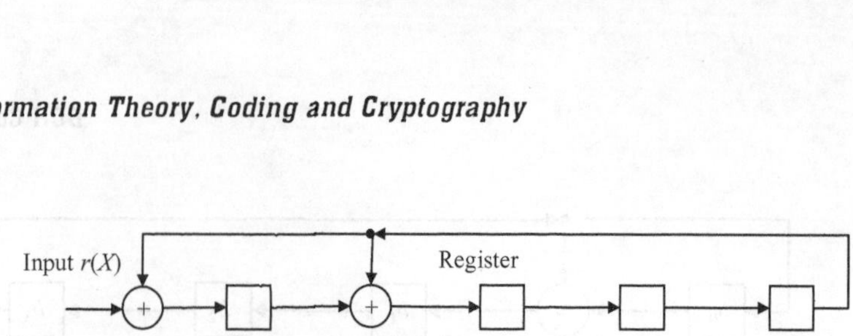

Figure 7.4 *Computation of $r(\alpha^i)$*

The received polynomial $r(\alpha)$ may be written as follows:

$$r(\alpha) = r_0 + r_1\alpha + r_2\alpha^2 + \cdots + r_{14}\alpha^{14}$$
$$= (\{[(r_{14})\alpha + r_{13}]\alpha + r_{12}\}\alpha + \cdots)\alpha + r_0) \quad (7.22)$$

After 15th shift at shift register shown in Figure 7.4, the register will contain $r(\alpha)$ in vector form. It may be noted that the figures explained for implementation of Galois field are not unique. Various circuits may be realized according to operator polynomials.

7.7 IMPLEMENTATION OF ERROR CORRECTION

As discussed earlier, corrected data at the receiver end require syndrome computation, error location polynomial search and error correction. These can be implemented either by digital hardware or by software programmed on a general purpose computer. The advantage of hardware implementation is faster computation; but software implementation is less expensive.

7.7.1 Syndrome Computation

Syndrome components $S_1, S_2, \ldots, S_{2t}$ for t-error correction BCH code may be obtained by substituting the field elements $\alpha, \alpha^2, \ldots, \alpha^{2t}$ into the received polynomials $r(x)$.

$$S_i = r(\alpha^i) = r_{n-1}(\alpha^i)^{n-1} + r_{n-2}(\alpha^i)^{n-2} + \cdots + r_1\alpha^i + r_0$$
$$= (\{[(r_{n-1})\alpha^i + r_{n-2}]\alpha^i + r_{n-3}\}\alpha^i + \cdots + r_1)\alpha^i + r_0 \quad (7.23)$$

The computation consists of $n-1$ additions and $n-1$ multiplications which can be achieved by the hardware as described in Section 7.6. Since the generator polynomial is a product of at most t minimal polynomials, to form $2t$ syndrome components it requires at most t feedback shift registers, each containing at most m stages. It takes n clock cycles for complete computation. A syndrome computation circuit schematic for double-error-correcting (15, 7) BCH code is shown in Figure 7.5. As soon as the entire $r(x)$ is received by the circuit, the $2t$ syndrome components are formed.

7.7.2 Computation of Error Location Polynomial

Since there are t numbers of error location polynomials $\sigma^{(\mu)}(x)$ and t numbers of discrepancies d_μ, computation of them requires $2t^2$ additions and $2t^2$ multiplications. Addition and multiplication circuits are already discussed which can be used to realize them. Figure 7.6 demonstrates *Chein's searching circuit*, the schematic for finding the error locations.

Error location polynomial $\sigma(x)$ of degree t is substituted by the field elements. Chein's searching circuit consists of t multipliers for multiplying $\alpha, \alpha^2, \ldots, \alpha^t$, respectively. Initially $\sigma_1, \sigma_2, \ldots, \sigma_t$ are loaded into the registers of multipliers. After lth shift, these register will contain $\sigma_1\alpha^l, \sigma_2\alpha^{2l}, \ldots, \sigma_t\alpha^{tl}$. The sum $1 + \sigma_1\alpha^l + \sigma_2\alpha^{2l} + \cdots + \sigma_t\alpha^{tl}$ is computed by m-input OR/NOR gate. If the sum is zero, the error location number is α^{n-1}. It requires n clock cycles to complete this step and k clock cycles to correct only the message bits.

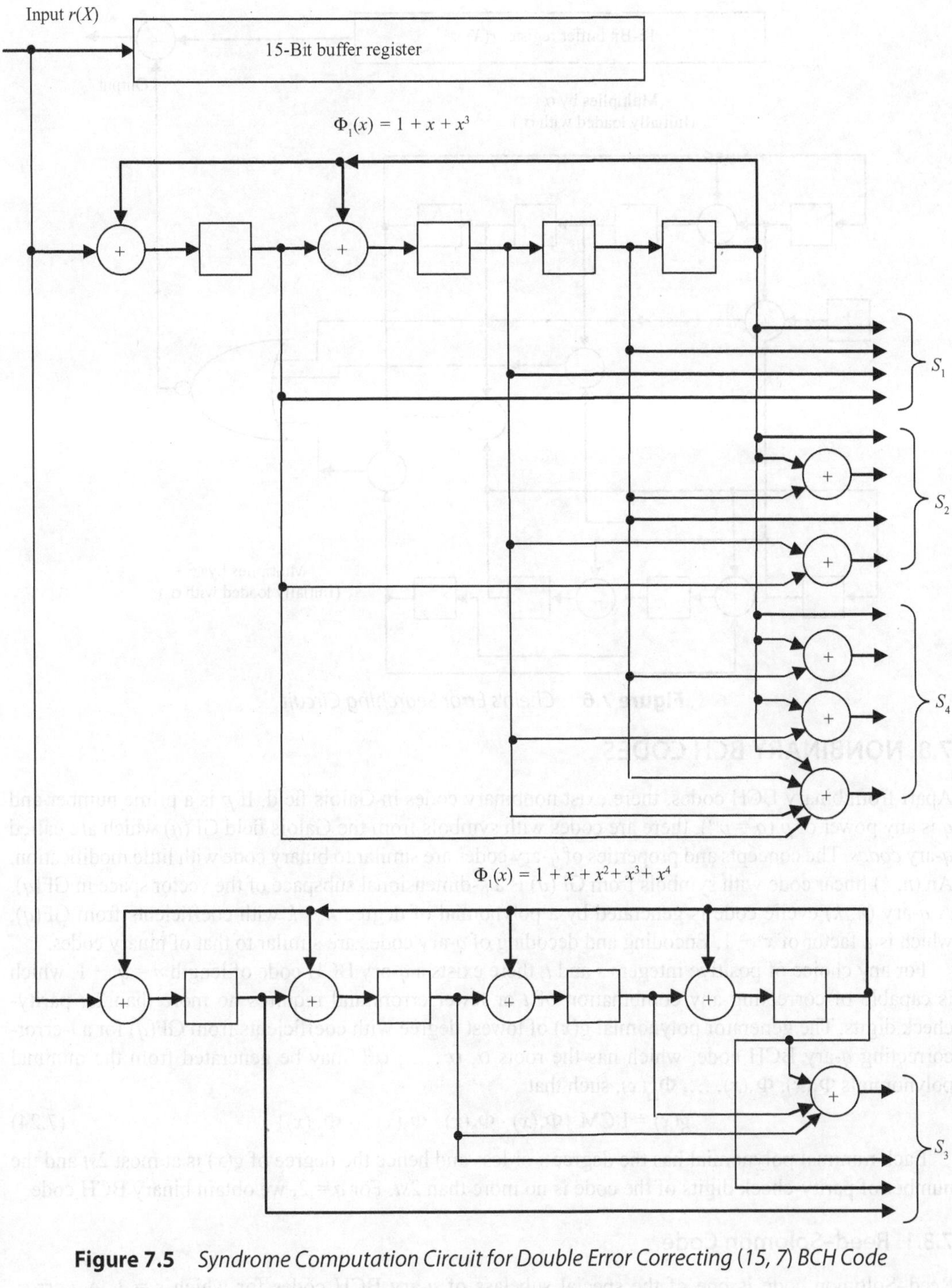

Figure 7.5 *Syndrome Computation Circuit for Double Error Correcting (15, 7) BCH Code*

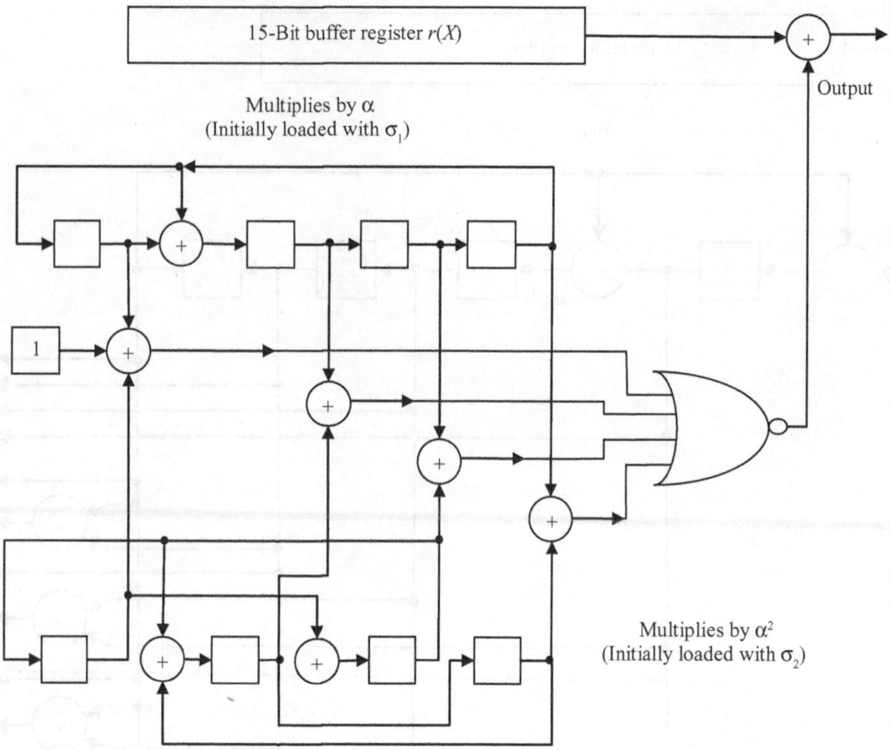

Figure 7.6 *Chein's Error Searching Circuit*

7.8 NONBINARY BCH CODES

Apart from binary BCH codes, there exist nonbinary codes in Galois field. If p is a prime number and q is any power of p ($q = p^m$), there are codes with symbols from the Galois field GF(q) which are called *q-ary codes*. The concepts and properties of q-ary codes are similar to binary code with little modification. An (n, k) linear code with symbols from GF(q) is a k-dimensional subspace of the vector space in GF(q). A q-ary (n, k) cyclic code is generated by a polynomial of degree $n - k$ with coefficients from GF(q), which is a factor of $x^n - 1$. Encoding and decoding of q-ary codes are similar to that of binary codes.

For any choice of positive integers s and t, there exists a q-ary BCH code of length $n = q^s - 1$, which is capable of correcting any combination of t or fewer errors and requires no more than $2st$ parity-check digits. The generator polynomial $g(x)$ of lowest degree with coefficients from GF(q) for a t-error-correcting q-ary BCH code, which has the roots $\alpha, \alpha^2, \ldots, \alpha^{2t}$, may be generated from the minimal polynomials $\Phi_1(x), \Phi_2(x), \ldots, \Phi_{2t}(x)$, such that

$$g(x) = \text{LCM}\ \{\Phi_1(x) \cdot \Phi_2(x) \cdot \Phi_3(x) \cdots \Phi_{2t}(x)\} \tag{7.24}$$

Each minimal polynomial has the degree s or less and hence the degree of $g(x)$ is at most $2st$ and the number of parity-check digits of the code is no more than $2st$. For $q = 2$, we obtain binary BCH code.

7.8.1 Reed–Solomon Code

Reed–Solomon code is one of the special subclass of q-ary BCH codes for which $s = 1$. A t-error-correcting Reed–Solomon code with primitive elements from GF(q) has the following parameters:

Block length:	$n = q - 1$
Number of parity digits:	$n - k = 2t$
Minimum distance:	$d_{min} = 2t + 1$

It may be noted that the length of this code is one less than the size of code symbols and minimum distance is one greater than the number of parity-check digits. For $q = 2^m$ with α as the primitive elements in GF(2^m), the generator polynomial $g(x)$ may be written as follows:

$$g(x) = (x + \alpha)(x + \alpha^2) \ldots (x + \alpha^{2t})$$
$$= g_0 + g_1 x + g_2 x^2 + \ldots + g_{2t-1} x^{2t-1} + x^{2t} \tag{7.25}$$

The code generated by $g(x)$ is an $(n, n - 2t)$ cyclic code consisting of the polynomials of degree $n - 1$ or less with coefficients from GF(2^m) that are multiples of $g(x)$. Encoding of this code is similar to the binary BCH code. If the message polynomial $a(x) = a_0 + a_1x + a_2x^2 + \cdots + a_{k-1}x^{k-1} + a_kx^k$ is to be encoded, where $k = n - 2t$, remainder $b(x) = b_0 + b_1x + b_2x^2 + \cdots + b_{2t-1}x^{2t-1}$ is obtained dividing $x^{2t}a(x)$ by $g(x)$. This can be accomplished by the schematic circuit as shown in Figure 7.7.

Here, the adders denotes the addition of two elements from GF(2^m) and multipliers perform multiplication of field element from GF(2^m) with a fixed element g_i from the same field. Parity digits will be generated in the registers as soon as the message bits entered in the circuit.

Decoding of Reed–Solomon code is performed in similar process as described for binary BCH code. Decoding of this code consists of four steps: (1) computation of syndrome, (2) determining error location polynomial $\sigma(x)$, (3) finding the error location numbers, and (4) evaluation of error values. The last step is not required in binary BCH code. If $r(x)$, $v(x)$, and $e(x)$ are the received, transmitted, and error polynomials, respectively, then $e(x) = r(x) - v(x)$. The syndrome components are obtained by substituting α^i into received polynomial $r(x)$ for $i = 1, 2, 3, \ldots, 2t$. Thus for $\alpha^{jl} = \beta_l$ for $0 < l < p$, we use Eq. (7.12) for q-ary BCH code and we have

$$S_1 = r(\alpha) = e_{j1}\beta_1 + e_{j2}\beta_2 + e_{j3}\beta_3 + \cdots + e_{jp}\beta_p$$
$$S_2 = r(\alpha^2) = e_{j1}\beta_1^{\,2} + e_{j2}\beta_2^{\,2} + e_{j3}\beta_3^{\,2} + \cdots + e_{jp}\beta_p^{\,2}$$
$$S_3 = r(\alpha^3) = e_{j1}\beta_1^{\,3} + e_{j2}\beta_2^{\,3} + e_{j3}\beta_3^{\,3} + \cdots + e_{jp}\beta_p^{\,3}$$
$$\vdots$$
$$S_{2t} = r(\alpha^{2t}) = e_{j1}\beta_1^{\,2t} + e_{j2}\beta_2^{\,2t} + e_{j3}\beta_3^{\,2t} + \cdots + e_{jp}\beta_p^{\,2t} \tag{7.26}$$

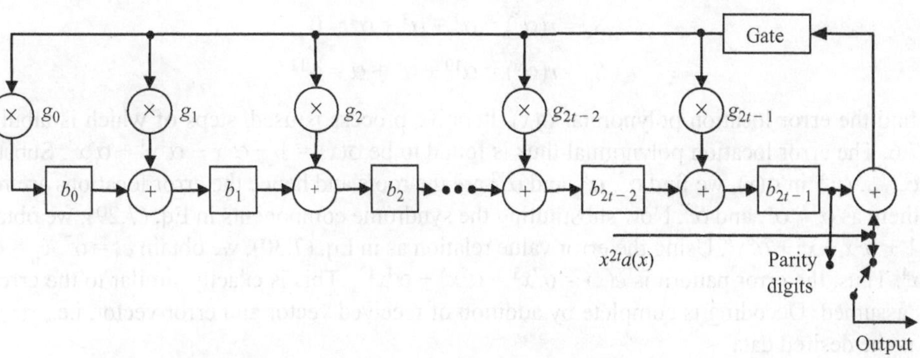

Figure 7.7 *Encoding Scheme for Nonbinary BCH Code*

The syndrome components S_i can also be computed by dividing $r(x)$ by $x + \alpha^i$, which results in the equality

$$r(x) = c_i(x)\,(x + \alpha^i) + b_i \tag{7.27}$$

The remainder b_i is constant in GF(2^m). Substituting α^i in both sides of Eq. (7.27), we obtain $S_i = b_i$.

The error location polynomial is computed by iterative method, where

$$\begin{aligned}\sigma(x) &= (1 + \beta_1 x)\,(1 + \beta_2 x)\,(1 + \beta_{31} x) \ldots (1 + \beta_p x)\\ &= 1 + \sigma_1 x + \sigma_1 x^2 + \ldots + \sigma_p x^p\end{aligned} \tag{7.28}$$

The error values can be determined by following computation. Let

$$\begin{aligned}z(x) = 1 + (S_1 + \sigma_1)x + (S_2 + \sigma_1 S_1 + \sigma_2)x^2 + \ldots\\ + (S_p + \sigma_1 S_{p-1} + \sigma_2 S_{p-2} + \sigma_p)x^p\end{aligned} \tag{7.29}$$

For $i \neq l$, the error values at location $\beta_1 = \alpha^{jl}$ is expressed as follows:

$$e_{ji} = \frac{z(\beta_l^{-1})}{\prod_{i=1}^{p}(1+\beta_i\beta_l^{-1})} \tag{7.30}$$

Example 7.4: Consider a triple-error-correcting Reed–Solomon code with symbols from GF(2^4). The generator polynomial of this code is

$$\begin{aligned}g(x) &= (x + \alpha)(x + \alpha^2)(x + \alpha^3)(x + \alpha^4)(x + \alpha^5)(x + \alpha^6)\\ &= \alpha^6 + \alpha^9 x + \alpha^6 x^2 + \alpha^4 x^3 + \alpha^{14} x^4 + \alpha^{10} x^5 + x^6\end{aligned}$$

Let all-zero transmitted vector be received as $r = (000\alpha^7 00\alpha^3 00000\alpha^4 00)$. Therefore, the received polynomial $r(x) = \alpha^7 x^3 + \alpha^3 x^6 + \alpha^4 x^{12}$. The syndrome components are calculated using Table 7.4 as follows:

$$S_1 = r(\alpha) = \alpha^{10} + \alpha^9 + \alpha = \alpha^{12}$$

$$S_2 = r(\alpha^2) = \alpha^{13} + 1 + \alpha^{13} = 1$$

$$S_3 = r(\alpha^3) = \alpha + \alpha^6 + \alpha^{10} = \alpha^{14}$$

$$S_4 = r(\alpha^4) = \alpha^4 + \alpha^{12} + \alpha^7 = \alpha^{10}$$

$$S_5 = r(\alpha^5) = \alpha^7 + \alpha^3 + \alpha^4 = 0$$

$$S_6 = r(\alpha^6) = \alpha^{10} + \alpha^9 + \alpha = \alpha^{12}$$

To find the error location polynomial $\sigma(x)$, iterative process is used, steps of which is tabulated in Table 7.6. The error location polynomial thus is found to be $\sigma(x) = 1 + \alpha^7 x + \alpha^4 x^3 + \alpha^5 x^3$. Substituting $1, \alpha, \alpha^2, \ldots, \alpha^{14}$ in $\sigma(x)$, we find α^3, α^9, and α^{12} are the roots and hence the error locations are reciprocal of them as α^{12}, α^6, and α^3. Now substituting the syndrome components in Eq. (7.29), we obtain that $z(x) = 1 + \alpha^2 x + x^2 + \alpha^6 x^3$. Using the error value relation as in Eq. (7.30), we obtain $e_3 = \alpha^7$, $e_6 = \alpha^3$, and $e_{12} = \alpha^4$. Thus, the error pattern is $e(x) = \alpha^7 x^3 + \alpha^3 x^6 + \alpha^4 x^{12}$. This is exactly similar to the error location as assumed. Decoding is complete by addition of received vector and error vector, i.e., $r(x) + e(x)$ which is the desired data.

Table 7.6 *Computation of Error Location Polynomial*

μ	$\sigma^{(\mu)}(x)$	d_μ	l_ρ	$\mu - l_\rho$
−1	1	1	0	−1
0	1	α^{12}	0	0
1	$1+\alpha^{12}x$	α^7	1	0 ($\rho = -1$)
2	$1+\alpha^3x$	1	1	1 ($\rho = 0$)
3	$1+\alpha^3x+\alpha^3x^2$	α^7	2	1 ($\rho = 0$)
4	$1+\alpha^4x+\alpha^{12}x^2$	α^{10}	2	2 ($\rho = 2$)
5	$1+\alpha^7x+\alpha^4x^3+\alpha^5x^3$	0	3	2 ($\rho = 3$)
6	$1+\alpha^7x+\alpha^4x^3+\alpha^5x^3$	–	–	–

Reed–Solomon codes are very effective for correction of multiple burst errors.

7.9 WEIGHT DISTRIBUTION

The minimum distance of a linear code is the smallest weight of any nonzero code word, and is important because it directly affects the number of errors the code can correct. However, the minimum distance says nothing about the weights of other code words in the code; and hence, it is necessary to look at the weight distribution of the entire code. It turns out that the weight distribution of many types of codes, including Hamming and BCH codes, is asymptotically normal (i.e., it approaches the normal distribution for large codes of a given variety). If A_i is the number of code vectors of weight i in (n, k) linear code C, the numbers $A_1, A_2, \ldots, A_n$ are called the weight distribution of C. If C is used only for error detection on a binary symmetric channel (BSC), the probability of undetected errors can be computed from the weight distribution of C. Since an undetected error occurs only when the error pattern is identical to nonzero code vector of C, the probability of undetected error $P(E)$ may be expressed as follows:

$$P(E) = \sum_{i=1}^{\infty} A_i p^i (1-p)^{n-i} \tag{7.31}$$

where p is the transition probability of the BSC. If the minimum distance of C is $d_{\min}$, then A_1 to $A_{d_{\min}-1}$ are zero. It has been observed that the probability of undetected error $P(E)$ for a double-error-correcting BCH code of length $2^m - 1$ has the upper bound of 2^{-2m} for $p \le ½$, where $2m$ is the number of parity digits of the code.

For t-error-correcting primitive BCH of length $2^m - 1$ with mt number of parity-check digits, where m is greater than certain constant $m_0(t)$, it has been observed that the weight distribution satisfies the following equalities:

$$\begin{aligned} A_i &= 0 && \text{for } 0 < i < 2t \\ &= (1+\lambda_0 n^{-1/10})\binom{n}{i}2^{-(n-k)} && \text{for } i > 2t \end{aligned} \tag{7.32}$$

where $n = 2^m - 1$ and λ_0 is the upper bounded by a constant. From Eqs. (7.31) and (7.32), we obtain the expression for probability of undetected error $P(E)$.

$$P(E) = (1+\lambda_0 n^{-1/10})2^{-(n-k)} \sum_{i=2t+1}^{n} \binom{n}{i} p^i (1-p)^{n-i} \tag{7.33}$$

For $\varepsilon = (2t + 1)/n$ and $p < \varepsilon$, the summation term of Eq. (7.33)

$$\sum_{i=2t+1}^{n} \binom{n}{i} p^i (1-p)^{n-i} \leq 2^{-nE(\varepsilon,p)} \tag{7.34}$$

where $E(\varepsilon, p) = H(p) - (\varepsilon - p)H'(p) - H(\varepsilon)$

$$H(x) = -x\log_2 x - (1-x)\log_2(1-x)$$

and $H'(x) = \log_2 \frac{1-x}{x}$

Therefore, for $p < \varepsilon$, the upper bound of $P(E)$ is given as follows:

$$P(E) \leq (1 + \lambda_0 n^{-1/10}) 2^{-nE(\varepsilon,p)} 2^{-(n-k)} \tag{7.35}$$

Similarly, for $p > \varepsilon$, since $\sum_{i=0}^{n} \binom{n}{i} p^i (1-p)^i = 1$, we have the upper bound of $P(E)$ as follows:

$$P(E) \leq (1 + \lambda_0 n^{-1/10}) 2^{-(n-k)} \tag{7.36}$$

It may be noticed that probability of undetected error reduces exponentially with number of parity-check digits, $n - k$. Therefore, incorporation of sufficiently large number of parity digits results in reduction of probability of undetected errors. For nonbinary case, the weight distribution of t-error-correcting Reed–Solomon codes of length $q - 1$ with symbols from GF(q) is as follows:

$$A_j = \binom{q-1}{j} \sum_{i=0}^{j-2t-1} (-1)^i \binom{j}{i} (q^{j-2t-i} - 1) \tag{7.37}$$

7.10 SOLVED PROBLEMS

Problem 7.1: Find the generator polynomial of a triple-error-correcting BCH code with block length $n = 31$ over GF(2^5).

Solution:

Block length: $n = 2^m - 1 = 31$, $m = 5$

Error-correction capability $t = 3$

Number of parity-check digits: $n - k \leq mt = 5 \times 3 = 15$

Minimum distance: $d_{\min} \geq 2t + 1 = 7$

The minimal polynomials have the degree of less than or equal to 5 and they divide $x^{2^5} + x$ or $x^{32} + x$. Triple-error-correcting BCH code of length 31 contains the lowest degree polynomial with the roots as $\alpha, \alpha^2, \alpha^3, \ldots, \alpha^6$. The generator polynomial $g(x)$ may be expressed as

$$g(x) = \text{LCM}\{\Phi_1(x) \cdot \Phi_3(x) \cdot \Phi_5(x)\}$$

As the degree of each polynomial is 5, the degree of $g(x)$ is at most 15. From Table 7.3, the minimal polynomials are

$$\Phi_1(x) = 1 + x^2 + x^5$$

$$\Phi_3(x) = 1 + x^2 + x^3 + x^4 + x^5$$

$$\Phi_5(x) = 1 + x + x^2 + x^4 + x^5$$

Therefore,

$$g(x) = (1 + x^2 + x^5)(1 + x^2 + x^3 + x^4 + x^5)(1 + x + x^2 + x^4 + x^5)$$

$$= 1 + x + x^2 + x^3 + x^5 + x^7 + x^8 + x^9 + x^{10} + x^{11} + x^{15}$$

Problem 7.2: Find the parity-check matrix of a double-error-correcting (15, 4) BCH code.

Solution: For double-error-correcting (15, 4) BCH code the generator polynomial is $\Phi_1(x) = 1 + x + x^4$ whose primitive element is α.

Then the parity-check matrix may be written as follows:

$$H = \begin{bmatrix} 1 & \alpha & \alpha^2 & \alpha^3 & \alpha^4 & \alpha^5 & \alpha^6 & \alpha^7 & \alpha^8 & \alpha^9 & \alpha^{10} & \alpha^{11} & \alpha^{12} & \alpha^{13} & \alpha^{14} \\ 1 & \alpha^3 & \alpha^6 & \alpha^9 & \alpha^{12} & \alpha^{15} & \alpha^{18} & \alpha^{21} & \alpha^{24} & \alpha^{27} & \alpha^{30} & \alpha^{33} & \alpha^{36} & \alpha^{39} & \alpha^{42} \end{bmatrix}$$

From the characteristics of primitive elements, we have $\alpha^{15} = \alpha^{30} = 1$, $\alpha^{18} = \alpha^{33} = \alpha^3$, $\alpha^{21} = \alpha^{36} = \alpha^6$, $\alpha^{24} = \alpha^{39} = \alpha^9$, and $\alpha^{42} = \alpha^{12}$. Due to conjugate elements of α, the Eq. (7.4) is reduced to

$$H = \begin{bmatrix} 1 & \alpha & \alpha^2 & \alpha^3 & \cdots & \alpha^{n-1} \\ 1 & (\alpha^3) & (\alpha^3)^2 & (\alpha^3)^3 & \cdots & (\alpha^3)^{n-1} \\ 1 & (\alpha^5) & (\alpha^5)^2 & (\alpha^5)^3 & \cdots & (\alpha^5)^{n-1} \\ \cdots & \cdots & \cdots & \cdots & \cdots & \cdots \\ 1 & (\alpha^{2t-1}) & (\alpha^{2t-1})^2 & (\alpha^{2t-1})^3 & \cdots & (\alpha^{2t-1})^{n-1} \end{bmatrix}$$

Using Table 7.4, the equivalent polynomial and its 4-tuple representation we obtain the following parity-check matrix.

$$H = \begin{bmatrix} 1&0&0&0&1&0&0&1&1&0&1&0&1&1&1 \\ 0&1&0&0&1&1&0&1&0&1&1&1&1&0&0 \\ 0&0&1&0&0&1&1&0&1&0&1&1&1&1&0 \\ 0&0&0&1&0&0&1&1&0&1&0&1&1&1&1 \\ 1&0&0&0&1&1&0&0&0&1&1&0&0&0&1 \\ 0&0&0&1&1&0&0&0&1&1&0&0&0&1&1 \\ 0&0&1&0&1&0&0&1&0&1&0&0&1&0&1 \\ 0&1&1&1&1&0&1&1&1&1&0&1&1&1&1 \end{bmatrix}$$

Problem 7.3: Construct a double-error-correcting BCH code over $GF(2^3)$.

Solution:

Block length: $n = 2^3 - 1 = 7, m = 3$

If t is the error-correction capability, then $n - k \le mt$.

For double-error-correction capability, $t = 2, k = 1$.

Minimum distance: $d_{\min} \ge 2t + 1 = 5$.

Polynomials of $GF(2^3)$ are $\Phi_1(x) = 1 + x + x^3$ and $\Phi_3(x) = 1 + x^2 + x^3$.

Double-error-correction code may be generated by the generator polynomial

$$g(x) = \text{LCM}\ \{\Phi_1(x) \cdot \Phi_3(x)\}$$
$$g(x) = (1 + x + x^3)(1 + x^2 + x^3)$$
$$= 1 + x + x^2 + x^3 + x^4 + x^5 + x^6$$

Problem 7.4: Construct the (15, 7) double-error-correcting BCH code and code word is $C(x) = 1 + x^4 + x^6 + x^7 + x^8$. Determine the outcome of a decoder when $C(x)$ incurs the error pattern $e(x) = 1 + x^2 + x^7$.

Solution:

Block length: $n = 2^4 - 1 = 15, m = 4$

If t is the error-correction capability, then $n - k \le mt$.

For double-error-correction capability, $t = 2, k = 7$.
Minimum distance: $d_{min} \geq 2t + 1 = 5$
The generated code is (15, 7) and the minimal polynomials over GF(2^4)

$$\Phi_1(x) = 1 + x + x^4$$
$$\Phi_3(x) = 1 + x + x^2 + x^3 + x^4$$
$$\Phi_5(x) = 1 + x + x^2$$

Double-error-correction BCH code is generated by the generator polynomial

$$g(x) = \text{LCM}\,\{\Phi_1(x) \cdot \Phi_3(x)\}$$
$$g(x) = (1 + x + x^4)(1 + x + x^2 + x^3 + x^4)$$
$$= 1 + x^4 + x^6 + x^7 + x^8$$

For the code word $C(x) = 1 + x^4 + x^6 + x^7 + x^8$ incurring error as $e(x) = 1 + x^2 + x^7$, the received vector $r(x) = C(x) + e(x)$, i.e.,

$$r(x) = 1 + x^4 + x^6 + x^7 + x^8 + 1 + x^2 + x^7$$
$$= x^2 + x^4 + x^6 + x^8$$

Therefore, the decoder output is $x^2 + x^4 + x^6 + x^8$.

Problem 7.5: Consider double-error-correcting code over GF(2^6) of the order of $n = 21$, where the element $\beta = \alpha^3$. Find the polynomial of minimum degree that has the roots β, β^2, β^3, and β^4. Which BCH code may be developed?

Solution: The elements β, β^2, and β^4 have the same polynomial, $\Phi_1(x) = 1 + x + x^2 + x^4 + x^6$.
The element β^3 has the minimal polynomial $\Phi_2(x) = 1 + x^2 + x^3$.
Therefore, the generator polynomial of minimum degree is

$$g(x) = \text{LCM}\,\{\Phi_1(x)\,\Phi_2(x)\}$$
$$= (1 + x + x^2 + x^4 + x^6)(1 + x^2 + x^3)$$
$$= 1 + x + x^4 + x^5 + x^7 + x^8 + x^9$$

The above polynomial divides $1 + x^{21}$. As $t = 2$ and $m = 6$, $k = n - mt = 9$. Therefore, a (21, 9) BCH code may be generated.

Problem 7.6: Consider a triple-error-correcting binary BCH (15, 5) code with generator polynomial $g(x) = 1 + x + x^2 + x^4 + x^5 + x^8 + x^{10}$. The received polynomial is $r(x) = x^3 + x^5$. Find the code word.

Solution: For t-error-correcting BCH code, the error location can be obtained by solving the following relation of syndrome matrix form.

$$\begin{bmatrix} S_1 & S_2 & S_3 & \cdots & S_{t-1} & S_t \\ S_2 & S_3 & S_4 & \cdots & S_t & S_{t+1} \\ \vdots & & & & & \\ S_t & S_{t+1} & S_{t+2} & \cdots & S_{2t-2} & S_{2t-1} \end{bmatrix} \begin{bmatrix} E_t \\ E_{t-1} \\ \vdots \\ E_t \end{bmatrix} = \begin{bmatrix} -S_{t+1} \\ -S_{t+2} \\ \vdots \\ -S_{2t} \end{bmatrix}$$

The syndromes are computed by substituting α^i in the received polynomial $r(x) = x^3 + x^5$ for $1 \leq i \leq 2t$, where t is error-correction capability. Using the Table 7.4, as $t = 3$, they are as follows:

$S_1 = \alpha^3 + \alpha^5 = \alpha^{11}$ $\quad$ $S_2 = (\alpha^2)^3 + (\alpha^2)^5 = \alpha^7$ $\quad$ $S_3 = (\alpha^3)^3 + (\alpha^3)^5 = \alpha^7$

$S_4 = (\alpha^4)^3 + (\alpha^4)^5 = \alpha^{14}$ $\quad$ $S_5 = (\alpha^5)^3 + (\alpha^5)^5 = \alpha^5$ $\quad$ $S_6 = (\alpha^6)^3 + (\alpha^6)^5 = \alpha^{14}$

The syndrome matrix is obtained as below (number or rows and columns are limited to $t = 3$)

$$M = \begin{bmatrix} S_1 & S_2 & S_3 \\ S_2 & S_3 & S_4 \\ S_3 & S_4 & S_5 \end{bmatrix} = \begin{bmatrix} \alpha^{11} & \alpha^7 & \alpha^7 \\ \alpha^7 & \alpha^7 & \alpha^{14} \\ \alpha^7 & \alpha^{14} & \alpha^5 \end{bmatrix}$$

Det $[M] = 0$, which implies that there are fewer than three errors are present in the received vector. Next matrix has generated for $t \le 2$, which given as

$$M = \begin{bmatrix} S_1 & S_2 \\ S_2 & S_3 \end{bmatrix} = \begin{bmatrix} \alpha^{11} & \alpha^7 \\ \alpha^7 & \alpha^7 \end{bmatrix}$$

where Det $[M] \ne 0$. Therefore, two errors have been occurred. Error location may be obtained from following matrix computation.

$$\begin{bmatrix} S_1 & S_2 \\ S_2 & S_3 \end{bmatrix} \begin{bmatrix} E_2 \\ E_1 \end{bmatrix} = \begin{bmatrix} -S_3 \\ -S_4 \end{bmatrix}$$

or

$$\begin{bmatrix} \alpha^{11} & \alpha^7 \\ \alpha^7 & \alpha^7 \end{bmatrix} \begin{bmatrix} E_2 \\ E_1 \end{bmatrix} = \begin{bmatrix} -\alpha^7 \\ -\alpha^{14} \end{bmatrix}$$

Solving the above equation, we obtain $E_2 = \alpha^8$ and $E_1 = \alpha^{11}$. Thus, error polynomial is $e(x) = 1 + \alpha^{11}x + \alpha^8x^2$. This may be written as $e(x) = (1 + \alpha^3x)(1 + \alpha^5x)$. Therefore, the error locations are at α^3 and α^5 or $e(x) = x^3 + x^5$. The code word may be computed as $c(x) = r(x) + e(x) = x^3 + x^5 + x^3 + x^5 = 0$. This means all-zero code word was sent.

MULTIPLE CHOICE QUESTIONS

1. For $m = 4$, what is the block length of the BCH code?
   (a) 16 (b) 15 (c) 16 (d) none of these

   Ans. **(b)**
2. What is the error-correction capability of a (15, 5) BCH code over GF(2^4)?
   (a) 1 (b) 2 (c) 3 (d) 4

   Ans. **(c)**
3. If t is the error-correction capability of a BCH code what is the minimum distance of the code?
   (a) $2t$ (b) $2t + 1$ (c) $2t - 1$ (d) none of these

   Ans. **(b)**
4. For BCH code, if the received vector and computed error vector are $r(x)$ and $e(x)$, then the error-free code vector can be calculated as
   (a) $r(x) \cdot e(x)$ (b) $r(x)/e(x)$ (c) $r(x) + e(x)$ (d) none of these

   Ans. **(c)**
5. For (15, 5) BCH code, if the roots of error location polynomial $\alpha(x)$ are α^2, α^7, and α^9, then error polynomial $e(x)$ is
   (a) $x^2 + x^7 + x^9$ (b) $x^6 + x^8 + x^{13}$ (c) $x^7 + x^{12} + x^{14}$ (d) none of these

   Ans. **(b)**
6. For a BCH code, if the minimal polynomials are $\Phi_i(x)$ $(1 \le i \le 7)$, the generator polynomial $g(x)$ of triple error correction is
   (a) LCM$\{\Phi_1(x)\Phi_2(x)\}$ (b) LCM$\{\Phi_1(x)\Phi_3(x)\}$
   (c) LCM$\{\Phi_1(x)\Phi_2(x)\Phi_3(x)\}$ (d) LCM$\{\Phi_1(x)\Phi_3(x)\Phi_5(x)\}$

   Ans. **(d)**

7. A BCH code over GF(2^6) can produce the code maximum error capability of
   (a) 6 (b) 8 (c) 10 (d) 12

   Ans. (c)

8. A (63, 15) BCH code over GF(2^6) can produce the code maximum error capability of
   (a) 6 (b) 8 (c) 10 (d) 12

   Ans. (b)

REVIEW QUESTIONS

1. Determine all generator polynomials for block length 31.
2. Decode the BCH code of block length 3, if the received polynomials are $r_1(x) = x^7 + x^{30}$ and $r_2(x) = 1 + x^{17} + x^{28}$.
3. Prove that the syndrome components related as $S_{2i} = S_i^2$.
4. If a BCH code of length $n = 2^m - 1$ has t-error-correcting capability and $2t + 1$ is a factor of n, prove that the minimum distance of the code is exactly $2t + 1$.
5. Using $p(x) = 1 + x^2 + x^5$ devise a circuit that is capable of multiplying two elements in GF(2^5).
6. Devise a syndrome computation circuit for a double-error-correcting (31, 21) BCH code.
7. A t-error-correcting Reed–Solomon code of GF(2^m) has the generator polynomial
   $g(x) = (x + \alpha)(x + \alpha^2)(x + \alpha^3) \ldots (x + \alpha^{2t})$.
   Show that it has error-correction capability of $2t - 1$, where α is the primitive element.
8. Device a syndrome computation circuit for single-error Reed–Solomon code of block length 15 from field of GF(2^4).
9. Find the generator polynomial of double-error-correcting Reed–Solomon code of block length 15 over GF(2^4). Decode the received polynomial $r(x) = \alpha x^3 + \alpha^{11}x^7$.

chapter 8

CONVOLUTION CODES

8.1 INTRODUCTION

Convolution code is an alternative to block codes, where n outputs at any given time unit depend on k inputs at that time unit as well as m previous input blocks. An (n, k, m) convolution code can be developed with k inputs, n output sequential circuit, and m input memory. The memory m must be large enough to achieve low error probability, whereas k and n are typically small integers with $k < n$. An important special case is when $k = 1$, the information sequence is not divided into blocks and can be processed continuously. This code has several practical applications in digital transmission over wire and radio channels due to its high data rate. The improved version of this scheme in the association with Viterbi algorithm led to application in deep sea and satellite communication.

8.2 TREE AND TRELLIS CODES

Very large block lengths have the disadvantage that the decoding procedure cannot be commenced unless the entire block of encoded data is received at the receiver. Hence, the receiving and decoding process become slow. *Tree* coding scheme is used to overcome this disadvantage, where uncoded information data is divided into smaller blocks or information frame of length k; information frame length may be as low as of 1 bit. These information frames are then encoded to code words frames of length n. To form a code word, the current information frame as well as the previous information frame is required. It implies that such encoding system requires memory which is accomplished by shift register in practice. The schematic diagram of encoding system for Tree codes is shown in Figure 8.1.

The information frame is stored in the shift register. Each time a new frame arrives, it is compared with the earlier frame in the logic circuit with some algorithm to form a code word and older frame is discarded, whereas new frame is loaded in the shift register. Thus for every information frame, a code word is generate for transmission.

Convolution code is one of the subclasses of Tree code. Tree code that is linear, time-invariant and having finite wordlength is called *Convolution Code*. On the other hand, time-invariant Tree code with finite wordlength is called *Sliding Block Code*. Therefore linear sliding block code is a covolution code.

Now consider a simple convolution encoder as shown in Figure 8.2 that encodes bit by bit. The input bits are loaded into registers S_1 and S_2 sequentially. The outputs of the registers are XORed with input bit and 3 bit output sequences are generated for each input bit. The outputs are tabulated in Table 8.1 for different input and register conditions. The clock rate of outgoing data is thrice as fast as the incoming data.

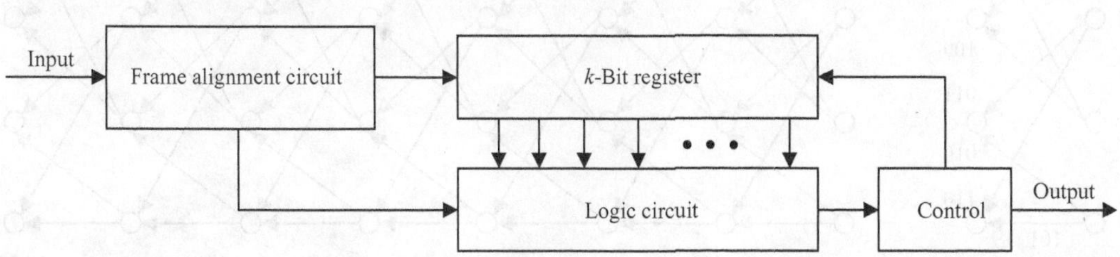

Figure 8.1 *Tree Code Encoding Scheme*

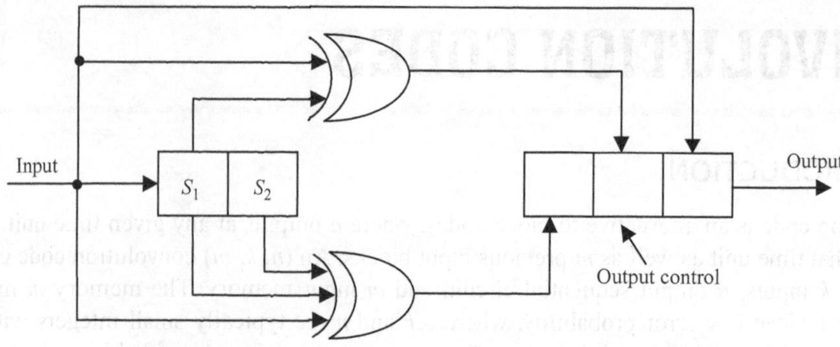

Figure 8.2 *Bit by Bit Convolution Code Encoder*

Table 8.1 *Bit by Bit Convolution Encoded Output*

Input	Registers		Output		
	S_2	S_1			
0	0	0	0	0	0
1	0	0	1	1	1
0	0	1	0	1	1
1	0	1	1	1	0
0	1	0	0	0	1
1	1	0	0	0	0
0	1	1	0	1	0
1	1	1	1	0	1

Here, we observe that the output sequence is generate from present input and previous two input bits. The same information can be represented by state diagram as shown in Figure 8.3a. This diagram is called *Trellis Diagram*. The diagram can be cascaded for the stream of input bits. The cascaded form is shown in Figure 8.3b. The code may be defined as binary (3, 1, 2) convolution code.

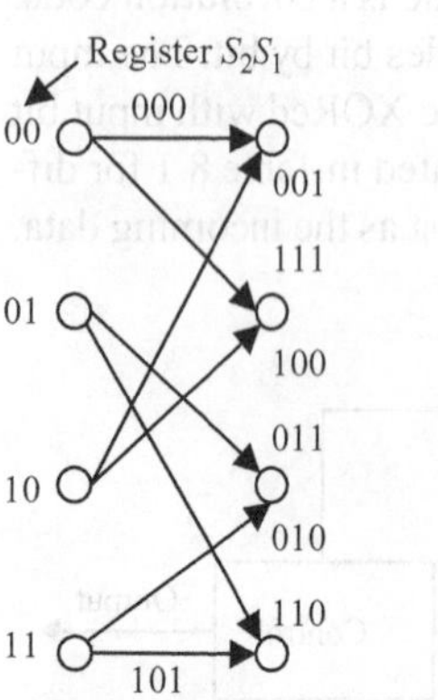

Figure 8.3a *Trellis Diagram for a Single Bit*

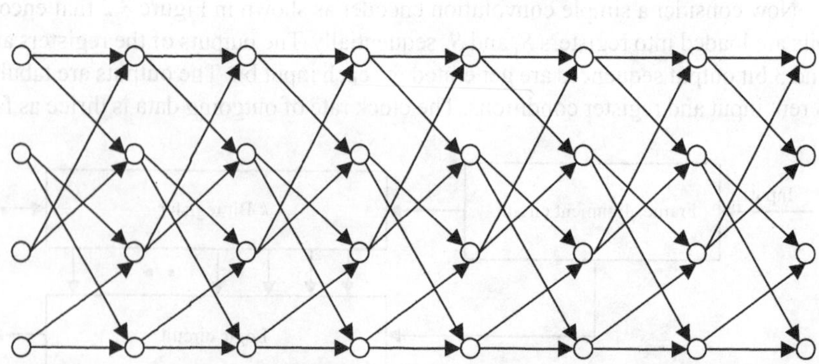

Figure 8.3b *Trellis Diagram for Stream of Input Bits*

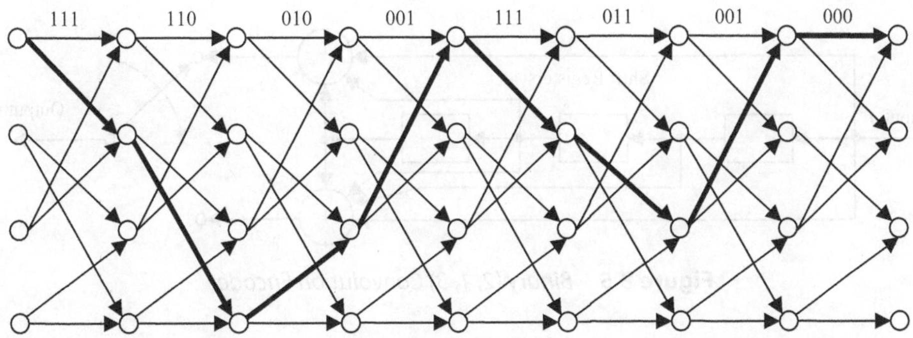

Figure 8.4a *Trellis Mapping for Input Sequence 11001000*

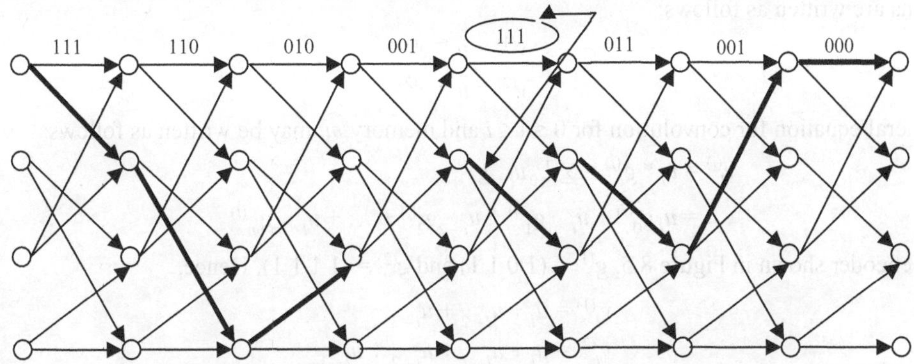

Figure 8.4b *Error Location from Trellis Mapping*

The name *Trellis* was coined because a state diagram of this technique, when drawn on paper, closely resembles the trellis lattice used in rose gardens. The speciality of this diagram is that for a sequence of input data it will follow the arrowed path. For example, let us consider the input data 11001000. Assuming initial register contents are 00, the trellis path is shown by thick lines in Figure 8.4a. Encoded bit sequence will be 111, 110, 010, 001, 111, 011, 001, and 000. If there is any break, it may be assumed that wrong data has arrived. For example, if received bit stream for the above data is 111, 110, 010, 001, 011, 011, 001 and 000, erroneous data is at the fifth sequence. There will be break at trellis mapping as shown in Figure 8.4b. It may be observed that error can be corrected by comparing the previous and succeeding data from the mapping. Therefore, at the receiver end error may be located and corrected.

8.3 ENCODING

Figure 8.5 presents schematic of an encoder for binary (2, 1, 3) code which contains linear feed-forward 3-stage shift register and modulo-2 adders (XOR). All convolution encoders can be implemented using this type of circuit. The information sequence u (u_0, u_1, u_2, …) enters the encoder bit by bit. Two sequences $v^{(1)}$ ($v_0^{(1)}$, $v_1^{(1)}$, $v_2^{(1)}$, …, $v_m^{(1)}$) and $v^{(2)}$ ($v_0^{(2)}$, $v_1^{(2)}$, $v_2^{(2)}$, …, $v_m^{(2)}$) are generated which are multiplexed and the final output v (v_0, v_1, v_2, …, v_m) is generated.

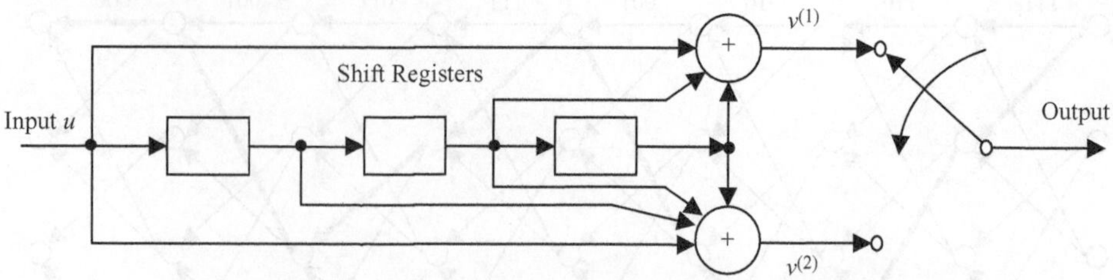

Figure 8.5 *Binary (2, 1, 3) Convolution Encoder*

Let us consider two sequences $v^{(1)}$ and $v^{(2)}$ are generated by the generator sequences (also called impulse sequences) $g^{(1)}$ $(g_0^{(1)}, g_1^{(1)}, g_2^{(1)}, \ldots, g_m^{(1)})$ and $g^{(2)}$ $(g_0^{(2)}, g_1^{(2)}, g_2^{(2)}, \ldots, g_m^{(2)})$. The encoding equations are written as follows:

$$v^{(1)} = u * g^{(1)} \tag{10.1}$$

$$v^{(2)} = u * g^{(2)} \tag{10.2}$$

The general equation for convolution for $0 \le 1 \le i$ and memory m, may be written as follows:

$$v_l^{(j)} = u_l * g_l^{(j)} = \sum_{i=0}^{m} u_{l-i} g_i^{(j)}$$

$$= u_l g_0^{(j)} + u_{l-1} g_1^{(j)} + u_{l-2} g_2^{(j)} + \ldots + u_{l-m} g_m^{(j)} \tag{10.3}$$

For the encoder shown in Figure 8.5, $g^{(1)} = (1\ 0\ 1\ 1)$ and $g^{(2)} = (1\ 1\ 1\ 1)$. Hence,

$$v_l^{(1)} = u_l + u_{l-2} + u_{l-3} \tag{10.4}$$

$$v_l^{(2)} = u_l + u_{l-1} + u_{l-2} + u_{l-3} \tag{10.5}$$

The output sequence or the code word is generated by multiplexing $v^{(1)}$ and $v^{(2)}$ as follows:

$$v_0^{(2)} = v = [v_0^{(1)} v_0^{(2)}, v_1^{(1)} v_1^{(2)}, v_2^{(1)} v_2^{(2)}, v_3^{(1)} v_3^{(2)}] \tag{10.6}$$

Let us consider another example of convolution encoder as shown in Figure 8.6. This is for (3, 2, 1) as this consists of $m = 1$ stage shift register, 2 inputs and 3 bits of output. The information sequence may be written as $u = [u_0^{(1)} u_0^{(2)}, u_1^{(1)} u_1^{(2)}, u_2^{(1)} u_2^{(2)}, \ldots]$ and the output sequence or code word may be considered as $v = [v_0^{(1)} v_0^{(2)} v_0^{(3)}, v_1^{(1)} v_1^{(2)} v_1^{(3)}, v_2^{(1)} v_2^{(2)} v_2^{(3)}, \ldots]$.

It may be noted that the number of memory or shift register may not be equal in every path. Encoder memory length is defined as m = maximum of m_i, where m_i is the number of shift register at ith path.

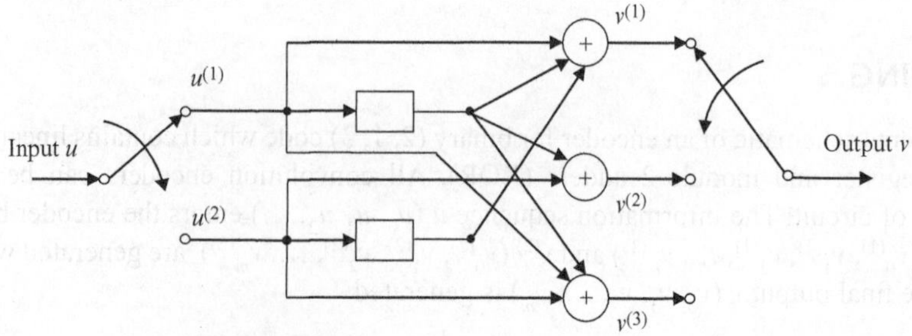

Figure 8.6 *(3, 2, 1) Convolution Encoder*

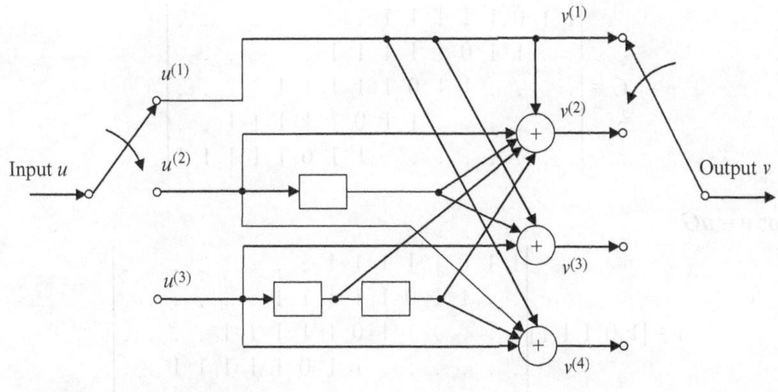

Figure 8.7 *(4, 3, 2) Convolution Encoder*

Figure 8.7 illustrates an example of (4, 3, 2) convolution code, where unequal numbers of shift registers exist at different input–output route. In this regard, it is useful to mention the following definitions:

1. The *constraint length* is defined as $n_A = n(m + 1)$.
2. The *code rate* is defined as $R = k/n$.

Now consider for an information sequence, there are L number of blocks each consisting of k bits with m memory locations. An information sequence will be of length of kL and code word has the length $n(L + m)$. The final nm outputs are generated after the last nonzero information block enters the encoder. The information sequence is terminated with all-zero block to allow the encoder memory clear. In comparison with the linear block codes, the block code rate of convolution code with generator matrix G is $kL/n(L + m)$. For $L >> m$, $L/(L + m) \approx 1$, the block code rate and convolution code rate are approximately equal. However, for small L, the effective rate of information transmission $kL/n(L + m)$ will be reduced by a fractional amount as follows:

$$\text{The fractional rate loss} = \frac{\frac{k}{n} - \frac{kL}{n(L+m)}}{\frac{k}{n}} = \frac{m}{L+m} \tag{8.7}$$

Hence, L is always is assumed to be much larger than m to keep the fractional loss small. For example, for a (2, 1, 3) convolution code of $L = 5$, the fractional rate loss is 3/8 = 37.5%. If $L = 1000$, the fractional rate loss is 3/1003 = 0.3%.

Example 8.1: If the message sequence is u = (10111) and generator sequences are $g^{(1)}$ = (1011) and $g^{(2)}$ = (1111), find the generated code word.

Solution:

$$v^{(1)} = (10111) * (1011) = (10000001)$$
$$v^{(2)} = (10111) * (1111) = (11011101)$$

The code word is (11, 01, 00, 01, 01, 01, 00, 11)

In the other method, the generator sequences can be interlaced and expressed in matrix form as follows:

$$G = \begin{bmatrix} 1\ 1\ 0\ 1\ 1\ 1\ 1\ 1 & . & . & . & . & . & . & . \\ . & . & 1\ 1\ 0\ 1\ 1\ 1\ 1\ 1 & . & . & . & . & . \\ . & . & . & . & 1\ 1\ 0\ 1\ 1\ 1\ 1\ 1 & . & . & . \\ . & . & . & . & . & . & 1\ 1\ 0\ 1\ 1\ 1\ 1\ 1 & . \\ . & . & . & . & . & . & . & . & 1\ 1\ 0\ 1\ 1\ 1\ 1\ 1 \end{bmatrix}$$

The code vector $v = uG$

$$v = [1\ 0\ 1\ 1\ 1] \begin{bmatrix} 1\ 1\ 0\ 1\ 1\ 1\ 1\ 1 & . & . & . & . & . & . & . \\ . & . & 1\ 1\ 0\ 1\ 1\ 1\ 1\ 1 & . & . & . & . & . \\ . & . & . & . & 1\ 1\ 0\ 1\ 1\ 1\ 1\ 1 & . & . & . \\ . & . & . & . & . & . & 1\ 1\ 0\ 1\ 1\ 1\ 1\ 1 & . \\ . & . & . & . & . & . & . & . & 1\ 1\ 0\ 1\ 1\ 1\ 1\ 1 \end{bmatrix}$$

Therefore, code word is $v = (11, 01, 01, 00, 01, 01, 00, 11)$.

Example 8.2: Consider a convolution code of two input sequences as $u^{(1)} = (101)$ and $u^{(2)} = (110)$. If the generator sequences are $g_1^{(1)} = (11)$, $g_1^{(2)} = (01)$, $g_1^{(3)} = (11)$, $g_2^{(1)} = (01)$, $g_2^{(2)} = (10)$, and $g_2^{(3)} = (10)$. Find the code word.

Solution: The coding equations are

$$v^{(1)} = u^{(1)} * g_1^{(1)} + u^{(2)} * g_2^{(1)} = (101) * (11) + (110) * (01) = (1001)$$
$$v^{(2)} = u^{(1)} * g_1^{(2)} + u^{(2)} * g_2^{(2)} = (101) * (01) + (110) * (10) = (1001)$$
$$v^{(3)} = u^{(1)} * g_1^{(3)} + u^{(2)} * g_2^{(3)} = (101) * (11) + (110) * (10) = (0011)$$

Therefore, the code word is $v = (110, 000, 001, 111)$.

8.4 PROPERTIES

As convolution encoder is a linear system, the encoding equations can be represented by polynomials and the convolution operation may be replaced by polynomial multiplication. This means the ith input sequence $u^{(i)}(D)$, jth output sequence $v^{(j)}(D)$, and generator g can be expressed in the following forms, where $1 \le i \le k$ and $1 \le j \le k$

$$u^{(i)} = u_0^{(i)} + u_1^{(i)}D + u_2^{(i)} D^2 + \dots$$
$$v^{(j)} = v_0^{(j)} + v_1^{(j)}D + v_2^{(j)} D^2 + \dots$$
$$g^{(ij)} = g_0^{(ij)} + g_1^{(ij)}D + g_2^{(ij)} D^2 + \dots \tag{8.8}$$

Therefore,

$$v^{(j)} = u^{(i)} \cdot g^{(ij)} \tag{8.9}$$

The indeterminate D can be interpreted as delay operator. The power of D denotes the number of time units delayed from initial bit. For a $(2, 1, m)$ convolution code after multiplexing the output will be

$$v(D) = v^{(1)}(D^2) + Dv^{(2)}(D^2) \tag{8.10}$$

In general, for an (n, k, m) convolution code, the output will be

$$v(D) = v^{(1)}(D^n) + Dv^{(2)} (D^n) + \dots + D^{n-1}v^{(i)} (D^n), \text{ for } 1 \le i \le k \tag{8.11}$$

Example 8.3: For encoder shown in Figure 8.5, for (2, 1, 3) convolution code, $g^{(1)} = (1\ 0\ 1\ 1)$ and $g^{(2)} = (1\ 1\ 1\ 1)$.

$$g(D) = g^{(1)}(D^2) + Dg^{(2)}(D^2) = 1 + D + D^3 + D^4 + D^5 + D^6 + D^7$$

For $u(D) = 1 + D^2 + D^3 + D^4$, the code word is

$$\begin{aligned} v(D) &= u(D^2)\, g(D) \\ &= (1 + D^4 + D^6 + D^8)(1 + D + D^3 + D^4 + D^5 + D^6 + D^7) \\ &= 1 + D + D^3 + D^7 + D^9 + D^{11} + D^{14} + D^{15} \end{aligned}$$

The generator polynomials of an encoder can be determined directly from its circuit diagram and generators of complex encoder system may be represented by matrix $G(D)$.

$$G(D) = \begin{bmatrix} g^{(11)}(D) & g^{(12)}(D) & g^{(13)}(D) & \cdots & g^{(1n)}(D) \\ g^{(21)}(D) & g^{(22)}(D) & g^{(23)}(D) & \cdots & g^{(2n)}(D) \\ \vdots & \vdots & \vdots & \ddots & \vdots \\ g^{(k1)}(D) & g^{(k2)}(D) & g^{(k1)}(D) & \cdots & g^{(kn)}(D) \end{bmatrix} \tag{8.12}$$

The *word length* of the code is max [deg $g^{(ij)}(D)$], for $1 \le j \le n$.
The *memory length* is max [deg $g^{(ij)}(D)$], for $1 \le j \le n$ and $1 \le i \le k$.
The *constraint length* is $\sum_{i=1}^{k} \max[\deg g^{(ij)}(D)]$, for $1 \le j \le n$.

Example 8.4: For (3, 2, 1) convolution code, the generator for the encoder shown in Figure 8.6 is expressed as $G(D) = \begin{bmatrix} 1+D & D & 1+D \\ D & 1 & 1 \end{bmatrix}$. Determine the code word for the inputs $u^{(1)} = 1 + D^2$ and $u^{(2)} = 1 + D$.

Solution:

$$\begin{aligned} V(D) &= [v^{(1)}(D), v^{(2)}(D), v^{(1)}(D)] = [1 + D^2 \quad 1 + D] \begin{bmatrix} 1+D & D & 1+D \\ D & 1 & 1 \end{bmatrix} \\ &= [1 + D^3 \quad 1 + D^3 \quad D^2 + D^3] \end{aligned}$$

By replacing D to D^3 (as $n = 3$) and using Eq. 8.12, we obtain the code word as

$$\begin{aligned} v(D) &= 1 + (D^3)^3 + D(1 + (D^3)^3) + D^2((D^3)^2 + (D^3)^3) \\ &= 1 + D + D^8 + D^9 + D^{10} + D^{11} \end{aligned}$$

8.4.1 Structural Properties

Since the encoder for convolution code is a sequential circuit, its operation can be described by a state diagram. The state of the encoder is defined by its shift register contents. State diagram describes the transition from one state to another. Each new block of k-inputs results in transition to a new state. There are 2^k branches leaving each state. Therefore, for $(n, 1, m)$ code, there will be only two branches leaving each state. Each transition is labelled with its input information bit and output. Figure 8.8 illustrates the state diagram for a (2, 1, 3) convolution code of encoder circuit of Figure 8.5.

Assuming that the encoder is initially at state S_0 (all-zero state), the code word for any given information sequence can be obtained from the state diagram by following the path. For example, for an information sequence of (11101) followed by nonzero bits, the code word with respect to Figure 8.8 will be (11, 10, 01, 01, 11, 10, 11, 11) and the shift registers contents return to initial state S_0.

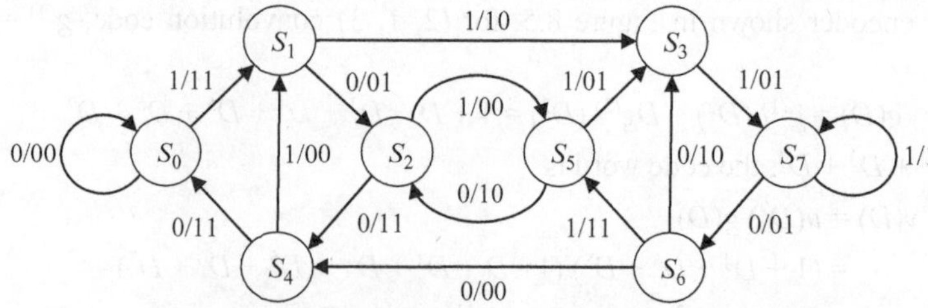

Figure 8.8 *State Diagram of (2, 1, 3) Convolution Code*

Similarly, a (3, 2, 1) convolution code shown in Figure 8.5 can be illustrated by the state diagram as shown in Figure 8.9. It may be noted that as $k = 2$, four branches are leaving from each state. There are two inputs and three outputs which are labelled in the diagram.

The state diagram can be modified to provide complete description with weight distribution function. However, the generating function approach to find the weight distribution of a convolution code is impractical. The performance may be estimated by distance properties as will be discussed in next section. An important subclass of the convolution code is the *systematic code*, where the first k output sequences are exactly similar to k input sequences. It will follow the condition as stated as follows:

$$V^{(i)} = u^{(j)} \quad \text{for } i = 1, 2, 3, \ldots, k \tag{8.13}$$

The generator sequences satisfy

$$\begin{aligned} g^{(j)} &= 1, \quad \text{for } i = j \\ &= 0, \quad \text{for } i \neq j \quad i = 1, 2, 3, \ldots, k \end{aligned} \tag{8.14}$$

The generator matrix is given as

$$G = \begin{bmatrix} I & P_0 & 0 & P_1 & 0 & P_2 & \cdots & 0 & P_m & & & & \\ & & I & P_0 & 0 & P_1 & \cdots & 0 & P_{m-1} & 0 & P_m & & \\ & & & & I & P_0 & \cdots & 0 & P_{m-2} & 0 & P_{m-1} & 0 & P_m \\ & & & & & & \ddots & & & & \vdots & & \end{bmatrix} \tag{8.15}$$

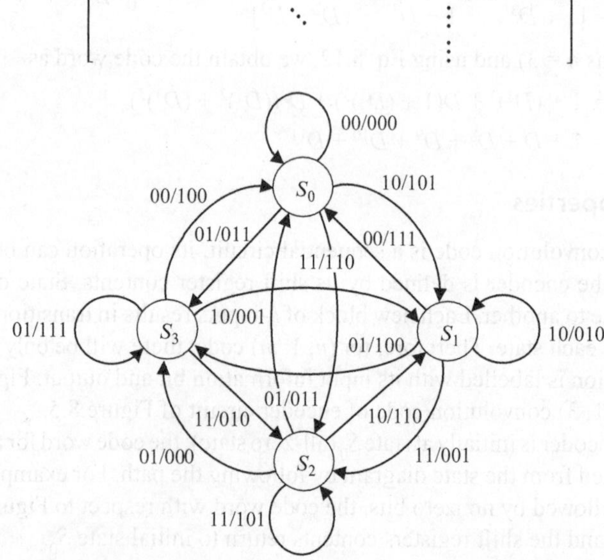

Figure 8.9 *State Diagram of (3, 2, 1) Convolution Code*

where I is $k \times k$ identity matrix, 0 is the $k \times k$ all-zero matrix and P_1 is the $k \times (n-k)$ matrix.

$$P_1 = \begin{bmatrix} g_{1,l}^{(k+1)} & g_{1,l}^{(k+2)} & g_{1,l}^{(k+3)} & \cdots & g_{1,l}^{(n)} \\ g_{2,l}^{(k+1)} & g_{2,l}^{(k+2)} & g_{2,l}^{(k+3)} & \cdots & g_{2,l}^{(n)} \\ \vdots & \vdots & \vdots & \ddots & \vdots \\ g_{k,l}^{(k+1)} & g_{k,l}^{(k+2)} & g_{k,l}^{(k+3)} & \cdots & g_{k,l}^{(n)} \end{bmatrix} \tag{8.16}$$

The transfer function matrix will be

$$G(D) = \begin{bmatrix} 1 & 0 & \cdots & 0 & g_1^{(k+1)}(D) & \cdots & g_1^{(n)}(D) \\ 0 & 1 & \cdots & 0 & g_2^{(k+1)}(D) & \cdots & g_2^{(n)}(D) \\ \vdots & \vdots & \ddots & \vdots & \vdots & & \vdots \\ 0 & 0 & \cdots & 1 & g_k^{(k+1)}(D) & \cdots & g_k^{(n)}(D) \end{bmatrix} \tag{8.17}$$

The first k output sequences equal the input sequences, and so they are called information sequences, whereas the next $n-k$ output sequences are parity sequences. It may be noted that only $k * (n-k)$ sequences must be specified to define a systematic code. Any code not satisfying the Eqs. (8.13) to (8.17) are called *nonsystematic*.

In short form Eq. (8.17) may be written as follows:

$$G(D) = [I \mid P(D)]$$

Parity-check matrix for a systematic code is

$$H(D) = [-P(D)^T \mid I]$$

It follows that

$$G(D)\, H(D)^T = 0 \tag{8.18}$$

A convolution code of transfer function matrix $G(D)$ has a feed forward inverse $G^{-1}(D)$ of delay l, if and only if

$$GCD\, [g^{(1)}(D), g^{(2)}(D), g^{(3)}(D), \ldots g^{(n)}(D)] = D^{(l)} \tag{8.19}$$

GCD denotes greatest common divisor. Code satisfying above equation is called *noncatastrophic convolution code*.

Hardware implementation is easier for systematic code as it requires no inverting circuit to recover the code word. It is to be noted that nonsystematic code can also be chosen for use in communication system, but catastrophic codes must be avoided.

Example 8.5: Consider a (2, 1, 3) systematic code for which the generator sequences are $g^{(1)} = (1000)$ and $g^{(2)} = (1101)$. Find the information sequence and parity sequence when the message sequence is $u = (1011)$.

Solution:

$$g^{(1)}(D) = 1 \text{ and } g^{(2)}(D) = 1 + D + D^3$$

The transfer function matrix is $G(D) = [1 \quad 1 + D + D^3]$

The information sequence is $v(D) = u(D)\, g^{(1)}(D) = (1 + D^2 + D^3) \cdot 1 = 1 + D^2 + D^3$.

The parity sequence is $P(D) = u(D)\, g^{(2)}(D) = (1 + D^2 + D^3)(1 + D + D^3)$

$$= 1 + D + D^2 + D^3 + D^4 + D^5 + D^6$$

Example 8.6: Consider the (3, 2, 2) systematic code of input sequences $u^{(1)}(D) = 1 + D$ and $u^{(2)}(D) = D^2 + D^3$ with transfer function matrix $G(D) = \begin{bmatrix} 1 & 0 & 1 + D + D^2 \\ 0 & 1 & 1 + D^2 \end{bmatrix}$. Find the information sequence and parity sequence.

Solution:

The information sequences are $v^{(1)}(D) = u^{(1)}(D)\, g_1^{(1)}(D) = 1 + D$

and $v^{(2)}(D) = u^{(2)}(D)\, g_2^{(2)}(D) = D^2 + D^3$

The parity sequence is given as $P(D) = u^{(1)}(D)\, g_1^{(3)}(D) + u^{(2)}(D)\, g_2^{(3)}(D)$

$$= (1 + D)(1 + D + D^2) + (D^2 + D^3)(1 + D^2)$$
$$= 1 + D^2 + D^4 + D^5.$$

8.4.2 Distance Properties

The performance of convolution code is governed by encoding algorithm and distance properties of the code. A good code must possess the maximum possible minimum distance. The most important distance measure for convolution codes is the minimum free distance d_{free} which is defined as the minimum distance between any two code words in the code.

$$d_{\text{free}} \triangleq \min[d(v', v''): u' \neq u''] \tag{8.20}$$

where v' and v'' are code words corresponding to information sequences u' and u'' respectively. If u' and u'' are of different lengths, then zeros are added to shorter sequence to make them equal length. In other words, d_{free} is the minimum weight code word of any length produced by a nonzero information sequence. Also it is the minimum weight of all paths in the state diagram that diverge from and remerge with all-zero state and it is the lowest power of X in the code generating function. For example, $d_{\text{free}} = 6$ for the (2, 1, 3) code in Figure 8.8 and $d_{\text{free}} = 3$ for the (3, 2, 1) code in Figure 8.9.

Another important distance measure for convolution codes is the *column distance function* (CDF), which is defined by the minimum weight code word over the first $i + 1$ time units whose initial information block is nonzero. Let $[u]_i$ and $[v]_i$ be the information sequence and code word sequence, respectively, with ith truncation.

$$[u]_i = (u_0^{(1)}\, u_0^{(2)} \ldots u_0^{(k)},\, u_1^{(1)}\, u_1^{(2)} \ldots u_1^{(k)},\, \ldots,\, u_i^{(1)}\, u_i^{(2)} \ldots u_i^{(k)})$$
$$[v]_i = (v_0^{(1)}\, v_0^{(2)} \ldots v_0^{(k)},\, v_1^{(1)}\, v_1^{(2)} \ldots v_1^{(k)},\, \ldots,\, v_i^{(1)}\, v_i^{(2)} \ldots v_i^{(k)})$$

The column distance function of the order of i, d_i is defined as

$$d_i \triangleq \min\{d([v']_i, [v'']_i): [u']_0 \neq [u'']_0\}$$
$$= \min\{w[v]_i : [u]_0 \neq 0\} \tag{8.21}$$

If $[G]_i$ is the generator matrix, $[v]_i = [u]_i\, [G]_i$, where

$$[G]_i = \begin{bmatrix} G_0 & G_1 & \cdots & G_i \\ & G_0 & \cdots & G_{i-1} \\ & & \vdots & \\ & & & G_0 \end{bmatrix} \quad \text{for } i \leq m \tag{8.22}$$

$$[G]_i = \begin{bmatrix} G_0 & G_1 & \cdots & G_{m-1} & G_m & & & & \\ & G_0 & \cdots & G_{m-2} & G_{m-1} & G_m & & & \\ & & \ddots & \vdots & \vdots & & & & \\ & & & G_0 & G_1 & \cdots & G_{m-1} & G_m & \\ & & & & G_0 & \cdots & G_{m-2} & G_{m-1} & \\ & & & & & \ddots & \vdots & \vdots & \\ & & & & & & G_0 & G_1 & \\ & & & & & & & G_0 & \end{bmatrix} \quad \text{for } i > m \tag{8.23}$$

If CDF d_i is the minimum weight code over first $i + 1$ time units with initial nonzero information block, it does not decrease with the increase of i. When $i = m$, CDF $= d_m$ is called the minimum distance and denoted as $d_{\min}$. For $i \to \infty$, CDF reaches d_{free} for noncatastrophic codes; however, this may not be true for catastrophic codes.

8.5 DECODING

Although convolution encoding is a simple procedure, decoding of a convolution code is much more complex task. Several classes of algorithms exist for this purpose:

- *Threshold decoding* is the simplest of them, but it can be successfully applied only to the specific classes of convolution codes. It is also far from optimal.
- *Sequential decoding* is a class of algorithms performing much better than threshold algorithms. Their main advantage is that decoding complexity is virtually independent from the length of the particular code. Although sequential algorithms are also suboptimal, they are successfully used with very long codes, where no other algorithm can be acceptable. The main drawback of sequential decoding is unpredictable decoding latency.
- *Viterbi decoding* is an optimal (in a *maximum-likelihood* sense) algorithm for decoding of a convolution code. Its main drawback is that the decoding complexity grows exponentially with the code length. Hence, it can be utilized only for relatively short codes.

8.5.1 Threshold Decoding

Threshold decoding, also termed as *majority logic decoding*, is based only on the constrain length of the received blocks rather than on the received sequence to make the final decision on the received information. Its algorithm is simple and hence it is simpler in implementation comparing to other decoding techniques. However, the performance is inferior when compared to other techniques and it mainly used telephony, HF radio, where moderate amount of coding gain is required at relatively low cost.

Let us consider the systematic code with $R = ½$, generator sequences $g^{(1)} = (1\,0\,0\,0\ldots)$ and $g^{(2)} = (g_0^{(2)}\, g_1^{(2)}\, g_2^{(2)}\ldots.)$. Therefore, the generator matrix i

$$G = \begin{bmatrix} 1 & g_0^{(2)} & 0 & g_1^{(2)} & 0 & g_2^{(2)} & \cdots & 0 & g_m^{(2)} & & & & \\ & & 1 & g_0^{(2)} & 0 & g_1^{(2)} & \cdots & 0 & g_{m-1}^{(2)} & 0 & g_m^{(2)} & & \\ & & & & 1 & g_0^{(2)} & \cdots & 0 & g_{m-2}^{(2)} & 0 & g_{m-1}^{(2)} & 0 & g_m^{(2)} \\ & & & & & \cdots & & & \cdots & \cdots & \cdots & & \\ & & & & & & & & \cdots & & \cdots & & \end{bmatrix} \tag{8.24}$$

For an information sequence u, we have the equations

$$v^{(1)} = u * g^{(1)} = u, \text{ and } v^{(2)} = u * g^{(2)} \tag{8.25}$$

The transmitted code word is $v = uG$. If v is send over a BSC, the received sequence r may be written as follows:

$$r = (r_0^{(1)} r_0^{(2)}, r_1^{(1)} r_1^{(2)}, r_2^{(1)} r_2^{(2)}, \ldots) = v + e \tag{8.26}$$

The received information sequence and parity sequences, respectively, are

$$r^{(1)} = (r_0^{(1)}, r_1^{(1)}, r_2^{(1)}, \ldots) = v^{(1)} + e^{(1)} = u + e^{(1)} \tag{8.27}$$

$$r^{(2)} = (r_0^{(2)}, r_1^{(2)}, r_2^{(2)}, \ldots) = v^{(2)} + e^{(2)} = u * g^{(2)} + e^{(2)} \tag{8.28}$$

where $e^{(1)} = (e_0^{(1)}, e_1^{(1)}, e_2^{(1)}, \ldots)$ and $e^{(2)} = (e_0^{(2)}, e_1^{(2)}, e_2^{(2)}, \ldots)$ are the information error sequence and parity error sequence, respectively.

The syndrome sequence may be defined as $s = (s_0, s_1, s_2, \ldots)$ may be defined as $s \triangleq rH^T$ (8.29)

where H is the parity-check matrix. H is given as

$$H = \begin{bmatrix} g_0^{(2)} & 1 \\ g_1^{(2)} & 0 & g_0^{(2)} & 1 \\ g_2^{(2)} & 0 & g_1^{(2)} & 0 & g_0^{(2)} & 1 \\ \vdots & \vdots & \vdots & \vdots & \vdots & \vdots \\ g_m^{(2)} & 0 & g_{m-1}^{(2)} & 0 & g_{m-2}^{(2)} & 0 & \cdots & g_0^{(2)} & 1 \\ & & g_m^{(2)} & 0 & g_{m-1}^{(2)} & 0 & \cdots & g_1^{(2)} & 0 & g_0^{(2)} & 1 \\ & & & & g_m^{(2)} & 0 & \cdots & g_2^{(2)} & 0 & g_1^{(2)} & 0 & g_0^{(2)} & 1 \\ & & & & & \ddots & \ddots & \ddots & \ddots & \ddots & \ddots & \ddots & \ddots \end{bmatrix} \tag{8.30}$$

We have seen that for block codes, $GH^T = 0$ and v is a code word if and only if $vH^T = 0$. However, unlike block codes, G and H are semi-infinite as information sequences and code word are of arbitrary length for convolution codes. Since $r = v + e$, the syndrome can be derived as

$$s = (v + e)H^T = vH^T + eH^T = eH^T \tag{8.31}$$

It may be noted that s depends only on the channel error and not on the code word. Hence, decoder may be designed to operate on s rather than r. Using the polynomial notation, we can write

$$v^{(1)}(D) = u(D)\, g^{(1)}(D) = u(D) \tag{8.32}$$

$$v^{(2)}(D) = u(D)\, g^{(2)}(D) = v^{(1)}(D)\, g^{(2)}(D) \tag{8.33}$$

$$r^{(1)}(D) = v^{(1)}(D) + e^{(1)}(D) = u(D) + e^{(1)}(D) \tag{8.34}$$

$$r^{(2)}(D) = v^{(2)}(D) + e^{(2)}(D) = u(D)\, g^{(2)}(D) + e^{(2)}(D) \tag{8.35}$$

$$\begin{aligned} s(D) &= r^{(1)}(D)\, g^{(2)}(D) + r^{(2)}(D) \\ &= [u(D) + e^{(1)}(D)]\, g^{(2)}(D) + u(D)\, g^{(2)}(D) + e^{(2)}(D) \\ &= e^{(1)}(D)\, g^{(2)}(D) + e^{(2)}(D) \end{aligned} \tag{8.36}$$

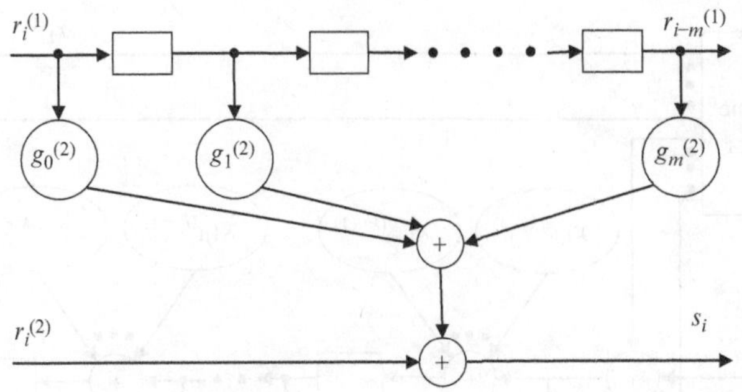

Figure 8.10 *Syndrome Generation*

Eq. 8.36 suggests that syndrome generation is equivalent to encoding of $r^{(1)}$ and then addition with $r^{(2)}$. The implementation of it is shown in Figure 8.10.

Threshold or majority logic decoding of convolution code is based on the concept of orthogonal parity checksums. Any syndrome bit or any sum of syndrome bits which represents the sum of channel error bits is called parity checksum. If received sequence is a valid code word, the error sequence is also a code word and hence the syndrome bits as well as all parity checksum bits must be zero. If the received sequence is not a code word, the parity checksums will not be zero. An error bit e_J is said to be checked if it is checked by checksum. A set of J checksums is orthogonal on e_J, if each checksum checks e_J, but no other error bit is by more than one checksum. The value of e_J can be estimated by majority logic decoding rule.

Majority logic decoding rule correctly estimates e_J, if the error bits are checked by J orthogonal checksums containing t_{ML} or fewer channel errors (1's) and estimates as $e_J = 1$, if and only if more than t_{ML} of the J checksums orthogonal e_J have value 1, where $t_{ML} \triangleq J/2$, t_{ML} is the *majority logic error–correcting capability* of the code. If the error bits checked by J orthogonal checksums contain t_{ML} or fewer channel errors, majority logic decoder correctly estimates e_J. The block diagram of decoder for self-orthogonal (n, k, m) code with majority logic decoding is given in Figure 8.11. The operation of the decoder is described as follows:

- First the constraint length of $(m + 1)(n - k)$ syndrome bits is calculated.
- A set of J orthogonal checksums on $e_0^{(1)}$ is formed on k information error bits from the syndrome bits.
- Each set of checksums is fed into majority logic gate, where output will be '1' if more than half of its inputs are '1'. If the output of ith threshold gate is '1' [$\hat{e}_0^{(i)} = 1$], $r_0^{(i)}$ is assumed to be incorrect. Correction is made by adding output of each of the threshold output to corresponding receiving bit. Threshold output is also fed back and subtracted from each of the affected syndrome bits.
- The estimated information $\hat{u}_0^{(i)} = r_0^{(i)} + \hat{e}_0^{(i)}$, for $i = 1, 2, \ldots, k$ is shifted out. The syndrome register is shifted once and receives next block of n received bits. The $n - k$ syndrome bits are calculated and shifted into leftmost stages of $n - k$ syndrome registers.
- The syndromes registers now contain the modified syndrome bits together with a new set of syndrome bits. The above steps are repeated to estimate the next block of information error bits. In the same way the successive blocks of information error bits are estimated.

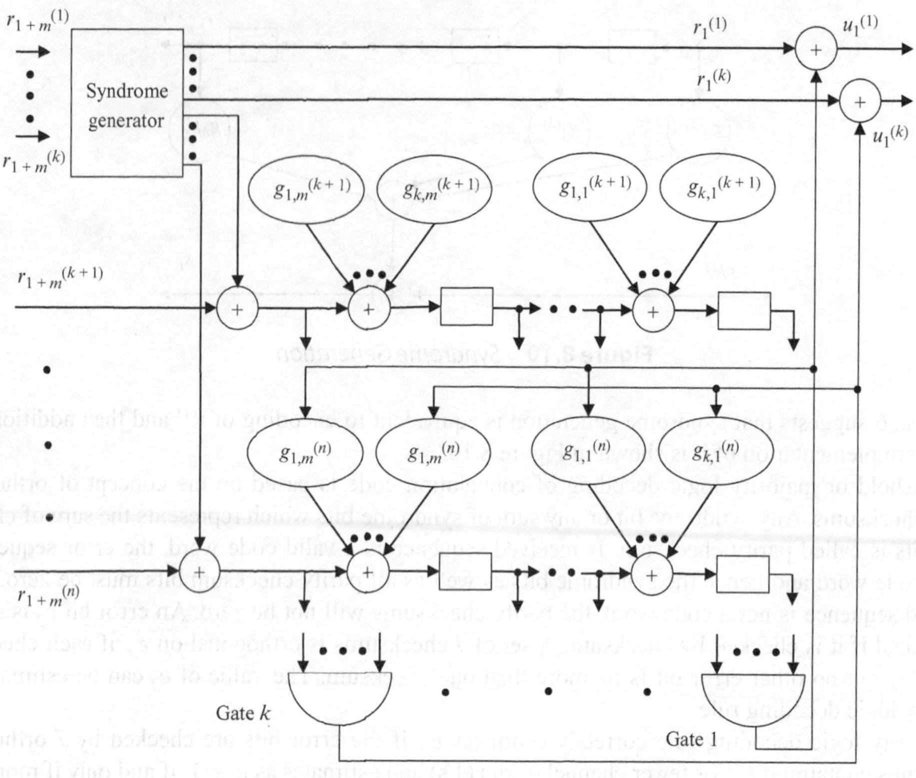

Figure 8.11 *Majority Logic Decoder Scheme*

Example 8.7: Consider systematic code with $g^{(1)}(D) = 1$ and $g^{(2)}(D) = 1 + D + D^4 + D^6$. Find the majority logic error correction capability (constraint length).

Solution: The parity-check matrix may be developed from $g^{(1)}(D) = 1$ and $g^{(2)}(D)$ as

$$H = \begin{bmatrix} 1 & 1 \\ 1 & 0 & 1 & 1 \\ 0 & 0 & 1 & 0 & 1 & 1 \\ 0 & 0 & 0 & 0 & 1 & 0 & 1 & 1 \\ 1 & 0 & 0 & 0 & 0 & 0 & 1 & 0 & 1 & 1 \\ 0 & 0 & 0 & 0 & 0 & 0 & 0 & 0 & 1 & 0 & 1 & 1 \\ 1 & 0 & 0 & 0 & 1 & 0 & 0 & 0 & 0 & 0 & 1 & 0 & 1 & 1 \end{bmatrix}$$

The syndrome polynomial is

$$s(D) = e^{(1)}(D)g^{(2)}(D) + e^{(2)}(D) = rH^T = (v + e)H^T = eH^T$$

Or $\quad s^T(D) = (eH^T)^T = He^T$

$$
= \begin{bmatrix} 1 & 1 \\ 1 & 0 & 1 & 1 \\ 0 & 0 & 1 & 0 & 1 & 1 \\ 0 & 0 & 0 & 0 & 1 & 0 & 1 & 1 \\ 1 & 0 & 0 & 0 & 0 & 0 & 1 & 0 & 1 & 1 \\ 0 & 0 & 0 & 0 & 0 & 0 & 0 & 0 & 1 & 0 & 1 & 1 \\ 1 & 0 & 0 & 0 & 1 & 0 & 0 & 0 & 0 & 0 & 1 & 0 & 1 & 1 \end{bmatrix} e^T
$$

The even number columns of H^T make an identity matrix. Therefore, the above equation may be rewritten by considering the odd number of columns.

$$
s^T(D) = \begin{bmatrix} s_0 \\ s_1 \\ s_2 \\ s_3 \\ s_4 \\ s_5 \\ s_6 \end{bmatrix} = \begin{bmatrix} 1 \\ 1 & 1 \\ 0 & 1 & 1 \\ 0 & 0 & 1 & 1 \\ 1 & 0 & 0 & 1 & 1 \\ 0 & 1 & 0 & 0 & 1 & 1 \\ 1 & 0 & 1 & 0 & 0 & 1 & 1 \end{bmatrix} \begin{bmatrix} e_0^{(1)} \\ e_1^{(1)} \\ e_2^{(1)} \\ e_3^{(1)} \\ e_4^{(1)} \\ e_5^{(1)} \\ e_6^{(1)} \end{bmatrix} + \begin{bmatrix} e_0^{(2)} \\ e_1^{(2)} \\ e_2^{(2)} \\ e_3^{(2)} \\ e_4^{(2)} \\ e_5^{(2)} \\ e_6^{(2)} \end{bmatrix}
$$

It may be noted that $e_0^{(1)}$ is affected by the syndromes s_0 to s_6. The above matrix which multiplies the error sequence is called *parity triangle*. The parity triangle matrix is used to find out the orthogonal sets of checksums on e_j. No syndrome bit can be used for more than one orthogonal checksum as parity bit should not be checked more than once. The selection of syndrome bits is indicated by arrows as under.

$$
\begin{array}{l}
\longrightarrow 1 \\
\longrightarrow 1\ \boxed{1} \\
\ 0\ 1\ 1 \\
\ 0\ 0\ 1\ 1 \\
\longrightarrow 1\ 0\ 0\ \boxed{1}\ \boxed{1} \\
\ 0\ 1\ 0\ 0\ 1\ 1 \\
\longrightarrow 1\ 0\ \boxed{1}\ 1\ 0\ \boxed{1}\ \boxed{1}
\end{array}
$$

The syndrome equations may be expressed as follows:

$$
\begin{aligned}
s_0 &= e_0^{(1)} && + e_0^{(2)} \\
s_1 &= e_0^{(1)} + e_1^{(1)} && + e_1^{(2)} \\
s_4 &= e_0^{(1)} + e_3^{(1)} + e_4^{(1)} && + e_4^{(2)} \\
s_6 &= e_0^{(1)} + e_2^{(1)} + e_5^{(1)} + e_6^{(1)} && + e_6^{(2)}
\end{aligned}
$$

It may be noted that no other than $e_0^{(1)}$ appears in the checksum more than once. Each checksum is single syndrome bit and so it is self-orthogonal. Since 11 different channel errors have been checked here, the effective constraint length is 11. In this case, the majority logic or threshold decoding technique can correctly estimate 2 ($t_{ML} = 2$) to 11 channel errors.

Example 8.8: Consider (3, 1, 4) systematic code with $g^{(2)} = 1 + D$ and $g^{(3)} = 1 + D^2 + D^3 + D^4$. Find constraint length.

---

*The arrows indicate syndrome bits and boxes indicate which information error bits checked other than $e_0^{(1)}$. At most one arrow can point each row and at most one box appear in each column.

Solution: In this case, there are two syndrome sequences $s_0^{(2)}, s_1^{(2)}, s_2^{(2)}, s_3^{(2)}, s_4^{(2)}$ and, $s_0^{(3)}, s_1^{(3)}, s_2^{(3)}, s_3^{(3)}, s_4^{(3)}$ generated by two generator polynomials. Removing the elements of parity matrix H due to $g^{(1)}$, the syndrome equations in matrix form is as follows:

$$S^T(D) = \begin{bmatrix} s_0^{(2)} \\ s_1^{(2)} \\ s_2^{(2)} \\ s_3^{(2)} \\ s_4^{(2)} \\ s_0^{(3)} \\ s_1^{(3)} \\ s_2^{(3)} \\ s_3^{(3)} \\ s_4^{(3)} \end{bmatrix} = \begin{bmatrix} 1 & & & & \\ 1 & 1 & & & \\ 0 & 1 & 1 & & \\ 0 & 0 & 1 & 1 & \\ 0 & 0 & 0 & 1 & 1 \\ 1 & & & & \\ 0 & 1 & & & \\ 1 & 0 & 1 & & \\ 1 & 1 & 0 & 1 & \\ 1 & 1 & 1 & 0 & 1 \end{bmatrix} \begin{bmatrix} e_0^{(1)} \\ e_1^{(1)} \\ e_2^{(1)} \\ e_3^{(1)} \\ e_4^{(1)} \end{bmatrix} + \begin{bmatrix} e_0^{(2)} \\ e_1^{(2)} \\ e_2^{(2)} \\ e_3^{(2)} \\ e_4^{(2)} \\ e_0^{(3)} \\ e_1^{(3)} \\ e_2^{(3)} \\ e_2^{(3)} \\ e_2^{(4)} \end{bmatrix}$$

Now two parity triangles are used to investigate the checksums. Useful syndromes are indicated by arrows. The checksums $s_0^{(2)}, s_0^{(3)}, s_1^{(2)}, s_2^{(3)}, s_2^{(2)} + s_4^{(3)}$ and $s_1^{(3)} + s_3^{(3)}$ form six orthogonal sets of $e_0^{(1)}$.

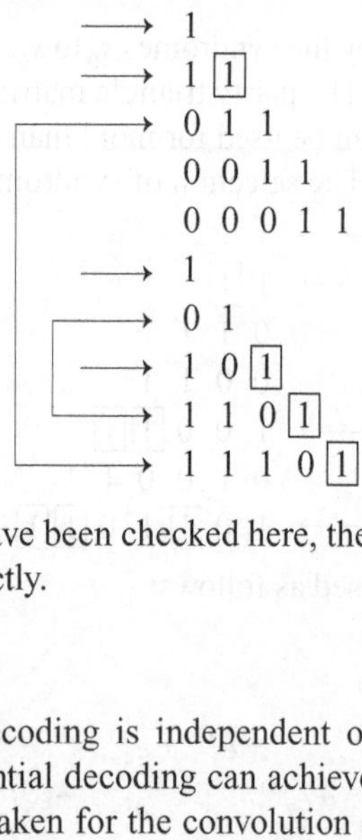

Since 13 different channel errors have been checked here, the effective constraint length is 13. It can estimate 3 (t_{ML} = 3) to 13 errors correctly.

8.5.2 Sequential Decoding

The decoding effort of sequential decoding is independent of encoder memory k and hence large constraint lengths can be used. Sequential decoding can achieve a desired bit error probability when a sufficiently large constraint length is taken for the convolution code. We shall see that decoding effort of it is also adaptable to the noise level. Its main disadvantage is that noisy frame requires large amount of computation and decoding time occasionally exceed some upper limit, causing information to be lost or erased.

The 2^{KL} code words of length $N = n(L + m)$ for an (n, k, m) code and an information sequence of length KL as paths may be conveniently represented by code-tree containing $L + m + 1$ time units or levels. The code-tree is an expanded version of trellis diagram where every path is distinct and totally different from every other path. The code-tree for (3, 1, 2) code with $G(D) = [1 + D, 1 + D^2, 1 + D + D^2]$ is given at Figure 8.12 for information sequence length $L = 5$. The number of tree levels is $L + m + 1 = 5 + 2 + 1 = 8$ which is labelled as 0 to 7. The leftmost node in the tree is called origin node representing

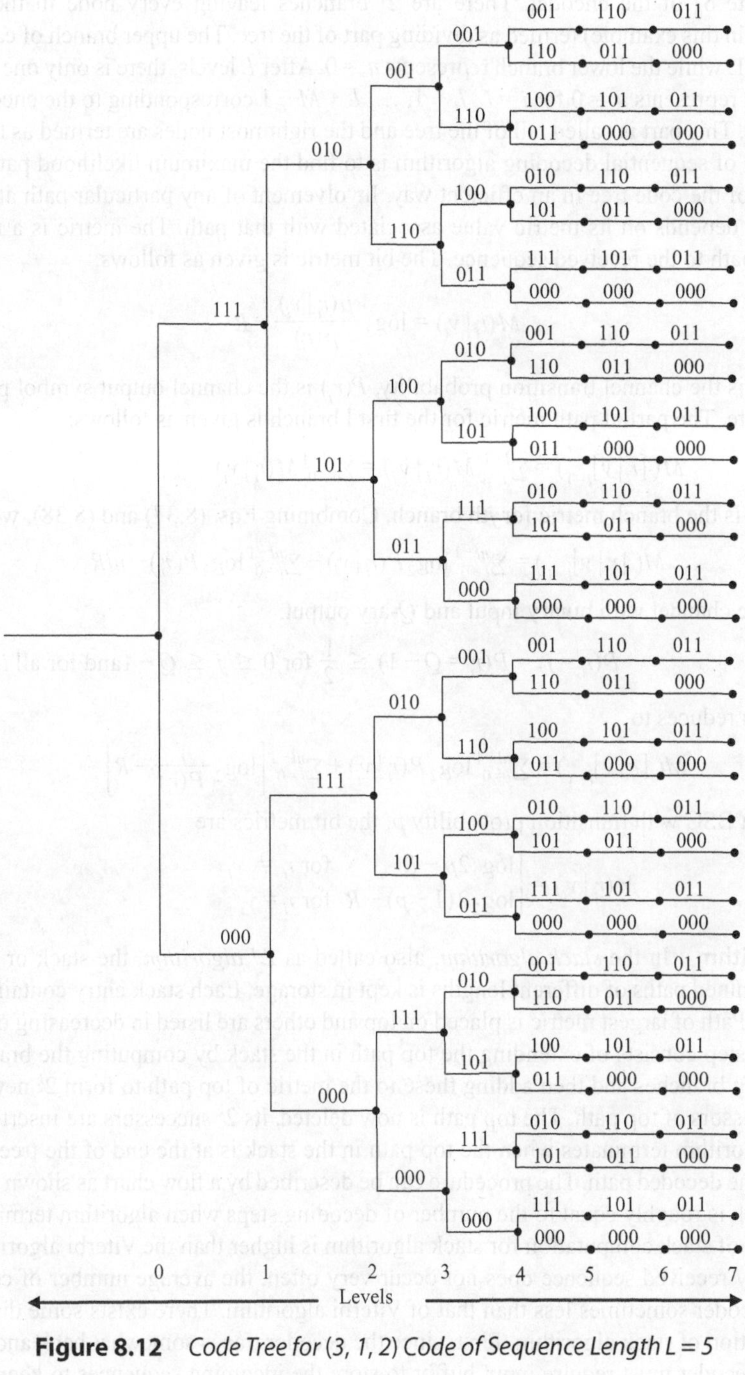

Figure 8.12 *Code Tree for (3, 1, 2) Code of Sequence Length L = 5*

the starting state S_0 of the encoder. There are 2^k branches leaving every node in the first L levels (i.e., five levels in this example) termed as dividing part of the tree. The upper branch of each node represents input $u_i = 1$, while the lower branch represents $u_i = 0$. After L levels, there is only one branch leaving each node. This represents $u_i = 0$ for $i = L, L + 1, \ldots, L + M - 1$ corresponding to the encoder's return to all-zero state S_0. This part is called tail of the tree and the rightmost nodes are termed as terminal nodes.

The purpose of sequential decoding algorithm is to find the maximum likelihood path by searching through nodes of the code tree in an efficient way. Involvement of any particular path at the maximum likelihood path depends on its metric value associated with that path. The metric is a measure of the closeness of a path to the received sequence. The bit metric is given as follows:

$$M(r_i \mid v_i) = \log_2 \frac{p(r_i \mid v_i)}{p(r_i)} - R \tag{8.37}$$

where $P(r_i \mid v_i)$ is the channel transition probability, $P(r_i)$ is the channel output symbol probability, and R is the code rate. The partial path metric for the first l branch is given as follows:

$$M([r \mid v]_{l-1}) = \Sigma_{j=0}^{l-1} M(r_j \mid v_j) = \Sigma_{i=0}^{nl-1} M(r_i \mid v_i) \tag{8.38}$$

where $M(r_j \mid v_j)$ is the branch metric for jth branch. Combining Eqs. (8.37) and (8.38), we obtain

$$M([r \mid v]_{l-1}) = \Sigma_{i=0}^{nl-1} \log_2 P(r_i \mid v_i) - \Sigma_{i=0}^{nl-1} \log_2 P(r_i) - nlR \tag{8.39}$$

For a symmetric channel with binary input and Q-ary output,

$$P(r_i = j) = P(r_i = Q - 1) \leq \frac{1}{2} \text{ for } 0 \leq j \leq Q - 1 \text{and for all } i.$$

Then Eq. (8.39) reduces to

$$M([r \mid v]_{l-1}) = \Sigma_{i=0}^{nl-1} \log_2 P(r_i \mid v_i) + \Sigma_{i=0}^{nl-1} \left[\log_2 \frac{1}{P(r_i)} - R\right] \tag{8.40}$$

In general, for a BSC with transition probability p, the bit metrics are

$$M(r_i \mid v_i) = \begin{cases} \log_2 2p - R & \text{for } r_i \neq v_i \\ \log_2 2(1-p) - R & \text{for } r_i = v_i \end{cases} \tag{8.41}$$

A. Stack Algorithm In the *stack algorithm*, also called as *ZJ algorithm*, the stack or ordered list of previously examined paths of different lengths is kept in storage. Each stack entry contains a path along with its metric. Path of largest metric is placed on top and others are listed in decreasing order of metric. Each decoding step consists of extending the top path in the stack by computing the branch metrics of its 2^k succeeding branches and then adding these to the metric of top path to form 2^k new paths, which are called successors of top path. The top path is now deleted, its 2^k successors are inserted and stack is rearranged. Algorithm terminates when the top path in the stack is at the end of the tree. At this point, the top path is the decoded path. The procedure can be described by a flow chart as shown in Figure 8.13. The size of stack is roughly equal to the number of decoding steps when algorithm terminates.

The number of stack computation for stack algorithm is higher than the Viterbi algorithm. However, since very noisy received sequence does not occur very often, the average number of computation by a sequential decoder sometimes less than that of Viterbi algorithm. There exists some disadvantages in the implementation of stack algorithm. First, since the decoder traces somewhat back and forth through code tree, the decoder must require input buffer to store the incoming sequences to keep them at waiting. The speed factor of the decoder, ratio of speed of computation to the rate of incoming data, plays

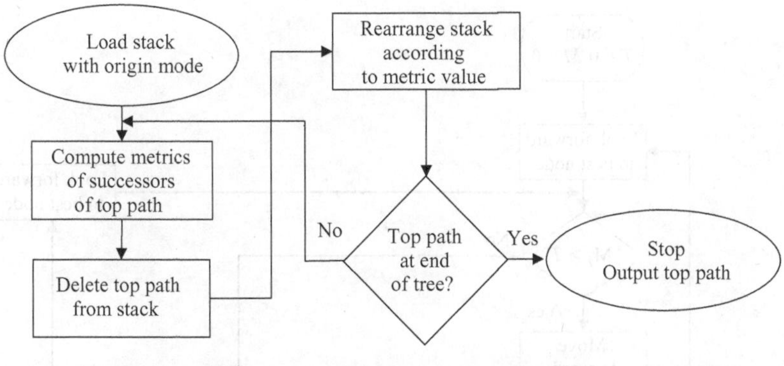

Figure 8.13 *Flow Chart for Stack Algorithm*

an important role. Second, the size of stack must be finite, otherwise there are always some probabilities that the stack will fill up before decoding is complete. The most common way of handling this problem is to push out or discard the path at the bottom of the stack on the next decoding step. Third, rearrangement of stack may be time-consuming if number of stack is high.

B. Fano Algorithm Fano algorithm approach of sequential decoding requires no storage with the sacrifice of speed compared to stack algorithm. In Fano algorithm, the decoder examines a sequence of nodes in the tree starting from the origin node and ending at terminal node. The decoder never jumps from node to node as in stack algorithm, but moves to adjacent node. The metric at each node is calculated at that instant by addition or subtraction of metric of connecting branch. Thus need of storing the metrics is eliminated. However, some nodes are revisited and metrics are recalculated. The decoder will move forward as long as the metric value along the path examined continues to increase. When the metric value dips below a certain threshold, the decoder selects another path to examine. If no path is observed below threshold, the threshold value is lower and examination procedure is started again. The decoder eventually reaches the end of the tree, where the algorithm terminates. This operation is described by a flow chart as shown in Figure 8.14. The decoder starts at origin with threshold $T = 0$ and metric value $M = 0$. It looks forward to the best of the 2^k succeeding nodes, i.e., the one with largest metric. If M_F is the metric of forward node being checked and if $M_F > T$, decoder moves in this node. Threshold modification or threshold tightening is performed if the node is visited first time. Threshold T is increased by largest possible multiple of a threshold increment Δ so that the new threshold does not exceed current metric. Threshold tightening is not required if the node is visited previously.

If $M_F < T$, the decoder looks backward to the proceeding node. If M_B is the metric of backward node being examined, and if $M_B < T$, then T is decreased by Δ and looks forward to the best node. If in this checking process $M_B > T$ and this backward move is from worst of the 2^k succeeding nodes, the decoder again looks back to the preceeding node, else the decoder looks forward to the next best of 2^k nodes. If the decoder ever looks backward from origin node, it is assumed to be metric value of ∞.

The number of computations in Fano algorithm depends on the selection of threshold increment Δ. If it is too small, the number of computations is large. It may be noted that the metrics are scaled by a positive constant so that they can be closely approximated as integers for easier implementation. For example, for $R = 1/3$ and $p = 0.10$, from Eq. (8.37) we get

$$M(r_i \mid v_i) = \begin{cases} \log_2 2p - R = -2.65 & \text{for } r_i \neq v_i \\ \log_2 2(1-p) - R = 0.52 & \text{for } r_i = v_i \end{cases} \tag{8.42}$$

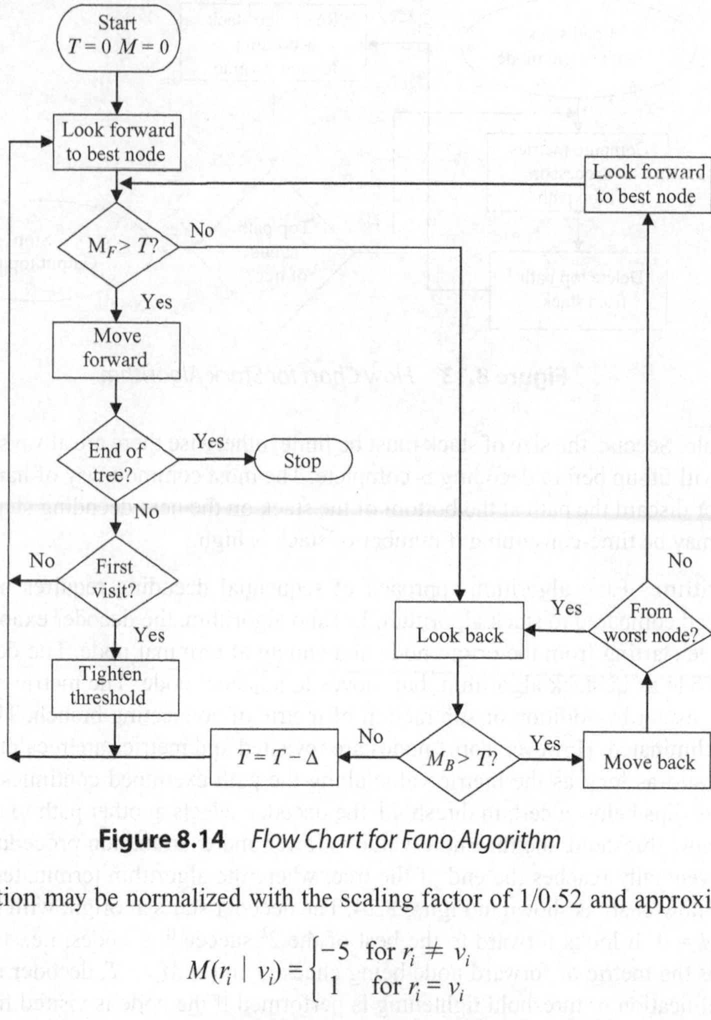

Figure 8.14 *Flow Chart for Fano Algorithm*

The above equation may be normalized with the scaling factor of 1/0.52 and approximated to integers as follows:

$$M(r_i \mid v_i) = \begin{cases} -5 & \text{for } r_i \neq v_i \\ 1 & \text{for } r_i = v_i \end{cases} \tag{8.43}$$

C. Performance Let the jth incorrect subset of the code tree be the set of all nodes branching from jth node on correct path, $0 \leq j \leq L - 1$, where L is the length of the information sequence in branches. If C_j represents the number of computations performed in the incorrect subset, the average probability distribution of the ensemble of all convolution codes satisfies

$$\Pr[C_j \geq \eta] = A\,\eta^{-\rho} \quad \text{for } 0 < \rho < \infty \tag{8.44}$$

where A is a constant for particular version of sequential decoding. For channel capacity of C, ρ is related to code rate R and Gallager function $E_0(\rho)$ as follows:

$$R = \frac{E_0(\rho)}{\rho} \quad \text{for } 0 < R < C \tag{8.45}$$

For any binary input discrete memoryless channel (DMC), $E_0(\rho)$ is given as follows:

$$E_0(\rho) = \rho - \log\frac{1}{2}\Sigma_j\left[P(j \mid 0)^{\frac{1}{1+p}} + P(j \mid 1)^{\frac{1}{1+p}}\right]^{1+p} \tag{8.46}$$

where p is the channel transition probability. If $\rho \leq 1$, the mean number of computations per decoded branch is unbounded. Therefore, R is bounded to R_0, when $\rho = 1$. R_0 is called *computational cutoff rate* of the channel. Hence, R must be less than R_0, for finite number of computation. The probability distribution of Eq. (8.44) may also be used to calculate the probability of buffer overflow or the *erasure probability*. When B is the capacity of input buffer i branches (nB bits), μ is the speed factor of decoder and L is information length, the erasure probability is given as follows:

$$P_{\text{erasure}} = LA(\mu B)^{-\rho} \tag{8.47}$$

It may be noted that erasure probability does not depend on code constraint length.

For high rates ($R > R_0$), the undetected error probability in sequential decoding is same as in maximum likelihood decoding and is therefore optimum. The average error probability in sequential decoding is suboptimum at low rates when $R < R_0$ and it can be compensated using higher values of constraint length K, as the computational behaviour of sequential decoding is independent of K. The overall performance can be optimized by obtaining trade-offs among three governing factors of performance characteristics—average computational cutoff, erasure probability, and undetected error probability.

8.5.3 Viterbi Decoding

Viterbi decoding algorithm is the most optimum to decode convolution code to produce the maximum likelihood estimate of the transmitted sequence over a band limited channel with intersymbol interference. It may be observed that in a convolution code, the channel memory that produces the intersymbol interference is analogous to the encoder memory. The Viterbi algorithm is a dynamic programming algorithm for finding the most likely sequence of hidden states—called the Viterbi path—that results in a sequence of observed events. The forward algorithm is a closely related algorithm for computing the probability of a sequence of observed events. These algorithms belong to the realm of probability theory. The algorithm makes a number of assumptions:

- First, both the observed events and hidden events must be in a *sequence*. The sequence is often temporal, i.e., in time order of occurrence.
- Second, these two sequences need to be *aligned*: An instance of an observed event needs to correspond to exactly one instance of a hidden event.
- Third, computing the most likely hidden sequence (which leads to a particular state) up to a certain point t must depend only on the observed event at point t, and the most likely sequence which leads to that state at point $t - 1$.

The above-mentioned assumptions can be elaborated as follows. The Viterbi algorithm operates on a state machine assumption. This means, at any time the system being modelled is in one of a finite number of states. While multiple sequences of states (paths) can lead to a given state, at least one of them is a most likely path to that state, called the *survivor path*. This is a fundamental assumption of the algorithm because the algorithm will examine all possible paths leading to a state and only keep the one most likely. This way, it is sufficient that the algorithm keeps a track of only one path per state and not necessary to have a track of all possible paths.

A second key assumption is that a transition from a previous state to a new state is marked by an incremental metric, usually a number. This transition is computed from the event. The third key assumption is that the events are cumulative over a path in some sense, usually additive. So the crux of the algorithm is to keep a number for each state. When an event occurs, the algorithm examines moving forward to a new set of states by combining the metric of a possible previous state with the incremental

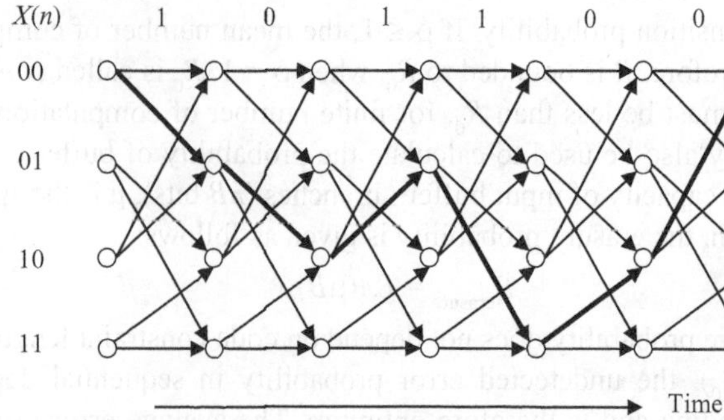

Figure 8.15 *Trellis Diagram*

metric of the transition due to the event and chooses the best. The incremental metric associated with an event depends on the transition possibility from the old state to the new state. For example in data communications, it may be possible to transmit only half the symbols from an odd numbered state and the other half from an even numbered state. Additionally, in many cases, the state transition graph is not fully connected. After computing the combinations of incremental metric and state metric, only the best survives and all other paths are discarded.

The trellis provides a good framework for understanding decoding and the time evolution of the state machine. Suppose we have the entire trellis in front of us for a code, and now receive a sequence of digitized bits. If there are no errors (i.e., the noise is low), then there will be some path through the states of the trellis that would exactly match up with the received sequence as shown in Figure 8.15.

That path (specifically, the concatenation of the encoding of each state along the path) corresponds to the transmitted parity bits. From there, getting to the original message is easy because the top arc emanating from each node in the trellis corresponds to a '0' bit and the bottom arrow corresponds to a '1' bit. When there are errors, finding the most likely transmitted message sequence is appealing because it minimizes the BER. If the errors introduced by going from one state to the next are captured, then accumulation of those errors along a path comes up with an estimate of the total number of errors along the path. Then, the path with the smallest such accumulation of errors is the desired path, and the transmitted message sequence can be easily determined by the concatenation of states explained above. Viterbi algorithm provides a way to navigate the trellis without actually materializing the entire trellis (i.e., without enumerating all possible paths through it and then finding the one with smallest accumulated error) and hence provides optimization with dynamic programming.

A. Viterbi Decoder The decoding algorithm uses two metrics: The branch metric (BM) and the path metric (PM). The branch metric is a measure of the 'distance' between the transmitted parity bits and the received ones, and is defined for each arc in the trellis. In hard decision decoding, where a sequence of digitized parity bits are transmitted, the branch metric is the Hamming distance between the expected parity bits and the received ones.

An example is shown in Figure 8.16, where the received bits are 00. For each state transition, the number on the arc shows the branch metric for that transition. Two of the branch metrics are 0, corresponding to the only states and transitions where the corresponding Hamming distance is 0. The other nonzero branch metrics correspond to cases when there are bit errors. The path metric is a value associated with a state in the trellis (i.e., a value associated with each node). For hard decision decoding, it corresponds to the Hamming distance over the most likely path from the initial state to the current state

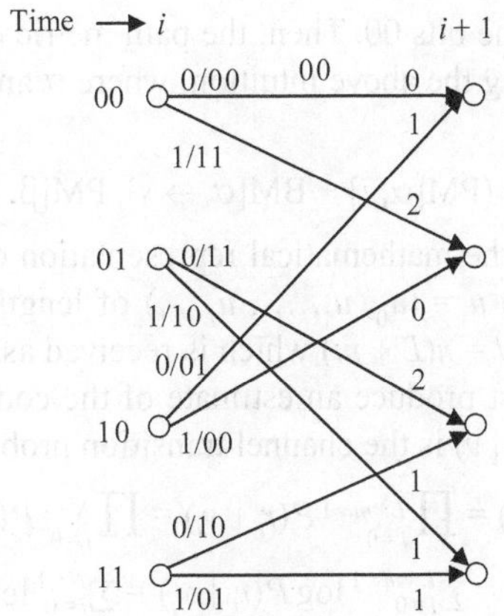

Figure 8.16 *Branch Metric and Path Metric*

in the trellis. *Most likely path* is referred to the path with smallest Hamming distance between the initial state and the current state, measured over all possible paths between the two states. The path with the smallest Hamming distance minimizes the total number of bit errors, and is most likely when the BER is low.

B. Computation of Path Metric The key insight in the Viterbi algorithm is that the receiver can compute the path metric for a (state, time) pair incrementally using the path metrics of previously computed states and the branch metrics. Suppose the receiver has computed the path metric PM[s, i] for each state s (of which there are 2^{k-1} states, where k is the constraint length) at time step i. The value of PM[s, i] is the total number of bit errors detected when comparing the received parity bits to the most likely transmitted message, considering all messages that could have been sent by the transmitter until time step i (starting from state '00').

Among all the possible states at time step i, the most likely state is the one with the smallest path metric. If there is more than one such state, they are all equally good possibilities. Now, to determine the path metric at time step $i + 1$, PM[s, $i + 1$], for each state s, it is first to be observed that if the transmitter is at state s at time step $i + 1$, then it must have been in only one of two possible states at time step i. These two predecessor states, labelled α and β, are always the same for a given state. In fact, they depend only on the constraint length of the code and not on the parity functions. Figure 8.16 shows the predecessor states for each state (the other end of each arrow). For instance, for state 00, α = 00 and β = 01; for state 01, α = 10 and β = 11. Any message sequence that leaves the transmitter in state s at time $i + 1$ must have left the transmitter in state α or state β at time i. For example, in Figure 8.16, to arrive at state '01' at time $i + 1$, one of the following two properties must hold:

1. If the transmitter is in state '10' at time i and the ith message bit is a 0, then the transmitter sents '11' as the parity bits and there are two bit errors, because we receive the bits 00. Then, the path metric of the new state, PM['01', $i + 1$] = PM['10', i] + 2, because the new state is '01' and the corresponding path metric is larger by 2 because there are two errors.
2. The other (mutually exclusive) possibility is that if the transmitter is in state '11' at time i and the ith message bit is a 0, then the transmitter sents 01 as the parity bits and there is one bit

error, because we receive the bits 00. Then, the path metric of the new state, PM['01', $i + 1$] = PM['11', i] + 1. Formalizing the above intuition, where α and β are the two predecessor states, we can easily say that

$$PM[s, i + 1] = \min (PM[\alpha, i] + BM[\alpha \rightarrow s], PM[\beta, i] + BM[\beta \rightarrow s]) \tag{8.48}$$

In general, for a Q-ary system, the mathematical representation can be given as below. Let us consider that an information sequence $u = (u_0, u_1, \ldots, u_{L-1})$ of length kL is encoded into a code word $v = (v_0, v_1, \ldots, v_{L+m-1})$ of length $N = n(L + m)$ which is received as the Q-ary sequence $r = (r_0, r_1, \ldots, r_{L-1})$ over a DMC. A decoder must produce an estimate of the code word which maximizes the log-likelihood function $\log P(r \mid v)$. $P(r \mid v)$ is the channel transition probability.

$$P(r \mid v) = \prod_{i=0}^{L+m-1} P(r_i \mid v_i) = \prod_{i=0}^{N-1} P(r_i \mid v_i) \tag{8.49}$$

Or

$$\log P(r \mid v) = \sum_{i=0}^{L+m-1} \log P(r_i \mid v_i) = \sum_{i=0}^{N-1} \log P(r_i \mid v_i) \tag{8.50}$$

If the term $P(r_i \mid v_i)$ is denoted as $M(r_i \mid v_i)$, which is called branch metric, and hence the path metric $M(r \mid v)$ may be written as follows:

$$M(r \mid v) = \sum_{i=0}^{L+m-1} M(r_i \mid v_i) = \sum_{i=0}^{N-1} M(r_i \mid v_i) \tag{8.51}$$

The above equation holds good to find a path v that maximizes $M(r \mid v)$.

In the decoding algorithm, it is important to remember which arc corresponds to the minimum, because it is required to traverse this path from the final state to the initial one, keeping track of the arcs used, and then finally reverse the order of the bits to produce the most likely message.

C. Finding the Most Likely Path Initially, state '00' has a cost of 0 and the other $2^{k-1} - 1$ states have a cost of ∞. The main loop of the algorithm consists of two main steps: Calculating the branch metric for the next set of parity bits and computing the path metric for the next column. The path metric computation may be thought of as an add–compare–select procedure:

1. Add the branch metric to the path metric for the old state.
2. Compare the sums for paths arriving at the new state (there are only two such paths to compare at each new state because there are only two incoming arcs from the previous column).
3. Select the path with the smallest value, breaking ties arbitrarily. This path corresponds to the one with fewest errors.

Figure 8.17 shows the algorithm in action from one time step to the next. This example shows a received bit sequence of 11 10 11 00 01 10 and how the receiver processes it. It may be noted that the paths of minimum path metric have been chosen and two likely paths or survivor paths are shown with

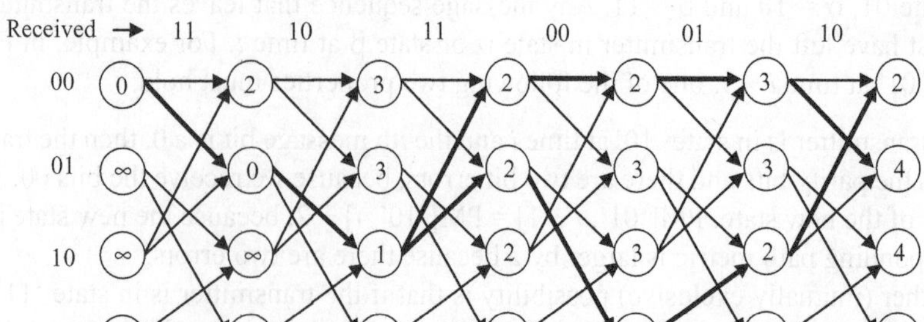

Figure 8.17 *Trellis Diagram for Received Bit Sequences 11 10 11 00 01 10*

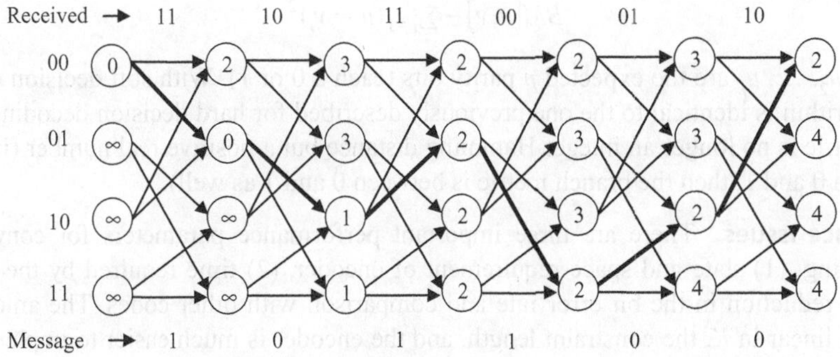

Figure 8.18 *Selection of Least Values of Path Metric*

thick lines. It may also be observed that all four states at fourth stage have the same path metric. At this stage, any of these four states and the paths leading up to them are most likely transmitted bit sequences (they all have a Hamming distance of 2). After final stage, the path following least values of path metric is chosen as shown at Figure 8.18. The corresponding message bits are 101100.

A survivor path is one that has a chance of being the most likely path; there are many other paths that can be pruned away because there is no way in which they can be most likely. The reason why the Viterbi decoder is practical is that the number of survivor paths is much, much smaller than the total number of paths in the trellis. Another important point about the Viterbi decoder is that future knowledge will help it break any ties, and in fact may even cause paths that were considered 'most likely' at a certain time step to change.

Example 8.9: The received code word of binary (3, 1, 2) convolution code follows the trellis diagram as (000, 111, 110, 010, 100, 011, 001, 000) as survival path. Assuming the trellis diagram (Figure 8.3b), find the information code after decoding.

The survival path has been shown as thick lines in the trellis diagram (Figure 8.19). The decoded information vector is $v = (01101000)$.

Viterbi algorithm is also applicable to soft decision decoding where decoding deals with the voltage signals. It does not digitize the incoming samples prior to decoding. Rather, it uses a continuous function of the analogue sample as the input to the decoder. Soft decision metric is the square of the difference between the received voltage and the expected one. If the convolution code produces p parity bits, and the p corresponding analogue samples are $v = (v_1, v_2, \ldots, v_p)$, one can construct a soft decision branch metric as follows:

Figure 8.19 *Survival Path of Example 8.9*

$$BM[u,v] = \Sigma_{i=1}^{p}(u_1 - v_i)^2 \tag{8.52}$$

where $u = u_1, u_2, \ldots, u_p$ are the expected p parity bits (each a 0 or 1). With soft decision decoding, the decoding algorithm is identical to the one previously described for hard decision decoding, except that the branch metric is no longer an integer Hamming distance but a positive real number (if the voltages are all between 0 and 1, then the branch metric is between 0 and 1 as well).

D. Performance Issues There are three important performance parameters for convolution coding and decoding: (1) state and space requirement of encoder, (2) time required by the decoder, and (3) amount of reduction in the bit error rate and comparison with other codes. The amount of space requirement is linear in K, the constraint length, and the encoder is much easier to implement than the Viterbi decoder. The decoding time depends mainly on K. We need to process 2^K transitions each bit time, so the time complexity is exponential in K. Moreover, as described, we can decode the first bits of the message only at the very end. A little thought will show that although a little future knowledge is useful, it is unlikely that what happens at bit time 1000 will change our decoding decision for bit 1, if the constraint length is, say, 6. In fact, in practice, the decoder starts to decode bits once it has reached a time step that is a small multiple of the constraint length; experimental data suggests that $5K$ message bit times (or thereabouts) are reasonable decoding window, regardless of how long the parity bit stream corresponding to the message it.

The reduction in error probability and comparisons with other codes is a more involved and detailed issue. The answer depends on the constraint length (generally speaking, larger K has better error correction), the number of generators (larger this number, the lower the rate, and the better the error correction), and the amount of noise.

To analyze the performance bound, let us consider that a first event error occurred at time unit j which is in the incorrect path. The incorrect path emerges from correct path and remerges at j time unit. There may be a number of incorrect paths. The number of code word is A_d, and the first error probability is P_d, for the incorrect path weight of d. Then the *first error probability* at j time unit, $P_j(E, j)$ is bounded by the sum of all error probabilities, such that

$$P_j(E, j) < \Sigma_{d=d_{\min}}^{\infty} A_d P_d \tag{8.53}$$

Since the bound is independent of j, it holds for all time units and hence the first error probability at any time, $P_j(E)$ is bounded by

$$P_j(E) < \Sigma_{d=d_{\min}}^{\infty} A_d P_d \tag{8.54}$$

If the BSC transition probability is p, mathematical derivation shows that

$$P_j(E) < \Sigma_{d=d_{\min}}^{\infty} A_d [2\sqrt{p(1-p)}]^d \tag{8.55}$$

For an arbitrary convolution code with generating function, $T(X) = \Sigma_{d=d_{\min}}^{\infty} A_d X^d$, Eq. 8.51 may be written as follows:

$$P_j(E) < T(X)\,|_{X=2\sqrt{p(1-p)}} \tag{8.56}$$

Since the *event error probability* is equivalent to first error probability and independent of j at any time unit, it can be derived as follows:

$$P(E) < \Sigma_{d=d_{\min}}^{\infty} A_d P_d < T(X)\,|_{X=2\sqrt{p(1-p)}} \tag{8.57}$$

For small p, the above equation is approximated as follows:

$$P(E) \approx A_{d_{\min}}[2\sqrt{p(1-p)}]^{d_{\min}} \approx A_{d_{\min}}2^{d_{\min}}p^{d_{\min}/2} \tag{8.58}$$

The event error probability can be modified to provide *bit error probability*, $P_b(E)$, i.e., the expected number of information bit decoding errors per decoded information bit. Each event error causes a number of information bit errors equal to the number of nonzero information bits on the incorrect path. If the number of information bit per unit time is k, and total number of nonzero information bits on all weight d path is B_d, the bit error probability is bounded as follows:

$$P_b(E) < \frac{1}{k}\Sigma_{d=d_{\min}}^{\infty} B_d P_d \tag{8.59}$$

Or

$$P_b(E) < \frac{1}{k}\Sigma_{d=d_{\min}}^{\infty} B_d[2\sqrt{p(1-p)}]^d \tag{8.60}$$

For small p, bound of bit error probability is

$$P_b(E) \approx \frac{1}{k}B_{d_{\min}}[2\sqrt{p(1-p)}]^{d_{\min}} \approx \frac{1}{k}B_{d_{\min}}2^{d_{\min}}p^{d_{\min}/2} \tag{8.61}$$

If E is the energy transmitted and N_0 is the one-sided noise spectral density, we have the maximum transition probability

$$p = \frac{1}{2}e^{-E/N_0} \tag{8.62}$$

If free distance for a convolution code is d_{free}, we may rewrite the Eq. (8.57) as follows:

$$P_b(E) \approx \frac{1}{k}B_{d_{\text{free}}}2^{d_{\text{free}}/2}e^{-(d_{\text{free}}/2)(E/N_0)} \tag{8.63}$$

When p is small, i.e., E/N_0 is large, *energy per information bit* is $E_b \triangleq E/R$, and transmitted symbols per information bit is $1/R$, we may write

$$P_b(E) \approx \frac{1}{k}B_{d_{\text{free}}}2^{d_{\text{free}}/2}e^{-(Rd_{\text{free}}/2)(E_b/N_0)} \text{ (with coding)} \tag{8.64}$$

Without coding, i.e., $R = 1$, the transition probability p is equivalent to $P_b(E)$ and hence

$$P_b(E) = \frac{1}{2}e^{-E_b/N_0} \text{ (without coding)} \tag{8.65}$$

Comparing Eqs. (8.64) and (8.65), we may calculate *the asymptotic gain*, $\gamma = Rd_{\text{free}}/2$. γ in decibel is calculated as follows:

$$\gamma = 10\log\frac{Rd_{\text{free}}}{2} \text{ dB} \tag{8.66}$$

For large E_b/N_0 at AWGN channel, the bound of $P_b(E)$ is approximated as follows:

$$P_b(E) \approx \frac{1}{k}B_{d_{\text{free}}}e^{-Rd_{\text{free}}E_b/N_0} \tag{8.67}$$

As the bit error probability at AWGN is approximately twice of BSC channel. At same bit error probability, AWSN channel has 3 dB power advantages over BSC channel. This illustrates the benefit of unquantized decoder where soft decision decoding may be done. However, the decoder complexity increases. It is observed that for quantization level Q of 8, performance within ¼ dB of optimum may be achieved as compared to analogue decoding. Random coding analysis has also shown the power advantage at soft decision over hard decision by 2 dB for small E_b/N_0. Over the entire range of E_b/N_0 the decibel loss associated for hard decision is 2 to 3 dB.

Example 8.10: An AWSN channel has the capacity of transmission of 10^6 information bits per second and noise power of 2.5 W. Information is transmitted over this channel with signal power of 20 W, d_{free} of 7, total number of nonzero information bits of 10^4. Every symbol is represented by 32 bits. What is the bit error probability of this channel with coding? What is the asymptotic gain?

Solution:

Maximum transition probability $p = \frac{1}{2}e^{-E/N_0} = \frac{1}{2}e^{-20/2.5} = 1.677 \times 10^{-4}$

Energy per information bit is $E_b = \frac{E}{R} = \frac{20}{32} = 0.625$

Bit error probability $P_b(E) = \frac{1}{k}B_{d_{\text{free}}} 2^{d_{\text{free}}/2} e^{-(Rd_{\text{free}}/2)(E_b/N_0)}$

$$= \frac{1}{10^6}10^4 2^{7/2} e^{-(37 \times 7/2)(0.625/2.5)} = 0.0115$$

The asymptotic gain $\gamma = 10\log\frac{Rd_{\text{free}}}{2}$ dB $= 10\log\frac{32 \times 7}{2}$ dB $= 20.49$ dB

8.6 CONSTRUCTION

The performance bound analysis suggests that to construct good convolution codes, free distance d_{free} is required to be as large as possible. Other governing factors are number of code words $A_{d_{\text{free}}}$ with weight d_{free}, and the total information sequence of all weight d_{free} code words, $B_{d_{\text{free}}}$. Under all circumstances the catastrophic codes should be avoided.

Most code construction for convolution codes are being done by computer search. It has been proved difficult to find the algebraic structures for convolution codes, which assure good distance properties, similar to the BCH construction for block codes. As most computer search techniques are time-consuming, construction of long convolution code is avoided and convolution code of relatively short constraint lengths is used. Computer construction techniques for noncatastrophic codes with maximum free distance has delivered quite a few number of codes for various coderates R. Basic rules of construction of good convolution codes are stated as under.

Let us consider $g(x)$ is the generator polynomial of any (n, k) cyclic code of odd length n with minimum distance d_g and $h(x) = (X^n - 1)/g(x)$ is the generator polynomial of $(n, n - k)$ dual code with minimum distance d_h. For any positive integer l, the rate $R = ½l$ convolution code with composite generator polynomial $g(D)$ is noncatastrophic and has $d_{\text{free}} \geq \min(d_g, 2d_h)$. Since the lower bound on d_{free} is independent of l, the best code will be obtained when l = 1, i.e., $R = ½$. The cyclic codes should be selected so that $d_g = 2d_h$, suggesting that cyclic codes within the range $1/3 \leq R \leq ½$ may be used for best performance.

For any positive integer l, convolution code of the rate $R = 1/4l$ with composite generator polynomial $g(D^2) + Dh(D^2)$ is noncatastrophic and has the characteristics of $d_{\text{free}} \geq \min(d_g + d_h, 3d_g, 3d_h)$. Since the lower bound on d_{free} is independent of l, the best code will be obtained when l = 1, i.e., $R = ¼$. The cyclic codes should be selected so that $d_g = d_h$, suggesting that cyclic codes with $R = ¼$ may be used for best performance. Some of the good convolution codes are given in Tables 8.2, 8.3, and 8.4.

Good Convolution Codes

Table 8.2 $R = 1/2$

m	n	g_1	g_2	d_{free}
3	6	5	7	5
4	8	15	17	6
5	10	23	33	7
6	12	53	75	8
7	14	133	171	10

Table 8.3 $R = 1/3$

m	n	g_1	g_2	g_3	d_{free}
3	9	5	7	7	8
4	12	13	17	17	10
5	15	25	37	37	12
6	18	47	75	75	13
7	21	133	175	175	15

Table 8.4 $R = 1/4$

m	n	g_1	g_2	g_3	g_4	d_{free}
3	12	5	7	7	7	10
4	16	13	15	15	17	15
5	20	25	27	33	37	16
6	24	53	67	71	75	18
7	28	13	135	147	163	20

Absence of good, long cyclic codes and dependence of the bound on the minimum distance of the dual cyclic codes are the factors that prevent construction of long convolution codes. In certain cases as observed by Justesen, construction yields the bound $d_{free} \geq d_g$, but a rather complicated condition on the roots of $g(x)$ is involved and in binary case, only odd values of n can be used to construct convolution codes.

8.7 IMPLEMENTATION AND MODIFICATION

The basic working of Viterbi algorithm has been discussed so far. But there involves several other factors in practical implementation of the algorithm.

- *Code Performance*—Performance of codes has been discussed in the earlier section. The bit error probability $P_b(E)$ with respect to E_b/N_0 is affected by encoder memory k, quantization levels Q, and code rate. E_b/N_0 decreases with the increase in encoder memory as well as quantization levels. Reduction in coderate increases the performance. Therefore, one has to consider all these aspects while considering a convolution code.
- *Decoder Synchronization*—In practice, decoder does not always commence its decoding process at the first branch transmitted after the encoder is set to all-zero state. It may begin with the encoder in an unknown state and decoding may start in the middle of trellis. Therefore, when memory truncation is used, the initial decision based on the survivor with the best metric is unreliable causing initial decoding errors. However, random coding arguments show that after about 5m branches of decoding the effect of initial lack of branch synchronization is negligible and can be discarded.

  Bit or symbol synchronization is also required by the decoder. An initial assumption is made by the decoder. If this assumption is incorrect, the survivor metrics remain relatively close together. This produces a stretch of data that seems contaminated by noisy channel. Such condition of long enough span is the indication of incorrect bit or symbol synchronization, as long stretches of noise is very unlikely. The symbol synchronization assumption is made reset until correct synchronization is achieved. It may be noted that at most n attempts are needed to acquire symbol synchronization.
- *Decoder Memory*—It may be observed that there are 2^k states in the state diagram of the encoder and hence the decoder must provide 2^k words of storage for the survivors. Each word must be capable of storing survivor paths along with its metric. As storage requirements increase exponentially with k, it is not practically feasible to use the codes of large values of k. The practical limit of k is considered to be about 8 for implementation of Viterbi algorithm. Thus available free distance also becomes limited. The achievable error probability cannot be made arbitrarily small for Viterbi algorithm accordingly the performance bounds as discussed above. In most cases of

soft decision decoding, the practical limit of coding gain and error probability are around 7 dB and 10^{-5}, respectively. The exact error probability depends on the code, its rate, free distance, signal-to-noise ratio (SNR) of the channel and the demodulator output quantization as well as the other factors.

- *Path Memory*—It has been noted that an encoder memory of order m, an information sequence of length kL and factor $m(L + m)$ govern the fractional loss in effective rate of transmission compared to the code rate R. Since, energy per information bit is inversely proportional to the rate, E_b/N_0 is required to be larger for lower effective rate to achieve a desired performance. Therfore, L is desired to be large as possible so that the effective rate is nearly R. Thus, the need of inserting m blocks of 0's into input stream is reduced after every blocks of information bits.

For very large L, it is practically impossible to implement as each of the 2^k words as storage must be capable of storing kL bits path with its metric. Some compromises are made by truncating the path memory of the decoder by storing only the most recent τ blocks of the information bits for each survivor, where $\tau = L$. Each τ blocks of the received sequence is processed by the decoder replacing the previous block. Decoder must decide at the previous block since they can no longer be stored. There are several strategies for making the decision:

1. An arbitrary survivor is selected and the first k bits on this path are chosen for decoded bits.
2. One of the survivor is selected which appears most often in the 2^k survivors from among the 2^k possible information blocks.
3. The survivor with the best metric may be selected and the first k bits on this path are considered as the decoded bits.

After the first decoding decision, next decoding decisions are made in the similar way for each new received block processed. Therefore, the decoding decision always lags the progress of the decoder an amount equal to τ blocks. The decoder in this case is no longer to be of maximum likelihood but results are almost as good if τ is not too small. It has been observed that if τ is in the order of five times the encoder memory or more, the probability of all survivors stem from the same information block τ time units back approaches to 1 and hence the decoding decision is unambiguous. If τ is large enough almost all decoding decisions will be equivalent to maximum likelihood and final decoded sequence is close to maximum likelihood path. It may be noted that the final decoded data may not be error-free, as the final path may not correspond to actual trellis path.

In truncated decoder memory, there are two ways that error can be introduced. Any branch decision at time unit j is made by selecting survivor at time unit $j + \tau$ with best metric becomes erroneous, if error is introduced at time unit j. As it is assumed the maximum likelihood path is best survivor at $j + \tau$ time unit, the truncated decoder will contain same error. Another source of error is when an incorrect path that is unmerged with correct path from time unit j through time unit $j + \tau$, is the best survivor at time unit $j + \tau$. Decoder error is observed at time unit j, though incorrect path is eliminated when it later remerges with correct path.

The limitation on practical application of Viterbi algorithm is the storage of 2^k words complexities of decoding process. Also 2^k comparisons must be performed in each time unit, which limits the speed of the processing. These leads to little modification in Viterbi algorithm. First, k is selected as 8 or less so that exponential dependence on k is limited. Second, the speed limitation can be improved by employing parallel decoding. Employment of 2^k identical parallel processing can perform all 2^k comparisons in single time unit instead rather than having one processor to perform all 2^k comparisons in sequence. Therefore, parallel decoding implies speed advantage of the factor of 2^k, but hardware requirement increases substantially.

One approach to reduce the complexities of Viterbi algorithm is to reduce the number of states in the decoder which is termed as *reduced code*. The basic idea is to design the decoder assuming less amount of encoder memory. This eventually reduces the effective free distance of the code. Another approach is to try to identify subclasses of codes that allow a simplified decoding structure. But this approach does not yield the optimum free distance codes.

8.8 APPLICATIONS

Convolution codes have been extensively used in practical error control applications on a variety of communication channels. Convolution encoding with Viterbi decoding is a forward error correction (FEC) technique that is particularly suited to a channel in which the transmitted signal is corrupted mainly by additive white gaussian noise (AWGN).

The Viterbi algorithm was conceived by Andrew Viterbi in 1967 as a decoding algorithm for convolution codes over noisy digital communication links. The algorithm has found universal application in decoding the convolution codes used in both CDMA and GSM digital cellular, dial-up modems, satellite, deep space communications, and 802.11 wireless LANs. It is commonly used even now in speech recognition, keyword spotting, computational linguistics, and bioinformatics. For example, in speech-to-text (speech recognition), the acoustic signal is treated as the observed sequence of events, and a string of text is considered to be the 'hidden cause' of the acoustic signal. The Viterbi algorithm finds the most likely string of text given the acoustic signal.

The Linkabit Corporation has designed and developed convolution encoder/Viterbi decoder codecs for a wide variety of applications. The Defense Satellite Communication System has employed soft decision hardware of the above, capable of operation at 10 Mb/s. NASA's CTS satellite system uses multiple-rate Viterbi coding system. High-speed decoder of the speed of 160 Mb/s has been employed in Tracking and Data Relay Satellite System (TDRSS) by NASA. Its concatenation schemes are found to have many applications at space and satellite communication.

Sequential decoding is also used in many of NASA application for deep space mission. One of these, a 50 Mb/s hard decision Fano decoder remains the fastest sequential decoder is used on a NASA space station-to-ground telemetry link. Another flexible Fano decoder is capable of handling memory orders from 7 to 47, systematic and non-systematic codes, variable frame lengths, hard or soft decisions with 3×10^6 computations per second, and is used in a variety of NASA applications including TELOPS programme, the International Ultraviolet Explorer (IUE) telemetry system, and International SUN-Earth Explorer (ISEE) programme. Hard decision Fano decoder hardware has also been deployed for US Army Satellite Communication Agency's TACSAT channel and NASA's digital television set. Extremely low frequency (ELF) band application of Fano decoder has been deployed in US Navy's project to facilitate the communication with submarines around the world where frequency of around 76 Hz and data rate as low as 0.03 bps has been used.

Majority logic decoder for self-orthogonal code is used in PCM/FDMA system (SPADE) with transmitting data rate of 40.8 kb/s over regular voice channels of INTELSAT system. This has the applications at PSK, FSK systems, terrestrial telephone lines, and airborne satellite communication.

8.9 TURBO CODING AND DECODING

Simple Viterbi-decoded convolution codes are now giving way to turbo codes, a new class of iterated short convolution codes that closely approach the theoretical limits imposed by Shannon's theorem with much less decoding complexity than the Viterbi algorithm on the long convolution codes that would be required for the same performance. Concatenation with an outer algebraic code [e.g., Reed–Solomon (R-S)] addresses the issue of error floors inherent to turbo code designs.

In information theory, turbo codes (originally in French *Turbocodes*) are a class of high-performance FEC codes developed in 1993, which were the first practical codes to closely approach the channel capacity, a theoretical maximum for the code rate at which reliable communication is still possible given a specific noise level. Turbo codes are finding the use in (deep space) satellite communications and other applications where designers seek to achieve reliable information transfer over bandwidth- or latency-constrained communication links in the presence of data-corrupting noise. Turbo codes are nowadays competing with LDPC codes, which provide similar performance.

Turbo codes are a quasi-mix between block code and convolution code. Like block codes, turbo codes require the presence of whole block before encoding can begin. However, the computation of parity bits is performed with the use of shift registers like convolution codes. Turbo codes typically use at least two convolution component encoders separated by *interleaver*. This is process is called *concatenation*. Three different arrangements are used for turbo codes which are as follows:

1. Parallel Concatenation Convolution Codes (PCCC)
2. Serial Concatenation Convolution Codes (SCCC)
3. Hybrid Concatenation Convolution Codes (HCCC)

Typically turbo codes are arranged in PCCC style, schematic of which is shown in Figure 8.20, where two encoders are used and interleaved. The reason behind use of turbo codes is that it gives better performance due to production of higher weight code words. The output $y_{1,i}$ may have low weight code word, but output $y_{2,i}$ has the higher weight code word due the interleaver. The interleaver shuffles the input sequence such that output from second encoder is more likely to be of high weight code word. Code word of higher weight results in better decoder performance.

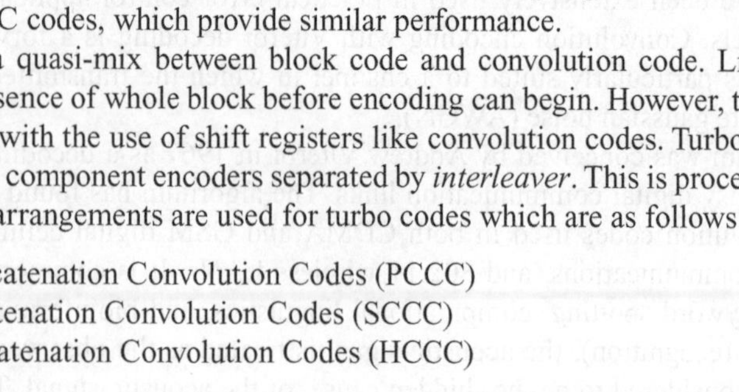

Figure 8.20 *Turbo Code Generator*

The key innovation of turbo codes is how they use the likelihood data to reconcile differences between the two decoders. Each of the two convolution decoders generates a hypothesis (with derived likelihoods) for the pattern of *m* bits in the payload sub-block. The hypothesis bit-patterns are compared, and if they differ the decoders exchange the derived likelihoods they have for each bit in the hypotheses. Each decoder incorporates the derived likelihood estimates from the other decoder to generate a new hypothesis for the bits in the payload. Then they compare these new hypotheses. This iterative process continues until the two decoders come up with the same hypothesis for the *m*-bit pattern of the payload, typically in 15–18 cycles.

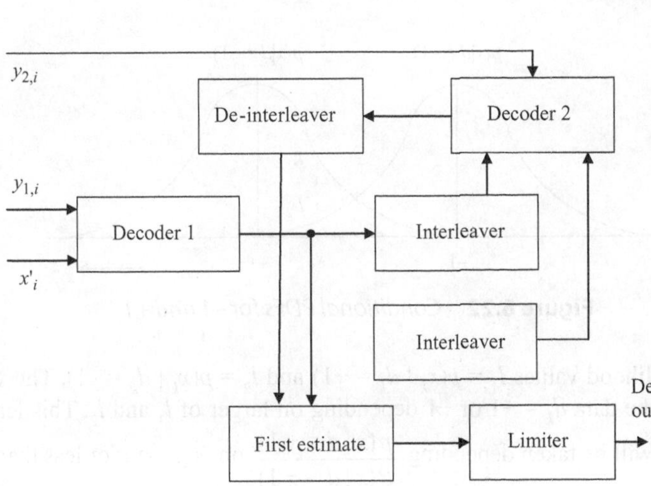

Figure 8.21 *Turbo Decoder*

Although the encoder determines the capability for the error correction, actual performance is determined by the decoder especially the algorithm used. Turbo decoding is an iterative process based on soft output algorithm like *maximum a posteriori* (MAP) or *soft output Viterbi algorithm* (SOVA). Soft output algorithm out-performs hard decision algorithms because soft output algorithm yields gradient of information about the computed information bits rather than just choosing a 1 or 0, resulting better estimate. The schematic of a turbo decoder is shown in Figure 8.21.

MAP algorithm is preferred to estimate the most likely information bit due to its better performance at low SNR conditions. However, it is complex enough as it focuses on each individual bit of information. Turbo decoding employs the iterative technique where the decoding process begins with receiving of partial information from x_i and $y_{1,i}$ at the first decoder. The first decoder makes an estimate of transmitted signal and interleaves to match the format of $y_{2,i}$ which is received by the second decoder. The second decoder now estimates based on the information from first decoder and the channel feeds back to first decoder for further estimation. This process is continued till certain conditions are met and the output taken out.

MAP or *maximum a posteriori* algorithm may be explained as a *minimum probability of error rule*. The general expression for the MAP rule in terms of a *posteriori probability* (APP) is as follows. Let x be the continuous valued random variable, $P(d = i \mid x)$ is the APP for $d = i$ representing the data d belonging to the ith signal class from a set of M classes, $P(d = i)$ is *a priori probability* (the probability of occurrence of the ith signal class and $p(x \mid d = i)$ is the probability density function (PDF) of received data with noise.

$$P(d = i \mid x) = \frac{p(x \mid d = i)P(d = i)}{p(x)} \text{ for } i = 1, 2, 3, \ldots, M \tag{8.68}$$

and

$$p(x) = \sum_{i=1}^{M} p(x \mid d = i)P(d = i) \tag{8.69}$$

If binary logical elements 1 and 0 (representing electronic voltages +1 and −1, respectively) are transmitted over AWGN channel, Figure 8.22 represents the conditional PDFs referred to as likelihood functions. The transmitted data bit is d and the test statistic variable x observed at time kth time interval

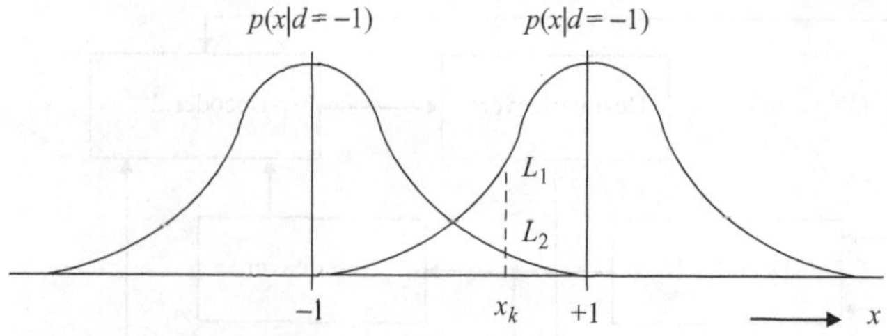

Figure 8.22 *Conditional PDFs for −1 and +1*

is x_k, yielding two likelihood values $l_1 = p(x_k \mid d_k = +1)$ and $l_2 = p(x_k \mid d_k = -1)$. The well-known hard decision rule chooses the data $d_k = +1$ or -1 depending on larger of l_1 and l_2. This leads to likelihood ratio test that decision will be taken depending $\frac{p(x \mid d = +1)}{P(x \mid d = -1)}$ on is greater or less than $\frac{p(x \mid d = -1)}{P(d = +1)}$, alternatively, $\frac{p(x \mid d = +1)P(d = +1)}{P(x \mid d = -1)P(d = -1)} \geq 1$. By taking the logarithm of likelihood ratio we obtain the log-likelihood ratio (LLR) as follows:

$$L(d \mid x) = \log\frac{p(d = +1 \mid x)}{p(d = -1 \mid x)} = \log\frac{p(x \mid d = +1)P(d = +1)}{p(x \mid d = -1)P(d = -1)}$$

or
$$L(d \mid x) = \log\frac{p(x \mid d = +1)}{p(x \mid d = -1)} + \log\frac{P(d = +1)}{P(d = -1)} \tag{8.70}$$

or
$$L(d \mid x) = L(x \mid d) + L(d) \tag{8.71}$$

where $L(x \mid d)$ is LLR of test statistic x obtained by measurement of the channel output x under alternate conditions $d = +1$ or $d = -1$ may have been transmitted and $L(d)$ is the priori LLR of the data bit d. If decoder extrinsic LLR $L_e(d)$ is considered, then after modification of Eq. (8.71), LLR of decoder output will be

$$L(d \mid x) = L(x \mid d) + L(d) + L_e(d) \tag{8.72}$$

The sign of $L(d \mid x)$ decides hard decision of logical elements 1 or 0. The value of $L_e(d)$ acts improvement of reliability of $L(d \mid x)$. In the iterative process, initially the term $(d) = 0$, the channel LLR value $L(x \mid d) = L_c(x)$ is measured according the values of L_1 and L_2 for a particular observation. The extrinsic LLR $L_e(d)$ is fed back to input to serve as a refinement of the priori probability of the data for the next iteration.

At high SNR, the performance of turbo code is dominated by the free distance of it. In this region, the iterative decoder converges rapidly within after two to three iterations. The performance in this region usually improves slowly with increasing SNR. At low to moderate SNR, there is a sharp drop in BER and relatively large number of iterations is required for convergence. At very low SNR, number of iteration increases providing gain in performance. The overall code performance which is poor at BER is certainly beyond the normal operating region for most communication systems. Turbo codes are used extensively in the following telecommunication systems.

- 3G and 4G_mobile telephony standards, e.g., in HSPA, EV-DO, and LTE.
- Media FLO, terrestrial mobile television system from Qualcomm.
- The interaction channel of satellite communication systems, such as DVB-RCS.

- New NASA missions such as Mars Reconnaissance Orbiter now use turbo codes, as an alternative to RS-Viterbi codes.
- Turbo coding, such as block turbo coding and convolution turbo coding, is used in IEEE 802.16 (WiMAX), a wireless metropolitan network standard.

8.10 INTERLEAVING TECHNIQUES: BLOCK AND CONVOLUTION

Wireless mobile communication channel as well as ionosphere and tropospheric propagation suffers from the phenomena of exhibiting mutually dependent signal impairments and multipath fading where signals arrive at the receiver over two or more paths of different lengths. The effect is that signals received are out of phase and distorted. These types of channels are said to have memory. Also some channels suffer from switching noise and other burst noise. All of these time-correlated impairments result in statistical dependence among successive symbol transmissions, i.e., burst errors. These errors are no longer characterized as single randomly distributed independent bit errors. Most block and convolution codes are designed to combat random-independent errors. But error performance for such coded signals is degraded in the channels with memory. Interleaving or the time diversity technique is adopted to improve the error performance, which requires the knowledge of the duration or span of the channel memory.

Interleaving the coded message before transmission and de-interleaving after reception causes bursts of channel errors to spread out in time and decoder handles them as random errors. Since the channel memory decreases with time separation in all practical cases, the idea behind interleaving is to separate code word symbols in time. The interleaving time is filled with the symbols of other code words. Separating the symbols in time, a channel with memory is effectively transformed to a memoryless channel and thereby enables the random-error-correcting codes to be useful in the channel with memory.

The interleaver shuffles the code symbols over a span of several block lengths or several constraint lengths. Span is determined by the burst duration. The detail of bit distribution pattern must be known to the receiver for proper extraction of data after deinterleaving. Figure 8.23 illustrates a simple interleaving example, where uninterleaved code words A to G, each code word comprising of seven code symbols. If the code word is of single-error-correcting capability and channel memory span is of one code word duration then the channel noise burst can destroy one or two code words. However, encoded data with interleaving can be reconstructed, though it is contaminated by burst noise. From Figure 8.23, it is clear that when the encoded data is interleaved and the memory span is enough to store one code word, though one code word is may be destroyed (as shown by xxxxxxx in the figure), this can be recovered from the seven code words after de-interleaving and decoding at the receiver end. Two types of interleavers are commonly used: (1) *block interleavers* and (2) *convolution interleavers.*

Block Interleavers—In this technique, the encoded code word of N code words, each of the M symbols, is fed to the interleaver in blocks columnwise to fill $M \times N$ array. After the array is completely filled, the output is taken out rowwise at a time, modulated and transmitted over the channel. At the receiver side, de-interleaver performs the reverse operation. Symbols are entered into the de-interleaver array through rows and taken out through columns. A 6×4 interleaving action is illustrated in Figure 8.24.

The most important characteristics of block interleaver are described as follows:

1. Any burst of less than N contiguous channel symbol errors results in isolated errors at the de-interleaver output which are separated from each other by at least M symbols.
2. Any bN burst of errors, where $b > 1$, results in the output burst from de-interleaver of no more than b_1 symbol errors. Each output burst is separated from the other bursts by no less than

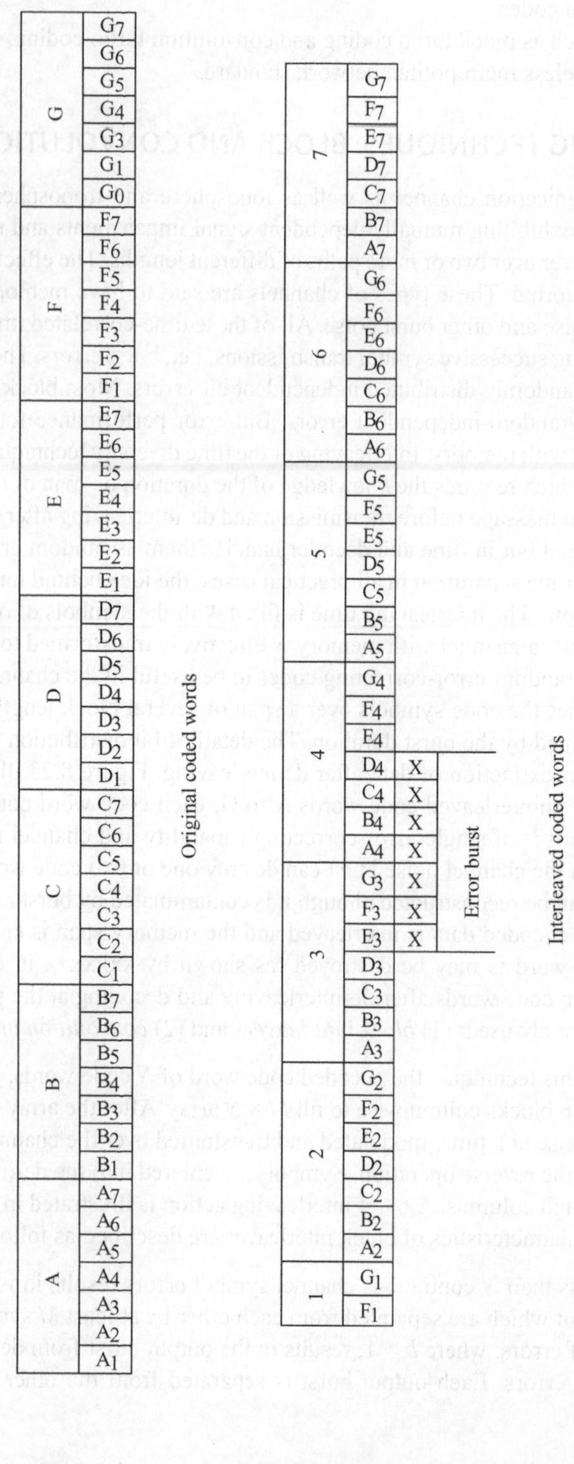

Figure 8.23 *Example of Interleave Operation*

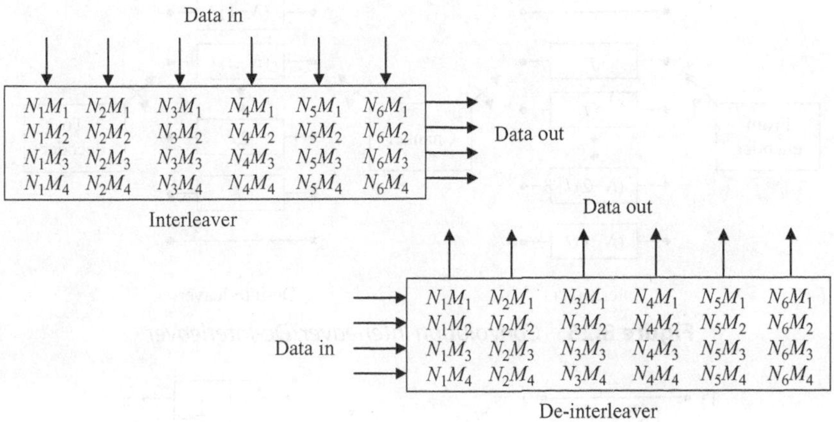

Figure 8.24 *Block Interleaver/De-interleaver Action*

$M - b_2$ symbols, where b_1 is the smallest integer no less than b and b_2 is the largest integer less than b.

3. A periodic sequence of single errors spaced N symbols apart causes single burst of errors of length M at the de-interleaver output.
4. The interleaver/de-interleaver end-to-end delay is approximately $2MN$ symbol times. $M(N-1)+1$ memory cells are required to be filled before the commencement of transmission as soon as the first symbol of last column of $M \times N$ array is filled. A corresponding number is to be filled at the receiver before decoding begins. Thus minimum end-to-end delay is $2MN - 2M + 2$ symbol times excluding the channel propagation delay.
5. Interleaver or de-interleaver memory requirement is MN symbols for each location. Since $M \times N$ array needs to be filled before it can be read out, memory of $2MN$ is generally implemented at each location.

Typically, the interleaver parameters are selected such that for single-error-correcting code the number of columns N is larger than expected burst length. The choice of number of rows M is dependent on the coding scheme. M should be larger than the code block length for block codes, while for convolution codes M should be greater than constraint length. Thus, a burst of length N can cause at most one single error in any block code word or in any constraint length for convolution codes. For t-error-correcting codes, N should be selected as greater than the expected burst length divided by t.

Convolution Interleavers—This type of interleaver uses N number of registers where code symbols are sequentially shifted. Each successive register has the storage capacity of J symbols more than the previous one. The zeroth register provides no storage, i.e., the symbol is transmitted immediately. Each new code symbol is fed to the new register as well as the commutator switches to this register. The new code symbol is shifted in while the oldest code symbol in that register is shifted out to modulator or transmitter. After the $(N-1)$th register the commutator returns to zeroth register and the process continues.

The de-interleaver performs the same operation, but in reverse manner. Synchronization must be observed for both interleaver and de-interleaver. A schematic diagram of convolution interleaver and de-interleaver is shown in Figure 8.25 and an example of their timing action for four regiters is given in Figure 8.26. Initially at transmitter code word 1 is taken out directly. Code word 2 is fed to the register

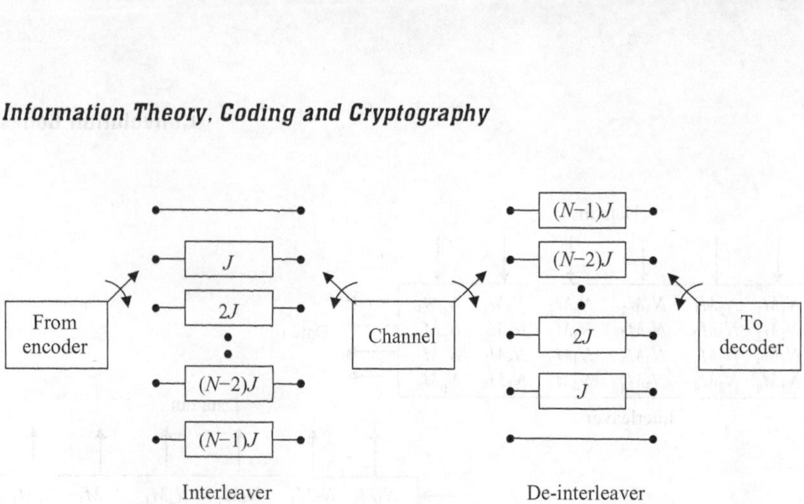

Figure 8.25 *Convolution Interleaver/De-interleaver*

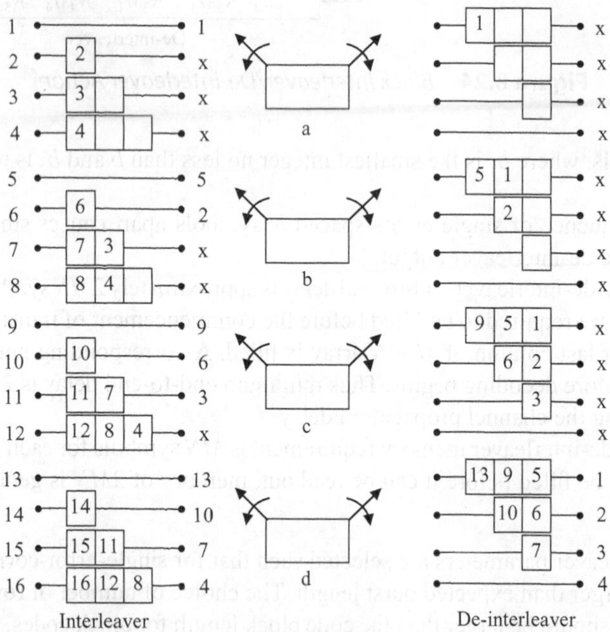

Figure 8.26 *Convolution Interleaver/De-interleaver with Register Contents*

of J memory; code word 3 is fed to the register of $2J$ memory; and code word 3 to the register of $3J$ memory. Now the commutator switch returns to first position and receives next four code words in similar sequence. This process continues. The register contents and the output of interleaver are shown at the left side of Figure 8.26.

In the receiver side, code word 1 is received first at the register of $3J$ memory and so there is no immediate output from de-interleaver. Next data is received at the register of $2J$ memory and the subsequent data at register of J memory while the following data is received directly. But there is no immediate valid output from de-interleaver. Now, the commutator switch returns to first position and receives next four code words while the previous stored symbols shift to next position of corresponding shift registers. De-interleaver will deliver valid code words from 13th time unit as indicated in Figure 8.26.

The performance of a convolution interleaver is very similar to that of block interleaver. However, the convolution interleaver has the advantage that it has end-to-end delay of $M(N - 1)$ symbol, where $M = NJ$, and the memory required $M(N - 1)$ at both ends which are ½ of the block codes.

8.11 CODING AND INTERLEAVING APPLIED TO CD DIGITAL AUDIO SYSTEM

A standard for the digital storage and reproduction of audio signals, known as the compact disc (CD) digital audio system, was defined by Philips Corp of the Netherlands and Sony Corp of Japan in 1979. This CD system has the world standard for achieving fidelity of sound reproduction of far quality compared to any other available technique. A plastic disc 120 mm in diameter is used to store the digitalized audio waveform which is sampled at 44.1 kilosamples/s to provide a recorded bandwidth of 20 kHz; each audio sample is uniformly quantized to one of 2^{16} levels (16 bits/sample), resulting in a dynamic range of 96 dB and a total harmonic distortion of 0.005%. A single disc of playing time of approximately 70 min stores about 10^{10} bits in the form of minute pits that are optically scanned by a laser.

There are several sources of channel errors. Small unwanted particles or air bubbles in the plastic material or pit inaccuracies arising in manufacturing cause errors in reproduction. Fingerprints or scratches during handling also introduce errors. It is difficult to predict actual cause of damage of a CD, but in the absence of an accurate channel model, it is safe to assume that the channel mainly has a burst-like error behaviour, since a scratch or fingerprint will cause errors on several consecutive data samples. A concatenated error control scheme called the *cross-interleave Reed–Solomon code* (CIRC) is an important aspect of the system design contributing to the high-fidelity performance. The data are rearranged in time so that digits stemming from contiguous samples of the waveform are spread out in time. In this way, error bursts are made to appear as single random events as explained in the earlier sections on interleaving. The protection of digital information is provided by adding parity bytes derived in two R-S encoders. Error control applied to the compact disc depends mostly on R-S coding and multiple layers of interleaving.

In digital audio applications, occasional detected failures are not so serious because they can be concealed, but an undetected decoding error is very serious since it results in clicks. The CIRC error-control scheme in the CD system involves both correction and concealment of errors. The performance specifications for the CIRC comprises of capability of maximum corrected burst length of 4000 bits (or a 2.5-mm track length on the disc), maximum interpolated burst length of 12000 bits (8 mm of track length), sample interpolation rate of one sample in every 10 h at $P_B = 10^{-4}$ and 1000 samples/min at $P_B = 10^{-3}$, undetectable error samples or clicks of less than one in every 750 h at $P_B = 10^{-4}$ and negligible at $P_B = 10^{-3}$. From the specifications it would appear that the CD can endure much damage (e.g., 8-min holes punched in the disc) without any noticeable effect on the sound quality. The CIRC system achieves its error control by a hierarchy of the following techniques:

1. The decoder provides a level of error correction.
2. The decoder provides a level of erasure correction, when the error correction capability is exceeded.
3. If the erasure correction capability is exceeded, the decoder attempts to conceal unreliable data samples by interpolating between reliable neighbouring samples.
4. The decoder blanks out of mutes the system for the duration of the unreliable samples, if the interpolation capability is exceeded.

8.11.1 CIRC Encoding and Decoding

Figure 8.27 illustrates the basic CIRC encoder block diagram (within the CD recording equipment) and the decoder block diagram (within the CD player equipment). Encoder consists of the encoding and interleaving steps designated as Δ-interleave, C2 encode, D* interleave, C1 encode, and D interleave. The decoder steps, consisting of de-interleaving and decoding, are performed in the reverse order of the encoding steps and are designated as D de-interleave, C1 decode, D* de-interleave, C2 decode, and de-interleave. CIRC system is characterized by the following five steps that are illustrated:

1. *Δ-interleave*—Two frames are formed by separating even-numbered samples and odd-numbered samples in order to scramble uncorrectable but detectable byte errors. Thus the interpolation process is facilitated.
2. C2 *Encode*—Four R-S parity bytes are added to Δ-interleaved 24-byte frame, resulting in total of $n = 28$ bytes. This (28, 24) code is called the outer code.
3. D* *Interleave*—In this section, each byte is delayed a different length, thereby facilitating spreading errors over several code words. C2 encoding together with D* interleaving have the function of providing for the correction of burst errors and error patterns that the C1 decoder cannot correct.
4. C1 *Encode*—Four R-S parity bytes are added to the $k = 28$ bytes of the D* interleaved frame, resulting in a total of $n = 32$ bytes. Thus (32, 28) code is formed which is called the inner code.
5. *D Interleave*—The even bytes of a frame with the odd bytes of the next frame are cross-interleaved here. By this procedure, two consecutive bytes on the disc will always end up in two different code words. The correction of most random single errors and the detection of longer burst errors are performed upon decoding, this interleaving, together with the C1 decoding.

Each of the inner and outer R-S codes with (n, k) values (32, 28) and (28, 24) as explained above uses four parity bytes. The code rate of CIRC is $(k_1/n_1)(k_2/n_2) = 24/32 = 3/4$. The minimum distance is $d_{min} = n - k + 1 = 5$. The error-correcting capability t and erasure correcting capability ρ may be expressed as follows:

$$t = \frac{d_{min} - 1}{2} = \frac{n - k}{2} \tag{8.73}$$

$$\rho = d_{min} - 1 \tag{8.74}$$

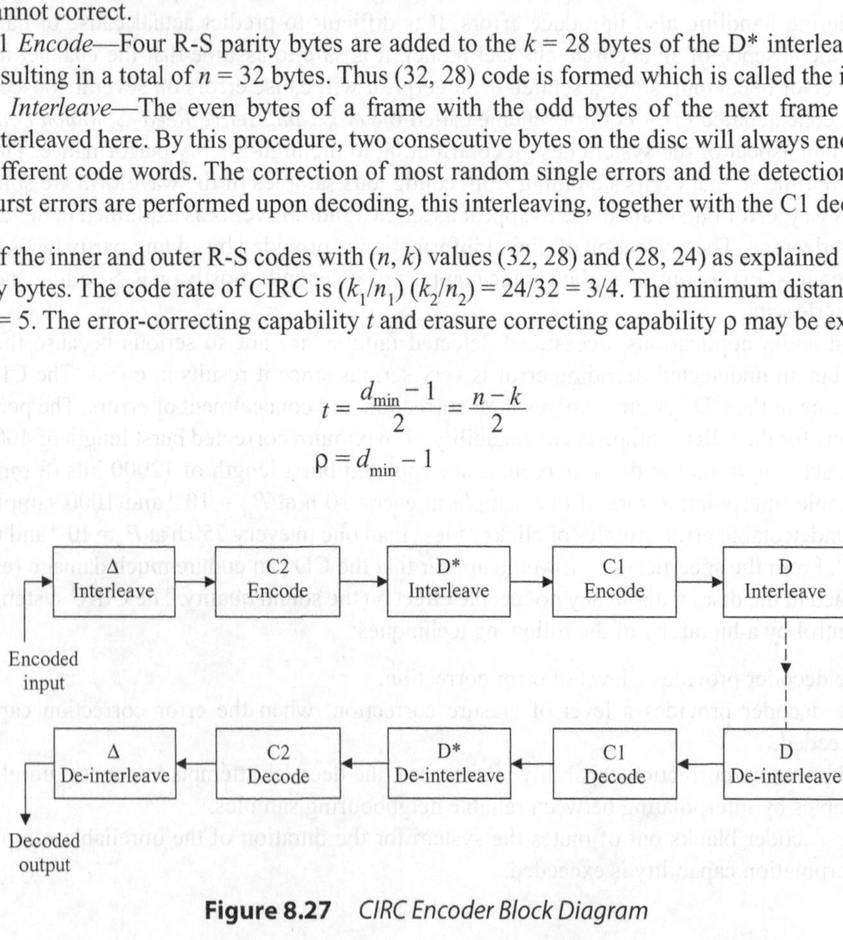

Figure 8.27 *CIRC Encoder Block Diagram*

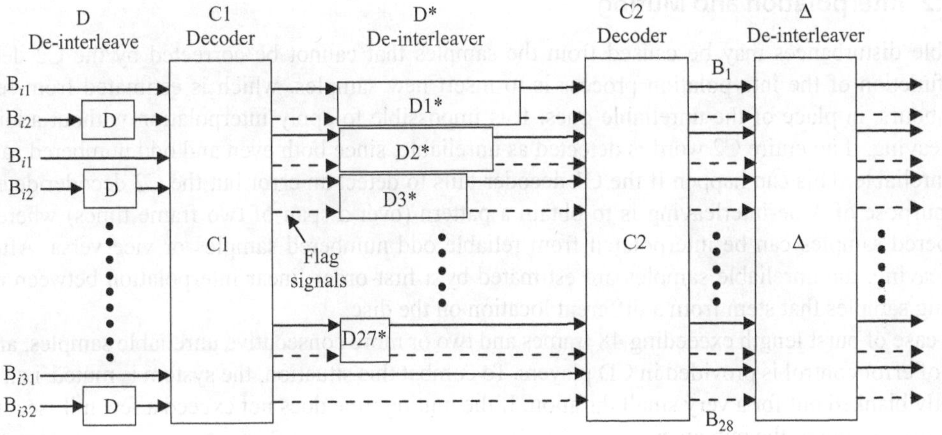

Figure 8.28 *CIRC Decoder*

It is possible to correct any pattern of α errors and γ erasures simultaneously provided that

$$2\alpha + \gamma < d_{\min} < n - k \tag{8.75}$$

Therefore, in above example, the scheme can correct two symbol errors and four symbol erasures per code word simultaneously. The decoding process is illustrated in Figure 8.28, where the processing is reverse manner.

1. *D Interleave*—Here 32 bytes of an encoded frame are applied to the 32 inputs of de-interleaver and every alternate byte of information is subjected to delay of one byte, so that even bytes are cross-de-interleaved with the odd bytes of next frame.
2. C1 *Decode*—The D de-interleaver and C1 decoder are designed to correct a single byte error in the block of 32 bytes. Larger burst errors are also detected here. However, multiple errors are passed unchanged through dashed lines attaching to all 28 remaining bytes with erasure flag. The parity bytes are no longer retained by C1 decoder.
3. *D* De-interleave*—Due to different lengths of de-interleaving delay lines, the errors that occurred in one word is spread over a number of words. Thus number of errors per unit word is reduced enabling C2 decoder to correct these errors.
4. C2 *Decode*—The burst errors that cannot be corrected by C1 decoder are corrected by C2 decoder. If C2 decoder cannot correct these errors, the 24-byte code word is passed unchanged to Δ-de-interleaver. Dashed output lines indicate the associated erasure flag.
5. Δ-*De-interleave*—The uncorrected but detected errors are finally corrected here by interpolation method using comparison with reliable neighbouring samples.

The output of C1 decoder consists of a sequence of 28-byte code words including extra one byte per code word for correction design. Each of the symbols in these code words is tagged with an erasure flag. Since a staggered delay is provided for each of the code words at D* de-interleave, the bytes of a give code word arrive in different code words at C2 decoder. C2 decoder is capable of four erasure corrections per code word and hence as many as four consecutive error bursts can be corrected. In the actual CD system, the delay increments are 4 byte, enabling maximum correction capability of 16 consecutive error bursts of C1 words.

8.11.2 Interpolation and Muting

Audible disturbances may be caused from the samples that cannot be corrected by the C2 decoder. The function of the interpolation process is to insert new samples, which is estimated from reliable neighbours, in place of the unreliable ones. It is impossible to apply interpolation without additional interleaving, if an entire C2 word is detected as unreliable, since both even and odd numbered samples are unreliable. This can happen if the C1 decoder fails to detect an error but the C2 decoder detects it. The purpose of Δ-de-interleaving is to obtain a pattern (over a span of two frame times) where even numbered samples can be interpolated from reliable odd numbered samples or vice versa. After de-interleaving, the unreliable samples are estimated by a first-order linear interpolation between neighbouring samples that stem from a different location on the disc.

In case of burst length exceeding 48 frames and two or more consecutive unreliable samples, another level of error control is provided in CD players. To combat this situation, the system is muted, i.e., audio is softly blanked out for a very small duration. If the muting time does not exceed a few milliseconds, it is not discernible to the human ear.

8.12 SOLVED PROBLEMS

Problem 8.1: Consider (3, 2, 1) convolution code of Figure 8.6. Find the composite generator polynomial $g_1(D)$ and $g_2(D)$. Find the code word for the input sequences $u(D) = [1 + D + D^3, 1 + D^2 + D^3]$

Solution: From the figure, the generator sequences are as follows:

$$g_1^{(1)} = (1\ 1) \qquad g_1^{(2)} = (0\ 1) \qquad g_1^{(3)} = (1\ 1)$$

$$g_2^{(1)} = (0\ 1) \qquad g_2^{(2)} = (1\ 0) \qquad g_2^{(3)} = (1\ 0)$$

Therefore, $G_1(D) = [1 + D,\ D,\ 1 + D]$ and $G_2(D) = [D, 1, 1]$. This can be written in composite form as follows:

$$G(D) = \begin{bmatrix} 1+D & D & 1+D \\ D & 1 & 1 \end{bmatrix}$$

Input sequences $u(D) = [1 + D + D^3, 1 + D^2 + D^3]$, i.e., $u_1 = (1101)$ and $u_2 = (1011)$.

The encoding sequences can be written as follows:

$$v^{(1)} = u^{(1)}g_1^{(1)} + u^{(2)}g_2^{(1)} = (1101) * (11) + (1011) * (01) = (10111) + (01011)$$

$$v^{(2)} = u^{(1)}g_1^{(2)} + u^{(2)}g_2^{(2)} = (1101) * (01) + (1011) * (10) = (01101) + (10110)$$

$$v^{(3)} = u^{(1)}g_3^{(1)} + u^{(2)}g_3^{(3)} = (1101) * (11) + (1011) * (10) = (10111) + (10110)$$

or $\quad v^{(1)} = (11100) \qquad v^{(2)} = (11011) \qquad v^{(3)} = (00001)$

Therefore, output sequence or code word $v = (110, 110, 100, 010, 011)$

Code word may be written as $v(D) = [1 + D, 1 + D, 1, D, D + D^2]$

Problem 8.2: The generator of (3, 1.5) systematic code are $g^{(2)} = (110101)$ and $g^{(3)} = (110011)$. Determine the generator polynomial and find the code word for information sequence $u = (1101)$.

Solution:

$$g^{(1)}(D) = 1,\ g^{(2)}(D) = 1 + D + D^3 + D^5, \text{ and } g^{(3)}(D) = 1 + D + D^4 + D^5$$

The transfer function matrix is $G(D) = [1, 1 + D + D^3 + D^5, 1 + D + D^4 + D^5]$

As $n = 3$, the composite generator polynomial is

$$\begin{aligned} G(D) &= g^{(1)}(D^3) + Dg^{(2)}(D^3) + D^2g^{(3)}(D^3) \\ &= 1 + D(1 + D^3 + D^9 + D^{15}) + D^2(1 + D^3 + D^{12} + D^{15}) \\ &= 1 + D^4 + D^5 + D^{10} + D^{14} + D^{16} + D^{17} \end{aligned}$$

The information code word $v(D) = u(D)\,G(D)$

$$= (1 + D + D^3)(1 + D^4 + D^5 + D^{10} + D^{14} + D^{16} + D^{17})$$

$$= 1 + D + D^3 + D^4 + D^6 + D^7 + D^8 + D^{10} + D^{11} + D^{13} + D^{14} + D^{15} + D^{16} + D^{17} + D^{18} + D^{19} + D^{20}.$$

MULTIPLE CHOICE QUESTIONS

1. For (n, k, m) convolution code, k represents
   (a) number of inputs (b) number of outputs
   (c) number of memory (d) none of these

   Ans. **(a)**

2. An encoder for a (4, 3, 2) convolution code has the memory of order of
   (a) 1 (b) 2 (c) 3 (d) 4

   Ans. **(b)**

3. For a (4, 2, 3) convolution code of length $L = 10$, the fractional loss is
   (a) 15.38% (b) 23.07% (c) 30.76% (d) 38.46%

   Ans. **(b)**

4. For generators $g_1 = (1010)$ and $g_2 = (1001)$ what is the output sequence of the input sequence $u = (0110)$ after convolution coding?
   (a) 00, 11, 10, 01, 11, 00, 11 (b) 00, 10, 01, 11, 11, 00, 10
   (c) 00, 11, 11, 10, 11, 01, 00 (d) 00, 01, 10, 11, 00, 01, 10

   Ans. **(c)**

5. For a majority logic decoder, if number of orthogonal checksum and number of checked channel errors are 4 and 9, respectively, how many errors can be estimated correctly?
   (a) 4 to 9 (b) 2 to 9 (c) 2 to 4 (d) only 4

   Ans. **(b)**

6. Approximately what is the interleaver/de-interleaver end-to-end delay of 8 × 6 block interleaver?
   (a) 6 symbol times (b) 8 symbol times
   (c) 48 symbol times (d) 96 symbol times

   Ans. **(d)**

7. What is the error correction capability of CIRC code of inner and outer codes of (32, 28) and (28, 24)?
   (a) 1 (b) 2 (c) 3 (d) 4

   Ans. **(b)**

8. For convolution code, if $s(D)$, H and e represent the syndrome, parity-check and error matrices the $s^T(D)$ is
   (a) H^Te (b) He^T (c) e^TH (d) eH^T

   Ans. **(b)**

9. Error control applied to the compact disc depends mostly on
   (a) R-S coding (b) multiple layers of interleaving
   (c) both of these (d) none of these

   Ans. **(c)**

REVIEW QUESTIONS

1. Define systematic code and noncatastrophic code.
2. Consider the (4, 3, 2) convolution code of Figure 8.7.
   (a) Find the generator sequence.
   (b) Find the generator matrix G.
   (c) Find the code word for the message sequence (11101).
3. Considering (3, 2, 1) code of Figure 8.6, find the composite generator polynomial. If input sequences are (1101) and (1011), what will be the code word?
4. A (3, 1, 5) systematic code has generator sequences as (101101) and (110011). Find the generator matrix and parity sequence for the input sequence (1101).
5. Consider the (2, 1, 11) systematic code with $g^{(2)} = 1 + D + D^3 + D^5 + D^8 + D^9 + D^{10} + D^{11}$ has been subjected to majority logic decoder. Find the parity-check matrix. Write down the first constraint length of syndromes. How many channel errors can be estimated?
6. For (2, 1, 3) code with $G(D) = [1 + D^2 + D^3, 1 + D + D^2 + D^3]$, draw the code tree. Find the code word if $u = (1001)$.
7. For (2, 1, 3) code with $G(D) = [1 + D^2 + D^3, 1 + D + D^2 + D^3]$ with Figure 8.5, draw the trellis diagram for length of 6.
8. Design a rate ½ convolution encoder with constraint length of 4 and minimum distance of 6. Construct the state diagram and trellis diagram of the encoder. What is the generator matrix of the code?
9. What are the advantages of Turbo code? Discuss how it is implemented.
10. What is interleaver? Discuss different types of interleaver. Also discuss the de-interleving process.
11. Compare the advantages and disadvantages of majority logic decoding, sequential decoding, and Viterbi decoding.
12. How the most likely path is decided for Viterbi decoding?

part

C

CRYPTOGRAPHY

chapter 9

CRYPTOGRAPHY

9.1 INTRODUCTION

Cryptography is the study of mathematical techniques related to aspects of information security such as confidentiality, data integrity, entity authentication, and data origin authentication. It is derived from the two Greek words *kryptos*', which means '*secret*', and '*graph*', which means '*writing*'. Cryptography is not the only means of providing information security, but rather one set of techniques. Cryptography helps to store sensitive information or transmit it across insecure networks (like the Internet) so that it cannot be read by anyone except the intended recipient.

While cryptography is the science of securing data, *cryptanalysis* is the science of analyzing and breaking secure communication. Classical cryptanalysis involves an interesting combination of analytical reasoning, application of mathematical tools, pattern finding, patience, determination, and luck. Persons or systems performing cryptanalysis in order to break a cryptosystem are also called *attackers*. Attackers are also known as *interlopers*, *hackers*, or *eavesdroppers*. The process of attacking a cryptosystem is called *hacking* or *cracking*.

In the early days, cryptography was performed manually. Though a lot of improvements have taken place in the implementation part, but basic framework of performing cryptography has remained almost same. Some cryptographic algorithms are very trivial to understand, replicate, and thus can be easily cracked. Alternatively there are some cryptographic algorithms which are really highly complicated and hence very difficult to crack. There is somewhat a false notion that cryptography is only intended for diplomatic and military communications. In fact, cryptography has different commercial uses and applications. Say, for example, when credit card information is used on the Internet (which we do very often), to secure that data from hackers, it needs to be encrypted. Basically, cryptography is all about increasing the level of privacy of individuals and groups.

Cryptology is the combined study of cryptography and cryptanalysis. The origin of the word *cryptology* is also from the two Greek words '*kryptos*', meaning '*secret*', and '*logos*', meaning '*science*'.

9.2 PLAIN TEXT, CIPHER TEXT, AND KEY

When we normally communicate, for example, with our family members, friends, or colleagues, we do not bother about its security aspects. We thus communicate in the normal language which is understandable by both the sender and the recipient. Such a message is called *plain text* message. Plain text is also called *clear text*.

Definition 9.1: *Plain text* or *clear text* refers to any message that is not encrypted.

However, there are situations when we are concerned with the secrecy of the message and we do not want any eavesdropper to get an idea of the message. In such situations we will not communicate in *plain text*. Hence, we will encrypt the data such that it is not understandable until it has been converted into plain text. The codified message is called *cipher text*.

Definition 9.2: *Cipher text* refers to any plain text message which is codified using any suitable scheme.

Another very important aspect of cryptography is the *key*. We define the key as follows.

Definition 9.3: A *key* is a value that causes a cryptographic algorithm to run in a specific manner and work on the plain text to produce a specific cipher text as an output. The security of the algorithm increases with the increase in key size.

Example 9.1: Our scheme is to replace each alphabet in the message with the alphabet that is actually four alphabets down the order. Hence, each A will be replaced by E, B will be replaced by F, and so on. The replacements are shown in Figure 9.1

A	B	C	D	E	F	G	H	I	J	K	L	M	N	O	P	Q	R	S	T	U	V	W	X	Y	Z
E	F	G	H	I	J	K	L	M	N	O	P	Q	R	S	T	U	V	W	X	Y	Z	A	B	C	D

Figure 9.1 *Replacements of Each Alphabet with an Alphabet Four Places Down the Line*

Now a plain text is taken as:

This is a basic course in cryptography.

Using the above-mentioned scheme, the cipher text becomes

Xlmw mw e fewmg gsyvwi mr gvctxskvetlc.

9.3 SUBSTITUTION AND TRANSPOSITION

There are two primary ways in which a plain text message can be coded to obtain the corresponding cipher text—*substitution* and *transposition*. When the two approaches are used together, the technique is called *product cipher*. An algorithm for transforming a plain text message into one that is cipher text by transposition and/or substitution methods is known as *cipher*.

Substitution—To produce cipher text, this operation replaces bits in the plain text with other bits decided upon by the algorithm. The substitution then has to be just reversed to get back the original plain text from the cipher text. Several substitution techniques are commonly used. To name a few are Caesar cipher, modified Caesar cipher, mono-alphabetic cipher, homophonic substitution cipher, poly-alphabetic substitution cipher, polygram substitution cipher, etc.

Caesar Cipher—The Caesar cipher is named after Julius Caesar, who, according to Suetonius, used it with a shift of three alphabets down the line to protect messages of military significance. While Caesar was recorded to be the first to use this scheme, other substitution ciphers are known to have been used earlier. Thus messages were sent, by replacing every A in the original message with a D, every B with an E, and so on, through the alphabet.

Example 9.2:

Plain text: *Meet me after the party*

Cipher text: *Phhw ph diwhu wkh sduwb*

Only someone who knew the 'shift by 3' rule could decipher the messages. The Caesar cipher is a very weak scheme of hiding plain text messages.

Modified Caesar Cipher—The scheme of Caesar cipher can be generalized and made more complicated by modifying it. The cipher text alphabets corresponding to the original plain text alphabets may not necessarily be three places down the order, but instead be any places down the order. Thus, the replacement scheme is not fixed; it has to be decided first. But once the scheme is decided, it would be constant and will be used for all other alphabets in the message. Thus A may be replaced by any other alphabet in the English alphabet set, i.e., B through Z. Hence, in the modified Caesar cipher, for each alphabet we have 25 possibilities of replacement.

Mono-alphabetic Cipher—Though modified Caesar cipher is better than Caesar cipher, yet a cryptanalyst has to try out maximum of 25 possible attacks to decipher the message. So, rather than using a uniform scheme for all alphabets in a plain text message, a dramatic increase in the key space can be achieved by allowing a scheme of *arbitrary substitution.* This means that in a plain text message each A can be replaced by any other random alphabet (B through Z), each B can also be replaced by any other alphabet (A or C through Z), and so on. The crucial point is that there is no relation between the replacements of A and that of B. In this way we can now have any permutation and combination of the 26 alphabets, which gives 26! or greater than 4×10^{26} possibilities.

Homophonic Substitution Cipher—The homophonic substitution cipher involves replacing each letter with a variety of substitutes, the number of potential substitutes being proportional to the frequency of the letter. For example, the letter A accounts for roughly 8% of all letters in English, so we assign eight symbols to represent it. Each time an A appears in the plain text it is replaced by one of the eight symbols chosen at random, and so by the end of the encipherment each symbol constitutes roughly 1% of the cipher text. The letter B accounts for 2% of all letters, so we assign two symbols to represent it. Each time B appears in the plain text either of the two symbols can be chosen, so each symbol will also constitute roughly 1% of the cipher text. This process continues throughout the alphabet, until we get to Z, which is so rare that is has only one substitute.

Poly-alphabetic Cipher—Poly-alphabetic substitution ciphers were first described in 1467 by Leone Battista Alberti in the form of discs. Johannes Trithemius, in his book *Steganographia* (Ancient Greek for 'hidden writing'), introduced the now more standard form of *tabula recta*, a square with 26 alphabets in it. Each alphabet was shifted one letter to the left from the one above it, and started again with A after reaching Z. A more sophisticated version using mixed alphabets was described in 1563 by Giovanni Battista della Porta. The Vigenére cipher is the best known and one of the simplest examples of poly-alphabetic substitution ciphers. The cipher uses multiple one-character keys. Each of the keys encrypts one plain text character. The first key encrypts the first plain text character; the second key does the same for the second plain text character; and so on. After all the keys are used they are recycled. Thus if we have 35 one-letter keys, every 35th character in the plain text would be replaced with the same key. This number (in this case 35) is called the *period* of the cipher.

Polygram Substitution Cipher—In a polygram substitution cipher, plain text letters are substituted in larger groups, instead of substituting letters individually. For example, sequences of two plain text characters (*digrams*) may be replaced by other digrams. The same may be done with sequences of three plain text characters (*trigrams*), or more generally using *n*-grams. In full digram substitution over an alphabet of 26 characters, the key may be any of the 26^2 digrams, arranged in a table with row and column indices corresponding to the first and second characters in the digram, and the table entries being the cipher text digrams substituted for the plain text pairs. There are then $(26^2)!$ keys.

Transposition—All the techniques discussed so far involve the substitution of a plain text alphabet with a cipher text alphabet. A very different kind of mapping is achieved by performing some sort of permutation on the plain text alphabets. This technique is referred to as a transposition cipher. We discuss here some of the transposition techniques.

Rail Fence Technique—The simplest transposition technique is the rail fence technique, in which the plain text is written down as a sequence of diagonals and then read off as a sequence of rows. Rail fence technique is not very sophisticated and is quite simple for a cryptanalyst to break into. Let us take an example to illustrate the rail fence technique.

Example 9.3: Suppose a plain text message is '*She is my best friend*'. Now first we arrange the plain text message as a sequence of diagonals, as shown in Figure 9.2.

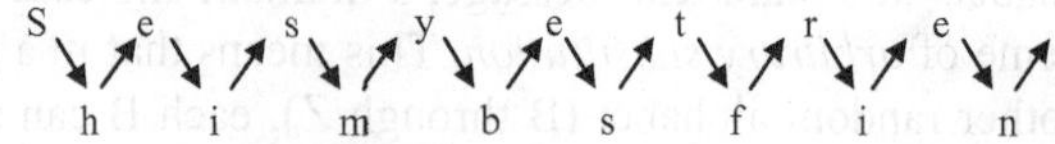

Figure 9.2 *Rail Fence Technique*

This creates a zigzag sequence as shown. Now read the text rowwise, and write it sequentially. Thus, we have the cipher text as follows:

sesyetredhimbsfin.

Columnar Transposition Technique—A more complex scheme is to write the message in a rectangle of pre-defined size, row by row, and read the message off, column by column, but permute the order of the columns. The order of the columns then becomes the key to the algorithm. The message thus obtained is the cipher text message.

Example 9.4: Let us illustrate the technique with the same plain text message '*She is my best friend*'. Let us consider a rectangle with seven columns. When we write the message in the rectangle rowwise (suppressing spaces), it appears as shown in Figure 9.3.

Column 1	Column 2	Column 3	Column 4	Column 5	Column 6	Column 7
s	h	e	i	s	m	y
b	e	s	t	f	r	i
e	n	d				

Figure 9.3 *Columnar Transposition Technique*

Now, let us decide the order of columns arbitrarily as, say 4 3 1 7 5 6 2. Then read the text in the order of these columns. Thus the cipher text becomes:

itesdsbeyisfmrhen.

A simple transposition cipher, as discussed above, is easily recognized because it has the same letter frequencies as the original plain text. For the type of columnar transposition discussed, cryptanalysis is fairly straightforward and involves laying out the cipher text in a matrix and trying out with various column positions. The transposition cipher can be made significantly more secure by performing more than one stage of transposition. The result is a more complex permutation that is not easily reconstructed.

Example 9.5: Thus, if the foregoing message is re-encrypted using the same algorithm with the order of columns as 4 3 1 7 5 6 2, we have the text as shown in Figure 9.4.

Column 1	Column 2	Column 3	Column 4	Column 5	Column 6	Column 7
i	t	e	s	d	s	b
e	y	i	s	f	m	r
h	e	n				

Figure 9.4 *Columnar Transposition Technique with Multiple Rounds*

Now the cipher text becomes:

sseinienbrdfsmtye.

This technique may be repeated as many times as desired. More the number of iterations more are the complexity of the produced cipher text.

One-Time-Pad—As an introduction to stream ciphers, and to demonstrate that a perfect cipher does exist, we describe the Vernam cipher, also known as the one-time-pad. Gilbert Vernam invented and patented his cipher in 1917 while working at AT&T. Joseph Mauborgne proposed an improvement to the Vernam cipher that yields the ultimate in security. He suggested using a random key which is as long as the message, so that the key need not be repeated. Additionally, the key is to be used to encrypt and decrypt a single message, and then is discarded (hence the name *one-time*). Each new message requires a new key of the same length as the new message. Such a scheme is unbreakable. It produces random output that bears no statistical relationship to the plain text. Because the cipher text contains no information whatsoever about the plain text, there is simply no way to break the code. An example should illustrate our point.

Example 9.6: The scheme is discussed first. Consider each plain text alphabet as a number in an increasing sequence as A = 0, B = 1, C = 2, … , Z = 25. Do the same for each character of the input key. Then add each number corresponding to the plain text alphabet to the corresponding input key alphabet number. If the sum produced is greater than 26, subtract 26 from the result. Translate each number of the sum back to the corresponding alphabet. This produces the cipher text as shown in Figure 9.5.

Plain text:	S	H	E	I	S	M	Y	B	E	S	T	F	R	I	E	N	D
	18	7	4	8	18	12	24	1	4	18	19	5	17	8	4	13	3
+																	
	15	23	11	12	21	12	18	24	3	14	5	20	24	17	21	25	22
Key:	P	X	L	M	V	M	S	Y	D	O	F	U	Y	R	V	Z	W
Initial sum:	33	30	15	20	39	24	42	25	7	32	24	25	41	25	25	38	25
Subtract 26: (if >25)	7	4	15	20	13	24	16	25	7	6	24	25	15	25	25	12	25
Cipher text:	H	E	P	U	N	Y	Q	Z	H	G	Y	Z	P	Z	Z	M	Z

Figure 9.5 *Vernam Cipher*

9.4 ENCRYPTION AND DECRYPTION

In the previous two sections we have already discussed the concepts of plain text and cipher text and also how to transform from one form to the other.

Definition 9.4: *Encryption* is the process of transforming information (referred to as plain text) using an algorithm (called cipher) to make it unreadable to anyone except those possessing special knowledge, usually referred to as a *key*.

The result of the process is an *encrypted* information (referred to as cipher text). Encryption has long been used by militaries and governments to facilitate secret communication. Encryption is now commonly used in protecting information within many kinds of civilian systems. Encryption can be used to protect data 'at rest', such as files on computers and storage devices. In recent years, there have been numerous reports of confidential data such as customers' personal records being exposed through loss or theft of laptops or backup drives. Encrypting such files at rest helps protect them when even physical security measures fail. Encryption is also used to protect data in transit, e.g., data being transferred via networks (e.g., the Internet), mobile telephones, wireless microphones, Bluetooth devices, bank automatic teller machines, etc. There have been numerous reports of data in transit being intercepted in recent years. Encrypting data in transit also helps to secure it as it is often difficult to physically secure all access to networks.

Decryption is exactly opposite of encryption. Encryption transforms a plain text message into cipher text, whereas decryption transforms the cipher text message back to plain text.

Definition 9.5: The reverse process of transforming cipher text messages back to plain text messages is known as *decryption*.

To encrypt a plain text message an encryption algorithm is applied. Similarly, to decrypt a received encrypted message, a decryption algorithm has to be applied. At the same time, it is to be noted that the decryption algorithm must be the same as the encryption algorithm. Otherwise, decryption would not be able to retrieve the original message. For example, if the encryption has been done using columnar transposition technique whereas the decryption uses rail fence technique, then decryption would yield a totally incorrect plain text. Hence, the sender and receiver must agree on a common algorithm for meaningful communication to take place.

We have already discussed what a *key* does with plain text and cipher text messages. A key is somewhat similar to the one-time-pad used in Vernam cipher. Anybody may use Vernam cipher to encrypt a plain text message and send it to the recipient who also posses the knowledge of the key being used. However, no one to whom the key is unknown can decrypt the message. In fact, cryptographic mechanisms may be broadly classified into two categories depending on the type of key used for encryption and decryption. The mechanisms are:

Symmetric-key Cryptography—This is the mechanism where the same key is being used for both encryption and decryption.

Asymmetric- or Public-key Cryptography—In this mechanism two different keys are used—one for encryption and the other for decryption. One key is held privately and the other is made public.

9.5 SYMMETRIC-KEY CRYPTOGRAPHY

Symmetric-key cryptography is known by various other terms, such as *Secret-Key Cryptography*, or *Private-Key Cryptography*. As already mentioned, symmetric-key algorithms have only one key that is used both to encrypt and to decrypt the message. Hence, on receiving the message, it is impossible to decrypt it unless the key is known to the recipient.

However, there are a few problems with symmetric-key algorithms. The first problem is that of *key distribution*. That is how to get the key from the sender. Either the recipient has to personally meet the sender to get the key; otherwise the key has to be transmitted to the recipient and hence is accessible by unauthorized persons. This is the main problem of symmetric key cryptography and is called the problem of *key distribution* or *key exchange* and it is inherently linked with symmetric-key cryptography.

The second problem is also very serious. Suppose X wants to communicate with Y and also with Z. There should be one key for all communications between X and Y and also a separate key for all communications between X and Z. The same key as used between X and Y cannot be used for communications between X and Z, since in such a situation there is a chance that Z may interpret messages going between X and Y. In a large volume of data exchange this becomes impractical because every sender and receiver pair would require a *distinct key*.

In symmetric-key cryptography, same algorithm is used by the sender and the recipient. However, the key is changed from time to time. Same plain texts encrypted with different keys result in different cipher texts. Since the encryption algorithm is available to the public, it should be strong enough so that an attacker should not be able to decrypt the cipher text.

9.5.1 Stream Ciphers and Block Ciphers

Cipher texts may be generated from plain texts using two basic symmetric algorithms—*stream ciphers* and *block ciphers*.

Stream Cipher—A *stream cipher* is one that encrypts a digital data stream one bit or one byte at a time. The decryption also happens one bit at a time. Examples of classical stream ciphers are the auto-keyed Vigenère cipher and the Vernam cipher.

Block Cipher—A *block cipher* is one in which a block of plain text is treated as a whole and used to produce a cipher text block of equal length. Typically, a block size of 64 or 128 bits is used. Decryption also takes one block of encrypted data at a time. Problem occurs with block ciphers when there are repeating text patterns. Since same cipher is generated for the same plain texts, it gives a clue to the cryptanalyst regarding the original plain text. The cryptanalyst can look for repeating strings and try to break them and thus there lies a chance that a large portion of the original message may be broken. To avoid this problem, block ciphers are used in *chaining mode*. In this mode, the previous block cipher is mixed with the current block, so as to obscure the cipher text. This avoids repeated patterns of blocks with the same plain texts.

We will discuss two of the most popular symmetric-key algorithms in this chapter. They are the *Data Encryption Standard* (DES) and the *International Data Encryption Algorithm* (IDEA). Both of them are block ciphers.

9.6 DATA ENCRYPTION STANDARD

The most popular encryption scheme widely used for over two decades is known as the *Data Encryption Standard* (DES). This had been adopted by the National Bureau of Standards, now known as the National Institute of Standards and Technology (NIST), in 1977. The algorithm itself is referred to as the *Data Encryption Algorithm* (DEA) by ANSI. Nowadays DES is found to be vulnerable against powerful attacks. However, DES still remains as a landmark in cryptographic algorithms.

In the late 1960s, IBM set up a research project in computer cryptography. The project concluded in 1971 with the development of an algorithm with the designation *LUCIFER*. LUCIFER is a block cipher that operates on blocks of 64 bits, using a key size of 128 bits. IBM then developed a marketable commercial encryption product which was a refined version of LUCIFER that was more resistant to cryptanalysis but that had a reduced key size of 56 bits. In 1973, the National Bureau of Standards (NBS) issued a request for proposals for a national cipher standard. IBM submitted the results of the refined version of LUCIFER. After intense criticism this was adopted as the *Data Encryption Standard* in 1977. Actually the users could not be sure that the internal structure of DES was free of any hidden weak points. However, subsequent events, particularly the recent work on differential cryptanalysis, show that DES has a very strong internal structure.

9.6.1 Basic Principle

DES encrypts data in blocks of size 64 bits each. It means that DES works on 64 bits of plain text to produce 64 bits of cipher text. The same steps, with the same key, with minor differences are used for decryption. For DES, data are encrypted in 64-bit blocks using a 56-bit key. Actually, the function expects a 64-bit key as input. However, only 56 of these bits are ever used; the other 8 bits can be used as parity bits or simply set arbitrarily. Every eighth bit of the key is ignored to produce a 56-bit key from the actual 64-bit key. This is illustrated in Figure 9.6. The ignored bits are shown shaded in the figure.

1	2	3	4	5	6	7	8
9	10	11	12	13	14	15	16
17	18	19	20	21	22	23	24
25	26	27	28	29	30	31	32
33	34	35	36	37	38	39	40
41	42	43	44	45	46	47	48
49	50	51	52	53	54	55	56
57	58	59	60	61	62	63	64

Figure 9.6 *Key Schedule Calculation*

The processing of the plain text proceeds in following phases:

1. First, the 64-bit plain text passes through an *initial permutation* (IP) that rearranges the bits to produce the *permuted input*.
2. Next, the IP produces two halves of the permuted block—*Left Plain Text* (LPT) and *Right Plain Text* (RPT).
3. This is followed by a phase consisting of 16 rounds of the encryption process, each with its own key, which involves both permutation and substitution functions.
4. The output of the last (sixteenth) round consists of 64 bits that are a function of the input plain text and the key.
5. At the end the left and right halves of the output are swapped to produce the **pre output**. Then, the pre output is passed through a *final permutation* (FP) that is the inverse of the IP function, to produce the 64-bit cipher text.

9.6.2 Initial Permutation

Before the first round takes place the Initial Permutation or IP happens. The IP is defined in Table 9.1. The table may be interpreted as follows. The input to a table consists of 64 bits which are numbered from 1 to 64. These 64 entries in the permutation table contain a permutation of the numbers from 1 to 64. Each entry in the permutation table indicates the position of a numbered input bit in the output,

Table 9.1 *Initial Permutation Table*

58	50	42	34	26	18	10	2
60	52	44	36	28	20	12	4
62	54	46	38	30	22	14	6
64	56	48	40	32	24	16	8
57	49	41	33	25	17	9	1
59	51	43	35	27	19	11	3
61	53	45	37	29	21	13	5
63	55	47	39	31	23	15	7

which also consists of 64 bits. The table is to be read from left to right, top to bottom. For example, during IP, the 58th bit of the original plain text will replace the 1st bit. Similarly, the 7th bit of the original plain text is found to replace the 64th bit position. The same rule applies for all other bit positions as shown in Table 9.1.

As already mentioned, after IP is done, the permuted 64-bit text block is divided into two halves of 32-bit block each. Then the 16 rounds of the encryption process are performed on these two blocks.

9.6.3 Details of Single Round

Each of the 16 rounds can be broadly divided into a step-by-step process. All the steps are discussed as follows:

Key Generation—We have already discussed that a 64-bit key is used as input to the algorithm. Every eighth bit of that key is ignored, as indicated by the shading in Fig. 9.6. The key is first subjected to a permutation as shown in Table 9.2. The resulting 56-bit key is then divided into two halves each of 28 bits. At each round, these halves are separately subjected to a circular left shift, or rotation, of 1 or 2 bits, as shown in Table 9.3. After the shift is over, 48 out of these 56 bits are selected. For this selection, Table 9.4 is used. From the table we find that bit numbers 9, 18, 22, 25, 35, 38, 43, and 54 are discarded. In this key transformation process, permutation as well as selection of a 48-bit sub-set of the original 56-bit key is done. Hence, it is also known as *compression permutation.* Due to this compression permutation technique, a separate subset of key bits is used in each round. This is the reason that DES is quite hard to crack.

Table 9.2 *Permuted Key Table*

57	49	41	33	25	17	9	1
58	50	42	34	26	18	10	2
59	51	43	35	27	19	11	3
60	52	44	36	63	55	47	39
31	23	15	7	62	54	46	38
30	22	14	6	61	53	45	37
29	21	13	5	28	20	12	4

Table 9.3 *Schedule of Left Shift of Keys per Pound*

Round	1	2	3	4	5	6	7	8	9	10	11	12	13	14	15	16
Number of key bits rotated	1	1	2	2	2	2	2	2	1	2	2	2	2	2	2	1

Table 9.4 *Compression Permutation*

14	17	11	24	1	5	3	28	15	6	21	10	23	19	12	4
26	8	16	7	27	20	13	2	41	52	31	37	47	55	30	40
51	45	33	48	44	49	39	56	34	53	46	42	50	36	29	32

Expansion Permutation—As already mentioned, the initially permuted 64-bit text block is divided into two halves of 32-bit block each known as *Left Plain Text* (LPT) and *Right Plain Text* (RPT). This RPT input is now expanded to 48 bits from 32 bits by using Table 9.5, which defines a permutation plus an expansion that involves duplication of 16 of the RPT bits. Hence, this process is known as *expansion permutation.*

Table 9.5 *Expansion Permutation of RPT*

32	1	2	3	4	5	4	5	6	7	8	9	8	9	10	11
12	13	12	13	14	15	16	17	16	17	18	19	20	21	20	21
22	23	24	25	24	25	26	27	28	29	28	29	30	31	32	1

The steps for the process are as follows:

1. First the 32-bit RPT is divided into eight blocks of 4 bits each as illustrated in Figure 9.7.
2. Now each of these 4-bit blocks is expanded to a corresponding 6-bit block. This is done by adding two more bits in each of these 4-bit blocks. These 2 bits are actually the repetition of the first and the fourth bits of the 4-bit block. The second and the third bits remain unchanged. This is illustrated in Figure 9.8. From the figure, we may see that the 1st input bit goes to the 2nd and

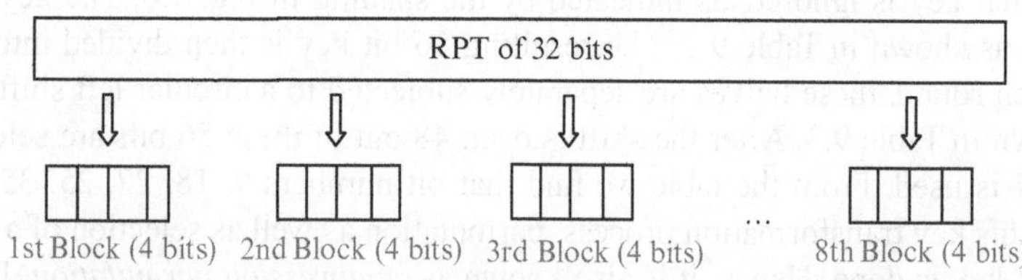

Figure 9.7 *Division of 32-Bit RPT into Eight Blocks of 4 Bits Each*

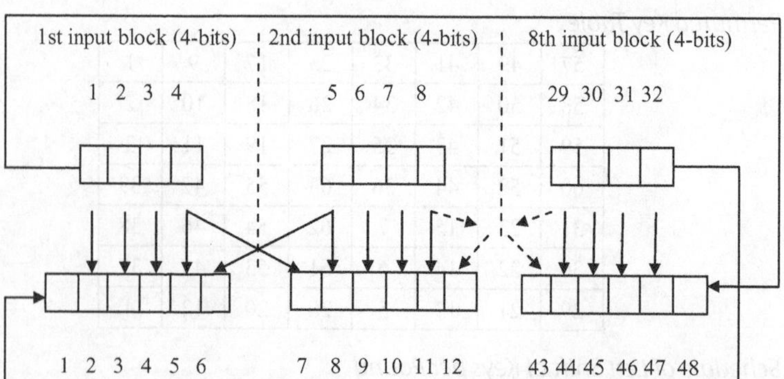

Figure 9.8 *Expansion Permutation of RPT*

48th position. The 2nd output bit goes to the 3rd position and so on. As a result, we observe that actually the expansion permutation process utilized Table 9.5.

We have already seen that by the *Key generation* process the 56-bit key is compressed to 48-bit key. On the other hand, by the *expansion permutation* process the 32-bit RPT is expanded into 48 bits. Now the 48-bit RPT is XORed with the 48-bit key. The resulting output is provided to the next step, which is known as *S-box substitution.*

S-Box Substitution—This is a process that accepts 48 bits from the XORed operation as mentioned earlier, and produces a 32-bit output using the substitution technique. The substitution consists of a set of eight *substitution boxes* also known as S-boxes. Each of the eight S-boxes accepts 6 bits as input and produces 4 bits as output. The 48-bit input block is divided into eight 6-bit sub-blocks. Each sub-block is given to an S-box. Each S-box may be considered to be a table having 4 rows (numbered 0 to 3) and 16 columns (numbered 0 to 15). At the intersection of every row and column, a 4-bit number is present. This is illustrated in Table 9.6a–h.

The interpretation of the table is as follows: The first and last bits of the input to every S-box form a 2-bit binary number. This is to select one of four rows in the table. The remaining four middle bits

Table 9.6 *S-Box Substitution*

(a) S-Box 1

14	4	13	1	2	15	11	8	3	10	6	12	5	9	0	7
0	15	7	4	14	2	13	1	10	6	12	11	9	5	3	8
4	1	14	8	13	6	2	11	15	12	9	7	3	10	5	0
15	12	8	2	4	9	1	7	5	11	3	14	10	0	6	13

(b) S-Box 2

15	1	8	14	6	11	3	4	9	7	2	13	12	0	5	10
3	13	4	7	15	2	8	14	12	0	1	10	6	9	11	5
0	14	7	11	10	4	13	1	5	8	12	6	9	3	2	15
13	8	10	1	3	15	4	2	11	6	7	12	0	5	14	9

(c) S-Box 3

10	0	9	14	6	3	15	5	1	13	12	7	11	4	2	8
13	7	0	9	3	4	6	10	2	8	5	14	12	11	15	1
13	6	4	9	8	15	3	0	11	1	2	12	5	10	14	7
1	10	13	0	6	9	8	7	4	15	14	3	11	5	2	12

(d) S-Box 4

7	13	14	3	0	6	9	10	1	2	8	5	11	12	4	15
13	8	11	5	6	15	0	3	4	7	2	12	1	10	14	9
10	6	9	0	12	11	7	13	15	1	3	14	5	2	8	4
3	15	0	6	10	1	13	8	9	4	5	11	12	7	2	14

continued

Table 9.6 *(Continued)*

(e) S-Box 5

2	12	4	1	7	10	11	6	8	5	3	15	13	0	14	9
14	11	2	12	4	7	13	1	5	0	15	10	3	9	8	6
4	2	1	11	10	13	7	8	15	9	12	5	6	3	0	14
11	8	12	7	1	14	2	13	6	15	0	9	10	4	5	3

(f) S-Box 6

12	1	10	15	9	2	6	8	0	13	3	4	14	7	5	11
10	15	4	2	7	12	9	5	6	1	13	14	0	11	3	8
9	14	15	5	2	8	12	3	7	0	4	10	1	13	11	6
4	3	2	12	9	5	15	10	11	14	1	7	6	0	8	13

(g) S-Box 7

4	11	2	14	15	0	8	13	3	12	9	7	5	10	6	1
13	0	11	7	4	9	1	10	14	3	5	12	2	15	8	6
1	4	11	13	12	3	7	14	10	15	6	8	0	5	9	2
6	11	13	8	1	4	10	7	9	5	0	15	13	2	3	12

(h) S-Box 8

13	2	8	4	6	15	11	1	10	9	3	14	5	0	12	7
1	15	13	8	10	3	7	4	12	5	6	11	0	14	9	2
7	11	4	1	9	12	14	2	0	6	10	13	15	3	5	8
2	1	14	7	4	10	8	13	15	12	9	0	3	5	6	11

select one of the sixteen columns. The decimal value in the cell selected by the row and column is then converted to its 4-bit representation to produce the output. Then the outputs of all the S-boxes are combined to form a 32-bit block. This is then supplied to the next stage known as the *P-box permutation*.

Let us now consider an example. Suppose in S-box 3 for input 110101, the row is 11 in binary (i.e., 3 in decimal) and the column is 1010 in binary (i.e. 10 in decimal). Thus the value at the intersection of row 3 and column 10 is selected which is 14. Hence, the output is 1110. Note that rows and columns are counted from 0 and not from 1.

P-Box Permutation—The 48-bit result from the output of S-boxes passes through a substitution function that produces a 32-bit output, which is permuted as defined in Table 9.7. In this permutation, there is no expansion or compression. This is known as *P-box permutation*.

Table 9.7 *P-box Permutation*

16	7	20	21	29	12	28	17
1	15	23	26	5	18	31	10
2	8	24	14	32	27	3	9
19	13	30	6	22	11	4	25

XOR and Swap—All the operations performed so far was on the 32-bit RPT of the original 64-bit plain text, whereas till now 32-bit LPT is untouched. Now an XOR operation is performed between the output of the P-box permutation and the LPT of the initial 64-bit plain text. Now a final swapping is done by which the result of the XOR operation becomes the new RPT and the old RPT becomes the new LPT.

9.6.4 Inverse Initial Permutation

Finally, at the end of all 16 rounds, the *inverse initial permutation* is performed. This is a simple transposition technique performed only once, based on Table 9.8. The output of the inverse IP is the 64-bit cipher text.

Table 9.8 *Inverse Initial Permutation*

40	8	48	16	56	24	64	32	39	7	47	15	55	23	63	31
38	6	46	14	54	22	62	30	37	5	45	13	53	21	61	29
36	4	44	12	52	20	60	28	35	3	43	11	51	19	59	27
34	2	42	10	50	18	58	26	33	1	41	9	49	17	57	25

9.6.5 DES Decryption

Decryption of DES uses the same algorithm as encryption, and hence the algorithm is reversible. Only difference between the encryption and the decryption process is that the application of the sub-keys is reversed. Say the original key K was divided into $K_1, K_2, \ldots, K_{16}$ for the 16 rounds of encryption. Then, for decryption the key should be used as $K_{16}, K_{15}, \ldots, K_1$.

9.6.6 Strength of DES

From the time of adoption of DES as a federal standard, there have been lingering concerns about the level of security provided by DES. These concerns, fall into two areas: key size and the cryptographic algorithm. However, as already discussed, the inner workings of the DES algorithm are known completely to the general public. Hence, the strength of DES mainly lies on its key.

The key length of DES is 56 bits. Thus, there are 2^{56} (or approximately about 7.2×10^{16}) possible keys. Hence, it may be said that a brute-force attack appears impractical. Assuming that, on average, half the key space has to be searched, a single computer performing one DES encryption per microsecond would take approximately 1,142 years to break the cipher. However, the assumption of one encryption per microsecond is too conservative. It has been postulated by Diffie and Hellman that a parallel machine with 1 million encryption devices, each of which could perform one encryption per microsecond, would bring the average search time down to about 10 h.

9.7 ADVANCE VERSIONS OF DES

Though DES proves to be quite secure, but due to tremendous advance in computing power it seems that DES is also susceptible to possible attacks. Hence, there has been considerable interest in finding an alternative. One of the approaches may be to write a new algorithm which is time-consuming as well as not easy. Moreover, that it has to be tested sufficiently before using it commercially. An alternative approach is to preserve the existing basic DES algorithm and make it stronger by using multiple encryptions and multiple keys. Consequently two advance versions of DES have emerged—*double DES* and *triple DES*.

9.7.1 Double DES

It is a very simple method where the encryption of the plain text is done twice before generating the final cipher text. In this method, two different keys, say K_1 and K_2, are used for the two stages of encryption. The concept is illustrated in Figure 9.9.

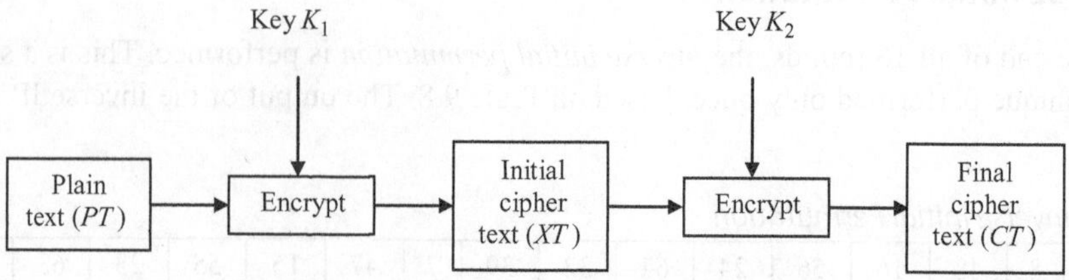

Figure 9.9 *Double DES Encryption*

From the figure we find that initially an encryption of the original plain text (*PT*) is done using the key K1, and the resultant is denoted as *XT*. Mathematically this may be expressed as $XT = E(K_1, PT)$. Again another encryption is performed on the already encrypted plain text with the second key K_2 resulting in the final cipher text (*CT*). This may be mathematically written as $CT = E(K_2, E(K_1, PT))$. For decryption, first the key K_2 will be used to produce the singly encrypted cipher text (*XT*). Then this cipher text block will be decrypted using the key K_1 to get back the original plain text (*PT*). Hence, the decryption may be mathematically denoted as $PT = D(K_1, D(K_2, CT))$. The process is shown in Figure 9.10.

Since, the key length of DES is 56 bits, this double DES scheme apparently involves a key length of $56 \times 2 = 112$ bits. Thus, it may be concluded that since the cryptanalysis for the basic version of DES requires a search of 2^{56} keys, double DES would require a key search of 2^{112} keys. However, that is not the case and there is a way to attack this scheme. In fact, the attacking scheme does not depend on any particular property of DES but will work against any block encryption cipher. The algorithm is known as *meet-in-the-middle attack.*

Let us assume that the attacker knows two basic pieces of information—the plain text block *PT* and the corresponding cipher text block *CT*. First, the attacker will encrypt *PT* for all 2^{56} possible values of K_1, which means that *XT* is calculated. These results are stored in a table and then the table is sorted by the values of *XT*. This means in this step the cryptanalyst computed $XT = E(K_1, PT)$.

Now the reverse operation will be performed, i.e., the known cipher text *CT* will be decrypted using all 2^{56} possible values of K_2. For each decryption, the result is compared with the table, which was computed earlier. In effect, in this step the cryptanalyst computes $XT = D(K_2, CT)$. If a match occurs, then the cryptanalyst now is able to find out the possible values of the two keys. Then the two resulting keys are tested against a new known plain text–cipher text pair. If the two keys produce the correct cipher text, then the keys are accepted as correct.

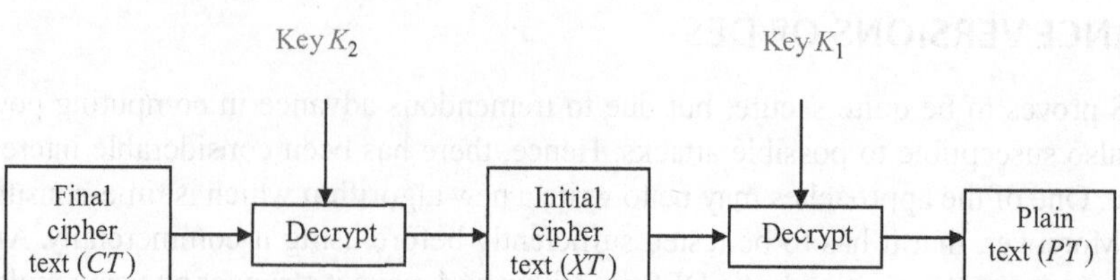

Figure 9.10 *Double DES Decryption*

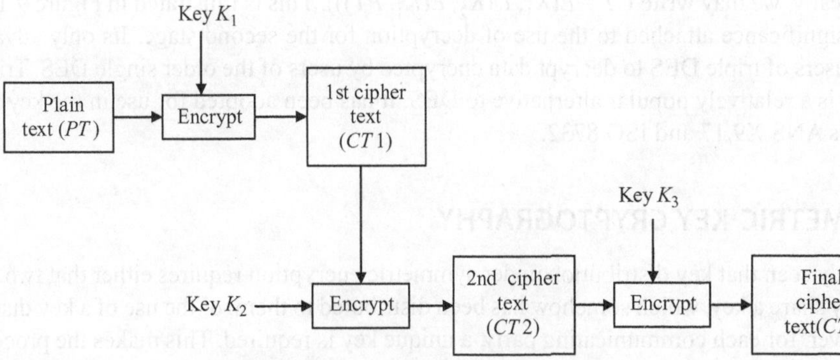

Figure 9.11 *Triple DES Encryption with Three Keys*

9.7.2 Triple DES

Though double DES is sufficient form of the standpoint of security for all practical purposes, still a better alternative may be *triple DES*. Depending on the number of keys used, triple DES is of two types—triple DES using three keys and triple DES using two keys.

Triple DES Using Three Keys—The basic idea of the method is to use three different keys, namely K_1, K_2, and K_3 for the encryption of the plain text. However, it suffers from the drawback that it requires a key length of $56 \times 3 = 168$ bits, which may be somewhat difficult for practical purpose. Mathematically it may be defined as $CT = E(K_3, E(K_2, E(K_1, PT)))$. This is illustrated in Figure 9.11. A number of Internet-based applications, including PGP and S/MIME, have adopted three-key triple DES. Decryption of the operation to be performed is given as $PT = D(K_3, D(K_2, D(K_1, CT)))$.

Triple DES Using Two Keys—To avoid the problem of a key of length 168 bits, Tuchman proposed a triple encryption method which uses only two keys. The algorithm follows an *encrypt–decrypt–encrypt* (*EDE*) sequence which means:

1. First encrypt the original plain text with key K_1.
2. Then decrypt the output of step 1 with key K_2.
3. Finally, again encrypt the output of step 2 with key K_1 (see Figure 9.12).

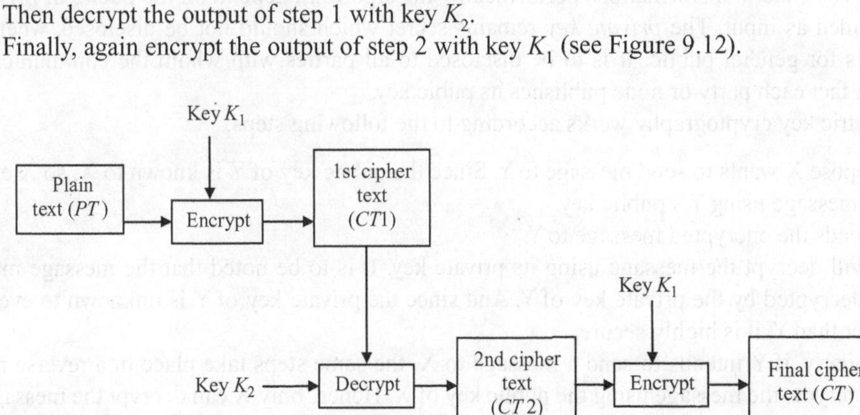

Figure 9.12 *Triple DES Encryption with Two Keys*

Mathematically, we may write $CT = E(K_1, D(K_2, E(K_1, PT)))$. This is illustrated in Figure 9.12. There is no special significance attached to the use of decryption for the second stage. Its only advantage is that it allows users of triple DES to decrypt data encrypted by users of the older single DES. Triple DES with two keys is a relatively popular alternative to DES. It has been adopted for use in the key management standards ANS X9.17 and ISO 8732.

9.8 ASYMMETRIC-KEY CRYPTOGRAPHY

We have already seen that key distribution under symmetric encryption requires either that two communicants already share a key, which somehow has been distributed to them, or the use of a key distribution centre. Moreover, for each communicating party, a unique key is required. This makes the process more cumbersome.

However, Whitfield Diffie, a student at the Stanford University along with his Professor Martin Hellman, first introduced the concepts of *asymmetric-key* or *public-key* cryptography in 1976. Based on the theoretical work of Diffie and Hellman, the first major asymmetric key cryptosystem was developed at MIT and published in 1978 by Ron Rivest, Adi Shamir, and Len Adleman. The method is known as *RSA algorithm* after the first letters of the surnames of the three researchers. As in this method every communicating party possesses a key pair known as *public key* and *private key*, hence the problem of key exchange and distribution is solved.

Asymmetric key cryptography relies on one key for encryption and a different but related key for decryption. It is very important to note that even with knowledge of the cryptographic algorithm and the encryption key, it is computationally infeasible to determine the decryption key. The advantage of the system is that each communicating party needs just a key pair for communicating with any number of other communicating parties. In addition, some algorithms, such as RSA, also exhibit an important characteristic, i.e., either of the two related keys can be used for encryption, with the other used for decryption.

9.8.1 Public and Private Key

This is a pair of keys that have been selected so that if one is used for encryption, the other is used for decryption. The exact transformations performed by the algorithm depend on the public or private key that is provided as input. The *private key* remains secret which should not be disclosed, whereas the *public key* is for general public. It is to be disclosed to all parties with whom the communication is intended. In fact each party or node publishes its pubic key.

Asymmetric key cryptography works according to the following steps:

1. Suppose X wants to send message to Y. Since the public key of Y is known to X, so X encrypts the message using Y's public key.
2. X sends the encrypted message to Y.
3. Y will decrypt the message using its private key. It is to be noted that the message may only be decrypted by the private key of Y. And since the private key of Y is unknown to everybody other than Y, it is highly secure.
4. Similarly, if Y intends to send a message to X, the same steps take place in a reverse manner. Y encrypts the message using the public key of X. Hence, only X can decrypt the message back using the private key.

9.9 RSA ALGORITHM

The RSA algorithm is the most popular asymmetric key cryptographic algorithm. The scheme is a block cipher. Here, the plain text and the cipher text are integers between 0 and N. A typical size for N is 1024 bits or 309 decimal digits. That is, N is less than 2^{1024}. We examine RSA in this section in some detail, beginning with an explanation of the algorithm.

Plain text is encrypted in blocks. For some plain text block M and cipher text block C, the total process may be summarized as follows:

1. Select two large prime numbers P and Q, such that $P \neq Q$.
2. Calculate $N = P \times Q$.
3. Calculate $\varphi(N) = (P-1)(Q-1)$.
4. Select an integer E as the public key (i.e., the encryption key) such that it is not a factor of $\varphi(N)$.
5. Calculate D as the private key (i.e., the decryption key) such that:
$$(D \times E) \bmod \varphi(N) = 1$$
6. From plain text M the cipher text is calculated as:
$$C = M^E \bmod N$$
7. This cipher text is sent to the receiver for decryption.
8. The cipher text is decrypted to the plain text as:
$$M = C^D \bmod N$$

9.9.1 Example of RSA

We now discuss the RSA with an example:

1. Select two prime numbers, $P = 17$ and $Q = 23$.
2. Calculate $N = P \times Q = 17 \times 23 = 391$.
3. Calculate $\varphi(N) = (P-1)(Q-1) = 16 \times 22 = 352$.
4. Select the public key E such that E is relatively prime to $\varphi(N) = 352$ and less than $\varphi(N)$. The factors of 352 are 2, 2, 2, 2, 2, and 11 (since $E = 2 \times 2 \times 2 \times 2 \times 2 \times 11$). Now we have to choose E such that none of the factors of E is 2 and 11. Let us choose E as 17 (it could have been any other number that does not have any of the factors 2 and 11).
5. Determine the private key D such that: $(D \times E) \bmod (352) = 1$.
We have $(D \times 17) \bmod (352) = 1$. After making some calculations, we find the correct value is $D = 145$, because $(145 \times 17) \bmod (352) = 2465 \bmod (352) = 1$.
6. Now calculate the cipher text C from plain text M as $C = M^E \bmod N$.
Let us assume that $M = 75$. Hence we have
$$C = 75^{17} \bmod 391$$
$$= (75^4 \bmod 391) \times (75^4 \bmod 391) \times (75^4 \bmod 391) \times (75^4 \bmod 391) \times (75^1 \bmod 391)$$
Now, $75^4 \bmod 391 = 123$
$75^1 \bmod 391 = 75$
Hence, $C = 75^{17} \bmod 391 = (123 \times 123 \times 123 \times 123 \times 75) \bmod 391$
$= 17166498075 \bmod 391 = 58.$

8. Send C as the cipher text to the receiver.
9. For decryption, calculate the plain text for the cipher text as $M = C^D \bmod N$.
   We have $M = 58^{145} \bmod 391$

$$= (58^{10} \bmod 391) \times (58^{10} \bmod 391) \times (58^{10} \bmod 391) \times (58^{10} \bmod 391) \times (58^{10} \bmod 391) \times (58^{10} \bmod 391) \times (58^{10} \bmod 391) \times (58^{10} \bmod 391) \times (58^{10} \bmod 391) \times (58^{10} \bmod 391) \times (58^{10} \bmod 391) \times (58^{10} \bmod 391) \times (58^{10} \bmod 391) \times (58^{10} \bmod 391) \times (58^{5} \bmod 391)$$

   Now, $58^{10} \bmod 391 = 2$
   $58^5 \bmod 391 = 317$

   Hence,

$$58^{145} \bmod 391 = (2 \times 2 \times 2 \times 2 \times 2 \times 2 \times 2 \times 2 \times 2 \times 2 \times 2 \times 2 \times 2 \times 2 \times 317) \bmod 391$$
$$= 5193728 \bmod 391 = 75.$$

9.9.2 Strength of RSA

There may be four possible approaches to attack the RSA algorithm. They are as follows.

Brute Force—This process involves trying out all possible private keys. The defense against the brute-force approach is basically to use a large key size. Hence, it is desirable that the number of bits in D should be large. However, we know that both in key generation and in encryption/decryption lot of calculations are involved. Thus, as the size of the key becomes larger the system becomes slower. Thus, we need to be careful in choosing a key size for RSA. However, development in algorithms and tremendous computing powers shows that for the near future a key size in the range of 1024 to 2048 bits seems reasonable.

Mathematical Attacks—This is equivalent in effort to factoring the product of two primes. This may be done in three possible ways:

1. Factor N into its two prime factors.
2. Determine $\varphi(N)$ directly, without first determining P and Q.
3. Determine D directly, without first determining $\varphi(n)$.

Of the above-mentioned methods, the most popular way is the task of factoring N into its two prime factors. But with the presently known algorithms, determining D for given E and N appears to be much time-consuming. For a large N with large prime factors, factoring is a hard problem. Researchers suggest that it may take more than 70 years to determine P and Q if N is a 100-digit number.

Timing Attacks—These types of attacks depend on the running time of the decryption algorithm. In fact, timing attacks are applicable to any public-key cryptography systems. Basically, the attack is only on the cipher text. With an analogy, we may say that a timing attack is somewhat like a burglar guessing the combination of a safe by observing how long it takes for someone to turn the dial from number to number. Although the timing attack is a serious threat, some simple counter measures might be implemented as follows:

1. It has to be ensured that all exponentiations take the same amount of time before returning a result.
2. Adding a random delay to the decryption algorithm will confuse the timing attack.
3. Before performing decryption, multiply the cipher text by a random number. This process prevents the attacker from knowing what cipher text bits are being processed inside the computer and hence prevents the bit-by-bit analysis essential to the timing attack.

Chosen Cipher Text Attacks—In this process, first a number of cipher texts are chosen. The attacker selects a plain text, encrypts it with the target's public key and then gets the plain text back by having it decrypted with the private key. This type of attack basically exploits properties of the RSA algorithm.

To overcome this type of attack, prior to encryption practical RSA-based cryptosystems randomly pad the plain text. This randomizes the cipher text. However, more sophisticated attacks are possible. Then a simple padding with a random value is not sufficient to provide the desired security. In such cases, it is recommended to modify the plain text using a procedure known as optimal asymmetric encryption padding (OAEP). A full discussion of the threats and OAEP are beyond the scope of this current book.

9.10 SYMMETRIC VERSUS ASYMMETRIC-KEY CRYPTOGRAPHY

After discussing both symmetric- and asymmetric-key cryptographies in detail, we saw that the techniques differ in certain aspects and both have some advantages compared to the other. We now want to compare between the two in brief:

1. In symmetric-key cryptography, the same key is being used both for encryption and for decryption, whereas in asymmetric-key cryptography we use separate keys for encryption and decryption.
2. In symmetric-key cryptography, the resulting cipher text is usually of the same size as the plain text, whereas in the other case, the size of the cipher text is more than the original plain text.
3. Symmetric-key cryptography is much faster than the asymmetric one.
4. The key exchange or agreement problem of symmetric-key cryptography is totally solved in asymmetric-key cryptography.
5. In symmetric-key cryptography number of keys required is equal to the square of the number of participants, whereas in asymmetric-key cryptography it is equal to the number of participants.

9.11 DIFFIE–HELLMAN KEY EXCHANGE

Whitefield Diffie and Martin Hellman were the first to publish a public-key algorithm which solved the problem of key agreement or key exchange. The algorithm is generally referred to as Diffie–Hellman key exchange. The main purpose of the algorithm is to enable two users to securely exchange a key which may then be used for subsequent encryption of messages. But it is to be noted that the algorithm itself is limited only to the exchange of keys, and is not used for encryption or decryption of messages. We will discuss the algorithm in the following section.

9.11.1 The Algorithm

Let us assume that A and B want to make a key agreement for encryption and decryption of messages exchanged between them. For the scheme, A and B first choose two large prime numbers p and q. These two prime numbers can be made public. User A now selects another large random integer $X < p$ and computes $a = q^X \bmod p$. A sends the number a to B but keeps X value as private. In a similar manner, user B independently selects a random integer $Y < p$ and computes $b = q^Y \bmod p$. B then sends this number b to A and keeps Y value private. User A now computes the secret key as $K_1 = b^X \bmod p$ and user B computes the key as $K_2 = a^Y \bmod p$. Both the calculations produce an identical result which is shown as follows:

$$
\begin{aligned}
K_1 &= b^X \bmod p \\
&= (q^Y \bmod p)^X \bmod p
\end{aligned}
$$

$$
\begin{aligned}
&= (q^Y)^X \bmod p && \text{(by the rules of modular arithmetic)}\\
&= q^{YX} \bmod p\\
&= (q^X)^Y \bmod p\\
&= (q^X \bmod p)^Y \bmod p && \text{(by the rules of modular arithmetic)}\\
&= a^Y \bmod p\\
&= K_2.
\end{aligned}
$$

This means that $K_1 = K_2 = K$ is the symmetric key, which must be kept secret and be used for both encryption and decryption of messages. Now it may seem so that if A and B can calculate K independently, then an attacker also can do the same. The fact is that an attacker only has the following ingredients to work with p, q, a, and b. Thus, the attacker is forced to take a discrete logarithm to determine the key.

For example, to determine the private key of user B, the attacker has to compute $Y = d\log_{q,p}(b)$. Then the key K may be calculated in the same manner as user B calculates it. The security of the Diffie–Hellman key exchange lies in the fact that, it is very difficult to calculate discrete logarithms. For large primes, this task is considered infeasible.

However, Diffie–Hellman key exchange fails in case of a *man-in-the-middle attack*. In this case, a third person C intercepts A's public-key value and sends his own public-key value to B. Again as B transmits his public-key value, C substitutes it with his own and sends it to A. A and C thus agree on one shared key and B and C agree on another shared key. Once this is done, C decrypts any messages sent out by A or B. This vulnerability of Diffie–Hellman key exchange may be avoided using asymmetric key operation.

9.12 STEGANOGRAPHY

A plain text message may be hidden in one of two ways—by cryptography or by steganography. Steganography is a technique for hiding a secret message within a larger message in such a way that the presence or contents of the hidden message is not understandable. The methods of steganography conceal the existence of the message, whereas the methods of cryptography render the message unintelligible to outsiders by various transformations of the text. Historically several techniques were used for steganography, namely character marking by overwriting in pencil, making small pin punctures on selected letters, writing in invisible ink etc., to name a few. However, different contemporary methods have been suggested for steganography. Of late, it is found that selected messages can be hidden within digital pictures. It has been shown that a 2.3-megabyte message may be hidden in a single digital snapshot. There are now a number of software packages available that take this type of approach to steganography.

Compared to encryption, there are a lot of drawbacks in steganography. It requires a lot of overhead to hide a relatively few bits of information. Also, once the system is discovered, it becomes virtually worthless. Alternatively, a message can be first encrypted and then hidden using steganography.

9.13 QUANTUM CRYPTOGRAPHY

Dr Charles Bennett and John Smolin were the first ever to witness the quantum cryptographic exchange using polarized light photons over a distance of 32 cm, at IBM's Thomas J. Watson Research Centre near New York in October 1989.

In the early 1980s, two computer scientists, Charles Bennett and Gilles Brassard, realized that the application of quantum theory in the field of cryptography could have the potential to create a cipher

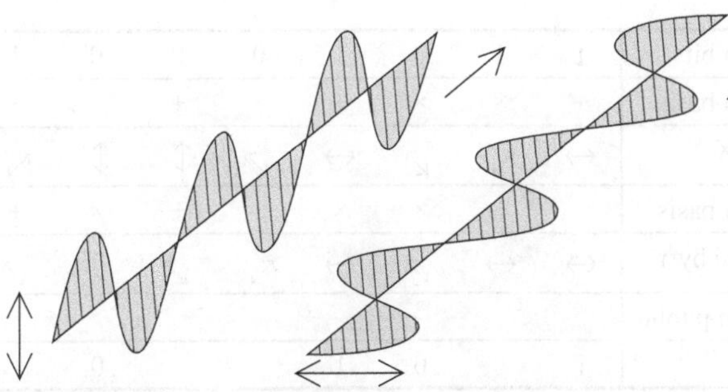

Figure 9.13 *Vertically and Horizontally Polarized Light*

giving absolute security. The cryptosystem developed by Bennett and Brassard uses polarized light photons to transfer data between two points. As a photon travels through space, it vibrates perpendicularly to its plane of movement and the direction of vibration is known as its polarization. For the sake of simplicity, the depicted directions of vibration are restricted to horizontal and vertical directions (Figure 9.13), although practically the photons will also move in all angles.

An observer will have no idea which angle of polarizing filter should be used for a certain photon to pass successfully through. The binary ones and zeroes of digital communication may be represented by either of the two schemes—rectilinear polarization or diagonal polarization. Rectilinear polarization may be vertically (↕) and horizontally (↔) polarized photons, while diagonal polarization represents left-diagonally (⤡) and right-diagonally (⤢) polarized photons. During transmission, the transmitter will randomly swap between the rectilinear (+) and diagonal (×) schemes, known in quantum cryptography as bases.

The key distribution is performed in several steps. The sender initially transmits a stream of random bits as polarized photons and continually swapping randomly between any of the four polarization states. The receiver at this point has no idea which schemes are being used for which bit, and hence will also swap randomly between either rectilinear or diagonal schemes. The receiver records the results of the measurements but keeps them secret. The transmitter will now contact the receiver insecurely and tell which scheme was used for each photon. The receiver can now say which ones were guessed correctly. All the incorrect guesses are discarded. These correct cases are now translated into bits (1's and 0's) and hence become the key. Both parties now share the secret key.

However, an eavesdropper attempting to intercept the photons will have no idea whether to use a rectilinear or diagonal filter. Around half of the time a totally inaccurate measurement will be made when a photon will change its polarization in order to pass through an incorrect filter. In fact, it will become immediately apparent to both if someone is monitoring the photons in transit, because their use of an incorrect filter is likely to change the polarity of photons before they reach the receiver. If, when comparing a small part of their shared secret key over a public channel, they do not match, it will be clear to both the transmitter and the receiver that the photons have been observed in transit.

The cryptosystem neatly takes advantage of one of the fundamental features of quantum theory, a manifestation of Heisenberg's uncertainty principle, that the act of observing will change the system itself. In this way, it is impossible for an attacker to make an accurate measurement of the data without knowledge of which scheme is being used, essentially the cryptographic key.

Example 9.7: Using quantum cryptographic technique, X wants to exchange a key with Y over an insecure channel. The 0° and 90° polarizations are denoted by ↕ and ↔, respectively, while 45° and 135° polarizations are denoted by ⤡ and ⤢ respectively. Show the steps followed.

X's choice of random bits	1	1	0	1	0	0	0	1	1	0
X's choice of random basis	+	×	×	+	×	+	+	×	+	×
Polarization sent by X	↔	⤡	⤢	↔	⤢	↕	↕	⤡	↔	⤢
Y's choice of random basis	+	+	×	×	×	+	×	+	+	×
Polarization measured by Y	↔	↔	⤢	↔	⤡	⤢	↕	⤢	↕	⤢
Discussion of basis in public										
Shared secret key	1		0	1			0			0

Now, X and Y will disclose a subset of the key and compare whether all the bits are identical. Suppose they compare 3rd and 5th bits. In the current example, all the bits match. Hence X and Y can use the remaining three bits (the 1st, 2nd, and 4th) as secret key. If eavesdropper was present, some of the bits in the key obtained by Y will not match with those of X.

9.14 SOLVED PROBLEMS

Problem 9.1: A message to encrypt and a message to decrypt are given. The modulus N is 851 and the encryption exponent $r = 5$ are given. Encrypt the message to encrypt 24; find the decryption exponent s, and decrypt the message to decrypt 111.

Solution: For the first part, we need to compute $24^5 \pmod{851}$.

$$24^5 \pmod{851}$$
$$= 7962624 - (9356 \times 851) = 668;$$

Hence the encryption of 24 is 668.

To do the second part, we first need to find the encryption exponent.

Here, $N = 851 = (23)(37)$

so $E = (22)(36) = 792.$

$\gcd(5; 792) = 1$ as desired.

We need to find the multiplicative inverse of $r = 5 \bmod 792$; this will be our decryption exponent s.

The idea is to use the Euclidean algorithm to solve $5x + 792y = 1$; the value of x that we find is the multiplicative inverse we are looking for.

$$792 - (158 \times 5) = 2;\ 5 - (2 \times 2) = 1;$$

so $5 - 2(798 - (158 \times 5)) = 1;$

there are $1 + 158(2)$ 5's here and -2 792's: $317(5) - 2(792) = 1$.

So the reciprocal of 5 mod 792 is 317.

317, 158, 79, 39, 19, 9, 4, 2 are the sequence of powers we need to compute (dividing by 2 each time and throwing away the remainder).

Now we set out to compute $111^{371} \pmod{851}$ (this will be the decryption we want).

$$111^2 = 12321;\ 12321 - (14)(851) = 407$$
$$111^4 = (111^2)^2;\ 407^2 = 165649;\ 165649 - (194)(851) = 555$$
$$111^9 = (111^4)^2(111);\ 555^2(111) = 34190775;\ 34190775 - (40177)(851) = 148$$
$$111^{19} = (111^9)^2(111);\ 148^2(111) = 2431344;\ 2431344 - (2857)(851) = 37$$

$$111^{39} = (111^{19})^2(111);\ 37^2(111) = 151959;\ 151959 - (178)\ (851) = 481$$
$$111^{79} = (111^{39})^2(111);\ 481^2(111) = 25681071;\ 25681071 - (30177)\ (851) = 444$$
$$111^{158} = (111^{79})^2;\ 444^2 = 197136;\ 197136 - 231 * 851 = 555$$
$$111^{317} = (111^{158})^2(111);\ 555^2(111) = 34190775;\ 34190775 - (40177)\ (851) = 148$$

The desired decryption is 148.

Problem 9.2: Write 1 as a linear combination of 7 and 18.

Solution: We first go through Euclid's algorithm:

$m_1 = 18$
$m_2 = 7$
$m_3 = r(18, 7) = 4$ so $18 = 2 \times 7 + 4$
$m_4 = r(7, 4) = 3$ so $7 = 1 \times 4 + 3$
$m_5 = r(4, 3) = 1$ so $4 = 1 \times 3 + 1$
$m_6 = r(3, 1) = 0$

Now we can use these steps to express 1 as a linear combination of 7 and 18, as follows:

$$1 = 4 - 3 = 4 - (7 - 4) = 2 \times 4 - 7 = 2 \times (18 - 2 \times 7) - 7 = 2 \times 18 - 5 \times 7$$

Problem 9.3: Find an integer d such that

$$13d \equiv 1 \bmod 220$$

Solution: We first express 1 as

$$1 = 13x + 220y$$

Using the Euclidean algorithm:

$m_1 = 220$
$m_2 = 13$
$m_3 = r(220, 13) = 12$ so $220 = 16 \times 13 + 12$
$m_4 = r(13, 12) = 1$ so $13 = 1 \times 12 + 1$
$m_5 = r(12, 1) = 0$

So using back-substitution we get

$$1 = 13 - 12 = 13 - (220 - 16 \times 13) = 17 \times 13 - 1 \times 220$$

so we can take $x = 17$, $y = -1$. As explained, we can now take $d = 17$.

Problem 9.4: Two prime numbers are given as $P = 17$ and $Q = 29$. Evaluate N, E and D in an RSA encryption process.

Solution: Here $P = 17$ and $Q = 29$.

Hence, $$N = P \times Q = 17 \times 29 = 493.$$

Now we calculate $\varphi(N) = (P - 1)\ (Q - 1) = 16 \times 28 = 448$.

We now select the public key E such that E is relatively prime to $\varphi(N) = 448$ and less than $\varphi(N)$. The factors of 448 are 2, 2, 2, 2, 2, 2, and 7 (since $E = 2 \times 2 \times 2 \times 2 \times 2 \times 2 \times 7$). Now we have to choose E such that none of the factors of E is 2 and 7. Let us choose E as 11 (it could have been any other number that does not have any of the factors 2 and 7).

Now we determine the private key D such that $(D \times E) \bmod (448) = 1$.

We have: $(D \times 11) \bmod (448) = 1$. After making some calculations, we find the correct value is $D = 285$, because $(285 \times 11) \bmod (448) = 3135 \bmod (448) = 1$.

MULTIPLE CHOICE QUESTIONS

1. The length of the key used in DES is
   (a) 128 bits (b) 64 bits (c) 32 bits (d) 96 bits
   Ans. (b)
2. A message that is sent in cryptography is known as
   (a) plain text (b) cipher text (c) cracking (d) decryption
   Ans. (b)
3. ________ is the science and art of transforming messages to make them secure and immune to attacks.
   (a) cryptography (b) cryptoanalysis
   (c) either (a) or (b) (d) neither (a) nor (b)
   Ans. (a)
4. The ________ is the original message before transformation.
   (a) cipher text (b) plain text (c) secret text (d) none of these
   Ans. (b)
5. The ________ is the message after transformation.
   (a) cipher text (b) plain text (c) secret text (d) none of these
   Ans. (a)
6. A(n) ________ algorithm transforms plain text to cipher text.
   (a) encryption (b) decryption
   (c) either (a) or (b) (d) neither (a) nor (b)
   Ans. (a)
7. A combination of an encryption algorithm and a decryption algorithm is called a ________.
   (a) cipher (b) secret (c) key (d) none of these
   Ans. (a)
8. The ________ is a number or a set of numbers on which the cipher operates.
   (a) cipher (b) secret (c) key (d) none of these
   Ans. (c)
9. In a(n) ________ cipher, the same key is used by both the sender and receiver.
   (a) symmetric key (b) asymmetric key
   (c) either (a) or (b) (d) neither (a) nor (b)
   Ans. (a)
10. In a(n) ________, the key is called the secret key.
    (a) symmetric key (b) asymmetric key
    (c) either (a) or (b) (d) neither (a) nor (b)
    Ans. (a)
11. In a(n) ________ cipher, a pair of keys is used.
    (a) Symmetric key (b) Asymmetric key
    (c) Either (a) or (b) (d) Neither (a) nor (b)
    Ans. (b)

12. In an asymmetric-key cipher, the sender uses the __________ key.
    (a) private (b) public
    (c) either (a) or (b) (d) neither (a) nor (b)

Ans. (b)

13. A ______ cipher replaces one character with another character.
    (a) substitution (b) transposition
    (c) either (a) or (b) (d) neither (a) nor (b)

Ans. (a)

14. The Caesar cipher is a(n) _______ cipher that has a key of 3.
    (a) transposition (b) additive (c) shift (d) none of these

Ans. (c)

15. A(n) _______ is a keyless substitution cipher with *N* inputs and *M* outputs that uses a formula to define the relationship between the input stream and the output stream.
    (a) S-box (b) P-box (c) T-box (d) none of these

Ans. (a)

16. A(n) ________ is a keyless transposition cipher with *N* inputs and *M* outputs that uses a table to define the relationship between the input stream and the output stream.
    (a) S-box (b) P-box (c) T-box (d) none of these

Ans. (b)

17. DES has an initial and final permutation block and _________ rounds.
    (a) 14 (b) 15 (c) 16 (d) 18

Ans. (c)

18. ______ DES was designed to increase the size of the DES key.
    (a) double (b) triple (c) quadruple (d) none of these

Ans. (b)

19. The ________ method provides a one-time session key for two parties.
    (a) Diffie–Hellman (b) RSA (c) DES (d) AES

Ans. (a)

20. The ________ attack can endanger the security of the Diffie–Hellman method if two parties are not authenticated to each other.
    (a) man-in-the-middle (b) cipher text attack
    (c) plain text attack (d) none of these

Ans. (a)

REVIEW QUESTIONS

1. Differentiate between block cipher and stream cipher.
2. What do you mean by symmetric-key and asymmetric-key cryptography? What is 'man-in-the-middle' attack?
3. What are the functions of P-box and S-box in case of DES algorithm?
4. Explain the Diffy–Hellman key exchange algorithm.
5. What do you mean by quantum cryptography?
6. What is steganography?
7. Define block cipher. What do you mean by cipher text?

8. Describe RSA algorithm.
9. What are the problems in symmetric-key cryptography?
10. Explain the main concepts of DES algorithm. What are the shortcomings of DES?
11. The following cipher text was obtained from an English plain text using a Caesar shift σ_d with offset $d \in Z_{26}$:

    TVSFP IQWLI IXRYQ FIVSR I

    (a) Find the plain text and the offset d.

    (b) Apply σ_d repeatedly to the cipher text. What happens?
12. Alice and Bob agreed on a secret key K by the Diffie–Hellman method using the (unrealistically small) prime $p = 2^{16} + 1$ and primitive root $g = 3 \in (Z/p)^*$. The data sent from Alice to Bob and vice-versa were $a = g^{\alpha} = 13242$ and $b = g^{\beta} = 48586$. The key $K = g^{\alpha\beta}$ was used to generate a byte sequence $z1, z2, z3, \ldots$ as a one-time-pad in the following way: With

    $$Z_i = K^i \bmod p = \sum_{j=0}^{16} b_{ij} 2^j, b_{ij} \in \{0, 1\} \quad \text{set} \quad z_i := \sum_{j=4}^{11} b_{ij} 2^{j-4}$$

    This one-time-pad was XORed with an ASCII–plain text. The resulting cipher text is

    F02B 1756 5C98 54C5 3923 109E 62E6 C89E 9F6E B9DE

    Calculate the values of α, β, K and decrypt the cipher text.
13. Transform the message 'Hello how are you' using rail fence technique.
14. Encrypt the following message using mono-alphabetic substitution cipher with key = 5.

    Cryptography is interesting subject
15. In RSA, the encryption key (E) = 5 and given N = 119. Find out the corresponding private key (D). Also calculate the cipher text C.
16. Two prime numbers are given as P = 23 and Q = 31. Evaluate N, D, and E in an RSA encryption process.

SOME RELATED MATHEMATICS

A.1 FERMAT'S LITTLE THEOREM

Fermat's Little Theorem is often used in number theory in the testing of large primes and simply states as follows.

Theorem A.1: Let p be a prime which does not divide the integer a, then $a^{p-1} = 1 \pmod{p}$.

In more simple language, it may be stated that if p is a prime that is not a factor of a, then when a is multiplied $(p - 1)$ times and the result is divided by p, we get a remainder of 1. For example, if we use $a = 5$ and $p = 3$, the rule says that 5^2 divided by 3 will have a remainder of 1. In fact, 25/3 does have a remainder of 1.

Proof: Start by listing the first $(p - 1)$ positive multiples of a:

$$a, 2a, 3a, \ldots, (p-1)a$$

Suppose that ra and sa are the same modulo p, then we have $r = s \pmod{p}$, so the $(p - 1)$ multiples of a above are distinct and nonzero; that is, they must be congruent to 1, 2, 3, …, $p - 1$ in some order. Multiplying all these congruences together we find

$$a \cdot 2a \cdot 3a \ldots (p-1)a = 1 \cdot 2 \cdot 3 \ldots (p-1) \pmod{p}$$

or

$$a^{(p-1)}(p-1)! = (p-1)! \pmod{p}$$

Dividing both side by $(p - 1)!$ we get

$$a^{(p-1)} = 1$$

Thus the theorem is proved.

Sometimes Fermat's Little Theorem is presented in the following form.

Corollary A.1: Let p be a prime and a any integer, then $a^p = a \pmod{p}$.

Proof: The result is trival (both sides are zero) if p divides a. If p does not divide a, then we can only multiply the congruence in Fermat's Little Theorem by a to complete the proof.

The theorem is 'necessary, but not sufficient'. It means that although it is true for all primes, it is not true just for primes, and will sometimes be true for other numbers as well. For example $3^{90} = 1 \pmod{91}$, but 91 is not prime.

We can test 3^{90} using Fermat's Little Theorem without even finding out what the actual value of 3^{90} is, by using the patterns of remainders for powers of 3 divided by 91.

$$3^1 = 3 = 3 \pmod{91}$$
$$3^2 = 9 = 9 \pmod{91}$$
$$3^3 = 27 = 27 \pmod{91}$$
$$3^4 = 81 = 81 \pmod{91}$$
$$3^5 = 243 = 61 \pmod{91}$$
$$3^6 = 729 = 1 \pmod{91}$$

Since $3^6 = 1 \pmod{91}$, then any power of 3^6 will also be $= 1 \pmod{91}$, and $3^{90} = (3^6)^{15}$.

Numbers which meet the conditions of Fermat's Little Theorem but are not prime are called *pseudoprimes*. Although 91 is a *pseudoprime* base 3, it does not work for other bases. There are, however, some numbers that are pseudoprimes to every base to which they are relatively prime. These pseudoprimes are called *Carmichael numbers*.

A.2 CHINESE REMAINDER THEOREM

The Chinese Remainder Theorem is one of the oldest theorems in number theory. This theorem originated in the book 'Sun Zi Suan Jing', or Sun Tzu's Arithmetic Classic, by the Chinese mathematician Sun Zi, or Sun Tzu, who also wrote 'Sun Zi Bing Fa', or Sun Tzu's The Art of War. The theorem is said to have been used to count the size of the ancient Chinese armies (i.e., the soldiers would split into groups of 3, then 5, 7, etc., and the 'leftover' soldiers from each grouping would be counted).

In fact, the theorem is used to speed up the modulo computations. If working modulo is a product of numbers, say mod $M = m_1 m_2 \dots m_k$, Chinese Remainder Theorem lets us work in each moduli m_i separately. Since computational cost is proportional to size, this is faster than working in the full modulus M.

Theorem A.2: Let $m_1, m_2, \dots, m_k$ be pair-wise relatively prime integers. That is, $\gcd(m_i, m_j) = 1$, for $1 \le i < j \le k$. Let $a_i \in Z_{m_i}$, for $1 \le i \le k$ and let $M = m_1 m_2 \dots m_k$. Consider the system of congruences:

$$\begin{aligned} x_1 &\equiv a_1 \pmod{m_1} \\ x_2 &\equiv a_2 \pmod{m_2} \\ &\vdots \\ x_k &\equiv a_k \pmod{m_k} \end{aligned} \tag{A.1}$$

Then there exists a unique $x \in Z_m$ satisfying this system.

x can be computed as follows:

$$x \equiv \left(\sum_{i=1}^{k} a_i c_i\right) \bmod M \tag{A.2}$$

where

$$c_i = M_i \times (M_i^{-1} \bmod M) \text{ and } M_i = M/m_i \text{ for } 1 \le i \le k. \tag{A.3}$$

Proof: We seek to solve the set of equations

$$\begin{aligned} x_1 &\equiv a_1 \pmod{m_1} \\ x_2 &\equiv a_2 \pmod{m_2} \\ &\vdots \\ x_k &\equiv a_k \pmod{m_k} \end{aligned}$$

where m's are relatively prime.

Let M = Product of the m's $= m_1 m_2 \dots m_k$.

Let $M_i = M/m_i$, for $i = 1, 2, \dots, n$, that is it is the product of all the m's except m_i.

Let M_i^{-1}, be such that $M_i \cdot M_i^{-1} \equiv 1 \pmod{m_i}$ (A.4)

So, $M_i^{-1} = 1/M_i$ = Multiplicative inverse (mod m_i).

Eq. (A.4) is always solvable, when $\gcd(M_i, m_i) = 1$, which is always true when the m's are relatively prime, because $\gcd(M/m_i, m_i) = 1$, because M has no factor m, and m is pair-wise relatively prime with all other m's.

The formulae (A.2) and (A.3) are known as Chinese remainder theorem. Now we wish to show that x is a solution to equation (A.1), and that is unique.

We can convert the equations (A.1) to a common modulus, when we can simply add them, by multiplying each equation by M_i. For example; multiplying the first equation of (A.1) by M_i gives:

$$M_1 x_1 = a_1 M_1 \pmod{M_1 \cdot m_1}$$

which gives

$$M_1 x_1 = a_1 M_1 \pmod{M}$$

because $\qquad (M/m_1) \cdot m_1 = M$

The new equation list becomes

$$\begin{aligned} M_1 x_1 &\equiv a_1 M_1 \pmod{M} \\ M_2 x_2 &\equiv a_2 M_2 \pmod{M} \\ &\vdots \\ M_k x_k &\equiv a_k M_k \pmod{M} \end{aligned}$$

Now multiply each equation by the respective multiplicative inverse of M_i, for $i = 1, 2, \ldots, n$.

$$\begin{aligned} M_1 M_1^{-1} x_1 &\equiv a_1 M_1 M_1^{-1} \pmod{M} \\ M_2 M_2^{-1} x_2 &\equiv a_2 M_2 M_2^{-1} \pmod{M} \\ &\vdots \\ M_k M_k^{-1} x_k &\equiv a_k M_k M_k^{-1} \pmod{M} \end{aligned}$$

Now sum all the equations and equate the right-hand side to x:

$$x \equiv a_1 M_1 M_1^{-1} + a_2 M_2 M_2^{-1} + \ldots + a_k M_k M_k^{-1} \pmod{M}$$

or

$$x \equiv \left(\sum_{i=1}^{k} a_i M_i M_i^{-1} \right) \bmod M$$

Now we note that in all cases, for $i = 1$ to n, $x \equiv x_i \equiv a_i (\bmod\ m_i)$, i.e., we get the original equations, so x is a solution to the set of equations (A.1).

For instance, taking modulo m_1, all the terms will disappear, because they have m_1 as a factor, except M_1, which is relatively prime to m_1. And M_1, multiplied by its inverse is 1, modulo m_1, so what remains is $x \equiv a_1 \pmod{m_1}$. The corresponding result occurs for all the divisors, m_i. Therefore, x is a solution to the set of equations (A.1).

Now we prove that the solution is unique.

Suppose y is another solution to the set of equations, which is unique modulo M, so that y and x are distinct. For each of the equations in (A.1)

$$y \equiv x \equiv x_i \equiv a_i \pmod{m_i}$$

or

$$y \equiv x \pmod{m_i}$$

Using a definition of modulus:

$$y = x + k \cdot m_i$$

y and x can differ only by a multiple of the modulus, which is zero modulo m_i; hence, y and x are equivalent modulo m_i.

Example A.1: What would be the least total number which gives the remainder 1, 2, and 3, when divided by 7, 9, and 11?

Then, the question becomes, what numbers satisfy the following equations:

$$x \equiv 1 \pmod 7$$
$$x \equiv 2 \pmod 9$$
$$x \equiv 3 \pmod{11}$$

Solution: Given $p_1, p_2, \ldots, p_n$, which are positive integers that are pair-wise relatively prime (i.e., say if i is not equal to j, $\gcd(p_i, p_j) = 1$), then the system of congruences

$$x \equiv a_1 \pmod{p_1}$$
$$x \equiv a_2 \pmod{p_2}$$
$$\vdots$$
$$x \equiv a_n \pmod{p_n}$$

has a solution that is unique modulo $p = p_1 * p_2 * \ldots * p_n$.

The proof of this actually finds the unique solution. First, we start by defining N_k to be n/n_n for each $k = 1, 2, \ldots, n$. That is N_k is all of the n_i multiplied together except n_n. Hence, for our problem, these would be

$$N_1 = 9 * 11 = 99$$
$$N_2 = 7 * 11 = 77$$
$$N_3 = 7 * 9 = 63$$

Next, we have to find the solutions x_k for each of the equations $N_k * x_k \equiv 1 \pmod{n_k}$. For our problem, this is

$$99 * x_1 \equiv 1 * x_1 \equiv 1 \pmod 7$$
$$77 * x_2 \equiv 5 * x_2 \equiv 1 \pmod 9$$
$$63 * x_3 \equiv 8 * x_3 \equiv 1 \pmod{11}$$

As a result, we have that $x_1 = 1$, $x_2 = 2$, and $x_3 = 7$. The simultaneous solution to our system then is the number

$$s = a_1 * N_1 * x_1 + a_2 * N_2 * x_2 + \ldots + a_n * N_n * x_n$$

In our case, $s \equiv 1730 \equiv 344 \pmod{693}$. Note that the 693 is from $693 = 7 * 9 * 11$.

Hence, x if of the form $693n + 344$ or lowest $x = 344$.

A.3 PRIME NUMBER GENERATION

Those numbers which are bigger than 1 and cannot be divided evenly by any other number except 1 and itself are known as prime numbers. If a number can be divided evenly by any other number not counting itself and 1, then it is not prime and is referred to as a composite number.

However, till 19th century, prime numbers was only an interesting area for mathematicians. But after the need for secrecy, especially during times of war, research in this field gained mileage. Prime numbers can also be used in pseudo-random number generators, and in computer hash tables. In computational number theory, a variety of algorithms make it possible to generate prime numbers efficiently. We discuss here the mostly used and the oldest known algorithm for generating primes, i.e., the Sieve of Erastothenes.

A.3.1 Sieve of Eratosthenes

We discuss here the steps involved to find all the prime numbers less than or equal to a given integer n by Eratosthenes' method:

1. Create a list of consecutive integers from 2 to n (2, 3, 4, …, n).
2. Initially, let p equal 2, the first prime number.
3. Starting from p, count up in increments of p and mark each of these numbers greater than p itself in the list. These numbers will be $2p$, $3p$, $4p$, etc.; note that some of them may have already been marked.
4. Find the first number greater than p in the list that is not marked. If there was no such number, stop. Otherwise, let p now equal this number (which is the next prime), and repeat from step 3.

When the algorithm terminates, all the numbers in the list that are not marked are prime.

As a refinement, it is sufficient to mark the numbers in step 3 starting from p^2, as all the smaller multiples of p will have already been marked at that point. This means that the algorithm is allowed to terminate in step 4 when p^2 is greater than n.

Another refinement is to initially list odd numbers only, (3, 5, …, n), and count up using an increment of $2p$ in step 3, thus marking only odd multiples of p greater than p itself. This actually appears in the original algorithm. This can be generalized with wheel factorization, forming the initial list only from numbers coprime with the first few primes and not just from odds, i.e., numbers coprime with 2.

Example A.2: Find all the prime numbers less than or equal to 20, proceed as follows.

Solution: First generate a list of integers from 2 to 20:

2 3 4 5 6 7 8 9 10 11 12 13 14 15 16 17 18 19 20

First number in the list is 2; cross out every second number in the list after it (by counting up in increments of 2), i.e., all the multiples of 2:

2 3 ~~4~~ 5 ~~6~~ 7 ~~8~~ 9 ~~10~~ 11 ~~12~~ 13 ~~14~~ 15 ~~16~~ 17 ~~18~~ 19 ~~20~~

Next number in the list after 2 is 3; cross out every 3rd number in the list after it (by counting up in increments of 3), i.e., all the multiples of 3:

2 3 ~~4~~ 5 ~~6~~ 7 ~~8 9 10~~ 11 ~~12~~ 13 ~~14 15 16~~ 17 ~~18~~ 19 ~~20~~

Next number not yet crossed out in the list after 3 is 5; cross out every fifth number in the list after it (by counting up in increments of 5), i.e., all the multiples of 5:

2 3 ~~4~~ 5 ~~6~~ 7 ~~8 9 10~~ 11 ~~12~~ 13 ~~14 15 16~~ 17 ~~18~~ 19 ~~20~~

Next number not yet crossed out in the list after 5 is 7; the next step would be to cross out every seventh number in the list after it, but they are all already crossed out at this point, as this number 14 is also multiple of smaller primes because 7 * 7 is greater than 20. The numbers left not crossed out in the list at this point are all the prime numbers below 20:

2 3 5 7 11 13 17 19

BIBLIOGRAPHY

1. Spiegel, M. R., Schiller, J. and Srinivasan, R. A., 2004, *Probability and Statistics*, 2nd Ed., *Schaum's Outlines Series* (Tata McGraw Hill).
2. Lipschutz, S., 1981, *Theory and Problems of Probability, SI (metric)*, Ed. *Schaum's Outlines Series* (Tata McGraw Hill).
3. Lathi, B. P. and Ding, Z., 2010, *Modern Digital and Analog Communication Systems*, International 4th Ed. (Oxford University Press).
4. Xavier, S. P. E., 1999, *Statistical Theory of Communication* (New Age International (P) Limited).
5. Hsu, H. P., 2010, *Analog and Digital Communications*, 3rd Ed. *Schaum's Outlines Series* (Tata McGraw Hill).
6. Carlson, A. B., Crilly, P. B. and Rutledge, J. C., 2002, *Communication Systems*, International 4th Ed. (McGraw Hill).
7. Singh, R. P., Sapre, S. D., 2010, *Communication Systems: Analog and Digital*, 2nd Ed. (Tata McGraw Hill).
8. Hsu, H. P., 1996, *Theory and Problems of Probability, Random Variables, and Random Processes*, *Schaum's Outlines Series* (Tata McGraw Hill).
9. Ghosh, P. K., 2008, *Principles of Electronic Communications: Analog and Digital* (University Press).
10. Chakrabarti, P., 2008–09, *Principles of Digital Communication*, 1st Ed. (Dhanpat Rai & Co).
11. Lin, Shu and Costello, Daniel J., Jr., 1983, *Error Control Coding: Fundamentals and Applications* (Prentice-Hall).
12. Gallager, Robert G., 1968, *Information Theory and Reliable Communication* (John Wiley & Sons).
13. Hamming, R. W., 1986, *Coding & Information Theory* (Prentice-Hall).
14. van Tilborg, Henk C. A., 2000, *Coding Theory A First Course* (Kluwer Academic).
15. Gravano, S., 2009, *Introduction to Error Control Codes* (Oxford University Press).
16. Bose, R., 2011, *Information Theory, Coding and Cryptography*, 2nd Ed. (Tata McGraw Hill).
17. Kahate, A., 2003, *Cryptography and Network Security* (Tata McGraw Hill).
18. Briffa, Johann, October 1999, *Interleavers for Turbo Codes* (Dissertation submitted for award of M.Phil., University of Malta).
19. Wesel, Richard D., Published Online: April 2003, *Convolutional Codes* (Wiley Encyclopedia of Telecommunications).
20. Han, Y. S. and Chen, Po-Ning, Published Online: April 2003, *Sequential Decoding of Convolutional Codes* (Wiley Encyclopedia of Telecommunications).
21. Sklar, Bernard, 2001, *Digital Communications: Fundamentals and Applications*, 2nd Ed. (Prentice-Hall PTR).
22. Roddy, D. and Coolen, J., 2000, *Electronic Communications*, 4th Ed. (Prentice-Hall India).
23. Kennedy, G. and Davis, B., 1992, *Electronic Communication Systems*, 4th Ed. (McGraw Hill).
24. Couch, L. W. II, 2007, *Digital and Analog Communication Systems*, 6th Ed. (Pearson Education).
25. Taub, H., Schilling, D. L. and G. Saha, 2008, *Principles of Communication Systems*, 3rd Ed. (Tata McGraw Hill).
26. Proakis, J. G. and Salehi, M., 2008, *Digital Communications*, 5th Ed. (McGraw Hill).
27. Tomasi, W., 2004, *Electronic Communications Systems*, 5th Ed. (Pearson Education).
28. Gonzalez, R. C. and Woods, R. E., 2011, *Digital Image Processing*, 3rd Ed. (Pearson).

29. http://site.iugaza.edu.ps/jroumy/files/Shanon-Fano.pdf
30. http://my.fit.edu/~vKepuska/ece5525/lpc_paper.pdf
31. http://eeweb.poly.edu/~yao/EE3414/audio_coding.pdf
32. http://erdos.csie.ncnu.edu.tw/~hychen/multimedia/mpeg audio coding.pdf
33. http://nptel.iitm.ac.in/courses/Webcourse-contents/IIT Kharagpur/Multimedia Processing/pdf/ssg_m9l28.pdf
34. http://www.beussery.com/pdf/beussery.dolby.pdf
35. http://dspace.mit.edu

INDEX